REGIONAL

COOKING

OF

ENGLAND

REGIONAL

COOKING

OF

ENGLAND

A culinary tour with more than 280 traditional recipes

EDITED BY

CAROL WILSON

LORENZ BOOKS

CONTENTS

FOREWORD

English cooking has a long and illustrious history, revealing a fascinating wealth of treasured recipes and cooking styles throughout the ages. The first written English recipes appeared in the *Forme of Cury* ('Cury' was the Old English word for cooking, derived from the French 'cuire' – to cook, boil, grill), and dates back to 1390.

New foods and ingredients were introduced to England at various times and were gradually incorporated into the cuisine. At first, these costly items were reserved for a wealthy elite. Spices and sugar (regarded as a spice), introduced in the Middle Ages, were prized and kept under lock and key.

The 17th century was a time of great changes, with orchards and market gardens yielding an abundance of fruits and vegetables. Sugar from Barbados became more plentiful, and cheaper, leading to an increase in the creation of preserves and confectionery. New beverages were welcomed, namely tea, coffee and chocolate. Coffee houses opened in London and tea drinking was made fashionable by Queen Catherine, wife of Charles II.

Although ingredients such as dried fruits, spices and sugar had become more affordable, with English cookbooks reflecting these changes in cooking and eating habits, they were still costly for most ordinary people and so were reserved for special occasions. Lavish fruitcakes, for instance, were regarded as treats for important holidays and celebrations – for Christmas, or the richly fruited and lightly spiced simnel cake still traditionally enjoyed at Easter.

Home baking really took off in the 18th century when enclosed domestic ovens were introduced into homes, and for the first time the cook could control the heat of the oven. Nonetheless, baking in the past remained time-consuming and laborious compared to nowadays: flour was likely to be damp from storage; stray pebbles, stones, stalks and seeds had to be removed from dried fruits, which then had to be washed and dried; and sugar had to be chipped off a hard block and sieved before use.

The 19th century brought major changes with the development of scientific farming and industrial growth. Improved transport by sea, road and railways meant that foods could be transported more quickly. The advent of refrigeration was also hugely influential, as foods remained fresh for longer. New kitchen equipment such as gas cookers and refrigerators, together with the creation of foods such as margarine, self-raising flour, compressed yeast and custard powder, revolutionised cooking. Many of the recipes we enjoy today were developed during the Industrial Revolution, when the families of northern mill workers and miners depended on satisfying dishes such as pies and puddings.

In this book you'll find everything from old-fashioned favourites and current classics to less well-known, almost forgotten historical dishes, along with lots of wonderful regional recipes, a few of which might raise an eyebrow but are included for their intriguing novelty or curiosity value.

There are so many English recipes, often handed down and adapted through the generations, and coming with (of course) countless regional tweaks and variations, and different local names. It would be impossible to include them all, but this collection offers a glorious illustration of England's splendid culinary diversity. All the recipes are easy to follow, with accessible ingredients, and achievable in today's modern kitchens. Together they offer a real taste of England, and a fascinating glimpse of the past.

RIGHT *A quintessential English afternoon tea, in a classic setting – Gold Hill, Shaftesbury, in the county of Dorset.* OVERLEAF *Sunset at Mam Tor in the Peak District in Derbyshire, with a winding view down to Hope Valley.*

INTRODUCTION

This book is a celebration of the food and cooking of England. Blessed with a mild and variable climate, the country boasts a mixed landscape of fertile valleys, undulating downs and dales, rugged moors and rocky mountains. There are beautiful lakes, rushing rivers and flat, salty marshlands, as well as a long and varied coastline, much of which is dramatic and distinctive. The English diet has been influenced not only by the landscape and the climate but also by invasion and immigration, a global empire, social development, trade and technology, politics and economics, and of course food fashion.

The food of England has a history that stretches back more than six thousand years. Before that time this temperate, wooded country would have provided an abundance of small, edible mammals and fish, plus vegetation, roots, fruits and nuts that were seasonally available to early hunter-gatherers. As a group of islands, isolated off the north-west of Europe, Britain was cut off by the sea from the migration of plants and animals, and from the casual spread of new ideas and techniques as people moved about to find homes. On the other hand, for adventurous Europeans this land over the sea promised a rich living, with its fertile soil and mineral resources, and settlers arrived in wave after wave. Farming began with the herding and subsistence farming techniques of one of those groups of settlers, the Celts. Keen to borrow and adapt the ideas of trading partners and incomers, goods were imported from mainland Europe and beyond. In return for raw materials, such as tin and copper, corn and wool, the English were importing wine and luxury foodstuffs from southern Europe even before the arrival of the Romans. With the Roman occupation came new varieties of plants and animals, and even more exotic ingredients such as spices from Asia.

Other influences were added to the mix in later centuries: from the occupying Vikings, Saxons and Normans, and from the Arabs via trade with southern Europe. In the age of exploration, ingredients from the New World made their debut in European cuisine – foodstuffs such as beans and tomatoes, which are now regarded as staples of local cookery. Of these, the most important was the potato, which was to have such a profound influence on the history of Ireland in the 19th century. To begin with, it was more popular there than in England, as it proved a more reliable crop than oats and barley, and

LEFT *An English village thatched cottage.*
RIGHT *Chinese-inspired blue and white porcelain became very fashionable in the 19th century.*

it was from Ireland that the trend for planting potatoes spread to areas like Lincolnshire and Lancashire. More exotic ingredients and cooking styles arrived as Britain's international reach grew. Tropical luxuries such as spices, sugar, coffee, tea and chocolate became daily necessities, and the administrators of the far-flung empire acquired a taste for the foods they had eaten in India and the Far East. Worcestershire sauce, for example, now regarded as a typically British condiment, is a spiced fermented fish sauce that was created in the 1830s for a family who missed the cooking of Bengal. Ironically, Worcestershire sauce made its way back to the East via European restaurants in Hong Kong and Shanghai, and is now used in Chinese cookery.

In every age, the new foodstuffs were most readily accepted, and most easily purchased, by the wealthy and fashionable, the city dwellers and the travellers. In remoter rural regions, old cooking techniques and traditional ingredients persisted far longer, particularly in the north and west of England. A primitive method of cooking meat in a pit filled with water, which was kept boiling by the addition of stones heated in a fire, seems to have been current in the Bronze Age, but in some places the method was still being used in the early medieval period. In the 18th and 19th centuries, rural cottage dwellers continued to cook their daily soup of carrots, onions and cabbage in an iron pot over the kitchen fire, and bake their bannocks or potato cakes on a bakestone, while the wealthy and more cosmopolitan gentry were eating turtle soup, curries, ice cream and tropical fruits. Yet it is the traditional country recipes, refined over generations, of healthy, wholesome dishes from modest ingredients, that are now a valued part of England's culinary heritage.

Given the richness of its food traditions and the excellence of its ingredients, it seems surprising that for much of the 20th century England had a reputation for food that was plain and boring, consisting mainly of overcooked meat and vegetables and stodgy puddings. This decline probably stemmed

ABOVE *The English pub is at the heart of many a village or town; this is the Old Friends pub, in Ulverston, Cumbria.*

from the 19th century, as Victorian morality inculcated a disdain for the sensory pleasure of eating, and the largely urban population lost touch with the quality of fresh produce. The emerging middle classes, locked between the wealthy and the poor, strove to keep up appearances with grandiose but badly cooked meals, aided by the publications of Mrs Beeton (who, among other ill-judged recommendations, suggested boiling an egg for 20 minutes). The lowly status of cooks, who were regarded as 'below stairs' staff in the houses of the rich, the consequences of two world wars, food shortages and rationing, periods of economic depression and the influx of processed foods all took their toll on the quality of cooking. Recovery from this adverse perception of its cuisine has taken time, but today England takes deserved pride in its reputation for excellent food, and there is a welcome resurgence of interest in seasonal ingredients of high quality. The nation has the ability to embrace curry and pizza (even turning them into new national dishes) as well as delicacies from the Mediterranean and the Middle East, while nostalgically guarding and updating its inheritance of national and regional favourites: roast beef and Yorkshire pudding, fish and chips, stews, bubble and squeak, and the much-loved puddings that hold memories of childhood.

This beautiful book focuses on the many good things that England has to offer, although the culinary heritage is shared between much of England, Ireland, Scotland and Wales. It begins with an overview of the rich food history of the regions, each with its own characteristics and food specialities, and describes some of the festivals and customs and the food associated with them. There follows a section on classic English ingredients – vegetables, fruit, fish, meat, poultry, game and dairy produce. The major part of this book is devoted, of course, to cooking, with delicious traditional recipes to suit every occasion (including, naturally, breakfast, Sunday lunch and teatime). Many of these dishes can be traced back through the ages; some are common to all areas, such as roast meats, crumbles, fruit pies and cooked breakfasts, while others are unmistakably from a particular region, such as Lancashire hotpot, Staffordshire oatcakes, Cornish pasties or Shropshire soul cakes, to name just a few.

This collection of recipes offers something to suit everyone, along with an evocative journey into English food. Enjoy it, and eat well.

ABOVE *Fortnum & Mason, the famous luxury food store in Piccadilly, London.*

HISTORY & TRADITIONS

The food of England has been shaped partly by the temperate climate and geography of the British Isles, but also by the nation's history of invasion, settlement and immigration. The English have had a stream of foreign influences to enrich their culinary development, initially from the European mainland, but also from the Americas, Asia and the Far East. Local specialities and traditional recipes play a role in creating the distinctive food identity of each region.

PICTURED *The impressive copper* batterie de cuisine *of an 18th-century English country house.*

EARLY TIMES

In the days of the hunter-gatherers, before farming began, England was mostly covered by woodland. In the clearings, where trees had fallen or died, edible weeds and plants grew – including barberries, blackberries, crab apples, haws, hazelnuts and sloes. The woods were home to wild cattle, boar, cats, deer and elk, badgers, hedgehogs, shrews and other small mammals. The rivers and coastal waters were rich with fish and shellfish. Prehistoric pottery was made from coarse clay and shaped into crude vessels. Some pots were porous, and were used for storage, while others could withstand the sudden and intense heat of an open fire during cooking. The shift to farming from around 4000BCE led to the growth of larger, settled communities. Livestock remained all-important until the Bronze Age (*c.*2000BCE), from which time we find the first remains of grain crops and field systems. In the Iron Age, the Celts made the first metal cauldrons for cooking.

NEW FOODS FROM THE ROMANS

When the Romans arrived in England in 55BCE, simple meat and vegetable stews were the order of the day. The far more sophisticated Romans were to have a huge and long-lasting influence on English

ABOVE *The Neolithic standing stones of Stonehenge.*

ABOVE *Hadrian's Wall, the Roman boundary between England and Scotland.*

eating, as they introduced a large range of foods and flavours, elaborately seasoned dishes and specialised cooking methods such as roasting and baking.

The Romans brought pheasants, peacocks and guinea fowl, and they imported a host of vegetables, including asparagus, cabbage, carrots, celery, cucumber, endive, globe artichokes, leek, marrow, onion, parsnip, turnip, radish and shallots. There were herbs such as borage, chervil, coriander, dill, fennel, mint, parsley, thyme, rosemary, sage, savory and sweet marjoram. Spices included cinnamon, ginger and pepper, and there were almonds, dates, olives, olive oil, pine kernels, walnuts and wine – the customary drink of Roman soldiers. They also introduced orchard trees such as damson, cherry, medlar, mulberry and plum. As well as importing dried grapes in the form of raisins and sultanas, they established vines, using the grapes to make wine for drinking, must for cooking, and vinegar for drinks,

sauces and preserving. The Romans also brought their favourite fermented fish sauces, called liquamen and garum (similar to South-East Asian fish sauces, and the forerunners of modern concoctions such as Worcestershire sauce), which they used in savoury and sweet dishes. The Romans held extravagant banquets featuring foods that now sound outlandish, such as milk-fattened snails, stuffed dormice and wild boar stuffed with live birds. Most notoriously, some of them indulged in the habit of inducing vomiting after eating several courses of rich food before coming back for more.

Farming practices also changed with the Romans, who created hare gardens and game parks for red, roe and fallow deer. Beef was popular and cattle also provided milk, butter and cheese. Pigs were plentiful and ham was salted (with sea salt) or pickled in brine. Sheep and goats were kept for meat, and their milk was made into cheeses. The Romans also kept hens and honey bees. Oysters were highly prized and came from England's south-east coast. Wheat and cereal grains were made into porridge and gruel as well as being used in baking. Flour was mainly ground at home by hand, using a rotary quern, though it has been confirmed that commercial bakeries existed in large towns and that the Romans made a variety of breads.

ANGLO-SAXONS AND VIKINGS

The Anglo-Saxons – Germanic tribes who settled in England from the 5th century CE following the fall of the Roman Empire – ate what they grew. Their cereals included wheat and rye for bread, barley for brewing, and oats for porridge and animal food.

There were vegetables (beans, cabbages, carrots, parsnip, peas and onions) and fruit (apples, cherries and plums).

Meat was in fairly short supply. Though wild animals such as deer and wild boar were common, only landowners had the right to kill them. Pigs were the only animals kept solely for their meat – they produced large litters, which matured quickly in readiness for slaughter. Sheep provided wool as well as meat, while cows produced milk, meat, hides and glue. The Anglo-Saxons also ate fish, from both rivers and the sea. Everyone, even the children, drank weak ale, which was safer than the water from wells, streams and rivers. Wine was imported from Europe, but was drunk only by the wealthy. Other options were buttermilk and whey (by-products from butter and cheese-making), with mead for special occasions.

The Viking invaders of the 8th and 9th centuries also influenced eating habits in England. These new settlers were proud of their hospitality, and willingly shared their homes and food with strangers. They ate a wide variety of fruits, nuts and grains, as well as fish and shellfish. Meat was available to all, not just reserved for the rich, and game animals included hare, boar, deer, squirrel and wild birds.

Dairy products formed an important part of the Viking diet, with whole milk reserved for butter-making. Eggs were regularly supplied by chickens, geese, ducks and wild birds (gulls' eggs were a special delicacy).

Fish and meat were preserved for the winter months by salting, pickling, drying or smoking. Bread – both leavened and unleavened – was made in large quantities, and the Vikings made use of wild yeasts and raising agents such as buttermilk, sour milk and yeast left over from brewing. The bread was often flavoured with nuts, seeds, herbs or cheese, or used to wrap fish or meat.

LEFT *An English longhorn bull.*
RIGHT *Reconstruction of an Anglo-Saxon village in West Stow, Sussex; an interior view of one of the houses.*

MEDIEVAL EXTREMES

What people ate varied according to social standing in the medieval period, as did their place at the table. Most still prepared their own food, or traded it with others. Though some food shops were to be found in towns, the majority of people were peasants living in villages, where there were no traders. Potting and drying were ways of preserving food, and salt was an important ingredient, kept dry in a box by the fire.

In the Middle Ages bread was the staple food of all classes, though only rich farmers and lords ate white bread, for they were able to grow wheat, which required well-dug and manured soil. The most common bread, called 'maslin', was coarse and made with a mixture of wheat and rye. Rye and barley breads were heavy and dark and were eaten only by the poorest. Feudal laws often meant that peasants were not allowed to bake bread in their own huts by the central fire, but had to take their dough to the manor for baking, where they were obliged to give up a proportion to feed the lord's servants. At the medieval table, bread was used to make trenchers (rough plate shapes cut from stale loaves), which were not eaten by the diners, but might be offered to beggars or animals at the end of the meal.

Pottage, a soupy mixture of vegetables, meat, pulses, cereals, herbs and broth, was eaten by

ABOVE *A medieval banquet (here, Richard II entertains) was an opportunity to impress, and display the host's wealth.*

ABOVE *A moated medieval manor house, Baddesley Clinton near Warwick.*

everyone every day and was cooked in the basic utensil of the time – the cauldron, a three-legged cast-iron pot that stood or hung over the open fire.

Fish was very important in the diet, too. The population at that time were Roman Catholics, which meant there were many days in the year when meat, eggs or dairy foods were forbidden, so fish would be eaten instead. A huge herring industry existed in England and most people ate salted or pickled herrings year-round. Only landowners and the rich had a wider choice of fresh fish and shellfish, though villagers were sometimes granted permission to catch certain fish from local rivers.

Cattle, sheep and goats provided meat, but the mainstay of the poor was the pig. Pigs could forage for their own food, could be slaughtered at any time of year, and were suitable for sausage-making and for smoking and salting in readiness for winter consumption. Though game animals roamed in the woodland surrounding most villages, they remained

the privilege of the wealthy and the property of kings and nobles. Poachers faced mutilation or death, though many peasants did get permission to hunt hares, rabbits, hedgehogs and squirrels.

The main drink of medieval days was ale, though villagers were not allowed to sell it without permission and a paid-for licence from their lord. Cooked dishes for the wealthy were flavoured with expensive imported spices such as cardamom, caraway, ginger, nutmeg and pepper, and foods were dyed with vivid natural colourings such as sandalwood, saffron and boiled blood. There were other exotic imports such as sugar, citrus fruits, dried fruits and almonds – all treasured by the wealthy. Medieval banquets would have spectacular centrepieces such as roasted swans or peacocks complete with plumage, or lavish sugar sculptures.

The numerous French words that entered the English language following the Norman Conquest included the names of the meats that were eaten by

the Norman aristocracy, such as mutton, beef, veal and pork. Meanwhile, the old Anglo-Saxon names – sheep, cow and pig – continued to be used for the live animals, tended by the English peasants.

TUDOR ENGLAND

The Tudor period was a time of colour, splendour, pomp and ceremony. While the English nobility had a reputation for overeating, even the lower classes ate well compared with their European counterparts.

At the table, trenchers began to be made of wood rather than bread, but the foods that were enjoyed were similar to those of the Middle Ages, with bread, pottage, fish and meat underpinning the diet. Vegetables and fruit were treated with suspicion and left for the lower classes. They were often thought to be responsible for sickness and disease – during the plague of 1569, for example, the selling of fresh fruit became illegal. As a result, vitamin deficiencies were common.

Meanwhile, expeditions to the New World were bringing back new and exotic foods for the enjoyment of the rich: potatoes, tomatoes, maize, chocolate, peanuts, pepper, pineapples, tapioca, turkey and vanilla. From southern Europe came apricots, blackcurrants, lemons, oranges, melons, pomegranates, quinces, raspberries and redcurrants, all of which the wealthy attempted to grow in the gardens of their large houses.

Sugar, though still expensive, had become more widely available and was very popular with the wealthy – so much so that their teeth were often decayed, as were those of Queen Elizabeth I. A refinery was built in London and sugar was sold in large cone-shaped lumps that required grating or pounding before use. It was added to meat, fish and vegetable dishes as well as being used to make

syrups, preserves and sweetmeats such as marzipan and crystallised fruits.

Standards for cooking and eating were firmly set by royalty, and the palaces served enormous quantities of elaborate dishes every day. Huge kitchens were equipped with several fireplaces, with spits for roasting, and dozens of bronze pots and pans. They required large storage areas for food, ale, beer and wine, spacious bakehouses and extensive kitchen gardens, not to mention teams of domestic staff. This theme was replicated on a smaller scale in the large country houses of the major landowners. Whereas in the early medieval house the lord and his family had eaten in the great hall with all his retainers, private dining chambers now came into use. Sumptuous feasts were the order of the day, providing the aristocracy with the opportunity to display their wealth and manners.

LEFT *The Tudor kitchen at Hampton Court, one of the palaces of King Henry VIII.*
RIGHT *Tudor farmhouse of Mary Arden, in Warwickshire.*

CENTURIES OF UPHEAVAL

The 17th century was an era of political turmoil in England, and also saw enormous changes in food and eating. The dissolution of the monasteries in the previous century had created a new class of non-aristocratic landowner – the landed gentry, as they were to become known. It became fashionable for this affluent new class to visit towns, and London became the finest source of both social graces and luxury foods. While most of the foodstuffs we know today had already been introduced, the arrival of allspice, cochineal, sago, tea, coffee and chocolate caused great excitement. Coffee houses opened, first in Oxford and then in London. Interest in foreign foods and new cooking methods continued to grow.

Standards were still set by the royal household, with much of its influence drawn from France, and (fancy) French cuisine gained mass popularity. Fresh fruit and vegetables were now considered safe to eat and diners began to appreciate salads.

The English continued to enjoy their traditional foods, with meat forming a large part of the diet. Baking skills improved, as local specialities were developed in the form of cakes, biscuits, buns and pastries. The English pudding was born, with the invention of the pudding cloth, a square of muslin in which the ball of dough was tied and cooked slowly in a pot with the meat and vegetables. There were oven-baked puddings, too, based on rice or eggs.

ABOVE *Interior of an early London coffee house, c.1705; the customers were exclusively male.*

ABOVE *A Georgian kitchen (restored, in St George Street, Bristol) where the food was prepared below stairs.*

Every country house, no matter how modest, had a kitchen garden. Those on large country estates boasted raised beds, hot beds and hothouses, all of which produced a huge range of vegetables and fruit. Icehouses were built to store winter ice for cooling food and drink in summer, and ice cream began to be made. Beehive ovens and stoves appeared alongside the kitchen fireplaces in large houses, and an early pressure cooker, the 'steam digester', was invented in 1679. Ladies began to exchange recipes and compile recipe books. Buffet-style meals were served (with a range of dishes offered at the same time) and eating took place in the 'dining room'.

GEORGIAN PROGRESS

In the early 1700s, the English people were still growing and rearing their own food and eating off the land. But landowners began to enclose their land, driving off the peasants (who lost their homes as well as their vegetable plots), to free it up for commercial farming. As a result, the poor struggled to survive, moving to towns and cities to work in the new factories, living in slums (particularly in the Midlands and the south of England), and eating a diet of bread, potatoes and porridge. Town life throbbed with activity: shops, markets, cattle traffic, puppet shows, dog fights, fops, prostitutes and pickpockets all packed the streets. It was an age of gambling on both a large scale (on the stock market) and a small scale (in domino games or cockfighting). Spirits, such as gin, were cheap, and drunkenness was rife among the poor – men, women and children.

Much more meat was available, and cheap to buy, as a result of new winter feeding practices for livestock, land enclosure and better breeding methods. Improved transport meant that regional foods such as cheeses, fresh fish and oysters (which were plentiful) could be conveyed throughout the country. Sugar was now readily available, and replaced spices and herbs to make food palatable, leading to the development of pickles, ketchups and bottled sauces. Sugar was also added to drinks – wine, tea, coffee and chocolate.

Coffee and tea were still expensive treats for the wealthy (China tea was kept in a locked caddy), and smuggling was prevalent. Tea's popularity exploded in England in the early 18th century. Between breakfast (of bread, beef and ale) and dinner at the end of the day, there was a long gap, and to fill it the Georgians began to take afternoon tea, displaying their wealth in ornate teapots and tea sets.

By the mid-18th century, the dinner table looked much as it does today, with plates, bowls, knives, forks, serving spoons and wine glasses. Etiquette became important – not eating too quickly or too slowly, not sitting too close or too distant from the table, and no scratching or spitting!

Although the aristocracy employed French chefs, the swelling ranks of Middle England enjoyed simpler, plain fare such as roast and boiled meats and pies. Rebelling against fancy French sauces, the English became known for their preference for plain roast beef, and their love affair with puddings took hold. A huge variety was enjoyed – boiled, baked, stuffed with meat or game – and most were loaded with butter or suet. In fact, butter, though twice the cost of meat, was used copiously in most dishes.

This age of indulgence led to widespread health problems, with a high incidence of gout, diabetes, heart and liver diseases, and vitamin deficiencies. Many foods were secretly or unwittingly made with poisonous ingredients. Copper and lead were used to make pickles green, sweets multicoloured, and cheese rind red. Pepper was mixed with floor sweepings to bulk it out, and alum (a toxic mineral salt) was added to bread to whiten it. Copper and brass pans, when used to cook acidic food, produced a poisonous layer of verdigris. Perhaps as a result of all this, towards the end of the century spa towns became very fashionable as people tried to improve their health.

ABOVE *Billingsgate in 1861 painted by G. E. Hicks; the famous fish market in London still exists today in a different location.*

Labels within illustration: Pine Apple and Grapes. Ice Pudding. Lemon Jelly. Macédoine of Fruits. Jelly with whipped Cream. Strawberries. Cherries. Charlotte of Pommes. Mixed Fruits. Melon and Green figs. Candied Oranges. Apricots. Plums. Chantilly Basket. Christmas Plum Pudding. Ribbon Jelly. Chocolate Cake. Rice Croquettes. Custards. Ices. Meringues. Sponge Cake. Tartlets. Red and white Currants. Greengages. Open Tart. Wedding Cake. Compote of Pears. Neapolitan Cake. Trifle. Plum Cake. Compote of Apples. Gâteau.

ABOVE *Some popular Victorian puddings, as featured in Mrs Beeton's cookbook of 1861.*

THE VICTORIAN AGE

The reign of Queen Victoria was a period of burgeoning industrial development, during which the gap between rich and poor widened even further, and poverty and plenty sat side by side. It was a time of factories, railways, pollution, gadgets, extravagance, mass poverty, destitution and starvation, exacerbated by poor harvests, crop diseases and famine. The growing population continued to move from the country to the city in search of work, with the poor supplying cheap labour for the factories and the growing middle classes holding higher-status jobs. For some, life became so difficult that it prompted a humanitarian movement that offered charity in the hardest-hit areas, and there were cookery books directed at feeding the poor.

However, the invention of the steam engine improved transportation of fresh foodstuffs such as milk and other dairy produce, fish and meat. In addition, the discovery of bacteria led to advances in medicine and food preservation, and to a greater awareness of food hygiene. As a result, the quality of produce in the cities improved, and international trade also took off. With more tea and wheat in England than ever before, prices dropped. Tea had been a valuable delicacy in the previous century; now it became the staple drink of the poor, who drank it in copious quantities as they ate their bread or potatoes. The development of roller mills meant that white flour (and therefore white bread) was available to all. And the canning process, patented in 1810,

ABOVE *The Victorian kitchen range, polished to perfection, at Audley End House in Saffron Waldon.*

meant that cheap meat could be shipped from the other side of the world and all kinds of produce – vegetables, fruit, soups, stews – could be preserved without being salted or pickled. Street food was popular in towns and cities and the first fish and chip shop opened in London in 1860.

Victorian kitchens were large – able to hold the new cast-iron ranges, with their open fires, ovens, water tank and hot plate. They burned coal (wood had previously been the main fuel) and, for the first time, cooks were able to control the temperature in their ovens. Cooks in middle-class houses could now prepare the complicated meals and delicate dishes that had been the reserve of grand kitchens in wealthy homes. *Mrs Beeton's Book of Household*

Management, published in 1861, was popular with young, middle-class families, and was followed by many other recipe books. Cast-iron and tin-plated equipment replaced brass and copper. Kitchens were filled with mass-produced equipment such as pastry cutters, baking tins, pie moulds and jelly moulds, and gadgets such as graters, potato peelers, mincers and bean slicers. There was usually a walk-in pantry to keep food cool and plenty of storage space for the vast array of packets, cans and bottles – all of which were prized by the urban middle class, who no longer grew their own food. The fishmonger, greengrocer and milkman delivered straight to the door. The end of the 19th century saw the introduction of gas stoves, electric kettles and facilities for chilling and freezing meat. In the country, meanwhile, where railway lines had not yet been laid, the people continued to live off the land.

THE MODERN AGE

At the beginning of the 20th century the English population ate very poorly. Vitamins and their importance in a healthy diet had only recently been discovered, and the government now began to invest in dietary research. After a period of recovery from World War I came the General Strike, during which soup kitchens were set up to feed communities, and a time of great depression and poverty followed. At the same time, the middle classes began to eat out: Indian restaurants opened in London and the first 'sit-down' fish and chip cafe appeared in Guiseley, near Leeds. Milk was pasteurised and bottled, and sliced bread and instant coffee went on sale.

In spite of the shortages, World War II is now considered to have been a period of healthy eating in England. Food rationing was introduced in 1940, with the Ministry of Food advising the nation on eating healthily and allotments popping up on every corner. Children were given free milk and vitamins, calcium was added to flour, and the brown National Loaf was introduced. The development of freezing and freeze-drying led to food scientists finding new ways to enhance and preserve foods. Ready-made meals became popular, and shoppers were able to buy food that was convenient – if also homogenised, high in emulsified fat and high in salt.

Today, alongside the continued growth of supermarkets with an ever-increasing range of ingredients, and eating-out venues that offer every kind of cuisine, there is also renewed interest in traditional cooking, in seasonal foods and where they come from. It is fun as well as instructive to rediscover the best of the great heritage of English cooking, and its wonderful regional dishes.

ABOVE *A 1930s kitchen/dining room in a back-to-back terrace house in the Black Country, West Midlands.*

FEASTS AND FESTIVALS

Many of the more traditional feast days and festivals of England are linked to the Christian calendar, although their origins often stretch back to pre-Christian times, when pagan celebrations were inextricably linked with agriculture and seasonal change. Nowadays, in England's multicultural society, many other festivals are celebrated as well.

SHROVE TUESDAY The last day before Lent, a period of fasting and reflection before the Christian celebration of Easter, is now often called Pancake Day. Shrove Tuesday is meant to be a day when everyone 'shrives' or confesses their sins and receives

absolution. It is also the last chance to feast before the period of abstinence. Pancakes are the customary treat, made with a batter containing the eggs, butter and milk that would otherwise go off during the 40 days of Lent. The traditions of tossing pancakes and pancake races are still kept up.

GOOD FRIDAY The day when Jesus Christ was crucified is a day of mourning in the Christian calendar, when churches are stripped of all decoration. It is traditional to eat fish on Good Friday, and hot cross buns are eaten warm for breakfast. Though the buns predated Christianity,

ABOVE *1940s housewives toss pancakes at the start of the Olney pancake race.*

they were adopted as a symbol of the cross on which Christ died. In Tudor times spiced buns could, by law, be sold only on special days. Years ago hot cross buns were thought to have holy powers, and a bun would be hung from the ceiling to protect people in the house from harm. Bits of the stale bun would be grated off and used as a cure for illness, but if the bun went mouldy bad luck was to be had by all. There is a pub in the East End of London (The Widow's Son) where, in the early 19th century, a widow lived who was expecting her sailor son back home for Easter. On Good Friday she put out a hot cross bun ready for him. Though the son never returned, his mother left the bun waiting and added a new one each year. When the house became a pub, the landlords continued the tradition.

EASTER DAY Christians celebrate the resurrection of Jesus Christ on Easter Sunday, but many of the festival's symbols and traditions predate Christianity. Traditional foods include lamb (with rosemary for remembrance), simnel cake (a fruit cake layered with marzipan) and eggs (which are forbidden during Lent). Customs include decorating eggs and egg hunts. In the north of England there is 'egg jarping', when children tap their opponents' hard-boiled eggs with their own and the last to break is the champion, and 'pace-egging', when they dress up and blacken their faces to go knocking on doors, asking in rhyme for Easter eggs. Egg rolling, still practised in England, is when hard-boiled eggs are rolled down a hill. The winner might be the one that rolls the farthest or the one that survives best. Today chocolate eggs are given as gifts.

ST GEORGE'S DAY The patron saint of England, St George, is acknowledged on 23rd April (also Shakespeare's birthday!). Though there are no national celebrations, people sometimes wear a red rose (the national flower), and some regions organise parades and concerts, while pubs and restaurants offer traditional English dishes.

ABOVE *The start of an Easter Egg hunt, in a daffodil-filled field in Lancashire.*

MOTHERING SUNDAY Also called Mother's Day, this was originally the day when people visited the 'mother' church. In the 17th century it became the occasion to acknowledge mothers. Children, mainly daughters, who had gone away to work as domestic servants were given a day off to visit their mother with flowers and simnel cake. Today it is a day when children give flowers, gifts and homemade cards to their mothers, and the family gathers for a meal.

MAY DAY The first day of May is the time to celebrate spring and the coming of summer. It once marked the time when livestock was moved to the hills to graze after a winter in the lowlands. It was

ABOVE *Dancing round the spring maypole in Wells, Somerset (left), and autumn harvest by a church in Kent (right).*

customary to dance around the maypole (a surviving pagan symbol of virility from the festival of Beltane) and a May queen would be crowned with hawthorn blossoms. Houses were decorated with flowers, and young girls washed their faces in morning dew for a beautiful complexion. There might be processions and Morris dancing.

HARVEST FESTIVAL A successful harvest has been an occasion for celebration and feasting for centuries. The harvest feast is an English custom, with its origins in feudal England, when the lord of the manor provided special food and drink as a thank you to the workers, who toiled from dawn to dusk in the fields. As time passed, this custom passed to farmers and their wives, who were responsible for feeding the large numbers of casual workers and their families who were taken on at harvest time.

Special cakes and breads were prepared – the earliest were made from leftover bread dough enriched with fat and eggs, studded with dried fruits

and spices. As sugar, dried fruits and spices became cheaper and more easily available to almost everyone, each county and region developed their own unique breads and cakes.

At the end of the 19th century, the feasts developed into church suppers. The first 'Harvest Thanksgiving' took place in 1843 and was the idea of a Cornish vicar, the Rev Hawker, who, during a service of thanksgiving invited his parishioners to take communion made from the 'bread of the new corn'. After the service he blessed the crops and everyone enjoyed a communal meal in the church hall, after which some of the produce was given to the poor; thus the modern 'Harvest Festival' was created which still takes place in most English towns and villages today.

HALLOWEEN The night of 31st October is All Hallows' Eve, or Halloween. It is traditionally a night of witches, goblins, ghouls and ghosts, a time of mischief, magic and mystery, with customs that can be traced back to the Celts. Fires would be lit on the hillsides to ward off evil spirits, and families huddled together at home out of harm's way. These days parties are held where lanterns with menacing faces are carved from pumpkins and swedes, and games such as apple bobbing are played, when participants must remove apples from a bowl of water using only their teeth.

ALL SOULS' DAY

Also with Celtic origins, All Souls' Day, on 2nd November, was traditionally a solemn day of fasting, when Christians offered prayers for the dead. Flowers were put on graves, and candles and bonfires were lit to light the souls' way to the afterlife. It was the custom for the poor to offer prayers in return for money or food –

especially fruit buns, which were called soul cakes. Spiced ale was served to the 'soulers', and there were souling songs and plays.

BONFIRE NIGHT

The anniversary of the gunpowder plot on 5th November 1605 – when Guy Fawkes attempted (but failed) to blow up the Houses of Parliament in London with barrels of gunpowder – is still celebrated in England with bonfires and fireworks. It is traditional to burn an effigy, made by children from old clothes, paper and straw, to represent Guy Fawkes, and children would take their effigies on to the street asking for 'a penny for the guy' with which to buy fireworks. Traditionally, bonfire toffee (hard and treacly), toffee apples and parkin (a solid, spicy gingerbread) are enjoyed.

ABOVE *A traditional torchlit procession in Tudor dress on Bonfire Night in Lewes, East Sussex.*

CHRISTMAS As Christians honour the birth of Jesus Christ at Christmas, families and friends come together to share customs and traditions that are centuries old. On Christmas Eve, Midnight Mass is celebrated in churches all over the country, and children hang up stockings to be filled with gifts by Father Christmas (provided they have been well behaved all year).

On Christmas Day there is much feasting and good cheer. The boar's head was the centrepiece of the medieval feast before goose, beef, chicken and today's turkey replaced it.

A Yule log was burned in every home, and is now represented by a cake. Plum pudding (made with prunes, eggs and meat) was the forerunner to Christmas pudding, with its rich mixture of dried fruit and spices. Similarly, mince pies were originally filled with a mixture of meat, dried fruit and spices; the meat survives in the form of suet in today's recipe (though that is often vegetable-based now as well). Mince pies were thought to bring good luck if you ate one on each of the twelve days of Christmas.

Wassailing was once practised all over England. 'Waes hael' was an Anglo-Saxon toast meaning 'Good health', and a large bowl (the wassail bowl), filled with ale, spices and honey, would be passed round. It would be taken from door to door, and gifts of Christmas fare, drink or money were offered in exchange for a goodwill toast. Greetings cards, crackers and decorated trees became fashionable in Victorian times.

TWELFTH NIGHT Medieval England celebrated the 12 days of Christmas, culminating with festivities on January 6th, to mark the end of the Christmas season. As time passed, Twelfth Night

ABOVE *The flaming plum pudding is brought in as the finale to this grand Christmas dinner (artist Charles Green, 1896).*

ABOVE *The Goose Fair, 1908, still held annually in Nottingham.*

became a hugely popular festive occasion, with masked balls, plays, singing, gambling and other jollities. Samuel Pepys noted in his diary that he hosted such an event. A rich fruitcake lavishly decorated with stars, castles and kings, often painted with edible colourings, was the central point of the celebrations. The cake contained a dried bean and a pea; the man who found the bean became king for the evening and the woman who found the pea was queen. Over the years, Twelfth Night became a time of disorderly behaviour and overindulgence. Around 1860, Queen Victoria announced that she felt it was inappropriate to hold such an unchristian festival and Twelfth Night celebrations were banned. The confectioners who made Twelfth Night cakes lost income by the cancellation of the events, so they began to decorate the cakes with snowy scenes and sold them at Christmas instead; consequently, the modern Christmas cake is the direct descendant of the Twelfth Night cake.

FAIRS AND WAKES Fairs have been popular events in England since the Middle Ages, with celebrations connected to religious festivals. People congregated at the fairs to join in the entertainments,

music and dancing, and to buy luxury food items such as toffee apples, brandy snaps and ginger biscuits known as 'fairings', sold from booths and stalls. White foods were considered luxurious in medieval England and junket was one such treat that featured so often at fairs held on religious holidays that the holidays themselves became known as 'junketing days'.

The Stourbridge fair, authorised by King John by royal charter in 1199, became the largest medieval fair in Europe. Some medieval fairs still take place today, such as Ilkeston Charter Fair, held in the Derbyshire town since 1252; Hull Fair, granted a charter in 1278; and Nottingham Goose Fair, held annually (with only three cancellations) since 1284.

In Lancashire, fairs were known as 'wakes'. The origin of the wakes is probably that they were intended to commemorate the anniversary of a church or chapel in the local area, when it was traditional to keep watch, or 'wake', in church on the eve of the celebration. However, by the 19th century, the wakes had mostly lost their religious associations. During Lancashire's industrial era, the most eagerly awaited time of the year was the annual summer holiday, known as Wakes Week.

SUNDAY LUNCH

The simple phrase 'Sunday lunch' paints a picture of a sizzling piece of meat, rich gravy, succulent vegetables and a delicious dessert. This well-loved occasion is said to have originated in medieval times, when the lord of the manor was sometimes good enough to provide a feast for his local militia and farm workers after church and archery practice. In later centuries, Sunday lunch gradually became a ritual – an ideal opportunity to roast a good-sized piece of meat slowly in the oven while the family was at church, followed by frantic activity – cooking vegetables and making gravy – the minute the cook arrived home around midday. The leftovers would feed everyone for days afterwards. To many people,

the aroma of a roast wafting from the kitchen still means 'home' and 'Sunday'. In these hectic days of the 21st century, it is sometimes difficult to find a time when all the members of a family can sit down to a meal together, and the dishes may have changed to suit diets and tastes, but Sunday lunch as a ritual is still thriving.

THE SUNDAY ROAST

Traditionally, the most typical Sunday lunch consists of a small starter such as soup or potted shrimps, followed by a huge and mouthwatering piece of roast beef, crisp roast potatoes, Yorkshire pudding, plenty

ABOVE The Roast Beef of Old England *by Frank Moss Bennett is named after a patriotic ballad by Henry Fielding.*

ABOVE *Traditional roast for Sunday lunch, whether beef (left) or crackling pork (right).*

of vegetables and lots of gravy. However, some great variations on this theme have arisen over the years in various parts of England. Northern cooks tend to serve Yorkshire pudding as a starter – it sits in splendid isolation on the plate with the tasty, meaty gravy poured into the centre. This fills up hungry stomachs and whets the appetite for the rich and costly meat to follow. Lancashire is particularly renowned for its savoury pies and puddings, which eke out a small amount of meat with a lot of gravy and some appetising pastry. Originally, meat puddings with a suet crust would be boiled in a cloth for several hours – the same length of time as a roast takes to cook and more convenient for those without an oven at home.

Until the 20th century, farming families in the rural areas had access to more meat than their town-dwelling counterparts, and enjoyed roast pork with its crisp crackling during the colder months of the year and tender lamb in the spring. Chicken and turkey are cheap and widely available now, but they were rare a hundred years ago and far more expensive than beef. In those days, poultry dishes were more likely to consist of goose or duck, served frequently at the tables of the rich, but only as an

occasional treat for the less affluent. Goose was traditional at Christmas, often roasted in the local baker's oven on the day. Nowadays fish, vegetarian or vegan dinners are served as well, of course.

SOMETHING SWEET

Finally, there would be a stunning dessert of the kind that British cooks have made their speciality, served with custard or cream. The magnificent puddings and desserts that traditionally end a Sunday lunch include hot fruit pies and crumbles, tarts, and hot and cold puddings. These were typically based either on fruits of the season – for instance, apple pie or poached pears – or on creamy mixtures such as rice pudding. The trend for eating sweet dishes such as trifle and fruit jelly at the end of a meal started in the 19th century (these dishes are now perhaps more typically served at teatime), and Victorian cooks really threw themselves into the task of devising ever more elaborate recipes with wonderful decorations. Nowadays the dishes tend to be simpler, but everyone still looks forward to a seasonal treat such as a beautiful summer pudding or warming winter fruit crumble.

TEATIME TRADITIONS

Whether teatime is a quick cuppa and a biscuit at 4pm, a children's tea with sandwiches and cake, or a proper afternoon meal, the idea of teatime is embedded in the English psyche. Teatime might have had several changes since the 1600s, when leaf tea first arrived in England, but is still a familiar and well-loved ritual.

HIGH TEA

In the 19th century, as the working classes flocked to the cities to work in factories, the working day lengthened and the main meal of the day was served when they returned home in the evening at around 7pm. Breakfast was a modest affair, followed by a portable meal at midday. The evening meal often consisted of stews or meat puddings made with suet pastry – dishes that could be left all day to cook. Alternatively, it might be something that could be prepared quickly at the end of the working day, such as chops, kippers or perhaps cold meats, cheeses and pickles. Apple tart or milk pudding would follow, and it would all be washed down with tea, which was by now England's most popular drink. It came to be known as high tea because it was eaten sitting 'up' at the table, unlike afternoon tea.

AFTERNOON TEA

The quintessential English ritual of afternoon tea is said to have begun in the 1840s, and is usually attributed to the 7th Countess of Bedford. The fashionable hour for dinner, the main meal of the day, had moved to around 8pm, instead of 3 to 4pm, and a light meal at this time helped to ward off hunger pangs. When afternoon tea was introduced, it soon became an elegant social event with specific etiquette and smart dress, and was an ideal opportunity to show off fine china and silver. The meal was a light and leisurely affair that was conducted in the drawing room, front parlour or sitting room. China or Indian tea would be offered, together with a selection of sandwiches and cakes, the latter often made with fruit.

At first the gatherings were made up mainly of middle- and upper-class ladies, and provided an opportunity to gossip. Many of the scenes in Oscar Wilde's most enduring play, *The Importance of Being Earnest* (1895), revolve around the afternoon tea table, its cakes and cucumber sandwiches, and, when accused by a friend of eating too much, Algernon is able to respond with complete assurance, 'I believe it is customary in good society to take some slight refreshment at five o'clock.'

Initially a purely domestic phenomenon, by the end of the 19th century the serving of afternoon tea had been adopted by the large hotels which were springing up all over Britain – and in far-flung reaches of the British Empire. Fashionable cafes followed suit, and, even when silver cake stands and cucumber sandwiches were no longer to be found in homes, they could still be found in these sophisticated hotels and cafes, and today we can enjoy afternoon tea in one form or another in teashops in towns and villages throughout England.

THE TEA TABLE

The new 19th-century phenomenon of afternoon tea was not only good for tea importers; it heralded a growth in several attendant industries, such as the production of fine china and porcelain tea services and the manufacture of silverware.

RIGHT *Beautiful vintage tea services displayed on a traditional kitchen dresser.*

The East India Company made huge profits out of the tea that they brought from China, and so did the government, who applied hefty taxes to the product. To increase sales, the importers quickly realised that their new customers needed something in which to brew the tea. The Chinese were used to brewing tea in powdered form in a teacup, but towards the end of the 14th century larger-leaved teas had become popular, requiring a brewing vessel, and the Chinese, who had made growing and brewing tea a skill akin to that of wine production, had adapted their traditional wine pots to this purpose, adding a handle and a spout.

This appealing Chinese design found favour with the English when they became interested in drinking tea, and many stoneware pots of this kind were exported back to England. These in turn spawned imitators, principally in Staffordshire, and the familiar 'Brown Betty' teapot evolved, a utilitarian vessel, with a high sheen glaze, reputed to make the best pot of tea. While not the most elegant of teapots, it had the virtue of durability – and, given the sheer quantity of tea being brewed in Britain at the time, that was not to be underestimated. The design of the Brown Betty has stood the test of time and can be seen in many households to this day, although nowadays in every colour imaginable.

The teapot always was and remains the undisputed star of the proceedings at the tea table. Over the years endless sleek styling and technical innovations in design have been dedicated to the teapot during its illustrious career. Nonetheless, in Britain at least, the ever-reliable earthenware teapot remains the default pot style of choice in many households – and for that we have to thank an anonymous 14th-century Chinese craftsman.

ABOVE *Afternoon tea in the garden, with a Willow-patterned tea service.*

Such workaday items as the Brown Betty teapot, however, were not suited to the elegant style of service that tea drinking demanded among the fashionable, well-heeled set. Consequently, it was Chinese porcelain which lent the most lustre to the new custom in Britain. This was the era of the craze for chinoiserie, when Chinese silks, wallpapers, screens and porcelain were the must-have items for any distinguished household. The East India Company's merchants started to exploit these markets, eventually involving themselves in the design and production process in China. Many a noble house in the 18th century would display dinner services of fine porcelain emblazoned with their coats of arms, hand-painted on the other side of the world. Teapots, teacups and saucers were now added to the shopping list among a growing range of other tea-serving items.

The Chinese dominance of the porcelain industry, could not last, however. German alchemists discovered the formula for making porcelain, and later Josiah Wedgwood of England was credited with industrialising the production of pottery on a scale never seen before. Other manufacturers followed suit, and the distinctive elements of Chinese designs such as the ubiquitous Willow Pattern and Blanc de Chine were shamelessly plundered, remaining popular even now.

It was not just the demand for teapots that fuelled the porcelain boom. During the 18th century British tea drinkers discovered a taste for black teas (as opposed to the green teas they had drunk initially) and found that these bitter teas worked particularly well with the addition of milk and sugar. This was good news for dairy farmers, West Indian sugar planters and porcelain manufacturers, who produced suitable vessels for the new additions. Then, in the 19th century, along came the idea of afternoon tea with its cakes and sandwiches, and yet more items were required to make up a tea service.

Others benefited commercially from the fashion for tea. Silver manufacturers were required to create

ABOVE *Teatime by Miles Birket Foster (1825–1899).*

sugar tongs, strainers, teaspoons, cake stands and small cutlery to enhance the daintiness of the offering, as well as teapots, milk jugs and sugar bowls for the top-notch tearooms. Linen mills, embroiderers and lacemakers did well, likewise, in producing tablecloths and napkins — even the innovation of the humble doily was a spin-off from the unstoppable growth in demand for tea.

THE ETIQUETTE OF AFTERNOON TEA

Over two centuries of tradition have led to a wealth of customs and codes of behaviour that are considered the way to display proper teatime manners in genteel society. Smart clothes and good manners are always welcomed at the tea table.

When serving afternoon tea, the host or hostess should bring all the essential items to the tea table on a large tray. The tray should be set down on the table and the individual items arranged appropriately. Platters of sandwiches and cake stands should be placed in the middle of the table and the teapot should be positioned with the spout facing the pourer. In front of each guest a teacup should be placed on a saucer with a teaspoon resting on the right side, a small plate with a fork for eating cake (or knife if you are serving anything that requires spreading) and a napkin. The milk jug and sugar bowl should be arranged near the centre.

Pouring the tea perfectly A warm teapot should be filled immediately when the water boils, and be brought to the table on a tray where it can stand while the tea brews. When the tea is ready to pour, the pourer should take the teapot to each guest and pour carefully into each cup. Tea is traditionally served in a cup holding 120ml/4fl oz of liquid and should be three-quarters filled with tea. The size is not imperative, but a teacup should be shallower and

wider than a coffee cup to allow the tea to cool slightly before drinking.

Demure tea drinking Once the tea has been poured, guests may add milk or lemon (offered in delicate slices) and sugar. It is preferable to use gentle to-and-fro movements with the spoon rather than wide, noisy circular motions. The teaspoon should be placed on the saucer to rest. If seated at the table, the correct etiquette is to lift the teacup only to drink the tea and replace it on the saucer between sips. If there is no table, the saucer should be held in the left hand on your lap and the teacup in your right hand. It should be returned to the saucer when not in use. The cup should be held daintily by the handle between the thumb and fingers, with the little finger extended for balance. Never hold the teacup in the palm of your hand or loop your fingers through the handle, and by no means should you wave the cup around. Tea should be drunk in small, silent sips from the cup with as much grace and elegance, and as little slurping, as possible.

Elegant eating The correct size of plate to use for serving sandwiches, cakes, pastries and other delicacies at afternoon tea is between 15cm and 20cm/6in and 8in. The hostess must ensure that guests are provided with the necessary cutlery for the food that is served. It is customary to serve wafer-thin sandwiches, cut into triangles and with crusts removed, from purposely designed bread and butter plates. Finger food can also be served. A slice of cake, scones with jam and cream, or a selection of biscuits, are appropriate, in dainty sizes. When enjoying afternoon tea at a table, place the napkin on your lap and, if you leave the table temporarily for any reason, set the napkin on the seat. All food should be eaten in delicate bites. When not in use, forks should be rested on the side of the plate with

LEFT *A traditional stove-top simple enamel kettle to boil the water for making tea.*

ABOVE *Loose-leaf tea is brewed in the pot, and poured through the strainer into the tea cup.*

the tines down. Never place them back on the table once they have been used. Similarly, place used knives on the side of the plate.

A social event Above all, afternoon tea is a sociable occasion to be enjoyed with friends and family. So, smile and make polite conversation (between mouthfuls, of course) and savour this most quintessential of English traditions.

BREWING A PERFECT POT OF TEA

Whether your preference is for green, black, herbal or flavoured, there is nothing more refreshing in the afternoon than a pot of freshly brewed tea. Aficionados have maxims of their own on what constitutes the perfect cup of tea, and what is the best blend, but they all agree that utmost care should be taken in making it.

The key ingredient of a perfect cup of tea is easily taken for granted – it is none other than water. This should be freshly drawn, which means that the cold tap should be allowed to run for at least half a minute before the kettle is filled. Likewise, twice-boiled water is dull and lifeless, so empty the kettle before filling it with fresh. The hardness of your water supply has a great influence on the quality of your tea. Some manufacturers even go to the lengths of making specific blends for specific areas. Very soft water mutes the nuances of flavour in a tea, and very hard water tends to dull the appearance of the brew and can create an unpleasant scum. Filtering the water before boiling always improves its performance.

1 Always warm the teapot before measuring in the tea. Either hold the inverted pot over the spout of the kettle as it boils, or swill the teapot with boiling water before adding the tea leaves.

2 There is no fixed amount of tea that should be used. Large-leaf teas occupy more volume than small-leaf ones, so adjust the measure accordingly.

3 Tea brews best at boiling point, so pour the water onto the tea leaves as soon as the water boils. Stir briskly. Allow to stand for at least 3 minutes.

4 Pour the tea through a strainer once it has brewed to your preferred strength. Add lemon, milk and/or sugar as desired.

Adding lemon Many people drink black tea with a slice of lemon for added zest – though some tea purists feel you shouldn't add anything.

Adding milk Milk can temper the bitterness of black tea. It doesn't matter whether you add the milk before or after the tea – adding first helps it to mix, but adding after gives more control of the colour.

Adding sugar Sweetness is a matter of individual preference. White sugar (loose or in lumps) can be added to black, milk and lemon tea.

ENGLAND'S REGIONAL FOOD

The distinctive food of England gradually developed over generations from the ingredients available locally, shaped by the temperate climate and geography. The traditional recipes of each region, and the customs that surround them, play a role in creating the identity of English cooking. There are dishes that are found all over the country, and some rarely outside their original locality.

PICTURED *The gloriously green Yorkshire Dales.*

SCOTLAND

NORTHERN
IRELAND

NORTH SEA

SIX REGIONS

*This chapter groups England into six broad
areas for the purposes of culinary overview.
These don't have official boundaries, but are
recognisable regions with distinctive food
traditions. Within England are 48 counties,
each with its own specialities and
recipes to explore.*

Newcastle-upon-Tyne

Carlisle

Durham

NORTH-
WEST

NORTH-EAST

Isle of Man

Leeds   York

Lancaster

Liverpool

Sheffield

Manchester

Lincoln

Derby   Nottingham

Stoke-on-Trent

MIDLANDS

Norwich

WALES

Birmingham   Coventry

Cambridge

Northampton

EASTERN COUNTIES

Hereford

Ipswich

Gloucester

Oxford

London

Bristol

SOUTH-EAST

Canterbury

Salisbury

Southampton

Brighton

Dover

SOUTH-WEST

Portsmouth

Isle of Wight

Exeter

ENGLISH CHANNEL

Plymouth

Penzance

IRISH SEA

A COOK'S TOUR OF ENGLAND

Every region in England has its own historic food specialities. Transportation of perishable foods was difficult, and people relied mostly on local produce, shaped by the landscape. Wheat grown in the south-east was used to make bread, while barley was much used in Devon and Cornwall; oats grown in Staffordshire, Yorkshire and Lancashire were the staple grain used for their breads and griddle cakes. These regional recipes survived often unchanged for centuries. Many of these traditional specialities, redolent with flavours of times past, are still enjoyed today.

Some dishes instantly evoke the region they originated in, even though they are found and eaten around the country. The south-west boasts the classic clotted cream tea, with scones, jam and rich cream; one of the south-east's specialities is delicious Kentish cherry batter pudding. London is known for its sticky fruity Chelsea buns; in East Anglia, summer pudding is made with the luscious berries of the eastern counties. The Midlands is renowned for raised pork pies. The north has a strong baking tradition, and northerners are known for their sweet tooth: sticky toffee pudding, treacle tart and liquorice Pontefract cakes are just three of their creations that have become popular throughout England. A north-eastern speciality is the satisfying toad in the hole (sausages baked in batter) with pease pudding; one of the north-west's most famous dishes is hearty Lancashire hotpot. Many more are described in this chapter, and most are given as recipes in the cooking part of the book, although there is not room to detail every single one.

These regional specialities have survived through the years, sometimes undergoing adaptation to meet the tastes of a particular time, incorporating new ideas, cooking methods and ideas along the way. There are dishes that are found all over the country, with regional twists and variations, but also those that are rarely spotted outside their original locality. Some dishes are familiar and more everyday, and some are fascinating reminders of what people used to eat. There's great pleasure to be found in making the dishes that our ancestors took pride in, and in discovering ones we hadn't come across before. These recipes are all a cherished part of England's culinary heritage.

RIGHT *A country pub in a Cotswold village, in the south-west, and a classic car to tour in.*

THE SOUTH-EAST

This corner of England features chalk downs, dramatic cliffs and large seaports, and at its centre sprawls the capital city, London. In spite of its dense population the region's mild climate and warm, rich soil make it a prime source of fresh produce, high-quality meat and fish, and dairy products.

GRAZING THE FIELDS Sheep have always grazed the lowlands, and quality lamb and mutton come from the South Downs. The Romney sheep is a pure breed that feeds on the salt marsh pastures of Sussex and Kent, producing meat with a fine, distinctive flavour. Pig farms abound in Hampshire in particular, and the county hosts one of the largest sausage competitions in the country. Hampshire haslet (a pork loaf) is a local speciality.

Poultry has always been important in this area, both for eggs and for the rearing of table birds. As far back as the 1600s, the Surrey town of Dorking was said to host the greatest poultry market in England. The White Dorking chicken is famous for its unusual fifth claw and was a favourite with Queen Victoria. The Aylesbury duck, with its white plumage and orange legs and feet, is the largest of the domestic ducks and has been popular for two centuries.

Game in south-east England includes venison from the New Forest, a medieval enclave established by William the Conqueror for the preservation of deer for royal hunts, which is still largely in the possession of the Crown. In addition, pheasant, partridge and hare are shot in the region.

Historically, the area is better known for dairy farming than for beef. Until the mid-1800s Londoners were supplied with milk from herds that grazed on Clapham Common and Hampstead Heath. Though there is no ancient tradition of cheese-making, some fine farmhouse cheeses are now made in the area, such as Spenwood, Sussex Slipcote and Oxford Blue.

COAST AND RIVER While the long Kent coastline has seen a huge decline in the fishing industry, there are still fine Dover sole and a variety of fish and shellfish to be bought direct from little huts and harbours along the seafront. In Sussex, fishing is still an important business, and sea bass, red and grey mullet and conger eels are caught.

LEFT *Dappled fallow deer in Richmond Park.*
RIGHT *A flowering apple orchard, with oast house and Saxon church behind, in the Kent countryside.*

Whitstable, on the Kent coast, has long been known as the oyster centre of England, and an annual oyster festival is still celebrated. Smokehouses and fish farms, mainly for rainbow trout, are dotted around.

The River Thames was once full of eels, and its tributary the Wandle, now submerged under the streets of south London, was one of the finest trout streams. In Hampshire, the River Test still yields wild trout, pike and zander.

MARKET GARDENS Known until recently as the 'Garden of England', Kent grows much of the country's fruit. Spring blossoms promise apples (Cox's Orange Pippin and Bramley both originated in Kent), pears, plums and cherries, and the National Fruit Collections are based at Brogdale. There are soft fruits too, and cobnuts, a variety of hazelnut, are a local treat. Market gardens along the Sussex Weald produce large amounts of fruit (particularly gooseberries), vegetables and salad crops. Sussex is also known for its mushroom farms. Hampshire and the Isle of Wight produce cereals, root vegetables and watercress.

HOPS, APPLES AND VINES Many of the oast houses in which hops for beer-making were dried still stand in the Kent countryside. Harvest is celebrated at Faversham's hop festival. The area is dotted with breweries, and Kent and Sussex are also cider-making centres, making the most of local apples. South-facing slopes in the area are increasingly being planted with vines, following a tradition of viticulture first brought to England by the Romans.

BAKES AND CAKES The Bedfordshire clanger – originally a portable midday meal for farm labourers – is a hefty suet pastry with a savoury filling at one end and a sweet one at the other. St Clement's cake, made with butter, currants, spice, candied peel and sugar, is special to Berkshire, where until the late 1800s it was sold at the sheep fair in Lambourn on St Clement's Day (23rd November). Oxfordshire has Banbury cakes (oval pastries filled with mixed dried fruit) and, since 1874, has been associated with Frank Cooper's distinctive Oxford marmalade.

ABOVE *Fisherman's hut and eel traps on the River Test in Hampshire.*

ABOVE *London's East End is well known for cockle and whelk stalls; Tubby Isaacs was famous.*

Kent has its Kentish huffkins – small bread rolls made with a dimple for holding jam or cream. Flead cakes, similar to lardy cakes, were traditionally made at pig-killing time. In the Kent village of Biddenden, little cakes bearing a picture of the village's famous medieval conjoined twins, the Biddenden Maids, are distributed at Easter as part of an ancient charity set up by the sisters. In Surrey, lardy cakes, also known there as dough cakes or breakfast cakes, traditionally contained caraway seeds as well other spices and dried fruit. Guildford manchets are soft buttery rolls. Sussex has its lemony Sussex pond pudding, and the Isle of Wight is known for its doughnuts.

THE STREETS OF LONDON Until the early 1900s, London resounded to the cries and bell-ringing of street traders, such as the muffin man, who came bearing a tray of fresh muffins and crumpets on his head. Well into the 20th century

there were barrows selling shellfish – cockles, prawns, winkles and whelks – and roasted chestnuts are still sold in the streets at Christmas. The famous Chelsea buns were originally sold in the 18th century by a company called Chelsea Bun House, in Pimlico.

Since the 18th century, the East End of London has been home to eel and pie shops, selling stewed or jellied eels and meat pies. London is also famous for dishes such as whitebait (tiny fish deep-fried and eaten whole), and boiled beef and carrots. All types of pies were sold by pie men in taverns and on London's streets, right up to the middle of the 19th century, when the opening of pie shops brought about their gradual end. London still has pubs, chop houses and grill rooms serving specialities such as steak and kidney pudding and game pies. Its ancient food markets include Covent Garden for fruit and vegetables (now moved to east London), Billingsgate for fish, and Smithfield for meat and poultry.

THE SOUTH-WEST

This fertile region enjoys the mildest climate in England. It remains a popular holiday destination, with thatched cottages, fishing villages, shady creeks and glorious beaches. The seas are warmed by the Gulf Stream and spring always arrives early.

CREAM, CHEESE AND BUTTER Rich dairy pastures produce milk with a high butterfat content – ideal for making the cream, cheese, butter and ice cream for which the region is famous. The area is probably best known for its clotted cream, which is extremely thick and yellow, with a wrinkled, grainy crust and a distinctive flavour. Clotted cream keeps well and is sent as a souvenir all over the world. Local cream teas would not be correct without it.

There are cheeses galore. From Gloucestershire, where a traditional cheese-rolling race is still held in spring, come Single and Double Gloucester, some still made with milk from the now rare Gloucester cattle. Stinking Bishop, with its perry-washed rind and potent smell, is also made with this milk. Farther south, there is Dorset Blue Vinney and, in Somerset, perhaps the most copied of English cheeses – Cheddar. Meanwhile, Devon is proud of its blue cheeses: Devon Blue from cow's milk, Beenleigh Blue from ewe's milk and Harbourne Blue from goat's milk. Cornish Yarg, a tangy, white cheese made with cow's milk, has a distinctive rind made from nettle leaves.

VEGETABLES AND FRUIT Dorset produces delicious watercress, lettuces, peas and cabbage, as well as carrots, Brussels sprouts and onions. From the famous chalk-stone cliffs come sea kale, samphire and sea holly, the root of which was once candied and thought to be an aphrodisiac.

Cornwall's warm climate produces early fruit and vegetables, including new potatoes, peas, broad beans and, from the Tamar Valley, strawberries. Gooseberries grow well there and are traditionally served with the locally caught mackerel. Apple orchards flourish throughout the region and pear orchards are a feature of Devon.

COAST AND RIVER The extensive coastline is dotted with bustling harbours. In Devon, large numbers of fishing boats used to go out of Brixham, Plymouth and the tiny fishing villages where shoals of mackerel and herring were once landed. Today's catches are small, but may include haddock, mullet (red and grey), mackerel, turbot and sea bream, as well as crabs, lobsters and shellfish (scallops in

LEFT *Freshly baked scones packed with strawberry jam and clotted cream.*
RIGHT *The harbour at Polperro, Cornwall.*

particular). Off the Cornish coast, pilchards (large sardines) were once the largest catch of the region, and they are the filling for stargazy pie, the whole fish arranged with their heads sticking out of the pastry as if gazing at the stars. Mackerel is now the main catch, but at Newlyn and Falmouth monkfish, sole, hake, skate and other varieties are landed. The River Severn is known for its salmon fishing and has been fished for elvers (baby eels) for hundreds of years: until 1990, annual elver-eating contests were held at Frampton-on-Severn.

PIGS IN ORCHARDS While there is excellent beef and early lamb from the rich inland pastures of Dorset and Devon, pig farming is the tradition of the south-west and of Wiltshire in particular. Many local food specialities are based on pork and bacon, and as always every part of the

animal is utilised. Bradenham ham has a distinctive black skin and a sweet subtle flavour, which comes from being soaked in molasses flavoured with spices and juniper berries before being smoked and matured. Bath chaps are cured pig's cheeks, traditionally from the famous Gloucester Old Spot pigs who enjoy eating windfall apples during the autumn. Bath chaps are salted, smoked, then boiled; they are then served cold, or coated in breadcrumbs and fried. Other pork dishes include sausages, pies, faggots, brawn, chitterlings and trotters. Jellied stock goes into pork pies, lard is rendered, and blood goes into black puddings (blood sausages). Pork fat mixed with oatmeal is made into white puddings.

CREAM TEAS AND BAKES Cream teas are legendary in the south-west, with scones or splits (soft dough buns), strawberry jam and, of course,

ABOVE *Large Cheddar cheese truckles ripening in the cellar of a Devon farm cheesemaker.*

ABOVE *The eponymous eating house in Bath still serves the Sally Lunn bun; the Plymouth Gin Distillery opened in 1793.*

clotted cream. Wiltshire's lardy cake is made from white bread dough, rolled and folded with lard, sugar and dried fruit. Wiltshire fairings and Cornish fairings are similar to brandy snaps but more lace-like. They were originally sold at the town fairs, which were held for the purpose of hiring agricultural workers.

Apple cakes are particularly popular in Dorset and Devon. Dorset knobs are crisp, roll-shaped biscuits, and Devon flats are biscuits that are made with clotted cream.

From the Georgian city of Bath comes the Bath Oliver biscuit, developed by the doctor who founded the Mineral Water Hospital in the city; the Bath bun, made with rich yeast dough topped with currants and crushed lump sugar; and the Sally Lunn, reputedly of 17th-century origin – a round, light, yeast cake, traditionally split and spread with butter or clotted cream.

There are cakes made with fruit and honey (the monks of Buckfast Abbey look after bee colonies in Devon and Cornwall and sell the honey in the Abbey shop). Spices would arrive at West Country ports from all over the world, with saffron remaining a favourite baking ingredient to this day.

Last but not least is the Cornish pasty, a portable meal of meat, root vegetables and onions wrapped in thick pastry, originally designed for farmers and miners to carry to work. Authentic pasties are made with cubed (not ground) beef, although legend has it that the devil would not cross the River Tamar into Cornwall for fear that the people there would put anything into their pasties.

CIDER, SCRUMPY AND GIN With apples so abundant, cider has always been, and still is, the traditional drink of the region, certainly in rural areas. Traditional dry ciders are made with sour cider apples, originally crushed using a horse-drawn stone wheel. Cider made on the farm from small apples or windfalls is known as scrumpy. Plymouth has the oldest gin distillery in England, which has been supplying the Royal Navy with gin for more than 200 years.

THE MIDLANDS

This large and varied region at the heart of England is an area of valleys, rugged hills, peat bogs and moors. While it is still the home of many industries, it also has rich agricultural land, which offers orchards laden with fruit, natural spring waters and some of the best reared beef in the country.

LOCAL MEAT The ginger-haired Tamworth pig is the traditional breed in the Midlands. Pork scratchings (slivers of the crisply cooked rind) remain a local delicacy and hot roast pork rolls are a favourite. For centuries, frugal cottagers used every part of their home-reared pigs, and the legacy of this practice is the wide range of pork products that remain popular, from home-cured bacon, chitterlings, tripe and trotters to faggots, haslet, brawn, black pudding (blood sausage), sausages and pies. The most famous pork pies have been made in Melton Mowbray, Leicestershire, since the 1850s. These raised pies with their crisp hot-water-crust pastry are stuffed with chopped fresh pork and savoury jelly. The Hereford, one of England's oldest and best-known breeds of beef cattle, dates back to the 17th century. The Derbyshire Dales are well known for sheep rearing, though sheep are farmed all over the region.

The Nottingham Goose Fair has been held in October since the 1200s. Today it is a funfair, but originally geese were brought to the fair to be sold before being herded to London.

ABOVE *The Tamworth pig.*

ABOVE *Plum blossom in the Vale of Evesham.*

A HAPPY ACCIDENT In the 1830s, the Worcester chemists Lea & Perrins tried to concoct a new spiced condiment at the request of one of their customers, but it was considered too strong to be edible and left in a barrel in the basement of their shop. When rediscovered some time later, it was found to have fermented and mellowed, and the partners bottled and sold it with great success.

CHEESES A mild climate and frequent rain produce rich pastures, making the Midlands one of the country's most prolific milk-producing regions. Its abundance led to the region's fame in cheese-making, with Stilton the best known. Stilton has been popular since the 18th century and is still made with milk exclusively from Leicestershire, Nottinghamshire and Derbyshire.

Cheshire cheese is one of the oldest English cheeses, and it has been made continuously since the 12th century. In the 17th century, sage was added to Derby cheese for its alleged health-giving properties, creating Sage Derby. Shropshire Blue is a fairly modern cheese, and Red Leicester is named for its distinctive colour.

FRUITS AND VEGETABLES In the vast orchards of Worcestershire's Vale of Evesham, a large variety of apples grow, and apples feature on Worcester's coat of arms. Pears grow especially well in Herefordshire, and the area around Pershore forms the centre of English plum production, with Victoria plums the most popular and Pershore Yellow Egg the most interesting. The spring blossom is a beautiful sight and organised Blossom Trails guide visitors along the scenic routes of the Vale of Evesham.

Numerous vegetables grow in the market gardens of Herefordshire and Worcestershire, and the local asparagus is particularly famous. Leicestershire is proud of its Brussels sprouts and the Vale of Evesham produces fine salad crops and runner beans, as well as plums. There are also herb farms in this area and an increasing number of farms where vegetables are intensively grown.

RIVERS AND LAKES With little coastline, the area has always relied on rivers and lakes for local fish, though stocks are now severely depleted. The River Severn was formerly a rich source of salmon, eels and elvers (small eels, which were a local delicacy). The Dee and Wye are also well-known salmon-fishing rivers, with pike and grayling running in them too. There are several fish farms across the region.

CAKES AND PUDDINGS Brandy snaps and gingerbread are particularly popular, and for centuries have been sold at fairs throughout the

region. Staffordshire fruitcakes are enriched with treacle (molasses) and brandy, and the region is proud of its 'clangers' – hefty pastries with either savoury or sweet fillings, similar to the Bedfordshire clanger. To the north, in Northamptonshire, the making of little cheesecakes was traditional at sheep-shearing time.

Though barley and wheat are now the main crops of the region, oats were important in the 18th and 19th centuries. Still famous are Staffordshire oatcakes, made with yeast and fine oatmeal and resembling pancakes. Pikelets are thick, holey pancakes, traditionally served hot and oozing with melted butter at teatime.

Specialities from Midland towns include crisp, lemony Shrewsbury biscuits, which have been baked there for centuries, and Bakewell puddings, which it is claimed were invented in Bakewell in the Peak District in the 1860s; the original shop is still there. Coventry godcakes, triangular in shape to represent the Holy Trinity, were often presented by godparents to their godchildren for good luck.

ORCHARDS AND SPRINGS While the area is important for hop growing and brewing, it is far better known for its cider and perry, the latter made from the fermented juice of pears. There is also a lesser-known cider made from plums, called plum jerkum. The area produces some famous mineral waters, from the springs of Ashbourne and Buxton in the Peak District and the Malvern Hills.

BLACK COUNTRY FAGGOTS Faggots, which used to be known as 'poor man's goose' or 'savoury ducks', are made from a mixture of pork offal, onion, breadcrumbs and seasoning, wrapped in caul – the lining of the pig's stomach. 'Faggot' comes from the Latin word for 'bundle'.

LEFT *Crushed apples wrapped in stacked hessian (burlap) cloths to filter the juice to make cider.*
RIGHT *The original Melton Mowbray pork pie shop.*

THE EASTERN COUNTIES

This low-lying part of England facing the North Sea, with its cold winters and warm summers, is rich arable land. The area called the Fens spreads out from the Wash across Cambridgeshire, Lincolnshire and West Norfolk. Once a swampy wilderness, it was reclaimed with a network of tranquil waterways. The Norfolk and Suffolk Broads are Britain's largest protected wetland.

FIELDS AND MORE FIELDS The soil is fertile and warm and tends to be dry, and all sorts of crops thrive. There are plenty of vegetables: Lincolnshire is especially known for its peas and early crops, while East Anglia is famous for its asparagus. The salt marshes of Lincolnshire are home to succulent samphire. Numerous windmills (a few still working) are reminders of the importance of grain in this area: there are hundreds of fields growing wheat, barley and oil seed rape. The cultivation of sugar beet is important to the local economy and yellow fields of mustard have grown here ever since Jeremiah Colman started making his condiment near Norwich in 1814.

Soft fruits and orchards flourish in the region too, particularly around Wisbech in Cambridgeshire, and roadside stalls and pick-your-own farms are plentiful. Essex is a centre for jam-making, both cottage and commercial, and much of the produce is directed here. Then there are fruit juices and, in Lincolnshire, raspberry vinegar.

THE SEASIDE Fishing has always been an important industry in the east of England, with large ports including Grimsby and Lowestoft handling a

range of fish – cod, haddock, plaice, skate, sprats and turbot. In Southend, there is an annual festival celebrating whitebait, small quantities of which are still landed there. Great Yarmouth was once the centre for a huge herring fleet. The port bustled with workers dealing with up to 800,000 fish a day and there were large smokehouses at the docks sending smoked herrings, bloaters and kippers all over the world. As with many coastal towns, ecological influences and over-fishing have resulted in a major industry dwindling to almost nothing.

Shellfish thrive here, especially in the relatively shallow waters of the Wash. Cromer crabs, small but fleshy, can be bought at the roadside fresh or ready-dressed. There are cockles from Stiffkey and

LEFT *Cley Windmill at Cley next the Sea, Norfolk; a view across the reedbeds.*
RIGHT *Cooked crabs for sale at Aldeburgh, Suffolk.*

Leigh-on-Sea and whelks from Wells-next-the-Sea. Mussel beds are to be found along the coasts of Norfolk and Lincolnshire. The native oysters from the beds at Colchester (England's first recorded town) are world-famous, and the fishery here dates back to the Roman occupation. Farther north, at Brancaster, Pacific oysters are farmed.

In the Norfolk Broads, the eel industry was once big, and eels remain a local delicacy. Nowadays the waters are better known for pike and zander.

MALDON SALT The dry conditions on the Essex coast favour the production of sea salt, and the salt pans of Maldon are mentioned in the Domesday Book. The world-renowned Maldon crystal salt is soft and flaky, with a taste of the sea.

PIGS AND TURKEYS Though cattle and sheep are reared in East Anglia, pigs and poultry have always been preferred. In Essex, the Dunmow Flitch trials are still held every three years, at which a flitch (side) of bacon is presented to a married couple who can prove they have not quarrelled in the previous year. Fidget (fitchet) pies with bacon, onions and apples are popular. Lincolnshire pork sausages and haslet are flavoured with sage. Stuffed chine – salt pork, slashed and filled with herbs – is a favourite.

Norfolk has been famed for its turkeys since flocks of traditional Norfolk Blacks were driven on the three-month journey to London in time for the Christmas market. Now it is home to a huge turkey farm. Historically, chickens, ducks, geese and guinea fowl have been reared in the region and conditions are ideal for game birds such as pheasant, partridge, woodcock and duck. All kinds of meat and fish are cured in the smokehouses of the Norfolk village of Orford.

LEFT Two views of Norfolk: the promenade and pier at Cromer, and the salt marshes at Stiffkey.
RIGHT The Norfolk Black turkey, brought to England in the 1500s from Spain (and the New World).

BREAD, CAKES AND PUDDINGS

The people of Cambridgeshire are said to have been the first to use a pudding cloth for wrapping and cooking suet puddings. Lincolnshire is perhaps best known for its plum bread and Grantham has its own gingerbread – a crunchy, puffed-up sweet biscuit.

Apples feature as an ingredient, and there are cake recipes using saffron, which serve as a reminder that the purple saffron crocus was once grown around Saffron Walden in Essex, a town named for the spice in the 16th century.

BEER AND WINE The region boasts several independent breweries making beer by traditional methods. Norfolk cider is usually made with cooking or dessert apples rather than the cider apples used in the West Country, so is less astringent. The climate suits grape growing, and vineyards in Essex, Norfolk and Suffolk produce a range of interesting wines.

THE NORTH-EAST

This region is notable for its beautiful, craggy coastline, reaching up to the border of Scotland and dotted with castles facing the North Sea. The heather-covered, rocky mountains of the Pennines lie to the west and there are dales and moors, seaside resorts and quaint fishing villages. Traditional meals tend to be simple, cheap, tasty and, in the cold climate of the north, warming. Little is wasted.

FISH, CHIPS AND KIPPERS The North Sea has been a great source of sustenance for the people of this region, providing a selection of fish and shellfish including cockles, mussels, scallops, crabs

and lobsters. Whitby was once a great whaling port. The Yorkshire coble, a traditional 'off the beach' fishing boat designed to be launched from steep shingle, is still used to work the inshore waters. The strong fishing heritage has resulted in a love of fish and chips. This is the area to taste fish coated in a light, crisp batter, cooked in beef dripping, served with mushy peas and, of course, chips.

Northumberland has had a flourishing kipper industry based at Craster since the 19th century. It is still in business today, and herrings are split and hung from the rafters of the smokehouses before being smoked slowly and gently over the traditional fuel of smouldering oak chips.

LIVESTOCK AND GAME Plenty of high-quality beef is produced here – ideal for one of England's best-known meals: Roast Beef and Yorkshire Pudding. Yorkshire's famous batter pudding was originally cooked beneath the meat so that it caught and soaked up the juices. It was made as one large pudding and could be eaten as a first course, with gravy, before the roast: an idea developed in lean days to reduce the appetite for meat. In pubs and restaurants today, Yorkshire puddings are filled with sausages and gravy, mince or stew.

Sheep are the principal livestock of the region, and the Yorkshire Moors and Yorkshire Dales are still home to some hardy breeds. Mutton was traditionally used in sausages, stews and pies, and sheep's milk is made into interesting, distinctively flavoured local cheeses.

As elsewhere, pigs have always played an important role too, with lard going to make cakes and pork

LEFT *Kippers hung up to smoke in Fortunes Kippers Smokehouse, Whitby, in North Yorkshire.*
RIGHT *Sheep on a frosty day in the Yorkshire Dales.*

pies. The famous York ham, traditionally eaten at Christmas, is prepared using the meat of the Large White pig, dry-salted, smoked and hung.

The moors are ideal habitat for game, with fine grouse, partridge, pheasant, hare and deer to be had. Local dishes include jugged hare, game pies, pâtés and sausages.

DOCK PUDDING

A springtime speciality enjoyed in West Yorkshire's Calder Valley is a pudding made with oatmeal, onions, nettles and 'dock', or bistort, a species of knotweed. Once boiled, the pudding is thickly sliced and fried in bacon fat. An annual Dock Pudding Championship is held in Mytholmroyd.

DALES CHEESES

Cheese was made here in the Middle Ages by Cistercian monks, who brought cheese-making skills from Roquefort in France (there is a Yorkshire Blue). Crumbly white Wensleydale cheese, made in Hawes in North Yorkshire, is traditionally eaten with rich fruitcake or Christmas cake. Wensleydale almost went out of production in the 1990s, but, as the favourite cheese of Wallace and Gromit, it is now enjoying renewed success. Cotherstone, made in Teesdale, is a tangy, yellow cheese.

VEGETABLES AND FRUIT

While most of the land is best suited to grazing, some is arable. Leeks grow especially well in this area and there

ABOVE *Picking rhubarb in a candlelit barn, Wakefield, West Yorkshire.*

ABOVE *Lindisfarne Castle on the Northumberland coast.*

are local competitions to discover the largest. Traditionally, leeks might be cooked in a pudding with suet pastry and served alongside meat stew. Pulses are popular and dishes containing dried peas were eaten regularly during Lent, when meat was forbidden. In the 1800s, pease pudding was sold as street food.

Rhubarb growing is traditional in Yorkshire, notably in the 'Rhubarb Triangle' between Pontefract, Wakefield and Leeds, which supplies the country with some of the finest forced rhubarb in early spring. Gooseberry showing is a tradition at the annual show in Egton Bridge, North Yorkshire. Growers return year after year to display traditional varieties and take part in a competition for the heaviest fruit. Bilberries (a small blueberry) grow wild on the moors in late summer.

BAKES Baking is a strong northern tradition and the region's teashops serve buttered teacakes, rich fruitcakes, cakes and biscuits. Many puddings are enjoyed, including Yorkshire curd tart. Parkin, made with oatmeal and treacle (a dark molasses), is traditionally eaten on Guy Fawkes Night on 5th November.

Bakestone cooking was popular here for oatcakes, drop scones, Newcastle singin' hinnies and crumpets. Stottie cake, a savoury bread made with flour and milk, is traditional for assembling bacon or chip butties. Local sweets include Harrogate toffee and Pontefract cakes, made from liquorice, which was once grown prolifically and is still made into confectionery. There is an annual liquorice festival.

BEER AND HOLY BREW The region has a robust tradition of family-owned, independent breweries making strong beer. In pubs, customers can be heard asking for 'Newkie' or 'brown dog' – Newcastle's famous brown ale. On Lindisfarne, just off the Northumberland coast, the monks of the 7th century brewed mead, which is still made there today.

THE NORTH-WEST

This is a region of beautiful lakes, mountains and a dramatic coastline. It is protected by the Pennine range in the east and the Cheviots to the north. Between the hills and the Irish Sea lies the stunning area of the Lake District, together with manufacturing towns and plenty of farming land. Northern dishes were devised with hard-working people and big appetites in mind. They tend to be hearty and are often based on economical ingredients.

MEAT, PUDDINGS AND PIES The climate of the north-west of England is milder and wetter than that of the north-east and most of the land is given to grazing. Hardy breeds of sheep, chosen to withstand the cold and wind of the uplands, dot the hills and moorlands. Butchers' shops sell choice local lamb, which goes into classic dishes such as Lancashire Hotpot and Shepherd's Pie. Mutton, which was once a staple throughout the country, is

seeing a revival and is now reared in Cumbria. Wild game, including the succulent Derwentwater duck, also thrives on uncultivated moors and mountains.

There is plenty of pork and bacon. Cumberland hams are dry-cured, salted and rubbed with brown sugar. Meaty Cumberland sausage, seasoned with herbs and spices, is sold in a coil and bought by the length rather than by weight. Meats and sausages are often served with Cumberland sauce, made with redcurrant jelly, port, orange and spices. There is offal to be found that is now seldom seen in southern England: tripe and onions, brains, chitterlings (pig's intestines), elder (pressed cow's udder), lamb's fry (testicles) and sweetbreads. Pig's trotters and cow heel are used to enrich stews and to make jellied stock for pies.

The north-west is black pudding (black sausage) country. The sausage-shaped puddings, made from pig's blood and oatmeal, vary in texture and taste according to their maker. Secret recipes abound and there are competitions to discover the best. Faggots, potted meats, pressed tongue and brisket of beef are popular too.

Hot pies, both savoury and sweet, can be bought from stalls (especially popular at football matches), butchers, and fish and chip shops.

THE DAIRY The lush pastures of this region mean there is plenty of milk to make fine cream, butter and cheese. Dairy breeds such as Friesians are chosen for their high milk yields and are left to graze on the lowlands. Lancashire cheese has been made since the early 1900s and has a soft, crumbly texture

LEFT *Saddleback pigs on a farm in Wigglesworth, Lancashire.*
RIGHT *A view of Thirlmere from Raven Crag fell, in the Lake District.*

and buttery flavour. Goats and sheep are kept for their milk too – and for yogurt and cheeses. In Cumberland, rum butter is a speciality that was traditionally served with oatcakes to visitors who had come to celebrate the birth of a baby.

BAYS AND LAKES Fishing has always been important to the region, with the industry centred in Fleetwood. Flatfish (such as plaice and sole), hake and herring (often stuffed and served with mustard sauce) are particularly popular. Morecambe Bay is famous for its small brown shrimps, which are potted in butter and sent all over the world.

Freshwater fish include trout and salmon in the lakes and rivers. It was traditional to catch them in the estuaries in wide 'heave' or 'haaf' nets, held by the fishermen standing in the water. Char is a fish special to the Lake District and is potted or used in pies. Found in the deep waters of the lakes, it is

caught with long fishing lines. The Isle of Man is famed for kippers and tiny scallops.

HARDY CROPS Lancashire is one of the few areas sheltered enough to grow vegetables. Varieties are chosen to suit the harsh climate, especially potatoes, root vegetables and some salad plants. Little fruit is grown in the cold climate of this region, but damsons (known as witherslacks and grown around Lake Windermere) and gooseberries are notable exceptions.

BAKED GOODS This region offers a host of special cakes and pastries, such as Eccles cakes – flaky pastry cases stuffed full of currants, sugar and spices – and the Cumberland rum nicky, a pie with a similar filling doused in rum (rum was shipped here from the West Indies in the 1700s). Corners are large round pies cut into serving-size quarters. Chester

ABOVE *Trout fly fishing at Watendlath tarn, Cumbria, in the Lake District.*

ABOVE *A damson tree in fruit.*
RIGHT *Grasmere Gingerbread was created in Victorian times, and is still made and sold in the village.*

buns are made with yeast dough glazed with sugar and water. Chester cake is made with stale cake, treacle, currants and ginger, and cut into small squares. Gingerbread has been made in Grasmere since the mid-19th century (by a local cook, Sarah Nelson), and the gingerbread shop is still there. Westmoreland pepper cake is a fruitcake spiced up with pepper. Goosnargh cakes from Lancashire, biscuit-like and flavoured with caraway seeds or coriander, were traditionally sold at Easter and Whitsun and served with a jug of ale. There are also curd tarts similar to those made in Yorkshire. Manchester tart has a pastry base spread with jam, topped with custard and sprinkled with coconut.

Dense, chewy treacle toffee is popular here, while Everton toffee is crisp and flavoured with lemon. Kendal mint cake, the strongly peppermint-flavoured sweet, is taken on treks as a source of instant energy.

THE ENGLISH LARDER

There is an incredible range of foods grown and produced in England – sourced from its orchards and hedgerows to hillsides and lowland pastures, and from its rivers and lakes to extensive coastlines. The changing seasons offer the kitchen cook a fantastic variety of ingredients through the year, and a chance to explore all kinds of delicious regional dishes, both traditional and modern.

PICTURED *Food being prepared on the kitchen table at Lanhydrock, a stately home in Cornwall.*

THE KITCHEN GARDEN

In the past, most country gardens contained a few vegetables, a fruit tree or two and maybe a beehive or some chickens – all with one aim in mind: to put food on the table. Since the Romans brought their cultivated varieties to Britain in the 1st century BCE, vegetables and fruits have played an important role in the British diet. In a short time, the Celtic diet of wild plants and roots expanded to include a range of grown and harvested vegetables. Fields of beans and peas were common by the Middle Ages, and explorers returned from the New World with potatoes and other exotics. Medieval French monks introduced many previously unknown varieties of vegetables, such as spinach, green beans and cauliflower. When transport improved, produce could be enjoyed outside their traditional growing areas, and by the late 20th century they were being imported from all over the world, and most vegetables and fruits became available year-round.

While modern transport allows out-of-season foods to be imported from many parts of the world, discerning cooks still eagerly await the arrival of the new season's home-grown potatoes, asparagus and strawberries. Today there is revived interest in the growing and eating of local, seasonal produce, and more shops and farmers' markets are offering high-quality local produce.

VEGETABLES

In most kitchens, vegetables were simply boiled and served plain. Although vegetables and potatoes have always been important in the traditional English diet, they have usually been served as side dishes to accompany meat and fish, rather than being the central feature of a main dish. They were most often plain-boiled and usually dressed with butter. Traditional soups and stews depend upon a high vegetable and herb content, but this (and a tradition of one-pot cooking) tended to encourage the cooking of vegetables for too long, and this is a failing that many home cooks have remedied only in the last couple of generations. As well as accompanying main dishes, vegetables are used in soups, in first courses, as garnishes for entrées, as vegetarian dishes and in many savoury dishes. In traditional kitchens, carrot, onion, celery, leek, parsnip, swede (rutabaga) and

LEFT *A trug of freshly harvested vegetables.*
RIGHT *A kitchen garden on grand scale in the grounds of the Tudor Walmer Castle in Kent.*

ABOVE *Harvested onions drying (left) and freshly picked radishes (right).*

herbs such as fresh parsley, thyme, garlic and bay leaf, are the mainstays of many recipes. A mixture of these basic ingredients is at the heart of many stews and soups.

Beneath the soil Every cook's standby for a side dish to accompany meat or fish, carrots are also used to give their flavour and sweetness to soups and casseroles. In the days when sugar was still a costly imported luxury, most people relied on honey to sweeten their food, but they also used the natural sweetness of root vegetables, particularly carrots. Their inherent natural sweetness and moist texture once cooked made them a successful ingredient in many cakes, puddings, pies, tarts and preserves. They store well throughout the winter.

Parsnip has a distinctive, sweet flavour. Steam or boil it lightly, mash it (perhaps mixed with carrots or potatoes), roast it or add it to soups and stews. It takes very well to spices, and makes a delicious curried soup.

When the potato was introduced to Britain from America in the late 16th century, it took a long time to become accepted. However, it eventually became an important crop and by the 19th century had become a staple food. Boiled potatoes were cheap

and filling, and were sold from carts in some cities. The curiously named rumbledethumps, from the Border region, is made with potatoes and cabbage. The name comes from 'rumbled and thumped'. Today there are many varieties, and there is a potato to suit every cooking method and every meal. They are still eaten in huge quantities, boiled or steamed 'in their skins' (jackets) and dressed with butter. Potatoes are also mashed with milk (or cream) and butter, with added herbs or other mashed vegetables.

The sweet, peppery flavour of the white turnip is best appreciated in spring and early summer, when it goes especially well with lamb and duck. Turnips were first introduced via Scotland in the 18th century, although the Scots recognised them immediately as a tasty vegetable – unlike the English, who fed them to their cattle, but they are now enjoyed as the delicacy they are. The youngest, smallest turnips have the best flavour and texture. Larger than turnip and with a leathery purple skin, swede (rutabaga) has a firm flesh and a sweet taste that is quite distinctive. It is usually eaten mashed with plenty of butter.

The onion was one of the foods introduced to Britain by the Romans, and has been popular ever since. By the Middle Ages, onions, together with cabbage and beans, were one of the three main vegetables eaten by rich and poor, in all parts of the British Isles. Apart from their use in all kinds of soups and stews, they can be eaten raw in salads, fried, boiled in milk, roasted (sometimes with a cheese topping) or chargrilled. Sliced onions fried in butter until deep brown are a traditional accompaniment to steak.

When freshly grated and mixed with cream and seasoning, the pungent root horseradish makes a sauce that is a perfect accompaniment to roast beef.

Jerusalem artichoke (sunchoke) is a knobbly root that can be served roasted, boiled or made into soup. It has an affinity with game.

Often cooked and pickled, beetroot can also be boiled or roasted and served hot. When they are young, the tops of beet can be eaten as greens.

Above the soil With its delicate onion flavour, the leek is good in many dishes, including soups, pies, sauces and stews. Leek is often used to flavour fish in the same way that onion is used with meat. Slice leeks down the middle and wash very well to remove any sand or grit; chop and add to soups or stews.

Spring onions (scallions) are used to enhance traditional potato dishes such as champ or colcannon, and in salads.

Once known by the name of sparrowgrass, asparagus was popular with the Romans and has been grown in English country gardens ever since the 16th century. East Anglia and the Vale of Evesham are the traditional growing areas. It has a short, six-week growing season, which makes it a particular delicacy. Asparagus is wonderful served steamed with melted butter, or soft-boiled eggs to dip the spears into.

One of the oldest vegetables, cabbage is easy to grow. The English enjoy several varieties – green, white and red – with the wrinkly Savoy and young spring greens being particularly popular, though

RIGHT *Locally grown asparagus on a market stall. It has a short season, so shouldn't be missed.*

stewed red cabbage is a favourite accompaniment for goose and venison. Available all year round, cabbage can be boiled, steamed or stir-fried.

Thought to have originated in the eastern Mediterranean, cauliflower was bought to Britain by the Romans. Along with broccoli, these popular vegetables can be cooked in similar ways. Favourite dishes are the classic cauliflower cheese and a soup incorporating cheese and cream. Cauliflower grows particularly well in the south-west of England. Brussels sprouts look and taste like tiny cabbages. They are served as a side vegetable (traditionally mixed with chestnuts at Christmas) or thinly sliced and served raw or stir-fried.

Globe artichoke is an edible thistle, with layers of leaves surrounding the central heart. It was introduced to Britain from the Mediterranean, but flourishes in milder regions. It is good boiled and served with lemon butter, for dipping the base of the leaves and the hearts. In spite of the name, globe

artichokes are not related to Jerusalem artichokes (or sunchokes).

An essential pot-herb, celery is eaten raw (as crudités), braised (especially the hearts), often with cheese, or as an ingredient in soup. After the Romans brought celery to England, it grew wild and tough until the 18th century, when it was cultivated and blanched to keep its stems tender. Now we enjoy both pale green summer celery and white winter celery.

When spinach first arrived in Britain from Spain, where it was introduced by the Moors, it was referred to as 'the Spanish vegetable'. The small young leaves add a mildly peppery taste to salads, but it is more commonly cooked as a side dish and is especially good with fish. Though similar to spinach, chard has thick stems that can be tough when older and need to be cooked longer than the leaves. Ruby chard has vivid red stems. Kale grows on a long stem and has curly dark green leaves but no head. It has the advantage of flourishing in the harsher climate of

northern regions and is resistant to frost – in fact, the flavour improves after it has been nipped by a slight frost. Shred the leaves finely and cook for a few minutes in boiling salted water, as for cabbage.

Peas and broad (fava) beans have been grown in Britain since the Middle Ages, when they were planted in cottage gardens and dried, to feed families through the winter. In summer they are deliciously sweet when small and freshly picked.

Pumpkin adds colour to autumn, when they are hollowed out and carved into Halloween lanterns, while the flesh is used for soup. There are many other varieties of squash, which can be mashed or roasted.

SALAD

Lettuce first appeared in English gardens in the 16th century. Its main use is in salads, though it can be braised with peas, or made into soup. There are many varieties, from traditional round and butterhead lettuces to crisp Cos and the tightly packed hearts of Little Gem.

Cucumber was a favourite for growing in Victorian glasshouses, as the plants need plenty of warmth during their short growing period. They are grown in greenhouses and allotments and are typically enjoyed thinly sliced in salads and sandwiches.

In 16th-century England, the tomato (botanically a fruit) was thought to be poisonous – a far cry from today's appreciation of it. England grows delicious tomatoes in season, though it faces stiff competition from year-round cheap imports. Tomatoes are very versatile, ideal for salads, grilling, frying, roasting, soups, sauces and casseroles.

Watercress has been grown in the spring waters of the south-east for about 200 years. In Hampshire the Watercress Line railway delivered the crop to London, and watercress sandwiches played a major part in the diet of the working classes. Land cress

LEFT *Cucumbers can be harvested while still small and tender, when they are ideal for pickling.*

ABOVE *Watercress being harvested.*

closely resembles watercress in shape and flavour and was once prevalent in the wild. Recently its popularity has begun to increase again. It grows in winter, making it a useful standby when salad ingredients are in short supply. Mustard and cress (white mustard and garden cress) were first grown together in Victorian times for adding to sandwiches. Today it is most often used as a salad ingredient, or added to egg mayonnaise sandwiches.

The English have eaten radishes for hundreds of years. Their peppery flavour is best appreciated when eaten just as they are, with salt for dipping.

HERBS

The Romans introduced most of the herbs the English use today. In the 16th century, when explorers brought home new exotic plants, the gardens of country houses filled with herbs. Some were used for culinary or medicinal purposes, or to make pomanders and scent bags. In the Victorian era,

herbs remained essential to flavour food that was often stale or bad. With the 20th century came the development of artificial flavourings, and use of herbs waned until the revival of interest in seasonal and locally grown foods. Today there are thriving herb farms growing a huge variety of culinary plants.

The most versatile herb, parsley (the strongly flavoured curly leaved variety is traditional), has leaves, stalks and roots that can be used in countless ways. Its flavour goes particularly well with fish and vegetables, and it is often added to soups, sauces and stews. The strong flavour of sage goes well with cheese, potatoes and pork, and it is popular as a stuffing for chicken. Mint, a summer herb, is chopped and mixed with sugar and vinegar to make mint sauce for roast lamb, and it is also used in salads and with new potatoes. French tarragon is the culinary herb used with eggs and chicken, and to flavour butter, vinegar and olive oil. The aniseed taste of fennel and dill's feathery fronds has an affinity with fish and vegetables, and the seeds go well with cheese

ABOVE *A flourishing herb garden, with verbena, chives, tarragon, thyme and rosemary.*

or pork. With their delicate onion flavour, chives are good snipped into salads, soups, sauces and egg dishes, and the flowers look good in a green salad. The fleshy, hollow stems of angelica can be crystallised and used in cakes and desserts; its leaves can be infused in milk or cream for desserts. Borage's young, tender leaves can be added to salads, but it is the blue, star-shaped flowers that are so pretty for drinks or scattering over salads. To add a lemony flavour to custards and ice cream, steep some lemon balm leaves in the hot milk. Savory is often called the 'bean herb' – adding a sprig or two to the cooking water of any type of bean helps to prevent flatulence. Lavender leaves and flowers are used to flavour sweet dishes. Used in lawns instead of grass in the past for their apple-like scent, chamomile leaves make a relaxing infusion.

FRUIT

England's temperate climate is ideal for growing orchard and soft fruits, and many regions still grow the same varieties that they have for centuries.

Orchards have long been a distinctive feature of the English landscape, particularly in the heartlands of Kent, Gloucestershire and Herefordshire. Recent years have seen a severe decline in orchard-fruit crops and many old English varieties have disappeared. Fortunately, traditional fruit growers are now beginning to see a turnaround, with some supermarkets responding to consumers' demand for home-grown produce, and local shops and farmers' markets offering heirloom varieties.

The ancestor of the modern apple is the crab apple, with its small, sour fruits that make delicious jellies and other preserves. There is a huge range of traditional apple varieties, each with its own texture and unique flavour, and many are evocatively named. Dessert apples include Ashmead's Kernel, Blenheim Orange, Cox's Orange Pippin, Discovery, James Grieve, Knobby Russet and Worcester Pearmain. Varieties that are more suitable for cooking include Bramley's Seedling, Burr Knot, Golden Hornet, Norfolk Beauty and Smart's Prince Arthur. English cider apples include Bulmer's Norman, Hoary Morning and Slack-me-girdle. Apple traditions such as apple bobbing and toffee apples survive to this day.

The pear's history can be traced back almost as far as the apple and for a long time it was considered the superior fruit. By the 19th century, there were hundreds of varieties. Today the most popular English dessert pear is the Conference, long and thin with green skin tinged with russet, and sweet flesh. Williams pears (known as Bartlett in the USA and Australia), bred in Berkshire in the 18th century, are golden yellow or red-tinged, and are ideal for cooking.

Originally cultivated from hedgerow fruits – the cherry plum and the sloe – plums vary in colour from black to pale green and yellow, and can be sweet or tart. In England they were grown in the gardens of medieval monasteries. The Victoria plum was first cultivated in Sussex in the 1800s and, with its red and yellow skin, remains the most popular dessert plum. The greengage is a sweet amber-coloured plum that makes particularly good jam. Damsons are small plums with dark-blue to purple skins and yellow flesh. They give their colour and flavour to damson gin.

ABOVE *Apples ready for the pressing machine.*

Cherries are grouped into three main types: sweet, acid and sour (known as Dukes). Sweet cherries can be firm and dry, ideal for candying into glacé cherries, or soft and juicy. Acid cherries, of which the Morello is the best known, range in colour from pale to those with an intense crimson glow. Duke cherries are thought to be crosses between these two.

The quince is an apple- or pear-shaped fruit with scented yellow flesh. Because it is very hard, it needs long, slow cooking. It is lovely cooked with apples or pears, when only a small amount is needed to add its flavour. Quinces make good jams and jellies that go well with pork. Medlars, though rare today, are small brown fruits with a sharp flavour that can still be found in the warmer areas of England. They are only edible raw and only when overripe.

Local farmers' markets and pick-your-own farms are the best sources of classic English varieties of soft fruit. Strawberries are possibly England's most popular summer fruit. While Elsanta has become the most frequently grown variety, Cambridge Favourite, English Rose, Hapil and Royal Sovereign are becoming favoured again. Strawberries are a traditional feature of the Wimbledon tennis championships. Raspberries are soft, juicy, sweet yet acidic, and can be red, yellow, white and black. Fresh raspberries are enjoyed on their own, with cream, or can be added to desserts, sauces, ice creams, jams and flavoured vinegars. English cooks often mix blackberries with apples in fruit pies and puddings, and they make lovely jam and jelly. The cultivated fruits are larger and juicier than the wild bramble, but many people pick wild blackberries from the hedgerows in early autumn. It is considered bad luck to gather them after Michaelmas Day (29th September): according to folklore, it is the day on which Satan was cast out of heaven and fell into a blackberry bush; in vengeance, on that day every year, he spits or stamps on the berries. Mulberries look similar to, though larger than, blackberries, and can be used in the same ways. They are the fruit of large, long-lived trees of Asian origin, which have probably been grown in England since Roman times. Mulberries are very soft and easily damaged, so are not widely available commercially, but are delicious straight from the tree.

Blackcurrants, with their rich, slightly sour flavour, are enjoyed in summer, and red and white currants are lovely mixed with soft berries in a summer pudding. Gooseberries belong to the currant family and have always been especially popular in England. They can be round, long, hairy or smooth, and different varieties are suitable for cooking or eating raw.

Rhubarb is botanically a vegetable, but it is used like a fruit. The tender pink stems of early forced rhubarb are a spring treat, mostly grown in Yorkshire. Main crop rhubarb, with its thick stems, stronger colour and more acidic flavour, is eaten in pies and crumbles, or in compôtes.

LEFT *Apples coming into fruit, on a tree trained as an espalier to grow up an old wall.*
RIGHT *Fresh hand-picked raspberries.*

WILD FOODS

Throughout history, the English have hunted for wild food in the hedgerows, woodlands and roadsides, heaths and moorlands, riverbanks and fields, along the coastlines and even on wasteland in towns. Foraging for wild food can become an exciting and worthwhile pastime, but be sure to be careful of where and what you pick. Check you are allowed to pick, and collect sustainably – do not over-pick.

The leaves of many wild plants are edible and make delicious, interesting salads and soups, but the leaves need to be picked when young, in spring and early summer. Dandelions grow plentifully on hedge banks and roadsides. Their young leaves are ideal for salads, and their flowers were once used to make wine. Wild garlic, or ramsons, grows in abundance in spring, on shady riverbanks and in damp meadows, proclaiming

its presence with a pungent smell. Its pointed leaves have a mild garlic flavour and can be added to salads, stir-fries and soups. The white flowers look pretty in salads.

Young, tender nettle leaves appear in early spring. They can be made into an infusion reputed to purify the blood, or lightly cooked and served as a vegetable, or in soups or stews. Young nettle leaves can be cooked in the same way as spinach: wash them well and place in a pan with just the water clinging to the leaves, cook over a low heat for 7–10 minutes, chopping them as they cook in the pan, then add butter, salt and pepper to taste. They make a refreshing and restorative soup in early spring.

Wild rocket (arugula), a little peppery leaf, grows prolifically in many areas of the country, and can be picked, washed and added to stews or made into salad. Sorrel, which appears in hedgerows, and watercress are in the same family. Burdock grows on waste ground, in hedgerows and occasionally in woodland. The young stems, peeled, can be eaten in salads and the roots can be cooked, but their traditional use in England is as an ingredient in dandelion and burdock, a soft drink similar to American root beer.

Samphire, of which there are two unrelated species, grows around the coast. Marsh samphire, or glasswort, grows on salt marshes, and the green fleshy tips can be eaten raw or lightly cooked in salads, or hot with butter or with fish. It is very popular in Norfolk and Lancashire. Rock samphire, as its name suggests, grows on rocky coastlines and is added to salads or cooked as a vegetable, made into soup or pickled.

LEFT *Marsh samphire picked at Morecombe Bay.*
RIGHT *Wild garlic, in late spring. The leaves are used in all kinds of ways, although the flowers are edible as well.*

ABOVE *Wild rosehips, in West Yorkshire.*

Wild fruits and berries are abundant in late summer and autumn, and for centuries have been picked to turn into a variety of jams, jellies and other preserves to fill the winter store cupboard. Summer brings tiny wild strawberries and raspberries. In autumn, long branches of blackberries (or brambles) tumble from the hedgerows. Sloes, the small, round bluish-black fruit of the blackthorn tree, are also to be found in hedgerows. The fruit is bitter if eaten raw, but is used to flavour sloe gin and other wines. Bilberries, or wild blueberries, also known as whortleberries, grow on low bushes on open moors and heaths. The little dark blue-to-mauve berries are a seasonal treat in late summer.

Rowan berries display their vibrant orange colour on the mountain ash tree. They make delicious sauces and chutneys that are particularly good served with lamb, game and venison. In late summer the small, shiny, almost black berries of the elder tree make lovely pies, fools, jellies, cordial, wine and sauces that make a fine accompaniment to meat. (In late spring, the flowers of the elder tree add their distinctive perfume to refreshing drinks, and are used to make elderflower cordials and sparkling 'champagne'.) Rosehips are the dark red seedpods of wild roses. They are very rich in Vitamin C, and during World War II British schoolchildren were sent out to pick them for making into syrup while oranges were unobtainable.

A source of protein, and easy to store for months, wild nuts would once have been a very important part of the English peasant's winter diet. Hazelnuts are plentiful in autumn hedgerows. The hazel has been cultivated in England since the 17th century, particularly in Kent; other varieties are cobnuts and filberts. Walnuts are most common in the mild climate of the south and south-east of England. In early autumn the nuts are harvested when their husks are still soft, and are often pickled. Chestnuts, the fruit of the sweet chestnut tree, are traditionally roasted in their skins on an open fire. They are still sold on city streets during the winter months, particularly in December. They make delicious soups and stuffings. At Christmas, they are served with Brussels sprouts.

Though most mushrooms used in cooking today are cultivated, wild field mushrooms are still to be found all over England, in meadows and open spaces (and particularly in regions where horses graze) at the end of summer and in early autumn. Other types of edible wild fungi to be found in the woodlands of England include St George's, the prince, blewits, chanterelles, morels, ceps, milk caps, horse mushrooms, honey fungus, oyster mushrooms, puffballs and chicken (and hen) of the woods. Each type has its own particular colour, flavour and texture. (It's essential to make a positive identification or seek expert advice when picking wild fungi, as some edible species resemble others that are deadly poisonous.)

One of the oldest natural foods, honey is made by bees from the nectar of flowers. It has been collected from wild colonies since ancient times for use as a sweetener and medicine. The Romans used it in cooking, and monasteries often kept bees as a valuable source of sweetener and to supply wax for making candles. Honey remained the only way to sweeten food until sugar was imported to England in the Middle Ages. In the 18th century, sugar became readily available and cheap; as a result, honey was used less and less. Today, good honey is an 'artisan product', with beekeepers positioning their hives among local flowers and herbs, which impart their flavour to the honey and give it colour and texture.

ABOVE *Wild mushrooms – always pick with care.*

THE FISHMONGER

England has always enjoyed a wonderful variety of fish from its coastal waters, lakes and rivers. The earliest hunter-gatherers foraged the coastline for shellfish, and tidal zones of the seashore provided valuable sea vegetables, including seaweed. Recent years have seen fish stocks diminish, but an increase in fish farming has led to greater availability of certain species such as salmon and trout. Historically, fish was eaten on the Church's many 'fast days' (including Friday every week), and the lengthy fasts of Lent and Advent when meat was forbidden.

Freshwater fish from clean waters need only simple cooking and delicate herbs such as watercress or thyme, perhaps with melted butter, to bring out

their natural taste. Sea fish can take more robust accompaniments, such as samphire, sauces made from shellfish, and robust herbs. Oily fish such as herring and mackerel are often cooked coated in oatmeal, which absorbs their strong flavours. Some species are best cooked whole, while others are better filleted.

SEA FISH

Several species have been affected by overfishing and stocks are desperately low. Cod and haddock are two examples of species where reduced numbers have led to higher prices. Nevertheless, both fish remain popular, and are sold as steaks, cutlets and fillets. Haddock, while smaller than cod, has a pronounced flavour that many people consider to be finer, and in the north-east of England it is always the first choice for fish and chips. Both haddock and cod are good baked, poached, grilled or fried (with or without batter). Other white fish, which vary in availability and popularity, include hake, with its firm flesh, pollack, whiting and coley, all of which are excellent in pies, soups and stews.

Plaice is a flat fish with a good flavour and texture. Available whole or as fillets, it is suitable for rolling and stuffing, grilling, frying, steaming and poaching. Dover sole has a similarly firm texture and a fine flavour that is best appreciated when the fish is simply grilled on the bone, perhaps with melted butter, chopped parsley and lemon juice. Lemon sole has softer flesh and a flavour not quite as fine as that of Dover sole, but it too is popular, being less expensive, and suitable for serving with strongly

LEFT *Unloading the catch at Newlyn Harbour, Cornwall.* RIGHT *A traditional fishmonger displaying his fresh fish and seafood.*

flavoured sauces. Turbot is considered by many to be the aristocrat of fish, with a sweet flavour and firm white flesh that can stand up to robust kinds of cooking. Halibut is widely available; it is best for grilling, frying or baking, but it can be poached or steamed too.

Herrings, sprats, pilchards, sardines and whitebait are all members of the same family, with a similar texture and bold flavours. Britain's thriving herring industry ensured they were always cheap, and they remain good value today. The larger fish are delicious fried, grilled (especially on the barbecue) or baked. (Herring is often smoked, after which it is called a kipper.) Tiny whitebait are deep-fried and eaten whole, and remain a popular appetiser in restaurants, particularly in London, where they were once so plentiful that they were sold from barrows in the streets. The pilchard has long been a mainstay of the Cornish fishing industry, though in greater demand abroad than at home: most of the fish has traditionally been salted and exported to France and Italy. Nowadays, with smaller catches and higher prices, the fresh fish is being more alluringly re-marketed in England under the name 'Cornish sardine'. Mackerel has always been plentiful in England's coastal waters, remains inexpensive and is delicious when very fresh. Several other species are still caught around the coast, albeit in smaller quantities, including brill, dabs, skate, sea bass, monkfish, ling, John Dory, gurnard and red mullet.

FRESHWATER FISH

England's rivers used to teem with fish, and most large country estates would have had at least one pond stocked with perch, pike and other species. Salmon is one of today's most popular fish because of the dramatic increase in fish farming. It is perfect for

ABOVE *Fish is often packed into ice as soon as it has been landed on the boat, to keep it fresh until delivery.*

ABOVE *A freshly caught brown trout, Devon.*

cooking whole and is a favourite centrepiece for summer entertaining. Fillets and steaks are lovely pan-fried, grilled or barbecued.

Wild salmon is an early summer treat worth its high price. Sea trout, otherwise known as salmon trout, has firm pink flesh and a delicate flavour, combining the best qualities of salmon and trout, but in recent years it has become scarce and even more highly prized than salmon. It can be cooked in any of the ways suitable for salmon, but is best lightly poached whole, delicately flavoured with dill.

The native brown trout, which is biologically identical to the salmon trout but not migratory, is found in lakes and streams in several regions. Because of the success of fish farming, rainbow trout is now widely available and inexpensive. Both kinds of trout can be enjoyed poached, baked, fried or grilled. There is no better breakfast or supper than one or two of these freshly caught, small fish, simply dusted in seasoned flour and pan-fried whole in butter. English rivers and lakes are also home to grayling, pike, zander, perch, roach, tench, bream, crayfish, eels and elvers.

SMOKED FISH

Before the days of refrigeration, freezing and easy transport, smoking over peat or wood fires was one of the chief methods of preserving fish. Smoked fish could be kept for times when fresh food was not so plentiful and for the many days when Christians were obliged to abstain from eating meat. Nowadays, fish is smoked for the distinctive flavour it imparts rather than the need to preserve it. Fish are salted, rinsed and then strung up to air-dry, and finally smoked over smouldering woodchips or peat. The strength of the cure and length of smoking affects the colour and flavour of the fish, and adding sugar, juniper berries or other flavouring to the flesh will change its character.

Oily fish such as eel respond particularly well to smoking. Some fish, such as salmon, trout, mackerel or herring, is hot-smoked, which means it is gently cooked as it is smoked and is therefore ready for eating. Cold-smoking involves smoking the fish very gently over a long period over a smouldering fire. Cold-smoked fish needs either to be cooked first, as in the case of kippers or smoked haddock, or cut into wafer-thin slices and served raw, sprinkled with lemon juice, like salmon, trout or mackerel.

South-west England, and Cornwall in particular, is known for its smoked mackerel, kippers and bloaters. On the east coast, Great Yarmouth once bustled with fish workers and smokehouses producing bloaters and kippers. In Northumberland, smoked fish is also a speciality, especially salmon and kippers. In fact, oak-smoked kippers were first made in the fishing town of Seahouses, and kippers are still produced in traditional smokehouses there and down the coast at Craster.

Smoked herrings include bloaters, which are lightly smoked and dry-salted herrings that have had their heads, tails and bones removed; they are best grilled or fried. Buckling are whole, hot-smoked herrings that are ready to eat. Kippers, a very traditional breakfast dish, are herrings that have been split, slightly salted and cold-smoked; they are poached or grilled. Red herrings are whole herrings that have been heavily smoked and salted, and have a strong flavour. They are obtainable from a few artisan smokers and can be eaten cold or lightly grilled.

Smoked haddock is traditionally served poached for breakfast or supper. Smoked salmon is usually served as a starter in wafer-thin slices with lemon wedges for squeezing over, black pepper and brown bread. Smoked trout can be bought whole or in fillets and is good as an appetiser or made into spreads and pâtés. Smoked mackerel, with its rich flavour and smooth texture, is enjoyed in salads or made into spreads and pâtés. Smoked eel is a delicacy that was difficult to find, but now smokeries in East Anglia and Somerset are encouraging a revival by offering it in chunks, ready to eat.

SHELLFISH

In the past, some species of shellfish were so plentiful that they were considered food for the poor, but the English have always been partial to a bag of whelks,

ABOVE *Fresh mackerel hanging in the fish smoker.*

winkles or cockles, freshly cooked in a beach-side hut or bought from the street sellers in London.

The coastlines of the north-east and south-west in particular have been good sources of shellfish, including lobster, crab, scallops, clams and mussels. Morecambe Bay is famous for its tiny brown shrimps, and many sandy estuaries are home to razor clams. As with other fish, shellfish stocks have been in decline in recent years, and many sheltered bays and estuaries are now home to aquaculture farms.

Regarded as one of the tastiest shellfish, lobster has a rich, intense flavour. Originally eaten by the poor, it became a gourmet food in the 19th century. They are usually boiled but can also be grilled. The dark blue-green shell becomes scarlet when cooked.

Lobsters and crabs were originally fished by coaxing them from under the rocks with a stick. In the 1750s, creel fishing was introduced, using special baited pots. Langoustines (also known as Dublin Bay prawns, jumbo shrimp, Norway lobsters or crayfish) were regarded by fishermen as a nuisance until the 1960s, when increased foreign travel began to create a demand for them. As scampi (extra-large shrimp) they became a gourmet food, exported all over the world and a fixture on restaurant menus. Crabs are caught around the coasts of Britain and sold live or pre-boiled. There are two main types: the common brown crab or the rarer shore variety.

Scallops have a creamy white flesh with a mild flavour, enclosed in a shell that can measure up to 15cm/6in across. The orange coral is edible and has a rich flavour and smooth texture. Scallops need only a few minutes' cooking. It is important not to overcook them, as the meat will become tough and rubbery, losing its sweet taste. If possible, buy them in closed shells. Plentiful, inexpensive and easy to prepare, mussels make a wonderful main dish or first course. Mussels must have tightly closed shells; discard any that remain open when tapped (and any that stay closed once cooked), as this indicates that they are not still alive. Steam or boil them in white wine or water, or add to fish stews.

Once so plentiful that they were used to eke out other ingredients, and even as cat food (Pepys refers to them as such in his *Diary*), oysters are now celebrated as a delicacy. Eaten raw, they are at their best from late autumn to spring – traditionally eaten only 'when there is an "r" in the month'. Whitstable in Kent and Lindisfarne in Northumberland are both renowned for oysters. The Pacific oyster is often farmed, and is more elongated than the native oyster.

ABOVE *Lobsterman in Clovelly, Devon (left); a plate of a half-dozen oysters at Whitstable, Kent (right).*

THE BUTCHER

Central to the country diet, both domestically raised meat and wild game have always been a prime source of protein, if enjoyed more by the wealthy and middle classes. While there are plenty of traditional recipes for roast meat as the centrepiece of a special meal, many recipes call for the cheaper cuts of meat or offal, which work so well in rich, tasty stews and casseroles cooked gently and slowly.

Before the introduction of the modern oven, particularly in large houses, meat was cooked in huge pieces, roasted on a spit in front of the kitchen fire. Much of the population, meanwhile, would take their meat to be cooked in the baker's oven while they attended church on Sunday morning. It was customary to make the Sunday roast last for several days: it would be served hot or cold, and made into dishes such as pies, rissoles and bubble and squeak.

MEAT

Cattle are reared for both their milk and their meat, beef. Old breeds still raised in England today include the Shorthorn (in the north) and the Red Poll (in

eastern areas). The British White was always popular on the estates of large houses. Selective breeding means that there are now cattle suited to all kinds of terrain – lowlands, hills and moorlands – with breeds such as the Hereford, South Devon and Sussex providing meat that is marbled with fat and has an excellent flavour. These days prime cuts of beef are an expensive luxury, but roast beef with all the trimmings – Yorkshire pudding, mustard and horseradish sauce – is still a Sunday lunch favourite. The tougher cuts, which tend to be less expensive, make delicious stews (with or without dumplings), pot roasts (such as boiled beef and carrots) and traditional puddings and pies, as well as the modern burger. The Victorians were great believers in the virtues of meat extracts, and drank restorative 'beef tea', made by simmering steak in water, cooling to remove all fat and residue and then reheated to serve.

The pig has always played a most important role in England's eating. There was a time when at least one pig was reared in every cottage, farm and country house in every village and town, fed on household scraps and often on the whey left over from cheese-making. In some homes the pig was known as 'the gentleman who pays the rent'. The 'porker' would be kept from springtime until autumn, when it was slaughtered. In small communities, pigs would be killed a few at a time and the meat shared out between neighbours. This practice continued until the late 19th century, when it was no longer permissible to keep pigs near the home.

When there was plenty of meat, the people ate to 'lay on fat' before winter set in. The boar was saved for Christmas and went into mince pies, with the

LEFT *A majestic sirloin of beef, with undercut.*
RIGHT *Fresh meat and game from a traditional small butcher in the country village of Castle Combe, Wiltshire.*

head being reserved for the table centrepiece. In the new year, the long sides (flitches) of bacon cured in autumn saw the family through the lean months until spring. Most parts of the pig were cured to make bacon, though the offal would be eaten immediately, and some fresh pork would be cooked too. The legs were reserved for ham. Every part of the animal was eaten, including trotters, stomach wall (tripe), brain, tongue, ears and tail; the blood was used for black pudding (blood sausage). Traditional breeds are seeing a revival today – such as the ginger-haired Tamworth and Gloucester Old Spot, often called the orchard pig because it was fattened on windfall apples. British pig farms have a reputation for very high standards of animal care and welfare. Pork is enjoyed roasted, perhaps with a stuffing of sage and onion, and served with apple sauce. It is made into sausages, pork pies, black puddings, haslet and many other regional dishes.

As well as remaining the foundation of the traditional British breakfast, bacon is used to flavour all kinds of dishes, including soups, stews and stuffings. The hind leg from a side of pork is removed for curing separately as ham and, after brining, the rest of the side is divided into gammon (shoulder and collar joints) and back and belly bacon. Traditionally both were dry-cured; wet-curing by injecting brine into the meat was introduced in the 19th century, but dry-cured bacon and ham are now sought after by discerning consumers. Once the meat has matured over a period of weeks, some is then smoked. Many craft pork butchers and artisan

ABOVE *Home-made sausages in the cold room of a local butcher's shop.*

producers make speciality sausages for cooking at home. Other traditional pork products include brawn, made from various boiled and cooked cuts of pork, pigs' cheeks, tongue and feet set in aspic, haslet (a cooked pork 'loaf' popular in the north of England) and the Irish street food crubeens, which is brined pigs' feet, boiled until tender, then grilled. Black pudding (blood sausage) is a quintessential northern food, and a much-loved breakfast food in the Midlands. The main ingredient is pig's blood, mixed with diced back fat, onions, herbs and spices, and oatmeal or barley, and encased in intestines, then boiled. It can be served sliced, grilled or fried, and as an ingredient or garnish in dishes from salads to stews and casseroles, and it is sometimes served with fish or shellfish. White pudding is made with chopped offcuts of pork and bacon and offal. Though it has similar flavouring ingredients to black pudding, white pudding contains no blood.

Lamb as we know it today was once unheard of. Sheep have always been raised more extensively than pigs or cattle and almost always grazed on grassland. Originally, sheep were kept primarily for their wool. All sheep meat was mutton – with a strong flavour and texture that required slow cooking to tenderise it. Over the years, lamb has slowly replaced mutton: young, tender and sweet, it can be cooked quickly to suit modern lifestyles. Large cuts of lamb are roasted and served with mint sauce or redcurrant jelly, while chops and steaks are grilled, fried or barbecued.

Lamb is the basis of traditional dishes such as Lancashire Hotpot and Shepherd's Pie. Today, there is spring lamb from southern England, followed by hill lamb from northern areas and lamb (up to 18 months old) from all over the country. Hogget (one to two years old) and mutton (over two years) are experiencing a welcome revival. Specialist breeds are available from farmers' markets and traditional butcher shops, with interesting names such as Blackface, Blue-faced Leicester, Lincoln Longwool, Norfolk Horn, Texel and White-faced Woodland. There is Romney from the salt marshes of Kent,

and mutton in the shape of the Ryeland and Herdwick breeds.

Goat or kid meat is becoming more available, and considered a tasty and ethical meat choice, as the animals are usually reared in smaller free-range farms, predominantly for their milk.

POULTRY (AND EGGS)

Many a country garden, from the most prosperous farm to the tiniest cottage, once had a group of hens happily pecking in the dirt, jealously guarded by the resident cockerel, or a few ducks swimming on a tiny pond. These creatures were a fantastic source of eggs and meat and would be carefully protected from marauding foxes. Hens, ducks, geese, turkeys, sometimes guinea fowl, and less commonly pigeons, were kept and bred. Their flesh provided meat for the Sunday dinner, while their eggs provided nourishing breakfasts and were an essential ingredient for cakes and tarts.

At one time poultry was reserved for Christmas and other festivities. For the rich, peacock and swan were festive fare until the 16th century, after which turkey and goose became regular features at Christmas. Traditionally, the ducks and hens that pecked about in the yard were the province of the farmer's wife, and even in relatively grand families the mistress of the house usually took responsibility for the domestic fowl. An industrious woman could earn a good deal of 'egg money' selling her produce at markets or to local stores. The profits were reserved for luxuries, such as tea (once known as 'China ale'), dried fruit and spices, cloth for clothes or hair ribbons. From an early age, girls were taught to care for fowl, given a few chickens to rear and allowed to spend their own egg money.

For hundreds of years, chickens have been bred both for their meat and their eggs, and they would have been a familiar sight in farmyards, country estates and gardens all over Britain. Older hens, with their laying days behind them, used to be stewed

ABOVE *Free-range geese on a poultry farm in Leicestershire.*

with root vegetables or made into pies, but that was in the days when they ranged freely about the farmyard, fed on a variety of foods, grew slowly and developed a complex flavour. The methods of breeding and rearing the birds have changed drastically in the modern era, with the result that they are now plentiful and cheap. Though most chicken meat for sale is still produced by intensive methods, there is a steady increase in the demand for free-range and organic birds, which is being met by supermarkets as well as traditional butchers, and farmers' markets are offering birds reared by artisan producers.

Geese provide meat for festive roast dinners, as well as eggs for use in breakfasts and baked goods.

Roast goose was traditional fare on Michaelmas Day (29th September), sometimes called Goose Day, when eating it is said to bring good fortune to the diners. From September to Christmas, goose might also be served at wedding feasts and could be a regular Sunday roast for wealthy families. Most of the geese eaten today are raised on farms, ready for roasting and serving with sage and onion stuffing and apple or gooseberry sauce. There is no industrial production of geese, so the birds reared by artisan producers are a luxury food, but they are making a comeback as the bird for a special festive occasion.

There are several breeds of domesticated duck, of which the Aylesbury is one of the best. Some are more fatty than others and need longer cooking at a high temperature, so that the fat is rendered out and the skin crisps. A real farmyard duck is relatively rare now, although excellent ducks are sold by medium and small producers.

An American bird, turkey was known in Britain as early as the 17th century. Only in the 20th century, however, did it become the bird of choice for the Christmas dinner, ousting the goose as the farmyard bird most likely to generate a good income. This is curious, because turkeys are difficult to rear and more prone to disease than geese. Like chicken, modern intensive production has made it plentiful, cheap and rather bland. For the true taste of turkey, look out for birds reared by specialist producers and sold at farmers' markets and traditional butchers. The Christmas turkey is usually served with gravy, bread sauce, bacon rolls and small sausages, and, nowadays, accompanied by cranberry jelly.

Guinea fowl and quail were originally game birds but are now farmed and usually now classed as poultry. Quail, a small bird, used to be shot in the wild but grew so scarce that it eventually became a protected species; the majority of quails eaten today are farmed by artisan food producers. They also sell the tiny eggs, sometimes hardboiled. These can be served just lightly boiled, or as a garnish, or as a party nibble dipped in celery salt. They are sometimes preserved in mild, lightly spiced wine vinegar. The birds are delicious roasted, pot-roasted or casseroled.

There was a time when most farms and households kept poultry for eggs, and also for meat. After the corn harvest the flocks of birds were driven to the fields to feed on the stubble and scattered grain. In the past, several types of eggs were eaten, most of which would have been smaller than today's. While hen's eggs have always been the most numerous, those from bantams, ducks and geese have been popular too. Peacocks' eggs are known to have been

an occasional luxury for the rich. Until the introduction of laws to protect wild birds, it was customary for the poor to plunder the nests of thrush, blackbird, mallard, moorhen, plover, seagull, sparrow and wood pigeon.

Eggs were once only a seasonal food, so they would be preserved for winter use: they were either waxed (coated with lard), pickled in brine or vinegar, or put in isinglass (or waterglass), a form of gelatine. Today, of course, hens' eggs are available all year round. Though laying cages are still the most common method of commercial egg production, more and more are being supplied from barns and from free-range hens with daytime access to runs. Also available, in smaller numbers, are eggs from ducks (favoured by many for their stronger flavour), geese (a rich treat) and quail.

In Victorian times, eggs became a standard breakfast food, served boiled, poached, coddled, fried, rumbled (scrambled) or made into omelettes. These days they are an integral part of the traditional English breakfast, accompanied by bacon, sausages

RIGHT *A point-to-lay brown hen (of an age to start laying eggs), free to roam in the field.*

and other extras. Away from the breakfast table, eggs are used in numerous ways in English baking, to make cakes, puddings, flans, pancakes, sauces and custards. Eggs are superb for quick, healthy light meals – a cheese omelette takes just minutes to make, as does fried or poached egg on toast. And no English picnic is complete without hard-boiled eggs, peeled and dipped into salt and pepper.

GAME

Out in the woods and pastures, country people might have access to feathered game such as partridge, pheasant and grouse, which would be hunted and then cooked to make a tasty autumn or winter casserole, with their rich, dark flesh. The eating of game once helped to sustain families through the winter months when other types of fresh meat were not available. History books mention the eating of most small birds, including plover, ptarmigan, teal, widgeon and rook. In medieval times hunting became training for war, a rite of manhood and a traditional pastime. Hunting was then a privilege of the wealthy and the sport of kings. While aristocrats hunted prime animals and birds, such as deer, swans, peacocks and pheasant, the peasants were allowed to hunt only small creatures. Today, thanks to organised seasonal shoots, game is widely available from game dealers throughout the country. Almost all game must be hung to develop flavour and tenderise the flesh. Birds are hung by the neck, unplucked, in a cool place. Deer are gutted and skinned before hanging. The length of hanging time depends on the type of game, where it is hung and the weather: game spoils quickly when the weather is thundery, for example. Fresh, well-hung game is a seasonal treat, but frozen game is obtainable all year round.

Venison is the meat of the red, fallow or roe deer, which is now widely farmed, but the term once meant any furred game. In the 11th century, William the Conqueror reserved the right to hunt in the royal forests, and there were severe punishments for anyone caught killing or even disturbing the animals. Venison is therefore historically a food of the wealthy and landowning classes. The shooting seasons depend on the species, and are different for stags and hinds. Farmed venison is less expensive than wild, and the meat is more tender, with a delicate, less gamey flavour. All venison is lean and low in cholesterol. Some deer farmers have developed a trade in venison sausages and pies. Wild venison is usually marinated in alcohol and oil to tenderise the flesh and keep it moist as it cooks. The age of the animal and the hanging time greatly affect the flavour and texture of the meat. The haunch, saddle or leg are best for roasting. Chops from the ribs can be fried or grilled. The flank is best casseroled or minced. A strong-flavoured meat, venison needs to be matched with robust flavours such as spices, rowan berries, juniper berries and red wine.

LEFT *Red stag deer are hunted in the wild for their meat (and antlers). Shooting is strictly regulated.*

Rabbit is available all year round and is best eaten without hanging. Wild rabbit has a more pronounced flavour and a darker flesh than farmed rabbits, which are delicate in flavour and always tender. The meat tends to be dry, so it should be well basted or cooked with liquid. Rabbit is an essential ingredient in game terrines and pies. Thyme is its natural partner. Hare is available late summer to early spring and must be hung before cooking. Its blood is often saved to thicken the gravy in the traditional dish called jugged hare – a rich, dark stew.

A few enterprising farmers are producing wild boar. Unlike pork, it is a lean, red meat with a slightly gamey flavour, which becomes more pronounced as the animal ages. Prized cuts are the saddle and haunches, both of which can also be smoked to produce wild boar ham.

Pheasant, a choice game bird, is in its prime in mid-autumn and stays in season until early spring. If eaten without hanging, the flavour is similar to that of chicken; after hanging, the flesh develops a mild gamey taste. The hen bird is less dry than the cock and tends to have more flavour, but they are often sold as a brace – one hen and one cock bird. They can be grilled, roasted or casseroled. Roast pheasant is traditionally accompanied by bread sauce. Pheasant is a major ingredient of game pies, particularly at Christmas. Partridge is best in mid- to late autumn while young and tender. Young birds are roasted; older birds are best braised.

Wild duck is a rare treat today. It is less fatty than domesticated birds and has a more developed flavour. Mallards are the largest and most common wild ducks. Cook them in the same way as ordinary duck, but add extra oil. The smaller wild ducks, such as the teal, widgeon and pochard, are prized by gourmets.

Woodcock is in season from mid-autumn to late winter. It is traditionally roasted without drawing and with its head still in place, accompanied by berries and roasted vegetables. Pigeons, though not as popular as they once were, are making a comeback. For centuries, domestic pigeons were an

ABOVE *A male collared or ring-necked common pheasant, introduced to Europe as a game bird a thousand years ago.*

important source of meat, housed in purpose-built dovecotes on farms and country estates. Nowadays, wild wood pigeons are shot to keep them off growing crops. The young birds, or just their breasts, can be roasted or pan-fried; older ones go into game casseroles and pies. They are available all year round.

The red grouse inhabits the northern moors, where it feeds on heather, blueberries, grasses and herbs, which impart a unique flavour. The flavour varies according to the locality and the hanging time (usually two to seven days). Found in Scotland and the north of England, red grouse are shot from 12th August ('The Glorious Twelfth') until 10th December. Grouse flesh tends to be dry, and they were originally cooked on a spit so that they basted themselves as they turned. Before roasting, the bird can be stuffed with berries to keep it moist and complement the flavour. Wrap it in rashers of streaky bacon or brush with butter and baste during cooking.

THE DAIRY

The dairy has always played an important part in English country life. There was a time when even small households kept a cow in the garden to supply milk. In some areas a cow formed part of a labourer's wages, and cows were milked on the streets of London as late as the 19th century. As well as cows, ewes and goats would have had their place on most mixed farms. Today the most common breeds of dairy cow found in England are the Friesian, Friesian/Holstein cross, Guernsey and Jersey.

In lowland pastures, where there is plenty of rain and grass grows well, milk has been turned into cream, butter and cheese, and traditional English cookery books are laden with recipes that use dairy products. In some regions, cattle are raised on such fertile pastures that they produce milk with an extremely high butterfat content. These areas have become justifiably renowned for their rich cream, butter and cheeses – the clotted cream of the West Country is just one example.

In the 20th century, industrialisation led to a decline in the production of traditional dairy products, but the old skills are now being revived and a wealth of local products are available, including milk, yogurt, cream, butter and buttermilk. An incredible range of English cheeses – cottage, cream, curd and hard varieties – is being made with the milk of cows, sheep and goats. Locally made ice creams are very popular too.

CHEESE

In England, cheese has a long history, and there was a time when it was made in almost every farmhouse. During spring and summer, there was plenty of milk available (from ewes, goats and cows), and making it into cheese meant that it could be kept without spoiling to feed the family during the winter months. Cheese-making was a skill that was passed down through generations of families and farmers.

In the time of the Romans, cheese was an everyday food and soldiers were given a small ration every day. They are thought to have taken England's oldest cheese, Cheshire, back to Rome with them. In the 11th century, the Normans brought their cheese-making expertise to England, and much of it was made by monks. With the dissolution of the monasteries, the business of making cheese passed to the farmers' wives. The upper classes enjoyed rich, creamy cheeses, leaving very hard cheeses made from skimmed milk for the poor. In the Middle Ages, cheese made from surplus milk would be sold at cheese fairs and local markets, a tradition that continues today. By the 17th century, every region

LEFT *Freshly churned home-made butter.*
RIGHT *The dairy scullery as it looked in a period stately home; butter was made from the milk of the estate's cows.*

ABOVE *Cheeses on display in Stamford, Lincolnshire.*

was producing its own distinctive cheese, with characteristics depending on the breed of animal, pasture and individual recipes or preferences.

Commercial cheese-making began in England during the Industrial Revolution, when workers migrated from the country to the towns. To supply this new and growing market, creameries were set up with factories making cheese on a large scale from the milk of mixed cattle herds from a wide area. With farmers selling their milk direct to the manufacturers, the production of local cheeses began to go into decline. During World War II, farmhouse cheese-making was again severely reduced and what little cheese was made was mass-produced in factories. When rationing ended – and a greater choice of cheese became available – it became fashionable in some circles for a while to host cheese and wine parties.

While cheeses continue to be manufactured on a large scale, recent years have seen a revolution in the English cheese industry. In spite of commercial pressures and government regulations, a new generation is discovering the art of cheese-making. With skill and passion it is reviving traditional recipes, and developing new ones using old techniques, to produce an enormous range of handcrafted cheeses with styles and flavours that are varied and unique. Milk is being sourced from rare breeds, and regions that do not have a long tradition of cheese-making are creating exciting new products.

An increasing number of cheeses are now being granted PDO (Protected Designation of Origin), an endorsement intended to protect the name, heritage and tradition of regional foods from imitation by mass producers. Stilton, West Country Farmhouse Cheddar and Single Gloucester are all examples of PDO cheeses. An important part of the resurgence of locally produced, specialist cheeses is the growing number of dedicated cheese shops that sell a wide variety: cheeses made with the milk of cows, goats, ewes and even buffalo; hard-pressed and soft cheeses; cheeses wrapped in cloth, rolled in herbs or wrapped in leaves; and cheeses washed in cider, perry, brandy or brine. There are food trails featuring cheese, cheese festivals and annual cheese awards. The cheeseboards of more and more pubs and restaurants feature good local and regional English cheeses.

To make farmhouse cheese, the milk from the morning or evening milking (or a mixture of the two) may be left whole, skimmed, semi-skimmed or enriched with cream. The prepared milk is warmed and soured (or acidified) by adding a starter culture – a blend of bacteria that occur naturally in milk. When the correct acidity has been reached, rennet (or a vegetarian equivalent) is added, causing the milk to coagulate and separate into solid curds and liquid whey. The curd is cut to break it up (lightly for soft cheese and finely for hard cheese) and the whey is drained off. The curds are shaped or tipped into moulds, and left to finish draining or pressed to remove moisture. The more the curd is pressed, the firmer the cheese will be. Many English cheeses are 'ripened' or matured for some time (up to 18 months), during which a mould develops on the surface or the cheese develops a rind. Alternatively, they may be coated in leaves or wax.

Though much cheese available today is uniform and comes from industrialised dairies, there is a growing band of artisans using old-fashioned methods to make traditional cheeses with interesting characters that change alongside the seasons. Cheshire is one of the oldest English cheeses and is mentioned in the Domesday Book. It has a slightly crumbly, silky texture. Its tangy, salty flavour is due to the salt deposits found in the local pasturelands.

Mature cheddar is golden yellow with a firm, silky texture and full flavour. Despite extensive imitation in other counties, Cheddar is unequivocally associated with the West Country, where it was once

matured in the caves of the Cheddar Gorge in Somerset. West Country Farmhouse Cheddar has PDO status, meaning that it can only be made in the four counties of Dorset, Somerset, Devon and Cornwall. A good mature piece of Cheddar is ideal for the cheeseboard and to use in cooking.

Lancashire cheese can be traced back as far as the 13th century. A creamy white cheese with an open, crumbly texture and mild flavour, it can be crumbled into sandwiches and salads. Lancashire is one of the best melting cheeses and was formerly known as the 'Leigh toaster', after a small town near Manchester where it was made.

Single and Double Gloucester were traditionally made as a large wheel with a thick rind, able to withstand the county's annual cheese-rolling races, one of which, at Cooper's Hill, is still held. Its orange colour originally came from carrot juice or saffron; today, the vegetable dye annatto is used. Double Gloucester, made from whole milk, has a smooth,

RIGHT *Cornish Yarg, a semi-hard cow's cheese that is wrapped in nettle leaves to mature.*

buttery texture with a clean, creamy, mellow flavour. Double Gloucester is the most widely available, but Single Gloucester (half the size of Double) can, by law, only be made on farms in Gloucestershire that have a pedigree herd of Gloucester cattle. Both cheeses melt well.

Red Leicester is a rich, russet-coloured cheese with a flaky, slightly open texture and a mellow flavour. Its luxurious colour made it very popular in the Victorian period. It is good eaten with fruit or beer, and can be used in cooking, as it melts exceptionally well.

Wensleydale is a moist, crumbly and flaky cheese with a flavour that is mild, slightly sweet and refreshing. Usually eaten young – one to three months old – it goes very well with apple pie. A blue variety is also available.

Other traditional cheeses include Derby, which has a smooth, mellow texture and mild, buttery flavour (similar in taste and texture to Cheddar). It is delicious with fruit juice. Sage Derby, as its name suggests, is flavoured with the herb sage. Lincolnshire Poacher is a modern hard, unpasteurised cheese with a granite-like rind. Production began in 1992. Leafield is a sheep's milk cheese made in Oxfordshire. Once made by the monks of Abingdon Abbey on the same site, it has been faithfully revived from its original 16th-century recipe, and is dense and chewy with a full flavour.

Cornish Yarg is based on a cheese recipe from the 13th century. The cheese is pressed and brined before being wrapped in nettle leaves, which are brushed on in a prescribed pattern and attract natural moulds of white, green, grey and blue. These moulds help the cheese to ripen and as it matures the edible nettles impart a delicate flavour. It is a great addition to the cheeseboard. Stinking Bishop, said to be derived from a cheese once made by Cistercian monks, is made in the village of Dymock in Gloucestershire. It is washed with perry made with a local variety of pear called Stinking Bishop. The cheese has a sticky orange rind, a meaty flavour and

ABOVE *Cheeses being turned in the maturing room at Stockbeare Farm in Devon.*

an appropriately pungent aroma. Windsor Red is Cheddar cheese with marbling produced by the addition of red (often elderberry) wine to the curd. Curworthy is a hard Devon cheese based on a 17th-century recipe and made from unpasteurised milk. It has a creamy yet open texture and a mild, buttery taste. Devon Garland is an unpasteurised, semi-hard cheese made from the milk of (usually) Jersey cows. Its rind is firm and smooth with a greyish brown crust. A layer of fresh herbs is added before the cheese is matured. Cotherstone comes from Yorkshire. It is an unpasteurised, hard cheese with a slight acidity and a fresh, citrus tang.

Stilton is historically referred to as 'the king of cheeses'. It has narrow, blue-green veins and a wrinkled rind. Its texture is smooth and creamy and its flavour is rich and mellow with a piquant aftertaste. It was never actually made in the village of Stilton, in Huntingdonshire, but was first sold there. The cheese originated at Quenby near Melton Mowbray in the early 18th century. Its certification trademark and Protected Designation of Origin status allows it to be made only in the counties of Nottinghamshire, Derbyshire and Leicestershire, to a specified recipe. Crumble it over salads, cook with it or offer it as a dessert cheese. At Christmas, Stilton is traditionally served with port. A white variety is also available.

Other blue cheeses include Dorset Blue Vinney, which gets its name from an Old English word for mould. The popularity enjoyed by this cheese in the 18th and 19th centuries declined with the introduction of factory cheese-making, and it became extinct in the 1960s, but happily is now being made again. It is a hard cheese, light in texture with a mild flavour. Beenleigh Blue is made in Devon from unpasteurised sheep's milk. The rough, crusty, natural rind is slightly sticky, with patches of blue, grey and white moulds. It is moist and crumbly, with blue-green streaks through the white interior. It is good served with a glass of mead or sweet cider. Shropshire Blue is not from Shropshire at all: having

ABOVE *Stilton cheeses for sale at a farmers' market. Colston Bassett is famous for its hand-ladled Stilton.*

been invented in Scotland, it is now produced in Leicestershire. This distinctive orange-coloured cheese with its blue veins has a firm, creamy texture and a sharp, strong flavour. Eating Shropshire Blue with a cup of tea is said to bring out its flavour. Buxton Blue is a pale orange, lightly veined cheese. Appreciate its 'blue' flavour in soups, salads or spread on crackers. It is perfect with chilled sweet dessert wine. Oxford Blue was created as an alternative to Stilton; it is creamy with a distinct 'blue' flavour and is sold wrapped in silver foil. Dovedale is a creamy soft, mild blue cheese that has been dipped in brine. It is made in Derbyshire and takes its name from a beautiful valley in the Peak District.

THE BAKERY

Using only a few ingredients and with very simple equipment, bread-making was a skill every cook needed to acquire. Although bread at its simplest is just flour, water, yeast and a little salt and sugar, many country breads are made with numerous other additions, including wholemeal (wholewheat) flour, grains such as rye and barley, and oats or seeds added for extra texture and flavour. Plain, nutritious mixtures such as oatcakes were peasant standbys, eaten in place of bread when wheat was scarce or expensive.

STAPLE GRAINS

England has traditionally produced several staple grains, principally used for making bread. Loaves

made from wheat were the most desirable, but until the agricultural improvements of the 18th century it could only be grown in the milder, more fertile areas of southern England, and was too expensive for most people to use it to make their daily bread.

Two types of wheat are grown – hard and soft. The former is rich in gluten – ideal for bread-making – and the latter is rich in starch, good for all other baking, pancakes and sauces. Wholegrains, or berries, have just the husk removed and can be cooked whole or sprinkled on bread dough before baking. Wheat flakes are flattened wholegrains and are used in breakfast cereals. Malted wheat grains have a sweet, nutty flavour.

Spelt is a forerunner of modern wheat that has a unique, nutty wheat-like flavour. It was grown extensively in Britain from the Bronze Age to medieval times, when modern wheat varieties began to replace it. Spelt has recently been revived as a health food, and is mixed with other flours for specialist bread and used in breakfast cereals.

Barley was one of the earliest cereals to be cultivated. It makes moist, heavy bread, and these days it is rarely used for this purpose because it is low in gluten (the protein that makes dough elastic). Pot (or Scotch) barley has only its husk removed, while pearl barley is the steamed and polished grain. Both are good for soups, stews and salads. Barley flour is ground pearl barley, used for thickening sauces and soups. Barley flakes (pressed and flattened grains) are popular in breakfast cereals and for making milk puddings.

Rye is a hardy cereal that grows easily in cold climates and poor soil. The hard, brown grain is

LEFT *Stoneground flour has become popular again and produces a flavoursome and nutritious loaf.*
RIGHT *Display of fresh breads in a bakery window.*

ABOVE *The white batch loaf is one of the most traditional breads.*

available whole for adding to soups and stews or for sprouting. Rye flakes are added to breakfast cereals. Rye flour, with its distinctive, slightly sour flavour, is mixed with wheat flour to make bread. In the medieval period this mixed grain, known as maslin, went into the bread eaten by the ordinary people.

Oats have always been an important crop in England and other parts of the British Isles, growing well in the colder, wetter areas. Once considered by the English to be fit only for feeding horses, it is a very versatile grain. Oatmeal contains no gluten, so breads made entirely using oats were inevitably flat, baked on stones or on a griddle. Many parts of England have their own traditional oatmeal cakes, but the meal is also used for baking loaves, mixed with wheat flour. Oats are available as wholegrains (groats) and oatmeal (ground groats) in various grades. Pinhead oatmeal can be made into porridge and oatcakes and used to thicken stews; medium grade is suitable for making cakes such as parkin and for mixing with other flours; fine oatmeal is good for

pancakes and for coating foods such as fish before cooking. Rolled oats or oat flakes go into quick-to-cook porridge, breakfast cereals, flapjacks and biscuits. Oats do not contain gluten, so can be used to make leavened bread only in combination with other flours.

BREADS AND CAKES

The use of naturally occuring yeasts became overtaken in the Middle Ages by beer-based and commercial yeasts; there is less of a historical tradition of sourdough bread-making in England, though many bakers do now of course make wonderful sourdough breads. Traditional-shaped loaves include the 'Batch' – a loaf baked in a batch alongside others, rather than separately, so that it has soft sides; the 'Bloomer' – a thick, long, white loaf with cuts across the top that open out or 'bloom' during baking; the 'Cob' – a round, smooth, crusty loaf, often topped with cracked wheat; the

'Farmhouse' – a white loaf with a lengthwise cut along its top; the 'Sandwich' – a large even-shaped loaf with a flat top that results from being baked in a square tin with a lid; and the 'Tin' – a loaf with a domed top, baked in a rectangular tin without a lid.

The 'Cottage' must be among the oldest shapes of English breads. The distinctive arrangement of a smallish round loaf baked on top of a larger round loaf seems to be a peculiarity to England and Elizabeth David in her *English Bread and Yeast Cookery* suggests that it might have originated as an improvised way of economising on baking space in a small oven. The two loaves are wedded together by pushing a wooden spoon handle or fingers down the centre of the two rounds and sometimes the sides are snipped to give an extra crusty finish. Traditionally, cottage loaves would have been baked on the floor of the oven, and the best cottage loaves today have a thick, dark bottom crust.

The first cakes were simply bread dough with added eggs or butter; many country cakes also contained fruit, nuts and seeds gathered wild from the hedgerows. Before commercially refined sugar was available, honey was used to sweeten baked goods. Many recipes for substantial country fruit-cakes make the most of rather meagre ingredients, using very little flour, sugar and eggs with plenty of fruit and nuts, which gives a dark, moist cake that has a long storage life. Most of the best-loved, so-called 'fancy breads' were made from the dough left over from a weekly bread baking, with the addition of eggs, sugar, fruit or nuts to make sweetened loaves. Speciality breads with added spices and fruit were often made for celebrations or festivals: many had symbolic relevance, such as hot cross buns to mark the Easter holiday. No harvest festival church service is complete without a huge loaf of bread sculptured into the shape of a sheaf of wheat.

Country cakes do tend to be rather substantial, and

RIGHT *Hot cross buns, marked with a cross (cut into the dough, or as dough strips), eaten on Good Friday at Easter.*

based on simple but delicious ingredients rather than the elaborate cream-filled confections typical of pâtisserie. Baking day was a regular tradition, providing home-made cakes and muffins for the coming week. Tarts, pies and puddings are emblematic of the English kitchen, and sum up the best sort of comfort food. Steamed puddings were popular because they do not require an oven, being gently steamed in a covered bowl on the hob for an hour or two. These substantial puddings, often containing fruit inside the pastry crust, only need the addition of a jug of creamy custard.

Cornish saffron bread is yeast-leavened, enriched with fruit and spiced with nutmeg, cinnamon and saffron. Saffron was an important crop in England in the 16th century, and although it gradually declined, it continued to survive in the West Country, where numerous traditional breads and cakes include the tiny threads of saffron, adding a delicate flavour and pretty colouring.

English muffins – to differentiate them from American muffins, which more resemble a large cupcake – belong to the same tradition as crumpets,

although there are several differences, as enthusiasts would be only too keen to point out. Like crumpets, they are a part of an English folk memory that includes the muffin man, winter afternoons in front of the fire, toasting forks and teatime. Although muffins and crumpets are made from the same, or similar, basic recipes, muffins use a stiffer mixture and are consequently thicker, with a thin skin or crust on each side and without the characteristic holes of crumpets. Both are delicious toasted, either split and then toasted, or toasted and then split (it makes a difference!), and served with butter.

Recipes for crumpets date from the 18th century, and then, just as now, they were always toasted and eaten with lashings of butter. Today, crumpets are made using yeast and baking powder (or bicarbonate of soda and cream of tartar), which accounts for their characteristic holey surface.

Some people say 'pikelet' is just another name for crumpet and in some parts of the country the words are synonymous. However, while both pikelets and crumpets have the distinctive holey tops, pikelets are not cooked in rings but are free-form in shape, being cooked straight on the griddle (like Scotch pancakes

or the Welsh crumpets, *bara pyglyd*, pronounced 'piglet', from which pikelets may well get their name). The mixture for pikelets is very much the same as crumpets, but perhaps a bit thinner. They are popular in the counties of Leicestershire, Derbyshire, Yorkshire and Lancashire.

Harvest loaves are not really intended for eating but are made by bakers in the autumn to coincide with harvest festivals in churches and schools. It is a tradition that has happily endured in many of the smaller villages of England and bakers relish the opportunity to demonstrate their skill and expertise.

Small yeasted buns have been enjoyed in England since medieval times, and the small breads, enriched with eggs, currants and raisins and spiced with nutmeg and cinnamon, were typically served to accompany wine at the end of a feast. Hot cross buns are a popular Eastertime treat.

Lardy cake is found in many different versions, and all are very rich. Originally, lardy cakes were made for celebrations, notably harvest festivals, but as sugar and fruit became more affordable they became popular all year round. Various English counties lay claim to lardy cake. You can certainly eat delicious lardy cake in Lancashire and Yorkshire, and Northumberland, too, has its own speciality. The Midlands and Derbyshire are partial to a very sweet variety, while further south, in Surrey and Hampshire, there are versions of fruitless lardy cakes. The round, flattish breads are made using a basic white dough, which is layered with fat, sugar and fruit. Lardy cake, almost by definition, is very calorific and it contains pork lard (shortening) and is therefore not for vegetarians or vegans. The cake is still often sold by weight or by the piece.

Lincolnshire plum bread is perhaps the best known of many fruited teabreads found across the country; as with plum pudding, 'plum' means dried fruit in this context, namely currants, raisins and sultanas.

LEFT *A hot buttered crumpet. These yeast-based treats are cooked in metal rings on a griddle.*

Sally Lunn, a brioche-style cake, is a speciality of the West Country, or more particularly Bath, where supposedly a lass called Sally Lunn once sold her cakes to the townspeople. The story goes that Sally Lunn, a Huguenot, brought her recipe from France and adapted it to the English oven. Alternatively, although less romantically, the word is thought to be a corruption of the French *soleil et lune* or 'sun and moon' cake. It is a distinctive-looking bread with tall sides and a billowing top; although there is no one authorised version, Sally Lunn is always made using white flour and yeast, enriched with butter and cream. It can be lightly spiced and slightly citrusy, but should not be over-flavoured. It is often split and spread with butter or clotted cream.

Stottie (or Stotty, or Stottie Cake) is a flattish bread native to the north-east of England, where it is widely available, although almost unheard of anywhere else. Almost always white, it is flat with a soft, floury crust, often (but not always) scored with a single slash or cross. Local bakers explain that stotties were traditionally the last things to be baked in the oven at the end of the day, the name itself coming from the local word 'stott', meaning 'to throw to the ground'. The bread apparently was ready for eating if it rebounded from the floor! Stottie bread (perhaps as a result of such disrespectful treatment) is rather dry, with an open crumb and fairly chewy texture. It is, however, delicious served with another regional dish, ham and pease pudding (a mash based on split peas).

Staffordshire oatcakes are soft and floppy and are the size of small pancakes (unlike the smaller, crumbly Scottish oatcake). They are known locally as 'Tunstall tortillas' and they are indeed similar to a tortilla, although, unlike the Mexican bread, these are eaten in true English fashion with eggs and bacon for breakfast or butter and honey for tea. The oatcakes are made from a mixture of oatmeal and flour, yeast and milk or water. It is likely that they have been made in Staffordshire for centuries, as all sorts of oatcakes and griddle cakes were common in

ABOVE *Stotties are flat rounded buns, originally from Newcastle and found throughout the north-east.*

the north of England from Tudor times. With the Industrial Revolution, though, they became associated with the Staffordshire potteries; the best are those that are baked on the premises of local bakers in places such as Stoke-on-Trent.

Yorkshire farl is a round soda bread, similar to the Irish soda breads, that is cross-slashed into quarters (farls) before being baked.

Scones are of course an English favourite. Simple and quick to make, they may be plain, fruited, sweet or savoury. Buttermilk, left in the churn after butter-making, was considered a great delicacy as far back as the Tudor era, and its delicate but distinctive flavour and acidity produce wonderfully light scones.

Biscuits originated in the medieval 'biscuit bread', when surplus dough from bread-making was dried out in a low oven (the word 'biscuit' means 'twice cooked') Gradually, 'biscuit bread' lost its yeast, and the discovery that beaten egg was an efficient raising agent saw the creation of many recipes (usually spelled 'bisket') in the 17th and 18th centuries.

THE CELLAR AND PANTRY

With a beer industry dating back to the earliest times, cider drinking in the south-west, dark stouts in the north-east, wine imported from Europe long before the Romans came, and a long history of whisky appreciation, it is not surprising that many of England's favourite drinks are alcoholic. Much of the consumption of alcohol traditionally happens in public houses, or 'pubs', which evolved from the taverns and coaching inns of the past. In their various manifestations, from Georgian drinking dens, to the men-only smoking clubs of the 1900s, to the smartened-up gastropubs of today, pubs have held a central place in the social life of English adults. There are nonetheless plenty of delicious non-alcoholic drinks that make the most of English fruits and flowers, from cordials to ginger beer and lemonade.

Associated more with medieval and Tudor times, but enjoying an artisan resurgence, mead is a mixture of honey and water fermented with wild yeasts, and it is thought to be the oldest alcoholic drink in the world. The term 'honeymoon' is thought to have originated in Anglo-Saxon times, when, for a month after the wedding, the bride's father would supply his son-in-law with all the mead he could drink in the belief that it aided fertility. The art of making mead had been preserved for centuries in monasteries, until their dissolution during the reign of Henry VIII. By the 17th century, imports of cheap sugar from the West Indies had reduced the importance of honey as a sweetener and it was no longer essential for everyone to keep bees. Mead-making declined, but the drink can still be found, made by artisan producers all over the country.

Beer and ale are perhaps the drink of England. Ale is simply fermented grain and has been drunk throughout England's history as a healthy alternative to water, which was often contaminated. Taverns existed as far back as Roman times, but it was the Normans who first organised brewing on a larger scale, setting up breweries attached to abbeys and monasteries for the refreshment of monks and travellers. By the Middle Ages, the brewing of ale was largely the realm of women; alehouses were well established, and ale was the most common drink, even for children. There were strong ales, medicinal varieties and weak versions for children.

Until the 15th century, ale consisted of malted barley, water and yeast. Then merchants from Flanders and Holland introduced a new brewing method to England. The new hopped version was called beer. It had a bitter flavour and, unlike ale, kept well. By the 18th century, all beers were hopped. Most brewing took place in the home until

LEFT *A pint of beer in the classic dimpled glass tankard.*
RIGHT *The Garrick Inn has been serving ale since Tudor times, and is the oldest pub in Stratford-upon-Avon.*

the increase in commercial brewing in the 19th century. Various styles of beer have developed, with each differing according to the water supply – pale beer, dark beer, porter and stout. The 21st century saw a significant revival in specialist brews.

The pressing and fermenting of apples to make cider is an ancient art. New apple varieties reached England with the Romans, and later with the Normans. By the middle of the 17th century, cider-making had reached a peak and most farms had a cider orchard and an apple press. The drink was popular with all, and it became traditional to pay part of a farm labourer's wages in cider, with extra at hay-making time, though consumption declined as farming practices changed. As the population moved from the farms to the towns in the 19th century, commercial cider-making developed. Although beer is more widely drunk now, cider (and scrumpy, its stronger relation) is still very popular in England's south-west. Today, small-scale and artisan producers coexist happily with the large manufacturers.

PRESERVES FOR THE PANTRY

Smoking, drying, bottling or making jams and chutneys were essential activities in every English country kitchen. Eating your own preserves, made with best-quality, tasty fruits and vegetables, is a reminder of summer in the depths of winter.

Jams, jellies and marmalades Making delicious jams and jellies is the most common way to enjoy the summer's harvest all year round. Compôtes are simply soft-set jams made with a little less sugar, served fresh, as they will not keep for long. Many traditional jellies are made from hedgerow crops

ABOVE *Freshly picked blackberries and home-made blackberry jam.*

such as crab apple, mint and elderflower, and these delicately flavoured preserves are usually served with meats or cheese. Old-fashioned fruit butters and cheeses are preserves made with the fruit pulp left in a jelly bag after the juice has dripped. Making fruit butter requires less sugar than jam and the texture is softer – perfect for spreading. Fruit cheeses have a firmer texture and are made from well-sieved thick fruit purées, often from fruits with lots of pips or stones such as damsons or quince. In contrast, fruit curds are made with the addition of butter and eggs, gently cooking the fruit to create a thick, sweet conserve which has a shorter shelf-life than other preserves because of the dairy content. Piquant lemon curd is the best known, but other fruits such as gooseberries, apricots and quince also lend themselves well to this treatment. Marmalade is made in a similar way to jam, using citrus fruits. The fruit rind in marmalade needs longer cooking than the usual jam fruits, so water is added to the fruit and sugar while it is cooked. The marmalade can be flavoured with alcohol or fragrant spices such as ginger.

Pickles, chutneys and relishes Both fruits and vegetables are made into mouthwatering pickles and chutneys. Chutney is made with chopped fruit and/ or vegetables simmered with varying amounts of spices, sugar and vinegar to a thick pulp and then stored in jars. As it improves with age, chutney stores very well and has a long shelf-life. It is particularly useful for using up end-of-season fruits such as windfall apples and green tomatoes, mixed with dried vine fruits such as sultanas (golden raisins) and currants. In contrast, pickles are more often made with whole vegetables, such as baby onions, cauliflower florets or beetroot. The vegetables are first salted or soaked to remove excess moisture, then packed into jars and covered in vinegar, with the addition of strong herbs and spices to add a really zingy taste to the mixture. Pickles do not require the long cooking of chutney, and benefit from being kept

ABOVE *Traditional piccalilli is made from pickled cauliflower and other vegetables, mustard and turmeric.*

for a few weeks for the flavours to develop. Both pickles and chutneys are usually served straight from the jar with cold meats, terrines, pies or cheese, but they can also be regarded as an instant ingredient to add zest to many winter dishes; piccalilli is an English tradition, coloured yellow with turmeric. Pickled onions can be rinsed and added to a robust casserole or stew, for example. Relish is halfway between chutneys and pickles. It consists of coarsely chopped fruit or vegetables, spices and vinegar cooked together for a shorter time than chutney, so the vegetables tend to keep their shape.

As well as the classic savoury accompaniments to certain dishes (mint sauce or redcurrant jelly with lamb, horseradish sauce with beef, gravy with anything), other quintessentially English relishes include the traditional Gentleman's Relish (a butter blend with anchovies), hot yellow English mustard, brown sauce (a spicy sweet-sour blend) and salad cream. Mayonnaise is also popular, bought or home-made.

BREAKFASTS

In medieval days the people of England
simply ate bread and drank ale before a
day in the fields. Over the centuries breakfast
(or breaking the overnight fast) changed and,
by the late 19th century, it was a more elaborate
affair, with the tables of the wealthy laden
with food. Such ostentation ended with
two world wars, and a more restrained
approach followed, with regional variations
providing interest. The 'full English'
is enjoyed everywhere.

PICTURED *Dawn in a bluebell wood.*

FULL ENGLISH BREAKFAST

For most of us, a cooked breakfast is a special treat, harking back to the 19th century, when the buffet tables of the rich groaned with food. This is an adaptable meal, with regional variations. The basic requirements are bacon and eggs, but sausages, fried potatoes, grilled tomatoes, mushrooms, fried bread, baked beans (sometimes debated) and even black pudding can be added.

SERVES 4

225–250g/8–9oz small potatoes

oil, for grilling or frying

butter, for grilling and frying

4 large or 8 small good-quality sausages

8 rashers of back or streaky bacon, preferably dry-cured

4 tomatoes

4 small slices of bread, crusts removed

4 eggs

1 Thinly slice the potatoes. Heat 1 tbsp oil with a knob of butter in a large, preferably non-stick frying pan, add the potatoes and cook over a medium heat for 10–15 minutes, turning them occasionally until they are crisp, golden and cooked through.

2 Using a slotted spoon, lift the potatoes out of the pan and keep them warm on a dish in a low oven.

3 Meanwhile, grill or fry the sausages in a little oil until golden brown all over and cooked through (test by inserting a fork in the centre – the juices should run clear). Keep warm.

4 Grill the bacon or fry it in a little oil in the non-stick pan. Keep warm.

5 Halve the tomatoes and either top each half with a tiny piece of butter and grill until they are soft and bubbling, or fry in a little oil in the frying pan. Keep warm.

6 Fry the bread in a little oil and butter over a medium-high heat until crisp and golden brown. Keep warm.

7 Add extra oil if necessary to the hot frying pan. As soon as the oil is hot, crack the eggs into the pan, leaving space between them. Cook over a medium heat, spooning the hot fat over occasionally to set the yolks, until cooked to your liking.

8 In anticipation, arrange the breakfast ingredients on warmed plates and, as soon as the eggs are ready, add and serve immediately.

COOK'S TIP

For the best flavour, fry the bread and tomatoes in the fatty juices remaining in the pan from the sausages and bacon.

SCRAMBLED EGGS

Carefully cooked scrambled eggs are deliciously comforting. They cook best
in a pan with a heavy base. Serve them on hot buttered toast by
themselves or with bacon, sausages or smoked fish.

SERVES 2

4 eggs
salt and ground black pepper
25g/1oz/1½ tbsp butter

1 Break the eggs into a bowl and beat lightly with a fork until well
mixed. Season with salt and pepper.

2 Put a medium-sized heavy pan over a medium heat and add half
the butter. When the butter begins to foam, add the beaten eggs.
Using a wooden spoon, stir the eggs constantly as they cook and
thicken, making sure you get right into the angle of the pan to
prevent the eggs sticking there and overcooking.

3 When the eggs are quite thick and beginning to set, but still
creamy, remove the pan from the heat and stir in the remaining
butter. The eggs will finish cooking gently in the residual heat of the
pan as you keep stirring. When they are set to your liking, serve
immediately.

POACHED EGGS

This delicate method of cooking eggs has been popular in England since the Middle Ages.
Use poaching rings in the water if you have them, for a perfect shape. Only use fresh eggs.
Serve on toasted bread or muffins.

SERVES 2

2–4 eggs

1 Put a frying pan over a medium heat and add 5cm/2in of boiling
water. Add the poaching rings if you have them.

2 When tiny bubbles begin to gather in the water and gently rise to
the surface, break the eggs, one at a time, into a cup and slide them
carefully into the hot water. Leave the pan on the heat for 1 minute
as the water simmers very gently (on no account allow it to boil).
Then remove from the heat and leave the eggs to stand, uncovered,
in the hot water for 10 minutes.

3 Use a slotted spoon to lift the eggs out of the water and drain
briefly on kitchen paper. Serve immediately.

BOILED EGGS

Soft-boiled eggs are just made for dipping hot toast 'soldiers'. In summer,
they also make a delicious accompaniment to freshly cooked asparagus spears.

SERVES 2

2–4 eggs
hot buttered toast, to serve

1 Put the eggs into a pan just large enough to hold them in a single layer and cover with cold water. Bring to the boil, then simmer for 3 minutes for soft-boiled, 4 minutes for a just-set yolk or 8 minutes for hard-boiled.

2 Drain and serve immediately with hot buttered toast, crusts removed and cut into strips.

COOK'S TIP

To ensure eggs do not crack during cooking, use an egg pricker to make a tiny hole in the round end (where there is a pocket of air).

CODDLED EGGS

This method of soft-cooking eggs became very popular in the Victorian era, and special decorative porcelain pots with lids were produced by Royal Worcester from the 1890s.

SERVES 2

butter, for topping and greasing
2 large eggs
60ml/4 tbsp single (light) cream (optional)
freshly ground black pepper, to garnish
chopped fresh chives, to garnish

1 Butter two small ramekin dishes or cups and break an egg into each. Top with a spoonful of cream, if using, and a knob of butter. Cover with foil.

2 Put a wide, shallow pan over medium heat. Stand the covered dishes in the pan. Add boiling water to come halfway up the sides of the dishes.

3 Heat until the water just comes to the boil, then cover the pan with a lid and simmer gently for 1 minute.

4 Remove from the heat and leave to stand, still covered, for 10 minutes. Serve sprinkled with a grinding of black pepper and chopped chives.

OMELETTE ARNOLD BENNETT

This creamy, smoked haddock soufflé omelette was created for the post-theatre suppers
of the famous English novelist, who frequently stayed at the Savoy Hotel in London.
It is now served all over the world as a sustaining breakfast or supper dish.

SERVES 2

175g/6oz smoked haddock fillet,
poached and drained

50g/2oz/4 tbsp butter, diced

175ml/6fl oz/¾ cup whipping or
double (heavy) cream

4 eggs, separated

ground black pepper

40g/1½oz mature Cheddar
cheese, grated

watercress, to garnish

1 Remove and discard the skin and any bones from the haddock
fillet by carefully pressing down the length of each fillet with
your fingertips. Using two forks and, following the grain of the
flesh, flake the fish into large chunks.

2 Melt half the butter with 60ml/4 tbsp of the cream in a small
non-stick pan. When the mixture is hot but not boiling, add the fish.
Stir together gently, taking care not to break up the flakes of fish.
Bring slowly to the boil, stirring continuously, then cover the pan,
remove from the heat and set aside to cool for at least 20 minutes.

3 Preheat the grill or broiler to high. Mix the egg yolks with
15ml/1 tbsp of the cream. Season with ground black pepper,
then stir into the fish.

4 In a separate bowl, mix the cheese and the remaining cream.
Stiffly whisk the egg whites, then fold into the fish mixture.

5 Heat the remaining butter in an omelette pan until foaming. Add
the fish mixture and cook until it is browned underneath. Pour the
cheese mixture evenly over the top and grill until it is bubbling.
Serve immediately, garnished with watercress.

BUBBLE AND SQUEAK

The name of this dish, which is made from the leftovers from dinner the night before, is derived from the noises the mixture makes as it cooks. Originally, it included chopped, boiled beef and was sprinkled with vinegar. This version is traditionally served with cold roast meat and pickles, but also goes very well with bacon and eggs.

SERVES 4

60ml/4 tbsp oil

1 onion, finely chopped

450g/1lb cooked, mashed potatoes

225g/8oz cooked cabbage or Brussels sprouts, chopped

salt and ground black pepper

1 Heat half the oil in a heavy, preferably non-stick frying pan. Add the onion and cook, stirring frequently, until softened but not browned.

2 Mix together the mashed potatoes and cabbage or sprouts, and season to taste with salt and plenty of pepper.

3 Add the vegetable mixture to the pan, stir well to incorporate the cooked onions, then flatten the mixture out over the base of the pan to form a large, even cake.

4 Cook over a medium heat for about 15 minutes, until the cake is nicely browned underneath.

5 Hold a large plate over the pan, then invert the cake onto it. Add the remaining oil to the pan and, when hot, slip the cake back into the pan, browned side uppermost.

6 Continue cooking for about 10 minutes, until the underside is golden brown. Serve hot, cut into wedges.

COOK'S TIPS

◆ Though cabbage is traditional, other cooked vegetables could be added too.

◆ Using bacon fat or dripping in place of oil adds extra flavour.

GATESHEAD BACON FLODDIES

This Tyneside breakfast special is traditionally cooked in bacon fat and served with eggs and sausages. A kind of potato cake, floddies are said to have originated with canal workers, who cooked them on shovels over a fire. They should be served crisp and golden brown.

SERVES 4–6

250g/9oz potatoes, weighed after peeling

1 large onion

175g/6oz rindless bacon, finely chopped

6 tbsp self-raising (self-rising) flour

salt and ground black pepper

2 eggs

oil, for frying

1 Grate the potatoes onto a clean dishcloth, and then gather up the edges to make a pouch. Squeeze and twist the towel to remove the liquid.

2 Grate or finely chop the onion into a mixing bowl and add the potatoes, chopped bacon, flour and seasoning, mixing well.

3 Beat the eggs and stir into the potato mixture. Heat some oil in a large frying pan.

4 Add generous tablespoonfuls of the potato mixture to the hot oil and flatten them to make thin cakes. Cook over a medium heat for 3–4 minutes on each side or until golden brown and cooked through. Lift out, drain on kitchen paper and serve.

COOK'S TIP

Fry the floddies in oiled metal rings if you wish, for a neat circular shape.

MUSHROOMS ON TOAST

Cultivated or wild mushrooms make a delicious addition to a full English breakfast. They also make a meaty treat when cooked with cream and served on toast. For the best flavour and texture, cook them quickly and serve without delay.

SERVES 2

250g/9oz button (white) or closed-cup mushrooms

5ml/1 tsp oil

25g/1oz/2 tbsp butter, plus extra for spreading

60ml/4 tbsp double (heavy) cream

salt and ground black pepper

freshly grated nutmeg

2 thick slices of bread

chopped chives or parsley, to garnish

1 Pick over and trim the mushrooms and cut into thick slices.

2 Heat the oil and butter in a non-stick pan, add the sliced mushrooms and cook quickly for about 3 minutes, stirring frequently.

3 Stir in the cream and season with salt, pepper and a little nutmeg. Simmer for 1–2 minutes.

4 Toast the bread and spread with butter. Top with the mushrooms, sprinkle with chopped herbs and serve.

POOR KNIGHTS OF WINDSOR

Thickly sliced stale white bread is usually used for this traditional breakfast dish, a version of eggy bread. It was originally served as a pudding, with the bread being soaked in white wine or sherry and sugar before being dipped in beaten egg and cream. Serve with a selection of fresh summer fruits, if in season.

SERVES 4

2 large eggs
4 large slices of white bread
50g/2oz/4 tbsp butter
2 tbsp caster (superfine) sugar

1 Break the eggs into a bowl and beat with a fork, then tip them into a shallow dish. Dip the bread slices in the beaten egg, turning them to coat evenly.

2 Heat the butter in a large non-stick frying pan and add the bread slices. (You will probably have to do this in batches, depending on the size of the pan.) Fry over a medium heat for 2–3 minutes on each side, until golden brown.

3 Remove the bread slices from the pan and drain on kitchen paper. Cut the slices in half diagonally and dust with the sugar. Serve immediately.

GRILLED KIPPERS WITH MARMALADE TOAST

Wonderful kippers are produced around the English coast, in places such as East Anglia and Craster in Northumberland, where the herrings are still cured in the traditional smokehouses that were erected in the mid-19th century. In this recipe, the smokiness of the kipper is complemented with the tang of orange marmalade.

SERVES 2

2 kippers

soft butter, for spreading and greasing

2 slices of bread

orange marmalade, for spreading

1 Preheat the grill or broiler. Line the grill pan with foil to help prevent fishy smells from lingering in the pan, and brush the foil with melted butter to stop the fish sticking.

2 Using kitchen scissors, or a knife, cut the heads and tails off the kippers.

3 Lay the fish, skin side up, on the buttered foil. Put under the hot grill and cook for 1 minute. Turn the kippers over, brush the uppermost (fleshy) side with melted butter, put back under the grill and cook for 4–5 minutes.

4 Toast the bread and spread it first with butter and then with marmalade. Serve the sizzling hot kippers immediately with the marmalade toast.

VARIATION

Omit the marmalade and cook the kippers sprinkled with a little cayenne pepper. Serve with a knob of butter and plenty of lemon wedges for squeezing over.

KEDGEREE

Brought back by the British from India, kedgeree became popular
in 18th-century England, when the original dish of rice, lentils
and onion (khitchri) was adapted to English tastes by the addition
of flaked smoked fish and hard-boiled eggs. While it is traditionally
served for breakfast, this also makes a delicious lunch or supper dish.

SERVES 4–6

450g/1lb smoked haddock

300ml/½ pint/1¼ cups milk

175g/6oz/scant 1 cup long-grain rice

salt and ground black pepper

pinch each of grated
nutmeg and cayenne pepper

50g/2oz/4 tbsp butter

1 onion, finely chopped

2 hard-boiled eggs, shelled

chopped fresh parsley, to garnish

lemon wedges and
wholemeal (wholewheat) toast,
to serve

1 Gently poach the haddock in the milk, made up with just enough water to cover the fish, for about 8 minutes, or until just cooked. Lift out and skin the haddock, remove all the bones and flake the flesh with a fork. Set aside.

2 Bring 600ml/1 pint/2½ cups water to the boil in a large pan. Add the rice, cover closely with a lid and cook over a low heat for about 25 minutes, or until all the water has been absorbed by the rice. Turn off the heat. Season the rice with salt and a grinding of black pepper, and the grated nutmeg and cayenne pepper.

3 Meanwhile, heat a quarter of the butter in a pan and fry the onion until soft and transparent. Set aside. Roughly chop one of the hard-boiled eggs and slice the other into neat wedges.

4 Stir the remaining butter into the hot rice and add the flaked haddock, onion and the chopped egg. Season to taste and heat the mixture through gently, or until just cooked (this can be done on a serving dish in a low oven, if more convenient).

5 To serve, pile up the kedgeree onto a warmed dish, sprinkle generously with parsley and arrange the wedges of egg on top. Garnish with lemon wedges and serve hot with the toast.

VARIATION

Try using the same quantity of cooked salmon in place of the haddock.

DEVILLED KIDNEYS

In the 19th century, hot spicy flavours became very popular, due to the influence of Indian recipes and spices brought back to England during the British Raj. Recipes for devilled kidneys, for instance, were enjoyed at the breakfast table.

SERVES 4

8 slices of country bread

25g/1oz/2 tbsp butter

1 shallot, finely chopped

2 garlic cloves, finely chopped

115g/4oz mushrooms, halved

¼ tsp cayenne pepper

15ml/1 tbsp Worcestershire sauce

8 lamb's kidneys, halved and trimmed

150ml/¼ pint/⅔ cup double (heavy) cream

2 tbsp chopped fresh parsley

1 Preheat the grill or broiler and toast the bread slices until golden brown on both sides, and keep warm.

2 Melt the butter in the pan until it is foaming. Add the shallot, garlic and mushrooms, then cook for 5 minutes, or until the shallot is softened. Stir in the cayenne pepper and Worcestershire sauce and simmer for about 1 minute.

3 Add the kidneys to the pan and cook for 3–5 minutes on each side. Finally, stir in the cream and simmer for about 2 minutes, or until the sauce is heated through and slightly thickened.

4 Remove the bread from the rack and place on warmed plates. Top with the kidneys. Sprinkle with chopped parsley and serve immediately.

COOK'S TIP

If you prefer, the bread can be fried rather than toasted. Melt 25g/1oz/2 tbsp butter in a frying pan and fry until crisp and golden on both sides. Remove from the pan and drain on kitchen paper.

SOUPS

A pottage was any dish cooked in a pot using whatever was available – meat, vegetables and grains such as oatmeal, wheat or barley. In medieval England, pottage was a staple for everyone, rich or poor, although the wealthy enjoyed more luxurious versions. If a pottage was too thin, it was poured over a piece of bread to make a 'sop', the forerunner of the word 'soup'. In the 17th century, people began to serve the broth without bread and, in the early 18th century, it became a fashionable first course.

PICTURED *The view from Westminster Bridge; fog in Victorian London led to the name of the original 'pea-souper'.*

LONDON PARTICULAR

Victorian London was regularly covered with a thick winter fog, known
as a 'pea-souper', or 'London particular', because it had the colour and consistency
of pea soup. The original version of this soup would probably have
included pig's trotters and a marrow bone.

SERVES 4–6

350g/12oz/1½ cups dried
split yellow or green peas

25g/1oz/2 tbsp butter

6 rashers of rindless bacon,
finely chopped

1 medium onion, finely chopped

1 medium carrot, thinly sliced

1 celery stick, thinly sliced

1.75 litres/3 pints/7½ cups
ham or chicken stock

60ml/4 tbsp double (heavy) cream

salt and ground black pepper

croutons and fried bacon, to serve

1 Put the split peas into a large bowl, cover well with boiling water
(from the kettle) and leave to stand.

2 Meanwhile, melt the butter in a large pan. Add the bacon, onion,
carrot and celery and cook over a medium heat for 10–15 minutes,
stirring occasionally until the vegetables are soft and beginning to
turn golden brown.

3 Drain the peas and add them to the pan. Stir in the stock. Bring to
the boil, cover and simmer gently for about 1 hour or until the peas
are very soft.

4 Process or blend until smooth and return the soup to the pan. Stir
in the cream and season to taste. Heat until just bubbling and serve
with croutons and pieces of crisp bacon on top.

CREAM OF TOMATO SOUP

When the tomato first came to England, it was thought to be an aphrodisiac, but until the late 19th century it was viewed with great suspicion in case it caused sickness. When it was used, it was usually cooked in soups and stews, and was rarely eaten raw. This creamy soup owes its good flavour to a mix of fresh and canned tomatoes – of course, in summer you could use all fresh, but do make sure they are really ripe and full of flavour.

SERVES 4–6

25g/1oz/2 tbsp butter

1 medium onion, finely chopped

1 small carrot, finely chopped

1 celery stick, finely chopped

1 garlic clove, crushed

450g/1lb ripe tomatoes, roughly chopped

400g/14oz can of chopped tomatoes

30ml/2 tbsp tomato purée (paste)

2 tbsp sugar

600ml/1 pint/2½ cups chicken or vegetable stock

1 tbsp chopped fresh thyme or oregano leaves

600ml/1 pint/2½ cups milk

salt and ground black pepper

1 Melt the butter in a large pan. Add the onion, carrot, celery and garlic. Cook over a medium heat for about 5 minutes, stirring occasionally, until soft and just beginning to brown.

2 Add both the tomatoes, purée, sugar, stock and herbs, retaining some to garnish.

3 Bring to the boil, then cover and simmer gently for about 20 minutes until all the vegetables are very soft.

4 Process or blend the mixture until smooth, then press it through a sieve to remove the skins and seeds.

5 Return the sieved soup to the cleaned pan and stir in the milk. Reheat gently.

6 Stir, without allowing it to boil. Season to taste with salt and ground pepper. Garnish with the remaining herbs and serve.

JERUSALEM ARTICHOKE SOUP

Related to the sunflower and also known as root artichoke or sunchoke, Jerusalem artichoke was introduced to England in the 17th century. At first it was prized, but then became so common an ingredient that people began to lose their taste for it. The tubers can be knobbly; choose those with a fairly smooth surface for easier cleaning or peeling. Roasting the artichokes before making this soup brings out their sweet, nutty flavour.

SERVES 4–6

500g/1¼lb Jerusalem artichokes

1 onion, roughly chopped

4 celery sticks, roughly chopped

2 carrots, roughly chopped

4 garlic cloves

45ml/3 tbsp olive oil

1.2 litres/2 pints/5 cups vegetable or chicken stock

60ml/4 tbsp double (heavy) cream

salt and ground black pepper

1 Preheat the oven to 200°C/400°F/gas 6. Scrub the artichokes well and halve them lengthways.

2 Toss all the vegetables in the olive oil in a roasting pan and spread them out.

3 Put into the hot oven and roast for 30–40 minutes until they are soft and golden brown. Stir them once during cooking so that the edges brown evenly.

4 Tip the roasted vegetables into a large saucepan. Add the stock, bring to the boil and simmer for 15 minutes.

5 Process or blend until smooth, return to the pan, add the cream, season, and reheat gently. Serve with a grinding of black pepper.

COOK'S TIP

If you prefer the artichokes peeled before roasting, drop them into water after with a good squeeze of lemon to prevent them discolouring.

WATERCRESS SOUP

In Roman times, eating watercress was thought to prevent baldness, which may be debatable but it does have proven nutritional value. It became the food of the working classes and was often eaten for breakfast in a sandwich. Watercress has been cultivated in the south of England since the early 19th century. Both stalks and leaves are used in this soup for a lovely peppery flavour.

SERVES 6

2 bunches of watercress, about 175g/6oz in total

25g/1oz/2 tbsp butter

1 medium onion, finely chopped

1 medium potato

900ml/1½ pints/3¾ cups chicken or vegetable stock

300ml/½ pint/1¼ cups milk

salt and ground black pepper

single (light) cream, to serve

1 Roughly chop the watercress, reserving a few small sprigs to garnish.

2 Melt the butter in a large pan and add the onion. Cook over a medium heat for about 5 minutes, stirring occasionally, until the onion is soft and just beginning to brown.

3 Stir in the potato and the chopped watercress, then add the stock. Bring to the boil, cover the pan and simmer gently for 15–20 minutes until the potato is very soft.

4 Remove from the heat, leave to cool slightly and then stir in the milk.

5 Process or blend the mixture until the soup is completely smooth.

6 Return the soup to the pan and adjust the seasoning to taste. Reheat gently and top each serving with a spoonful of cream and a few watercress leaves.

VARIATION

Try adding a little finely grated orange rind and the juice of an orange in step 6.

COUNTRY VEGETABLE SOUP

Vegetable soups have always been particularly popular in the north of England. In the reign of Victoria, during extreme food shortages, vegetable soup kitchens were opened in Manchester. Soup-making is a good way to make the most of seasonal vegetables. Serve this one as an appetiser or with crusty bread and perhaps a wedge of cheese as a light meal.

  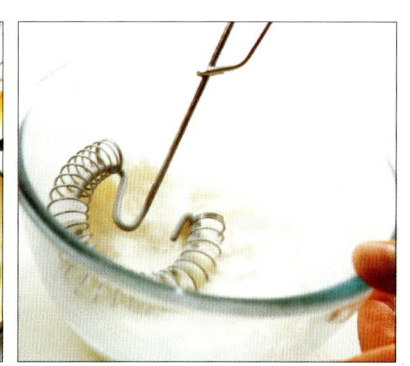

SERVES 6

15ml/1 tbsp oil

25g/1oz/2 tbsp butter

2 medium onions, finely chopped

4 medium carrots, sliced

2 celery sticks, sliced

2 leeks, sliced

1 potato, cut into small cubes

1 small parsnip, cut into small cubes

1 garlic clove, crushed

900ml/1½ pints/3¾ cups vegetable stock

300ml/½ pint/1¼ cups milk

25g/1oz/4 tbsp cornflour (cornstarch)

handful of frozen peas

salt and ground black pepper

2 tbsp chopped fresh parsley

1 Heat the oil and butter in a large pan and add the onions, carrots and celery. Cook over a medium heat for 5–10 minutes, stirring occasionally, until soft and just beginning to turn golden brown. Stir in the leeks, potato, parsnip and garlic.

2 Add the stock to the pan and stir into the vegetables. Bring the mixture slowly to the boil, cover and simmer gently for 20–30 minutes until all the vegetables are soft.

3 In a bowl, whisk the milk into the cornflour, making a paste. Stir this into the pan of vegetables.

4 Add the frozen peas, bring to the boil, and simmer for 5 minutes. Adjust the seasoning, stir in the parsley and serve.

CELERY SOUP WITH STILTON

Stilton — known as the 'king of English cheeses' — and celery are traditional partners, whether on the cheeseboard or in this warming winter soup. The two flavours complement each other beautifully, with the fresh, clean taste of the celery setting off the rich, creamy texture and tang of the famous blue-veined cheese.

SERVES 6

40g/1½ oz/3 tbsp butter

1 large onion, finely chopped

1 medium potato, cut into small cubes

1 whole head of celery, thinly sliced

900ml/1½ pints/3¾ cups vegetable or chicken stock

salt and ground black pepper

100g/3¾ oz Stilton cheese, crumbled

150ml/¼ pint/⅔ cup single (light) cream

1 Melt the butter in a large pan and add the onion. Cook over a medium heat for 5 minutes, stirring occasionally, until soft but not browned.

2 Stir in the potato and celery and cook for a further 5 minutes until the vegetables soften and begin to brown.

3 Add the stock, bring to the boil, then cover the pan and simmer gently for about 30 minutes, until all the vegetables are very soft.

4 Process or blend about three-quarters of the mixture until smooth, then return it to the pan with the rest of the soup.

5 Bring the soup just to the boil and season to taste with salt and ground black pepper.

6 Remove the pan from the heat and stir in the cheese, reserving a little for the garnish. Stir in the cream and reheat the soup gently without boiling.

7 Serve topped with the reserved crumbled cheese.

COOK'S TIP

In the place of Stilton, try using another cheese, either a blue-veined variety or a strong Cheddar.

PARSNIP AND APPLE SOUP

The Romans introduced apple orchards to England. Since then, the country has been proud of its wonderful range of apples, and many fine apple juices are now available, often made from single varieties. For this soup, choose a fairly sharp-tasting juice – it will complement the sweetness of the parsnips and the warmth of the spices.

SERVES 4–6

25g/1oz/2 tbsp butter

1 medium onion, finely chopped

1 garlic clove, finely chopped

500g/1¼lb parsnips, peeled and thinly sliced

1 tsp curry paste or powder

300ml/½ pint/1¼ cups apple juice

600ml/1 pint/2½ cups vegetable stock

300ml/½ pint/1¼ cups milk

salt and ground black pepper

thick natural plain yogurt, to serve

chopped fresh herbs such as mint or parsley, to garnish

1 Melt the butter in a large pan and add the onion, garlic and parsnips. Cook gently, without browning, for about 10 minutes, stirring often.

2 Add the curry paste or powder and cook, stirring, for 1 minute.

3 Add the juice and stock, bring to the boil, cover and simmer gently for about 20 minutes until the parsnips are soft.

4 Process or blend the mixture until smooth and return it to the pan.

5 Add the milk and season to taste with salt and pepper.

6 Reheat the soup gently and serve topped with a spoonful of yogurt and a sprinkling of herbs.

VARIATION

This recipe is also delicious when the parsnips are replaced with butternut squash or an equal mixture of the two.

SHROPSHIRE PEA AND MINT SOUP

Peas have been grown in England since the Middle Ages, while mint
was made popular by the Romans. Peas and mint picked fresh from
the garden are still true seasonal treats and make a velvety,
fresh-tasting soup. When fresh peas are out of season, use frozen peas.

SERVES 6

25g/1oz/2 tbsp butter

1 medium onion, finely chopped

675g/1½lb shelled fresh peas

¼ tsp sugar

1.2 litres/2 pints/5 cups
chicken or vegetable stock

handful of fresh mint leaves

salt and ground black pepper

150ml/¼ pint/⅔ cup
double (heavy) cream

snipped fresh chives (with chive
flowers if you have them), to garnish

1 Melt the butter in a large pan and add the onion. Cook over a low
heat for about 10 minutes, stirring occasionally, until soft and just
brown.

2 Add the peas, sugar, stock and half the mint. Cover and simmer
gently for 10–15 minutes until the peas are tender.

3 Leave to cool slightly. Add the remaining mint and process or
blend until smooth. Return the soup to the pan and season to taste.

4 Stir in the cream and reheat gently without boiling. Serve
garnished with snipped chives.

CELERIAC SOUP WITH CABBAGE, BACON AND HERBS

Often overlooked, celeriac is a traditional winter root vegetable that makes excellent soup. Savoy cabbage is used for the topping, but other greens, such as kale or spring greens, would also be suitable.

SERVES 4

50g/2oz/4 tbsp butter

2 onions, chopped

675g/1½lb celeriac, roughly diced

450g/1lb potatoes, roughly diced

1.2 litres/2 pints/5 cups vegetable stock

150ml/¼ pint/⅔ cup single (light) cream

salt and ground black pepper

FOR THE CABBAGE AND BACON TOPPING

1 small savoy cabbage

50g/2oz/4 tbsp butter

175g/6oz rindless streaky bacon, roughly chopped

1 tbsp chopped fresh thyme

1 tbsp chopped fresh rosemary

1 Melt the butter in a pan. Add the onions and cook for 4–5 minutes until softened. Add the celeriac. Put a lid on the pan and cook gently for 10 minutes.

2 Stir in the potatoes and stock, bring to the boil, reduce the heat and simmer for 20 minutes. Leave to cool slightly. Using a slotted spoon, remove half the celeriac and potatoes from the soup and set them aside.

3 Purée the soup in a food processor or blender. Return the soup to the pan with the reserved celeriac and potatoes.

4 Prepare the cabbage and bacon mixture. Discard the tough outer leaves from the cabbage. Roughly tear the remaining leaves, discarding any hard stalks, and blanch them in boiling salted water for 2–3 minutes. Refresh under cold running water and drain.

5 Melt the butter in a large frying pan and cook the chopped bacon for 3–4 minutes. Add the cabbage, thyme and rosemary, and stir for 5–6 minutes until tender. Season well.

6 Add the cream to the soup and season it well, then reheat gently until piping hot.

7 Ladle the soup into warmed bowls and pile the cabbage mixture in the centre of each portion.

MUSHROOM SOUP

Using a mixture of mushrooms gives this traditional soup character. Wild mushrooms grow all year round but most come up in the autumn, and they are perfect in a warming country soup. This will also make a flavoursome light meal served with fresh crusty bread.

SERVES 4–6

15g/½oz/1½ tbsp butter

15ml/1 tbsp oil

1 onion, roughly chopped

4 potatoes, about 250–350g/
9–12oz, roughly chopped

1 or 2 garlic cloves, crushed

350g/12oz mixed mushrooms,
roughly chopped

150ml/¼ pint/⅔ cup
dry cider or white

1.2 litres/2 pints/5 cups
good chicken stock

bunch of fresh parsley, chopped

salt and ground black pepper

whipped or sour cream, to serve

1 Heat the butter and oil in a large pan, over medium heat. Add the onion and potatoes. Cover and sweat over a low heat for 5–10 minutes until softened but not browned.

2 Add the garlic, mushrooms, white wine or cider and stock. Season, bring to the boil and cook for 15 minutes until all the ingredients are tender.

3 Put the mixture through a food mill, using the coarse blade, or blend in a liquidiser.

4 Return the soup to the rinsed pan, and add three-quarters of the parsley. Bring back to the boil, season and garnish with cream and the remaining parsley.

OXTAIL SOUP

This hearty soup is an English classic, stemming from the days when it was natural to make use of every part of an animal. Oxtail may start off tough and full of bone, but long, slow cooking produces a flavour that is rich and delicious, and meat that is beautifully tender.

SERVES 4–6

1 oxtail, cut into pieces, total weight about 1.3kg/3lb

25g/1oz/2 tbsp butter

2 medium onions, chopped

2 medium carrots, chopped

2 celery sticks, sliced

1 rasher of bacon, chopped

2 litres/3½ pints/8 cups beef stock

1 bouquet garni

2 bay leaves

salt and ground black pepper

2 tbsp flour

squeeze of fresh lemon juice

60ml/4 tbsp port, sherry or Madeira (optional)

1 Wash and dry the pieces of oxtail, trimming off any excess fat. Melt the butter in a large pan and, when foaming, add the oxtail a few pieces at a time and brown them quickly on all sides. Lift the meat out onto a plate.

2 To the same pan, add the onions, carrots, celery and bacon. Cook over a medium heat for 5–10 minutes, stirring occasionally, until the vegetables are softened and golden brown.

3 Return the oxtail to the pan and add the stock, bouquet garni, bay leaves and seasoning. Bring just to the boil and skim off any foam. Cover and simmer gently for about 3 hours or until the meat is so tender that it is falling away from the bones.

4 Strain the mixture, discarding the vegetables, bouquet garni and bay leaves, and leave to stand. When the oxtail has cooled sufficiently to handle, pick all the meat off the bones and cut it into small pieces.

5 Skim off any fat that has risen to the surface of the stock, then tip the stock into a large pan. Add the pieces of meat and reheat.

6 With a whisk, blend the flour with a little cold water to make a smooth paste. Stir in a little of the hot liquid, then stir the mixture into the pan. Bring to the boil, stirring, until the soup thickens slightly. Reduce the heat and simmer gently for about 5 minutes.

7 Season with more salt and pepper if needed, and lemon juice to taste. Just before serving, stir in the port or sherry, if using.

BROWN WINDSOR SOUP

Another hearty meaty soup, once considered a classic Victorian recipe, although it is now doubted among food historians whether the Queen herself did ever eat it! It's not mentioned by Mrs Beeton, or other Victorian cookbooks. The name 'Brown Windsor' seems to have appeared in the 1920s; it may have been confused with Potage à la Windsor, created by royal chef Francatelli, a white soup containing rice and cream.

SERVES 4

225g/8oz lean stewing steak

2 tbsp flour

25g/1oz/2 tbsp butter

1 medium onion, finely chopped

1 medium carrot, finely chopped

1 small parsnip, finely chopped

about 1 litre/1¾ pints/4 cups beef stock

1 bouquet garni

salt, black pepper and chilli powder

cooked rice, to serve

sprigs of thyme, to garnish

1 Cut the stewing steak into 2.5cm/1in cubes and coat them with the flour.

2 Melt the butter in a large saucepan over a medium heat. Add the steak a few pieces at a time and brown them on all sides. Lift the meat out and set aside.

3 Add the vegetables to the hot pan and cook over a medium heat for about 5 minutes, stirring occasionally until they are softened and golden brown.

4 Return the steak to the pan and add the stock, bouquet garni and seasoning.

5 Bring just to the boil, cover and simmer very gently for about 2 hours until the steak is very tender.

6 Process or blend the soup until smooth, adding a little extra hot stock or water to thin it if necessary. Return it to the pan, adjust the seasoning to taste and reheat.

7 When the soup is in the serving bowls, add a spoonful of cooked rice to each one. Garnish with a sprig of thyme.

BACON AND BARLEY BROTH

Use a good-sized bacon hock to flavour this soup, which is packed with barley and lentils.
This is a hearty peasant recipe, which makes a nutritious and comforting soup.
Serve with fresh brown bread.

SERVES 6–8

1 bacon hock (ham hock),
about 900g/2lb

75g/3oz/⅓ cup pearl barley

75g/3oz/⅓ cup lentils

2 leeks, sliced, or onions, diced

4 carrots, diced

200g/7oz swede (rutabaga), diced

3 potatoes, diced

small bunch of herbs
(thyme, parsley, bay leaf)

ground black pepper

1 small cabbage, trimmed,
quartered or sliced

chopped fresh parsley, to garnish

1 Soak the bacon in cold water overnight. Next morning, drain it and put it into a large pan with enough fresh cold water to cover it. Bring to the boil, skim off any scum that rises to the surface, and then add the barley and lentils. Bring back to the boil and simmer for about 15 minutes.

2 Add the vegetables to the pan with the herbs and some pepper. Bring back to the boil, reduce the heat and simmer for 1½ hours, until the meat is tender.

3 Lift the bacon hock from the pan with a slotted spoon. Remove the skin, then take the meat off the bones and break it into bitesize pieces.

4 Return to the pan with the cabbage. Discard the herbs and cook for a little longer, until the cabbage is cooked to your liking.

5 Adjust the seasoning and ladle into large serving bowls, garnished with parsley.

COOK'S TIP

Traditionally, the cabbage is simply trimmed and quartered, although it may be thinly sliced or shredded, if you prefer.

SPLIT PEA AND GAMMON SOUP

This traditional tasty winter soup is a perfect family filler, and is great for using up leftover cold ham and vegetables.

 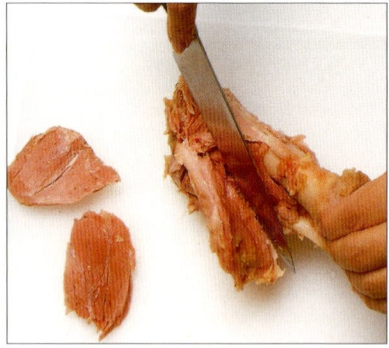 

SERVES 4–6

25g/1oz/2 tbsp butter

1 large onion, chopped

1 large celery stick with leaves, chopped

2 carrots, chopped

1 smoked gammon (smoked or cured ham) knuckle, about 450g/1lb

2 litres/3½ pints/8½ cups water

350g/12oz/1½ cups split peas

2 tbsp chopped fresh parsley, plus extra to garnish

½ tsp dried thyme

1 bay leaf

about 30ml/2 tbsp lemon juice

salt and ground black pepper

1 Melt the butter in a large heavy pan. Add the onion, celery and carrots and cook until soft, stirring occasionally.

2 Place all the remaining ingredients in the pan. Bring to the boil, cover and simmer gently for 2 hours.

3 After 2 hours, once the peas are very tender, remove the gammon knuckle. Leave it to cool a bit, then remove the skin and cut the meat away from the bones. Discard the skin and bones, then cut the meat into chunks as evenly sized as possible.

4 Return the chunks of gammon to the soup. Discard the bay leaf. Taste and adjust the seasoning with more lemon juice, salt and pepper. Serve hot, sprinkled with fresh parsley.

DEVON CRAB SOUP

Locals will tell you that crab caught around the Devon coastline is especially sweet. Although crab is available all the year round, it is at its best and is least expensive during the summer months – the perfect time to make this lovely creamy soup.

SERVES 4–6

25g/1oz/2 tbsp butter

1 medium onion, finely chopped

1 celery stick, finely chopped

1 garlic clove, crushed

1½ tbsp flour

225g/8oz cooked crab meat, half dark and half white

1.2 litres/2 pints/5 cups fish stock

salt and ground black pepper

150ml/¼ pint/⅔ cup double (heavy) cream

30ml/2 tbsp dry sherry

1 Melt the butter in a pan and add the onion, celery and garlic. Cook over a medium heat for about 5 minutes, stirring frequently, until the vegetables are soft but not browned.

2 Remove from the heat and quickly stir in the flour, then the brown crab meat. Gradually stir in the stock.

3 Bring the mixture just to the boil, then reduce the heat and simmer for about 30 minutes.

4 Process or blend the soup and return it to the cleaned pan. Season to taste with salt and pepper.

5 Chop the white crab meat and stir it into the pan with the cream and sherry. Reheat the soup and serve immediately.

STARTERS & SAVOURIES

The tradition of serving up a salty, savoury morsel reached its height in Victorian and Edwardian times, typically served at the end of a dinner. Nowadays we enjoy them at all times, to start a meal as well as to complete one. Delicious savouries whet the appetite, typically highlighting fine fish, meat and cheeses. Stand-alone savoury dishes are included here too, such as cheese pudding, the ultimate comfort food.

PICTURED *Cheddar Gorge in the Mendip Hills, Somerset, the origin of Cheddar cheese, which is the highlight of many savoury snacks and dishes.*

SMOKED MACKEREL PÂTÉ

The south-west of England and East Anglia in particular are known for smoking fish, especially freshly caught mackerel. This modern recipe provides an ideal way to use smoked mackerel – it's quick and easy, involves no cooking and is extremely versatile.

SERVES 4–6

225g/8oz/1 cup crème fraîche or thick strained plain yogurt

finely grated rind of ½ lemon and 15ml/1 tbsp lemon juice

few sprigs of parsley, and some chopped, for garnish

225g/8oz smoked mackerel fillets

1–2 tsp horseradish sauce

ground black pepper

crusty bread, hot toast or crisp plain crackers, and extra lemon wedges, to serve

1 Put the crème fraîche and lemon rind into a blender or food processor. Add a few sprigs of parsley.

2 Flake the mackerel, discarding the skin and any bones. Add the flaked fish to the blender. Blend on a medium speed until almost smooth.

3 Add the horseradish sauce and lemon juice and blend briefly. Season with pepper. Spoon into individual dishes. Cover and refrigerate until required.

4 Garnish with chopped parsley and serve with crusty bread, crackers or hot toast, and lemon wedges for squeezing over.

SALMON MOUSSE

This type of light and delicate mousse often features in English wedding feasts. It is ideal for a summer lunch or buffet, garnished with thinly sliced cucumber, cherry tomatoes and lemon wedges. Serve it with something crisp such as thin crackers or toast, and perhaps a garnish of cucumber strips and dill sprigs.

SERVES 6–8

300ml/½ pint/1¼ cups milk

1 small onion, thinly sliced

1 small carrot, thinly sliced

2 bay leaves

2 sprigs of dill or parsley

4 whole peppercorns

1 tbsp powdered gelatine

350g/12oz salmon fillet

75ml/5 tbsp dry white vermouth or white wine

25g/1oz/2 tbsp butter

25g/1oz/3 tbsp plain (all-purpose) flour

5 tbsp mayonnaise

salt and ground black pepper

150ml/¼ pint/⅔ cup whipping cream

crisp Melba toasts or crackers, to serve

1 Put the milk in a pan with half the onion, carrot, herbs and peppercorns. Bring slowly to the boil, remove from the heat, cover and leave to stand for 30 minutes to infuse.

2 Meanwhile, sprinkle the gelatine over 45ml/3 tbsp cold water and leave to soak.

3 Put the salmon in a pan with the remaining onion, carrot, herbs and peppercorns. Add the vermouth or wine and 60ml/4 tbsp water. Simmer, covered, for 10 minutes.

4 Flake the fish, discarding the skin and bones. Boil the juices in the pan to reduce by half, strain and reserve.

5 Strain the infused milk into a clean pan and add the butter and flour. Whisking continuously, cook until the sauce thickens, then simmer gently for 1 minute. Pour into a food processor or blender. Add the soaked gelatine and blend. Add the salmon and the reserved cooking juices and blend briefly.

6 Tip into a bowl and stir in the mayonnaise and seasoning. Whip the cream and fold in gently.

7 Pour into an oiled mould, cover and refrigerate for about 2 hours or until set. Turn the mousse out onto a flat plate to serve.

POTTED SHRIMPS

Tiny brown shrimps found in the seas around England (most famously those
from Morecambe Bay) have been potted in spiced butter since about 1800.
If your fishmonger doesn't have them, you can use small cooked prawns instead.

SERVES 4

225g/8oz cooked, shelled shrimps
225g/8oz/1 cup butter
pinch of ground mace
salt
pinch of cayenne pepper
dill sprigs, to garnish
lemon wedges and thin slices of
brown bread and butter, to serve

1 Chop a quarter of the shrimps.

2 Melt half of the butter slowly in a pan. Skim off any foam that
rises to the surface of the butter. Stir in all the shrimps, the mace,
salt and cayenne and heat gently without boiling. Pour the mixture
into four individual ramekins or dishes and leave to cool.

3 Melt the remaining butter in a small pan, then spoon the clear
butter over the shrimps, leaving the sediment behind. When the
butter is almost set, place a dill sprig in the centre of each dish.
Cover and chill.

4 Remove from the refrigerator 30 minutes before serving with
lemon wedges and brown bread and butter.

PRAWN COCKTAIL

This 1960s dinner-party appetiser is a delight, so long as it includes really crisp
lettuce and is assembled at the last minute. The traditional accompaniment
is thin slices of brown bread and butter.

SERVES 6

60ml/4 tbsp double (heavy)
cream, lightly whipped
4 tbsp mayonnaise
4 tbsp tomato ketchup
1–2 tsp Worcestershire sauce
juice of 1 lemon
450g/1lb cooked peeled
prawns (shrimp)
salt, ground black pepper and paprika
½ crisp lettuce, finely shredded
thinly sliced brown bread, butter
and lemon wedges, to serve

1 Mix the cream, mayonnaise, ketchup, Worcestershire sauce and
lemon juice in a bowl. Stir in the prawns and season with salt and
black pepper.

2 Place a little lettuce in the base of six glasses. Spoon the prawns
over and sprinkle with paprika. Serve immediately.

DEVILLED WHITEBAIT

Whitebait are the tiny, silver fry (young) of sprats or herring and are crisply fried and eaten whole. They used to be caught in large numbers every summer in the Thames Estuary, and, for most of the 19th century, an annual whitebait dinner was held at Greenwich to mark the end of each parliamentary session.

SERVES 4

450g/1lb whitebait

115g/4oz/1 cup plain (all-purpose) flour

salt and ground black pepper

pinch of cayenne pepper

150ml/¼ pint/⅔ cup milk

oil, for deep-frying

1 Spoon the flour into a paper bag or freezer bag and season the flour with salt, pepper, and a little cayenne.

2 Put the milk in a shallow bowl. Dip a handful of the whitebait into the milk, drain them well, then put them into the bag and shake gently to coat in the flour. Repeat until all the fish have been coated. Don't add too many of the fish at once or they will stick together.

3 In a large pan or deep fryer, heat the oil to 190°C/375°F or until a cube of stale bread browns in 20 seconds. Add a small batch of whitebait and fry for 2–3 minutes, until crisp and golden brown.

4 Lift out, drain and keep hot while you fry the rest. Sprinkle with more cayenne and serve very hot.

SUSSEX SMOKIES

England's smokehouses offer some fine products. The flavour and colour of this Sussex dish is best when made with pale, undyed smoked haddock rather than the bright yellow artificially dyed variety. A filling appetiser, this is good served with crusty bread as a light meal or snack.

SERVES 4

350g/12oz smoked haddock

450ml/¾ pint/scant 2 cups milk

25g/1oz/2 tbsp butter

25g/1oz/3 tbsp plain (all-purpose) flour

salt and ground black pepper

115g/4oz mature Cheddar cheese, grated

4 tbsp fresh breadcrumbs

crusty bread, to serve

1 Remove and discard all skin and bones from the haddock and cut the fish into strips.

2 Put the milk, butter, flour and seasoning into a pan. Over a medium heat and whisking constantly, bring to the boil and bubble gently for 2–3 minutes until thick and smooth.

3 Add the haddock and half the cheese to the hot sauce and bring it just back to the boil to melt the cheese.

4 Divide the mixture between individual flameproof dishes or ramekins. Toss together the remaining cheese and the breadcrumbs and sprinkle the mixture over the top of each filled dish.

5 Put the dishes under a hot grill or broiler until bubbling and golden. Serve immediately.

ANGELS ON HORSEBACK

This recipe dates back to the 19th century, when oysters were plentiful and cheap. It became fashionable in England to serve a savoury – a small, strongly flavoured dish – at the end of a meal, mainly to revive the palates of the gentlemen after dessert and before the arrival of the port. Nowadays, this little dish makes a delicious appetiser.

SERVES 4

16 oysters, removed from their shells
fresh lemon juice
8 rashers of rindless streaky bacon
8 small slices of bread
butter, for spreading
paprika (optional)

1 Preheat the oven to 200°C/400°F/gas 6. Sprinkle the oysters with a little lemon juice.

2 Lay the bacon rashers on a board, slide the back of a knife along each one to stretch it and then cut it in half crossways. Wrap a piece of bacon around each oyster and secure with a wooden cocktail stick or toothpick. Arrange them on a baking sheet.

3 Cook the oysters and bacon in the hot oven for 8–10 minutes until the bacon is just cooked through.

4 Meanwhile, toast the bread. When the bacon is cooked, butter the hot toast and serve the bacon-wrapped oysters on top. Sprinkle with a little paprika, if using.

DEVILS ON HORSEBACK

This is another popular savoury, designed to be served at the end of a lavish dinner, or as a party bite. The prunes are sometimes filled with pâté, olives, almonds or nuggets of cured meat. They may be served on crisp, fried bread instead of buttered toast.

SERVES 4

16 stoned (pitted) prunes
fruit chutney, such as mango
8 rashers of rindless streaky bacon
8 small slices of bread
butter, for spreading

1 Preheat the oven to 200°C/400°F/gas 6. Ease open the prunes and spoon a small amount of fruit chutney into each cavity.

2 Lay the bacon rashers on a board, slide the back of a knife along each one to stretch it and then cut in half crossways. Wrap a piece of bacon around each prune and lay them close together (if they touch each other, they are less likely to unroll during cooking) on a baking sheet.

3 Cook in the hot oven for 8–10 minutes until the bacon is cooked through.

4 Meanwhile, toast the bread. Butter the hot toast and serve the bacon-wrapped prunes on top.

SALAD WITH WARM BLACK PUDDING

Black pudding is a traditional sausage containing pig's blood that is flavoured with spices. In England it is considered a Lancashire speciality, but similar sausages are also found all over Britain, particularly in the Midlands. Fried rapidly so that the outside is crisp, and the inside still moist, slices of black pudding are delicious in salads.

SERVES 4

250g/9oz black pudding (blood sausage)

45ml/3 tbsp olive oil

1 small crusty loaf, plain or flavoured with herbs, cut into small chunks

1 Romaine lettuce, torn into bite-size pieces

250g/9oz cherry tomatoes, halved

FOR THE DRESSING

juice of 1 lemon

90ml/6 tbsp olive oil

1 tsp English (hot) mustard

1 tbsp clear honey

2 tbsp chopped fresh herbs, such as chives and parsley

salt and ground black pepper

1 Slice the black pudding with a sharp knife, then dry-fry the slices on both sides over a medium heat in a non-stick frying pan for 5–10 minutes, until crisp.

2 Remove the black pudding from the pan using a slotted spoon and drain the slices on kitchen paper. Keep warm.

3 Mix together the ingredients for the salad dressing and season to taste with salt and pepper.

4 Add the olive oil to the juices in the frying pan and cook the bread cubes in two batches, turning often, until golden on all sides. Drain the croutons on kitchen paper.

5 Mix together the croutons, black pudding, lettuce and cherry tomatoes in a large bowl. Pour the dressing over the salad, mix well and serve at once.

VARIATION

Try this salad with pieces of bacon, fried until crispy, or chunks of grilled, herby sausages in place of the black pudding.

PEARS WITH STILTON, CREAM AND WALNUTS

English cheeses and fruit taste wonderful together, as in traditional combinations such as apple pie with Wensleydale or fruitcake with Cheshire cheese. This dish needs pears that are fully ripe and juicy, yet firm – Comice, Conference or Williams all work well.

SERVES 6

115g/4oz/½ cup cream cheese or curd cheese

75g/3oz Stilton cheese

ground black pepper

30–45ml/2–3 tbsp single (light) cream

115g/4oz/1 cup roughly chopped walnuts

6 ripe pears

15ml/1 tbsp lemon juice

watercress sprigs, to garnish (optional)

FOR THE DRESSING

juice of 1 lemon and a little finely grated lemon rind

pinch of caster (superfine) sugar

60ml/4 tbsp olive oil

salt and ground black pepper

1 Mash the cream or curd cheese and Stilton together with a good grinding of black pepper, then blend in the cream to make a smooth mixture. Stir in the chopped walnuts. Cover the mixture and chill until required.

2 Halve the pears lengthways and scoop out the cores. Put them into a bowl of cold water with the lemon juice, to prevent them from browning.

3 Whisk the dressing ingredients together and season to taste.

4 Drain the pears well and pat dry with kitchen paper, then place hollow side up on serving dishes. Pile the cheese mixture into the pears and spoon over the dressing. Serve, garnished with watercress sprigs if you like.

VARIATION

Try other blue cheeses such as Beenleigh Blue or Oxford Blue, or for a milder taste use soft cream cheese.

POTTED CHEESE

The potting of cheese became popular in the 18th century, and it is still a great way to use up odd pieces left on the cheeseboard. Blend them with your chosen seasonings, adjusting the flavour before adding the alcohol. Serve with plain crackers, oatcakes or crisp toast.

SERVES 4–6

250g/9oz hard cheese, such as mature Cheddar

75g/3oz/6 tbsp soft unsalted butter, plus extra for melting

¼ tsp ready-made English (hot) mustard

¼ tsp ground mace

ground black pepper

30ml/2 tbsp sherry

fresh parsley, to garnish

crackers or crisp toast, to serve

1 Cut the cheese into rough pieces and put them into a food processor. Use the pulse button to chop the cheese into small crumbs.

2 Add the butter, mustard, mace and a little black pepper and blend again until smooth. Taste and adjust the seasoning. Finally, blend in the sherry.

3 Spoon the mixture into a dish just large enough to leave about 1cm/½in to spare on top. Level the surface.

4 Melt some butter in a small pan, skimming off any foam that rises to the surface. Leaving the sediment in the pan, pour a layer of melted butter on top of the cheese mixture to cover the surface. Refrigerate until required.

5 Garnish with parsley and serve spread on crackers or thin, crisp slices of toast.

VARIATIONS

◆ Use some crumbled Stilton in place of the Cheddar and the same quantity of port in place of sherry.

◆ Some finely chopped chives could be added instead of mustard.

CHICKEN LIVER PÂTÉ

This traditional English recipe is one of the simplest pâtés to make. The name 'pâté' is a medieval French term, originally describing a pastry case with a filling. Over time, in England the name came to mean just the filling without the pastry case. Depending on availability, chicken or duck livers can be used in this lovely country starter.

SERVES 4

115g/4oz/½ cup butter

4 shallots, finely chopped

2 garlic cloves, finely chopped

1 bay leaf

225g/8oz chicken livers, rinsed and trimmed

30ml/2 tbsp dry sherry

1 tsp chopped fresh herbs, such as thyme and parsley

300ml/½ pint/1¼ cups double (heavy) cream

salt and ground black pepper

toasts and red onion marmalade (optional), to serve

1 Melt half the butter in a large frying pan. Add the shallots and garlic and bay leaf, and cook until softened but not coloured.

2 Add the chicken livers and stir over a medium heat for 8–10 minutes, or until they are just firm and cooked through. Remove and discard the bay leaf.

3 Purée the chicken liver mixture in a blender with the remaining butter and sherry.

4 Add chopped fresh herbs and transfer the mix to a sieve. Press through the sieve into a bowl. This makes for a velvety smooth pâté.

5 Lightly whip the cream until it stands in soft peaks, then fold it into the chicken liver mixture with seasoning to taste. Spoon the pâté into a serving dish and chill until set.

6 Serve the pâté with thin toasts or warm crusty bread, perhaps with a red onion marmalade relish (see overleaf) on the side.

COOK'S TIP

Don't overcook the livers, or they may harden and become grainy in texture. They should be still very slightly pink in the centre.

GAME PÂTÉ WITH RED ONION MARMALADE

This English country pâté is typical; the blend of coarsely chopped and ground game, bolstered by liver and alcohol, makes a richly satisfying spread. Serve with plenty of crusty bread or toast, and sweet-sour onion marmalade.

SERVES 6–8

350g/12oz boned rabbit or hare, cut into small chunks

115g/4oz boned rabbit or hare, minced (ground) or blitzed in a food processor

the liver from the rabbit or hare, minced or blitzed in a food processor

225g/8oz fatty pork, minced

150ml/¼ pint/⅔ cup fortified wine

2 tsp green peppercorns, lightly crushed

1 tsp finely chopped thyme

1 tsp finely chopped marjoram

12 slices cured ham

salt and ground black pepper

2 bay leaves

FOR THE RED ONION MARMALADE

30ml/2 tbsp olive oil

675g/1½lb red onions, thinly sliced

1 sprig of thyme

salt and ground black pepper

45ml/3 tbsp balsamic vinegar

2 tsp caster (superfine) sugar

1 In a bowl, mix the rabbit or hare meat, minced liver and pork with the wine, green peppercorns, thyme and marjoram. Combine it all together with your hands and leave the mixture, covered, in the refrigerator overnight to marinate.

2 Next day, preheat the oven to 160°C/325°F/gas 3. Line a 450g/1lb loaf tin or pan with ham, arranging four slices along each side and one at each end. Reserve two slices for the top.

3 Re-mix the filling, seasoning with salt and pepper, and spoon it into the tin. Press down and smooth the top.

4 Lay the remaining two slices of ham along the top, then fold the side and end pieces of ham over to encase the filling completely

5 Place the bay leaves on top and cover with a double layer of foil. Scrunch the foil under the rim of the tin to seal it. Place the tin in an oven tray surrounded by a little water, and bake in the oven for 1½ hours. Remove, cool and refrigerate.

6 To make the onion marmalade, heat a heavy pan over high heat. Add the oil and allow to heat to near smoking before adding the onions. Allow them to sizzle and scorch, then cook vigorously, stirring, for a further 2 minutes. Add the thyme and some seasoning, turn the heat down to low, cover with a lid and simmer for 20 minutes.

7 Once the onions have softened, stir in the vinegar and sugar and cook gently, stirring, until the vinegar has been fully absorbed by the onions. Cool, and then serve with the chilled pâté.

VARIATION

Almost any game can be substituted in this recipe – pheasant, for example. Always include the fatty pork, however, as this is needed for flavour and texture.

DEVILLED EGGS

The expression 'devilled' dates from the 18th century. It was used to describe dishes or foods that were seasoned with hot spices, giving a fiery flavour that was lightheartedly associated with the devil and hellish heat.

SERVES 6

9 eggs, hard-boiled

50g/2oz/¼ cup finely chopped cooked ham

6 walnut halves, very finely chopped

1 tbsp very finely chopped spring onion (scallion)

1 tbsp Dijon mustard

1 tbsp mayonnaise

2 tsp white wine vinegar

salt and ground black pepper

¼ tsp cayenne pepper

ground paprika and slices of dill pickle, to garnish (optional)

1 Cut each egg in half lengthways. Place the yolks in a bowl and set the white halves aside.

2 Mash the yolks well with a fork, or push them through a sieve or strainer. Add all the remaining ingredients and mix well with the yolks. Season to taste with salt, pepper and cayenne.

3 Spoon the filling into the egg white halves, or pipe it in with a piping bag fitted with a wide nozzle.

4 Sprinkle the top of each stuffed egg with a little paprika and garnish with a small piece of dill pickle, if you like. Serve at room temperature.

SCOTCH EGGS

The origins of this tasty English snack, popularly served in pubs and at picnics, are unclear, but famous London store Fortnum & Mason claims it invented them in 1738 as a portable snack for wealthy coach travellers. The first printed recipe appeared in 1809 in Mrs Rundell's *A New System of Domestic Cookery*; in 1861, Mrs Beeton recommended serving them hot with 'a good gravy'. Despite their name, Scotch eggs are not actually Scottish. The name comes from the process of chopping or mincing the meat to wrap around the egg, which was known as 'scotching'.

MAKES 4

4 eggs

275g/10oz pork sausage meat

1 tsp dried sage

salt and freshly ground black pepper

50g/2oz/½ cup plain (all-purpose) flour

1 egg, beaten

85g/3½oz/1½ cups dried breadcrumbs

vegetable oil, for deep frying

1 Put the eggs, in their shells, in a pan of cold water. Bring to the boil, then simmer for 10 minutes. Cool under cold running water, then peel off the shells.

2 Mix together the sausage meat and sage. Season generously and divide the mixture into four.

3 Flatten each portion into ovals, large enough to enclose the eggs.

4 Season the flour with salt and pepper in a shallow bowl and dredge the boiled eggs in the flour.

5 Place an egg on each sausage meat oval, and wrap the sausage meat around the egg, making sure that it completely covers each egg.

6 Roll the coated eggs in beaten egg, and then in the breadcrumbs, to cover completely.

7 Heat the oil in a large pan or deep fryer, no more than half full for safety, to 190°C/375°F (or until a cube of stale bread browns in 20 seconds). Carefully place the eggs in the hot oil and cook for 8–10 minutes, until golden and crisp and the sausage meat is cooked through. Drain on absorbent kitchen paper.

CHEESE PUDDING

This is vegetarian comfort food, included in this savoury snack chapter, but it makes a substantial side or even supper dish by itself. Old recipes for this classic dish involved cooking layers of toasted bread and cheese in the custard mixture.
This version uses fresh breadcrumbs for a lighter result.

SERVES 4

225g/8oz/2 cups grated mature (strong) Cheddar-style cheese

115g/4oz/2 cups fresh breadcrumbs

40g/1½oz/3 tbsp butter, plus extra for greasing

600ml/1 pint/2½ cups milk

3 eggs, beaten

1 tsp wholegrain mustard

salt and ground black pepper

1 Preheat the oven to 200°C/400°F/gas 6. Butter the insides of a 1.2 litre/2 pint ovenproof soufflé dish.

2 Place three-quarters of the grated cheese in a bowl together with the breadcrumbs, and mix together.

3 Put the butter, milk, eggs, mustard and seasoning into a saucepan and stir well. Heat gently, stirring, until the butter has just melted (if the mixture gets too hot, the eggs will start to set).

4 Stir the warm liquid into the cheese mixture and then pour into the prepared dish. Scatter the remaining cheese evenly over the top.

5 Put into the hot oven and cook for about 30 minutes or until golden brown and just set (a knife inserted in the centre should come out clean).

VARIATIONS

- Stir a small handful of chopped fresh parsley into the mixture before cooking.
- Put a layer of soft-cooked leeks in the bottom of the dish.

BAKED MACARONI CHEESE

The first real collection of English recipes – *Forme of Cury* (1390) – included a recipe for 'macrows with cheese'. Macrows was an early form of pasta, the forerunner of macaroni. An early recipe for the now very well-known macaroni cheese was given by Elizabeth Raffald in 1769 in her book *The Experienced English Housekeeper*. This is the classic version made by families today.

SERVES 6

500ml/16fl oz/2 cups milk

1 bay leaf

3 blades mace, or pinch of grated nutmeg

50g/2oz/4 tbsp butter

35g/1½oz/4 tbsp plain (all-purpose) flour

salt and freshly ground black pepper

175g/6oz/1½ cups grated Cheddar cheese

40g/1½oz/⅓ cup breadcrumbs

450g/1lb dried macaroni or other short, hollow pasta

1 Make a white sauce by gently heating the milk with the bay leaf and mace in a small saucepan. Do not let it boil. Melt the butter in a medium-heavy saucepan. Add the flour, and mix it in well with a wire whisk. Cook for 2–3 minutes, but do not let the butter burn. Strain the hot milk into the flour and butter mixture all at once, and mix smoothly with the whisk. Bring the sauce to the boil, stirring constantly, and cook for another 4–5 minutes.

2 Season with salt and pepper, and the nutmeg if no mace has been used. Add all but 2 tbsp of the cheese, and stir over low heat until it melts. Place a layer of cling film (plastic wrap) right on the surface of the sauce, to stop a skin from forming, and set aside.

3 Bring a large pan of water to the boil. Preheat the oven to 200°C/400°F/gas 6. Grease an ovenproof dish, and sprinkle with some breadcrumbs. Add salt and the pasta to the boiling water, and cook until it is al dente, about 10–15 minutes. Do not overcook, as the pasta will get a second cooking in the oven.

4 Drain the pasta, and combine it with the sauce. Pour it into the prepared ovenproof dish. Sprinkle the top with the remaining breadcrumbs and grated cheese, and bake in the centre of the preheated oven for 20 minutes.

FISH & SHELLFISH

England has always enjoyed wonderful fish and shellfish from its coastlines, lakes and rivers. It has a proud history of smokeries dedicated to preserving fresh fish – herrings and mackerel in particular. Cooking methods vary from simple pan-frying, steaming and baking whole fish, to delicious combinations in soups, sauces, casseroles, pies and fishcakes. And let's not forget the favourite national dish of fish and chips!

PICTURED *The harbour at Mousehole, a fishing village in Cornwall.*

FRESH MACKEREL WITH GOOSEBERRY RELISH

Packed with beneficial oils, fresh mackerel is not only tasty but nutritious. The tart gooseberries in this recipe are a perfect accompaniment to any type of oily fish.

SERVES 4

4 whole mackerel, cleaned
salt and ground black pepper
60ml/4 tbsp olive oil

FOR THE SAUCE

250g/9oz gooseberries
25g/1oz/2 tbsp soft light brown sugar
1 tsp wholegrain mustard
salt and ground black pepper

1 For the sauce, wash and trim the gooseberries and then roughly chop them, so there are some pieces larger than others.

2 Cook the gooseberries in a little water with the sugar in a small pan. A thick and chunky purée will form. Add the mustard, and season to taste with salt and ground black pepper.

3 Preheat the grill or broiler to high, and line the grill pan with foil. Using a sharp knife, slash the fish two or three times down each side, then season and brush with the olive oil.

4 Place the fish in the grill pan and grill for about 4 minutes on each side until cooked. You may need to cook them for a few minutes longer if they are particularly large. The slashes will open up to speed cooking, and the skin should be lightly browned. To check that they are cooked properly, use a small sharp knife to pierce the skin and check for uncooked flesh.

5 Place the mackerel on warmed plates and spread generous dollops of the gooseberry relish over them.

COOK'S TIP

Turn the grill on well in advance, as the fish need a fierce heat to cook quickly.

HALIBUT FILLETS WITH PARSLEY SAUCE

The halibut, found in the North Atlantic, is one of the largest flat fish – the Norsemen considered it 'the fish of the gods'. Any firm white fish works well. Creamy parsley sauce is a traditional English accompaniment for white fish; use the curly variety rather than flat-leaved, for authenticity.

SERVES 4

900g/2lb halibut fillet

2 eggs, beaten

10ml/2 tsp water

75g/3oz/1½ cups fine fresh breadcrumbs

2 tsp salt

½ tsp white pepper

50g/2oz/4 tbsp butter

lemon wedges, to garnish

FOR THE PARSLEY SAUCE

50g/2oz/4 tbsp butter

35g/1¼oz/4 tbsp plain (all-purpose) flour

350ml/12fl oz/1½ cups milk

salt

3 tbsp finely chopped fresh parsley

1 Cut the halibut into four equal pieces. Whisk the eggs and water together in a shallow dish. Place the breadcrumbs in a second shallow dish. Dip the fish into the egg mixture, then into the breadcrumbs, to coat both sides evenly. Sprinkle with salt and white pepper. Allow the fish to rest at least 10 minutes before cooking.

2 To make the parsley sauce, melt the butter in a pan over a medium heat, and whisk in the flour. Reduce the heat and cook the roux for 3–5 minutes until pale beige. Slowly add the milk into the roux; cook, whisking constantly, for about 5 minutes, until the sauce comes to the boil and becomes smooth and thick. Season, add the parsley and simmer for 2 minutes. Cover and keep warm.

3 Melt the butter in a large frying pan over a medium-high heat. Cooking in two batches, place the halibut fillets in the pan, and cook for about 4 minutes on each side, turning once, until the coating is golden brown and the fish flakes easily with a fork.

4 Serve the halibut fillets with the sauce spooned over. Accompany with lemon wedges for squeezing over, and perhaps a portion of lightly boiled shredded cabbage.

PAN-COOKED SALMON WITH SORREL SAUCE

Native to England, sorrel leaves add their lovely tart lemony flavour to this traditional sauce for fresh fish. In its absence (because sorrel is at its best in spring and early summer), you could try using tender young spinach leaves. Small new potatoes are the perfect seasonal accompaniment.

SERVES 4

4 pieces salmon fillet, each weighing about 175g/6oz

15g/½oz/1½ tbsp butter

10ml/2 tsp olive oil

100g/3¾oz fresh sorrel leaves

150ml/¼ pint/⅔ cup double (heavy) cream

salt and ground black pepper

1 Heat the butter and oil in a pan, add the salmon and fry over medium heat for 3–5 minutes until golden brown.

2 Turn the fish over and continue cooking the second side for about 3 minutes until it is almost cooked through. Lift out and keep warm (the salmon will finish cooking while you make the sauce).

3 Chop the sorrel and add it to the hot pan. Cook, stirring, until wilted and soft. If the sorrel gives off lots of liquid, bubble it gently until reduced to a tablespoonful or two.

4 Stir in the cream, bring just to the boil and bubble gently for no more than 1 minute. Add seasoning to taste and serve the sauce with the salmon.

VARIATION

This recipe also works well with other fish, such as trout and sea bass.

POACHED SALMON WITH HOLLANDAISE SAUCE

A whole poached fish makes an elegant party dish and served cold is perfect for a summer buffet. Robert May, cook to the English upper classes, gave a recipe for poached salmon in *The Accomplisht Cook, Or the Art and Mystery of Cooking*, first published in 1660.

SERVES 8–10

2–2.5kg/4½–5½lb whole salmon, gutted, washed and dried

300ml/½ pint/1¼ cups dry (hard) cider or white wine

1 large carrot, roughly chopped

2 medium onions, roughly chopped

2 celery sticks, roughly chopped

2 bay leaves

a few black peppercorns

sprigs of parsley and thyme

watercress and lemons, to serve

FOR THE HOLLANDAISE SAUCE

175g/6oz/¾ cup unsalted butter

1 tsp sugar

3 egg yolks

10ml/2 tsp cider vinegar or white wine vinegar

10ml/2 tsp lemon juice

salt and ground white pepper

1 Put the cider, prepared vegetables and herbs into a large pan and add 1 litre/1¾ pints/4 cups water, bring to the boil and simmer gently for 30–40 minutes. Strain and leave to cool.

2 About 30 minutes before serving, pour the cooled stock into a fish kettle. Lay the salmon on the rack and lower it into the liquid.

3 Slowly heat the kettle until the stock almost comes to the boil (with small bubbles forming and rising to the surface), cover and simmer very gently for 20–25 minutes until the fish is just cooked through – test the thickest part with a knife near the backbone.

4 Meanwhile, to make the hollandaise sauce, heat the butter with the sugar (on the stove or in the microwave) until the butter has melted and is hot but not sizzling – do not allow it to brown.

5 Put the egg yolks, vinegar, lemon juice and seasoning into a processor or blender and blend on high speed for about 15 seconds, or until the mixture is creamy.

6 Keep the processor or blender on high speed and add the hot butter mixture in a slow stream until the mixture is thick, smooth and creamy.

7 Lift the salmon out of its cooking liquid. Remove the skin carefully, so the flesh remains intact, and lift the salmon onto a warmed serving plate. Serve with the warm hollandaise sauce, garnished with watercress, and lemon wedges for squeezing over.

VARIATION

To cook salmon that is to be served cold, in step 3 slowly heat until the stock just comes to the boil, let it bubble two or three times, then cover, remove from the heat and leave to cool completely (this will take up to 12 hours). When cold, lift out the fish and slide it onto a serving plate. Strip off the fins and peel away the skin, then garnish with wafer-thin cucumber slices arranged like scales. Serve the salmon with mayonnaise.

SOUSED HERRINGS

Cooking then storing fish in vinegar, or sousing, was a way to preserve the plentiful supplies of herring caught in the east of England, where these fish were once a staple food.

SERVES 4

4 large or 8 small filleted herrings

salt and ground black pepper

1 medium onion

200ml/7fl oz/scant 1 cup malt vinegar

1 tsp sugar

6 black peppercorns

2 bay leaves

½ tsp mustard seeds

½ tsp coriander seeds

pinch of ground ginger

1 small dried chilli

1 Preheat the oven to 150°C/300°F/gas 2. Lay out the herring fillets skin side down, and sprinkle the flesh with a little salt and pepper. Roll up the fillets from the head end and secure each one with a wooden cocktail stick or toothpick. Slice the onion horizontally and separate into thin rings.

2 Cover the bottom of a shallow ovenproof dish with a layer of onion rings, arrange the rolled herrings on top and scatter the remaining onion rings over them.

3 Mix the vinegar with 200ml/7fl oz/scant 1 cup water and pour over the herrings. Add the remaining ingredients to the dish and cover securely with a lid or a sheet of foil.

4 Put into the preheated oven and cook for 1–1¼ hours, or until the herrings are cooked through and the onion is very soft.

5 Leave the herrings to cool completely in the cooking liquid before serving.

VARIATIONS

◆ Use 1½–2 tsp ready-made pickling spice in place of the herbs and spices.

◆ Replace the vinegar and water with 400ml/14fl oz/1⅔ cups dry (hard) cider for a fruitier, less sharp flavour.

TROUT WITH ALMONDS

The shallow streams and rivers of southern England once supplied an abundance of wild trout. Their earthy flavour goes particularly well with buttery juices and toasted almonds.

SERVES 4

4 whole trout, cleaned

3–4 tbsp flour seasoned with salt and pepper

75g/3oz/6 tbsp butter

15ml/1 tbsp olive oil

50g/2oz/½ cup flaked (sliced) almonds

juice of ½ lemon

lemon wedges, to serve

1 Wash the fish, dry with kitchen paper and coat them with seasoned flour, shaking off any excess.

2 Heat half the butter with the oil in a large frying pan. When the mixture begins to foam, add one or two fish.

3 Cook over medium heat for 3–5 minutes on each side or until golden brown and cooked through. Lift out, drain on kitchen paper and keep warm.

4 Cook the remaining fish, then wipe the pan out with kitchen paper.

5 Add the remaining butter and, when foaming, add the almonds. Cook gently, stirring frequently, until the almonds are golden brown. Remove from the heat and add the lemon juice.

6 Sprinkle the almonds and pan juices over the trout, and serve immediately with lemon wedges for squeezing over.

VARIATION

The trout can be grilled or broiled if preferred. Omit the flour coating. Melt half the butter and brush over both sides of the fish. Put the fish under a medium-hot grill or broiler and cook for 5–7 minutes on each side until golden brown and cooked all the way through. Cook the almonds in butter, as in step 5 above.

PAN-FRIED DOVER SOLE

For many, Dover sole is one of the finest of the flat fish, often called 'the Englishman's fish of choice' because, in the days when transport was slow, its flavour actually improved during the journey from the Kent coast. Use herbs such as dill, parsley or tarragon.

SERVES 4

4 small Dover sole, dark skin and fins removed

2–3 tbsp flour seasoned with salt and pepper

45ml/3 tbsp olive oil

25g/1oz/2 tbsp butter

juice of 1 lemon

1 tbsp chopped fresh herbs

1 Spread the seasoned flour on a plate, and coat each fish, shaking off any excess. Heat a large non-stick frying pan and add the oil.

2 Add one or two fish to the frying pan and cook over a medium heat for 3–5 minutes on each side until golden brown and cooked through. Lift them out and keep them warm while you cook the remaining fish.

3 Add the remaining oil and the butter to the hot pan and heat until the butter has melted. Stir in the lemon juice and chopped herbs. Drizzle the pan juices over the fish and serve immediately.

COOK'S TIPS

◆ Leaving the white skin on one side of the fish helps to keep its shape during cooking; it is also full of flavour and good to eat, particularly the crisp edges.

◆ To grill or broil the fish, omit the flour coating and brush both sides with melted butter. Put the sole under a medium-hot grill or broiler and cook for 5–7 minutes on each side until golden brown and cooked through.

SKATE WITH BLACK BUTTER

Skate wings were especially popular in the early 20th century, and in southern England were once sold in fish and chip shops. Black butter, a traditional sauce, is in fact a deep nutty brown colour. As skate is now endangered, this recipe is included for historical interest, but can be adapted for any sustainably sourced white fish.

SERVES 4

4 pieces of skate wing or sustainably sourced flat white fish, total weight about 1kg/2¼lb

1 small onion

1 bay leaf

salt

50g/2oz/4 tbsp butter

30ml/2 tbsp cider vinegar or white wine vinegar

2–3 tsp capers, rinsed

1 tbsp chopped fresh parsley

1 Wash and dry the fish and put into a shallow pan large enough to accommodate the fish in a single layer. Thinly slice the onion and add to the pan with the bay leaf. Season with a little salt and pour over boiling water (from the kettle) to cover.

2 Heat until bubbles rise to the surface, then lower the heat and simmer gently for 10–15 minutes until the flesh parts easily from the bones.

3 Using a slotted fish slice or spatula, lift the skate wings out of the pan on to a warmed serving plate. Carefully peel off and discard any skin. Cover the fish and keep it warm while you cook the sauce.

4 Melt the butter in a small pan and cook gently until it turns golden brown. Drizzle it over the cooked fish.

5 Add the vinegar to the hot pan and allow it to bubble gently until slightly reduced. Drizzle this over the fish.

6 Scatter the capers and parsley over the top and serve immediately.

COOK'S TIP

If the fish is not already skinned, you will find it easier to remove the skin after cooking as in step 3.

FISH AND CHIPS

This is one of England's national dishes. A much-loved part of English culture, fried fish was sold on the streets of Victorian London and a 'fried fish warehouse' is mentioned in *Oliver Twist*. At that time, though, fried fish was sold with bread rather than potatoes. The first fish and chip shop in England is reputed to be Malin's of Bow in London's East End, which opened in 1860. Use white fish of your choice, sustainably sourced if possible – traditionally, cod, haddock, hake, huss, plaice, skate or whiting were used. Cook in batches so that each piece of fish and all the chips are perfectly crisp. Double cooking the chips ensures they are crisp and golden. Salt and vinegar are the traditional seasonings.

SERVES 4

675g/1½lb skinned cod fillet, cut into four pieces

115g/4oz/1 cup self-raising (self-rising) flour

salt and pepper

150ml/¼ pint/⅔ cup water

675g/1½lb potatoes

oil, for deep frying

lemon wedges, to serve

1 Stir the flour and a good pinch of salt together in a bowl, then make a well in the centre. Gradually whisk in the water to make a smooth batter. Leave for 30 minutes.

2 Using a sharp knife, cut the potatoes into strips about 1cm/½in wide and 5cm/2in long. Put the potatoes in a colander and rinse them with cold water, then drain and dry well.

3 Heat the oil in a deep-fat fryer or large heavy pan to 150°C/300°F (or until a cube of stale bread browns in 20 seconds); for safety, do not fill the pan more than half full with oil.

4 Using a wire basket, lower the potatoes in batches into the hot oil and cook for 5–6 minutes, shaking the basket occasionally until the chips are soft but not browned. Remove the chips from the oil and drain them thoroughly on kitchen paper.

5 Increase the heat of the oil in the fryer to 190°C/375°F. Season the pieces of fish with salt and pepper. Stir the batter, then dip the fish into it, one piece at a time, allowing the excess to drain off.

6 Working in two batches if necessary, lower the fish into the hot oil and fry for 6–8 minutes, until crisp and brown. Drain the fish on kitchen paper and keep warm.

7 Make sure the oil is hot again, then add a batch of chips, cooking for 2–3 minutes, until brown and crisp. Keep hot while cooking the other batches. Sprinkle with salt and serve with the fish, accompanied by lemon wedges.

HADDOCK IN CHEESE SAUCE

A relative of cod, haddock is one of the nation's preferred white fish, though unfortunately North Sea supplies have declined considerably in recent years. Other white fish can be used in place of haddock in this flavourful dish – try hake, coley or whiting. If using smoked haddock, look for naturally smoked rather than the bright yellow fish, which is dyed. If you prefer, the fish can be left whole, with the sauce spooned over before grilling.

SERVES 4

1kg/2¼lb haddock fillets

300ml/½ pint/1¼ cups milk

1 small onion, thinly sliced

2 bay leaves

a few black peppercorns

25g/1oz/2 tbsp butter

25g/1oz/3 tbsp flour

1 tsp English (hot) mustard

115g/4oz mature hard cheese such as Cheddar, grated

salt and ground black pepper

1 Put the fish in a pan large enough to hold it in a single layer. Add the milk, onion, bay leaves and peppercorns and heat slowly until small bubbles are rising to the surface.

2 Cover and simmer very gently for 5–8 minutes, until the fish is just cooked. Lift out with a slotted spoon, straining and reserving the cooking liquid. Flake the fish, removing any bones.

3 To make the sauce, melt the butter in a saucepan, stir in the flour and cook gently, stirring all the time, for about 1 minute (do not allow it to brown). Remove from the heat and gradually stir in the strained milk. Return the pan to the heat and cook, stirring, until the mixture thickens and comes to the boil. Stir in the mustard and three-quarters of the cheese, and season to taste.

4 Gently stir the fish into the sauce and spoon the mixture into individual flameproof dishes. Sprinkle the remaining cheese over the top. Put under a hot grill (broiler) until bubbling and golden, and serve.

VARIATION

This dish can be made with mildly smoked haddock, perhaps half smoked and half unsmoked.

SALMON FISHCAKES

Fishcakes are believed to have originated in the 19th century. Mrs Beeton recommended making fishcakes with leftovers, but the best results come from using equal quantities of freshly cooked fish and potatoes. Add a few well-chosen seasonings and fry them until they are crisp on the outside and meltingly soft inside.

SERVES 4

450g/1lb cooked salmon fillet

450g/1lb potatoes, boiled and mashed

25g/1oz/2 tbsp butter, melted

2 tsp wholegrain mustard

1 tbsp each chopped fresh dill and chopped fresh flat-leaf parsley

grated rind and juice of ½ lemon

salt and ground white pepper

1 tbsp flour

1 egg, lightly beaten

150g/5oz/generous 1 cup dried breadcrumbs

60ml/4 tbsp sunflower oil

rocket (arugula) leaves and fresh chives, to garnish

lemon wedges, to serve

1 Skin and flake the cooked salmon, watching carefully for, and discarding any, bones. Place the flaked salmon in a bowl with the mashed potato, melted butter and wholegrain mustard. Mix the fish and potato well (it is easiest to use your fingers), then stir in the chopped fresh dill and parsley, lemon rind and juice. Season to taste.

2 Divide the mixture into eight equal portions and shape each into a ball, then flatten into a thick disc.

3 Put the flour, egg and breadcrumbs into separate shallow bowls. Dip the fishcakes in flour, then in egg and finally in breadcrumbs.

4 Heat the oil in a frying pan until very hot. Fry the fishcakes in batches until golden brown and crisp all over. As each batch is ready, drain on kitchen paper and keep hot.

5 Arrange the fishcakes on warmed plates and garnish with rocket leaves and chives. Serve with lemon wedges.

VARIATIONS

◆ In place of salmon, try smoked cod or haddock, or a mixture of smoked and fresh fish. For a quick version you can also use tinned fish.

◆ Make your own fresh breadcrumbs instead of using dried.

FISH PIE

Fish pies have been popular in England since the Middle Ages, when the fish was combined with ingredients such as sugar, spices, rosewater and fruit. Although tastes have changed, fish pie is just as popular today. It is particularly good made with a mixture of fresh and smoked fish – ideal in the winter, when the fishing fleets are hampered by gales and fresh fish is in short supply. Cooked shellfish, such as mussels, can be included too.

SERVES 4–5

450g/1lb haddock or cod fillet

225g/8oz smoked haddock or cod

150ml/¼ pint/⅔ cup milk

150ml/¼ pint/⅔ cup water

1 slice of lemon

1 small bay leaf

a few fresh parsley stalks, plus 3 tbsp chopped fresh parsley

50g/2oz/4 tbsp butter

25g/1oz/3 tbsp plain (all purpose) flour

5ml/1 tsp lemon juice, or to taste

FOR THE POTATO MASH

450g/1lb potatoes, peeled and halved

50g/2oz/4 tbsp butter

60ml/4 tbsp double (heavy) cream

salt and freshly ground black pepper

1 Make the mash. Bring the potatoes to the boil in a large pan of water over a high heat, with a pinch of salt, then cover and cook for 20–25 minutes until tender. Drain in a colander and leave for 3–4 minutes, until the steam has evaporated. Put the potatoes in a large bowl and mash with a potato masher until smooth. Mix in the butter and cream, and season to taste with salt and pepper.

2 Preheat the oven to 190°C/375°F/gas 5. Put the fish into a pan with the milk, water, lemon, bay leaf and parsley stalks. Heat slowly until bubbles are rising to the surface, then cover and simmer gently for about 10 minutes until the fish is cooked.

3 Lift out the fish and strain and reserve 300ml/½ pint/1¼ cups of the cooking liquid. Leave the fish until cool enough to handle, then flake the flesh and discard the skin and bones. Set aside.

4 Melt half the butter in a pan, add the flour and cook for 1–2 minutes over low heat, stirring constantly. Gradually add the reserved cooking liquid, stirring well until smooth. Simmer gently for 1–2 minutes, then remove from the heat and stir in the fish, chopped parsley and lemon juice. Season to taste with black pepper.

5 Turn into a buttered 1.75 litre/3 pint ovenproof dish, top with the mashed potato and dot with the remaining butter. Cook for about 20 minutes, until heated through and golden brown on top.

SMOKED FISH SOUFFLÉ

The fluffy savoury soufflé comes from French cuisine, but was introduced into the grand English kitchens by 19th-century chefs such as Antonin Carême, who cooked for the Prince Regent. Serve it puffed up and straight out of the oven, before it has time to settle and fall.

SERVES 4

225g/8oz skinless smoked haddock

300ml/½ pint/1¼ cups milk

2 bay leaves (optional)

40g/1½oz/3 tbsp butter, plus extra for greasing

40g/1½oz/5 tbsp plain (all-purpose) flour

50g/2oz mature Cheddar cheese

1 tsp English (hot) mustard

ground black pepper

5 eggs, separated

1 Put the fish into a pan just large enough to hold it in a single layer, and add the milk and bay leaves (if using). Heat slowly until the milk is very hot, with small bubbles rising to the surface, but not boiling. Cover and simmer very gently for 5–8 minutes until the fish is just cooked.

2 Lift out the fish with a slotted spoon, reserving the cooking liquid, and remove any bones. Discard the bay leaves and break the fish into flakes. Preheat the oven to 190°C/375°F/gas 5 and butter a 20cm/8in soufflé dish.

3 Melt the butter in a pan, stir in the flour and cook gently for 1 minute, stirring. Remove from the heat and gradually stir in the reserved cooking liquid. Cook, stirring constantly until the sauce thickens and comes to the boil.

4 Remove from the heat. Stir in the cheese, mustard, and season with black pepper. Beat in the egg yolks, then gently stir in the flaked fish.

5 Whisk the egg whites until stiff. Stir a little egg white into the sauce, then use a large metal spoon to fold in the rest.

6 Pour the mixture into the prepared dish and cook in the hot oven for about 40 minutes until risen and just firm to the touch. Serve immediately.

FISHERMAN'S CASSEROLE

This simple recipe can be adapted according to the varieties of fish and shellfish that are obtainable on the day – it is delicious whatever mixture you choose.
Serve with a seasonal green vegetable of your choice.

SERVES 4

500g/1¼lb mixed fish fillets, such as salmon, haddock, bass and red mullet

500g/1¼lb mixed shellfish, such as squid strips, mussels, cockles and prawns (shrimp)

15ml/1 tbsp oil

25g/1oz/2 tbsp butter

1 medium onion, finely chopped

1 carrot, finely chopped

3 celery sticks, finely chopped

2 tbsp plain (all-purpose) flour

600ml/1 pint/2½ cups fish stock

300ml/½ pint/1¼ cups dry (hard) cider

350g/12oz small new potatoes, halved

150ml/¼ pint/⅔ cup double (heavy) cream

salt and ground black pepper

small handful of chopped mixed herbs such as parsley, chives and dill

1 Wash the fish fillets and dry on kitchen paper. With a sharp knife, remove the skin, feel carefully for any bones and extract them. Cut the fish into large, even chunks.

2 Prepare the shellfish, shelling the prawns if necessary. Scrub the mussels and cockles, discarding any with broken shells or that do not close when given a sharp tap. Pull off the black tufts (beards) attached to the mussels.

3 Heat the oil and butter in a large saucepan, add the onion, carrot and celery and cook over a medium heat, stirring occasionally, until beginning to soften and turn golden brown. Add the flour, and cook for 1 minute.

4 Remove the pan from the heat and gradually stir in the fish stock and cider. Return the pan to the heat and cook, stirring continuously, until the mixture comes to the boil and thickens.

5 Add the potatoes. Bring the sauce back to the boil, then cover and simmer gently for 10–15 minutes until the potatoes are nearly tender.

6 Add all the fish and shellfish, and stir in gently.

7 Stir in the cream. Bring back to a gentle simmer, then cover the pan and cook gently for 5–10 minutes or until the pieces of fish are cooked through and all the shells have opened. Adjust the seasoning to taste and gently stir in the herbs. Serve immediately.

DRESSED CRAB WITH ASPARAGUS

In Elizabethan England, crabs were often dressed and eaten cold. Juicy and flavourful, crab meat is cheaper than lobster, and is at its best when asparagus comes into season.

SERVES 4

4 dressed crabs

24 asparagus spears, washed

2 tbsp mayonnaise

1 tbsp chopped fresh parsley

1 Scoop out the white crab meat from the shells and claws and place it in a bowl. If you can't find fresh crabs, you can use the same amount of canned or frozen white crab meat. Ensure the meat is completely defrosted, and place onto kitchen paper to dry.

2 Trim the bases off the asparagus. Boil in a pan of water for about 7 minutes, until tender. Plunge the spears into iced water to stop them from cooking further. Drain them when cold, and pat dry with kitchen paper.

3 Add the mayonnaise and chopped fresh parsley, and combine with a fork.

4 Place the mixture into the crab shells and serve with the asparagus spears.

VARIATION

This dish can be enlivened with a splash of Tabasco sauce. This sauce, a fiery scarlet concoction, is made from ripe red peppers ground to a mash with salt, soaked in spirit vinegar and left to age for three years in white oak casks. Invented in Louisiana in the USA, it is recorded arriving in England in the 1880s, when it became a popular way of spicing up dishes.

SCALLOPS WITH BACON

Scallops have been enjoyed in England for hundreds of years and are the sweetest of all the shellfish, with a soft luscious texture. Like oysters, scallops are often believed to be an aphrodisiac. They are best when cooked quickly and briefly, and go well with bacon.

SERVES 4 (OR 2 AS A MAIN COURSE)

8 large or 16 small scallops

15ml/1 tbsp olive oil

4 rashers of streaky bacon, cut into 2.5cm/1in pieces

2–3 fresh sage leaves, chopped

small piece of butter

15ml/1 tbsp fresh lemon juice

100ml/3¾fl oz/scant ½ cup dry (hard) cider or dry white wine

1 Heat the oil in a frying pan. Add the bacon and sage and cook, stirring occasionally, until the bacon is golden brown. Lift out and keep warm.

2 Add the butter to the pan and, when hot, add the scallops. Cook quickly for about 1 minute on each side until browned. Lift out and keep warm.

3 Add the lemon juice and cider or wine to the pan and, scraping up any sediment remaining in the pan, bring just to the boil. Continue bubbling gently until the mixture has reduced to just a few tablespoons of syrupy sauce.

4 Serve the scallops and bacon with the sauce drizzled over.

COOK'S TIP

In summer, some fishmongers sell marsh samphire (glasswort), which grows around the coast of England and makes a good accompaniment to this dish. To prepare samphire, wash it well and pick off the soft fleshy branches, discarding the thicker woody stalks. Drop it into boiling water for just 1 minute before draining and serving.

MUSSELS IN TOMATO BROTH

Once considered fit only to feed the poor because they were so abundant, mussels remain reasonably plentiful and inexpensive, and are farmed along the east and south coasts of England. These days they appear in a myriad of dishes, from the simple to sophisticated. Serve with crusty bread.

SERVES 4

1.8kg/4lb mussels in their shells

1 medium onion

1 garlic clove

30ml/2 tbsp oil

1 tsp sugar

pinch of cayenne or chilli powder

150ml/¼ pint/⅔ cup dry (hard) cider

400g/14oz can of chopped tomatoes

salt and ground black peppe

small handful of chopped fresh parsley, chopped

1 Scrub the mussels in cold water, discarding any that have broken shells and any with open shells that do not close when given a sharp tap. Pull off the black tufts (beards) attached to the shells.

2 Finely chop the onion and garlic.

3 Heat the oil in a deep pan and add the onion, garlic and sugar. Cook, stirring occasionally, over medium heat for about 5 minutes, or until the onion is soft and just beginning to brown. Stir in the cayenne or chilli.

4 Add the cider, tomatoes and a little seasoning. Bring to the boil.

5 Add the mussels, all at once. Cover tightly with a lid and cook quickly for about 5 minutes, until the shells have opened, shaking the pan occasionally.

6 Serve in warmed shallow dishes with chopped parsley scattered over to garnish.

COOK'S TIP

Do not be tempted to prise open and eat any mussels that have not opened up during cooking; these should be discarded.

MEAT DISHES

England takes great pride in its Sunday roast – a succulent piece of beef, lamb or pork cooked to perfection in the oven and served with all the trimmings. Then there are pot roasts, stews and braises, and comforting puddings and pies, not to mention bacon, chops and steaks and a wonderful variety of sausages to grill, pan-fry or bake.

PICTURED *Sheep grazing in autumnal fields. The blackface sheep is the most common breed.*

RIB OF BEEF WITH YORKSHIRE PUDDINGS

Mention English food and most people think of this quintessential dish, which is traditionally served for Sunday lunch and on special occasions. In Victorian days in the north-east of England, roast beef would have been traditional fare on Christmas Day. The accompanying batter pudding was not served alongside it until well into the 18th century, and in Yorkshire it is still sometimes eaten with gravy before the meat course. For Sunday lunch, serve with roast potatoes (page 363) and a selection of vegetables. Horseradish sauce (see page 625) is a traditional accompaniment to roast beef.

SERVES 6–8

rib of beef, weighing about 3kg/6½lb

oil, for brushing

salt and ground black pepper

FOR THE YORKSHIRE PUDDINGS

115g/4oz/1 cup plain (all-purpose) flour

¼ tsp salt

1 egg

200ml/7fl oz/scant 1 cup milk

oil or beef dripping, for greasing

FOR THE GRAVY

600ml/1 pint/2½ cups good beef stock

1 Preheat the oven to 220°C/425°F/gas 7. Weigh the meat and calculate the cooking time required as follows: 10–15 minutes per 500g/1¼lb for rare beef, 15–20 minutes for medium and 20–25 minutes for well done.

2 Put the meat into a large roasting pan. Brush it all over with oil and season with salt and pepper. Put into the hot oven and cook for 30 minutes, until the beef is browned. Lower the oven temperature to 160°C/325°F/gas 3 and cook for the calculated time, spooning the juices over the meat occasionally during cooking.

3 For the Yorkshire puddings, sift the flour and salt into a bowl and break the egg into it. Make the milk up to 300ml/½ pint/1¼ cups with water and gradually whisk into the flour to make a smooth batter. Leave to stand while the beef cooks. Generously grease eight Yorkshire pudding tins (muffin pans are fine) measuring about 10cm/4in.

4 At the end of its cooking time, remove the beef from the oven, cover with foil and leave to stand for 30–40 minutes while you cook the Yorkshire puddings and make the gravy.

5 Increase the oven temperature to 220°C/425°F/gas 7 and put the prepared tins on the top shelf for 5 minutes until very hot. Pour in the batter and cook for about 15 minutes until well risen, crisp and golden brown.

6 To make the gravy, transfer the beef to a warmed serving plate. Pour off the fat from the roasting pan, leaving the meat juices. Add the stock to the pan, bring to the boil and bubble until reduced by about half. Season to taste.

7 Carve the beef and serve with the gravy and Yorkshire puddings, along with roast potatoes, vegetables, and horseradish cream if liked.

POT-ROASTED BEEF WITH STOUT

The pot roast is a descendant of meat cooked in a cauldron over a fire. Over time, vegetables and herbs were added and, later, potatoes, when those became common. A pot roast would have often formed part of the harvest supper prepared for workers on the farm. The stout helps to tenderise the meat and mingles with the juices. Boned and rolled brisket, silverside (top rump) and topside of beef, which are full of flavour, are perfect.

SERVES 6

900g/2lb rolled brisket of beef

30ml/2 tbsp vegetable oil

2 medium onions, roughly chopped

2 celery sticks, thickly sliced

450g/1lb carrots, cut into large chunks

675g/1½lb potatoes, peeled and cut into large chunks

2 tbsp plain (all-purpose) flour

450ml/¾ pint/scant 2 cups beef stock

300ml/½ pint/1¼ cups stout

1 bay leaf

3 tbsp chopped fresh thyme

1 tsp soft light brown sugar

2 tbsp wholegrain mustard

1 tbsp tomato purée (paste)

salt and ground black pepper

1 Preheat the oven to 180°C/350°F/gas 4. Heat the oil in a large flameproof casserole that will fit the brisket, and brown the beef until golden brown all over.

2 Lift the beef from the pan and drain on kitchen paper. Add the onions to the pan and cook for about 4 minutes, until just beginning to soften and brown.

3 Add the celery, carrots and potatoes to the casserole and cook over a medium heat for 2–3 minutes, or until they are just beginning to colour.

4 Add the flour and cook for a further 1 minute, stirring continuously. Gradually pour in the beef stock and the stout. Heat until the mixture comes to the boil, stirring frequently.

5 Stir in the bay leaf, thyme, sugar, mustard, tomato purée and seasoning. Place the meat on top, cover tightly and transfer the casserole to the hot oven.

6 Cook for about 2½ hours, or until the meat is tender. Adjust the seasoning to taste. To serve, carve the beef into thick slices and serve with the vegetables and plenty of the gravy.

BRAISED BEEF STEW WITH HERB DUMPLINGS

Dumplings, probably originally made from bread dough, have been added to English stews for centuries to satisfy hearty appetites, and are particularly associated with Norfolk.

SERVES 4

900g/2lb lean braising steak, cut into chunks

25g/1oz/2 tbsp butter

30ml/2 tbsp oil

115g/4oz rashers of streaky bacon

3 tbsp plain (all-purpose) flour

450ml/¾ pint/scant 2 cups beer

450ml/¾ pint/scant 2 cups beef stock

salt and ground black pepper

1 bouquet garni

8 shallots, peeled

175g/6oz/2 cups small mushrooms

FOR THE HERB DUMPLINGS

115g/4oz/1 cup self-raising (self-rising) flour

50g/2oz/scant ½ cup shredded suet

½ tsp salt

½ tsp mustard powder

1 tbsp chopped fresh parsley

1 tbsp fresh thyme leaves

1 In a large frying pan, melt half the butter with half the oil, add the beef chunks and fry quickly in batches. Transfer the meat to a casserole dish.

2 Chop the bacon into pieces and fry in the same pan, then transfer to the casserole using a slotted spoon.

3 Stir the flour into the fat in the frying pan. Add the beer, stock and seasoning and bring to the boil, stirring constantly.

4 Pour the liquid over the meat in the casserole and add the bouquet garni. Cover and place in a cold oven set to 200°C/400°F/gas 6. Cook for 30 minutes, then reduce the temperature to 160°C/325°F/gas 3 and cook for 1 hour.

5 Heat the remaining butter and oil in a frying pan and cook the shallots until golden. Lift out and set aside. Add the mushrooms and cook quickly for 2–3 minutes.

6 Stir the shallots and mushrooms into the stew in the casserole, cover and put back in the oven for 30 minutes.

7 In a bowl, mix together all the dumpling ingredients. Add just a little cold water, enough to make a soft, sticky dough. Roll into 12 balls and place on top of the stew. Cover, and cook in the oven for a further 25 minutes. Serve.

STEAK AND KIDNEY PUDDING

This classic savoury pudding is in fact a 19th-century invention that has, in a relatively short time, become one of England's most famous dishes. In Victorian days it would also have included oysters, then incredibly cheap, and some versions also contain mushrooms.

SERVES 6

500g/1¼lb lean stewing steak, cut into cubes

225g/8oz beef kidney or lamb's kidneys, skin and core removed and cut into small cubes

1 medium onion, finely chopped

2 tbsp finely chopped fresh herbs, such as parsley and thyme

2 tbsp plain (all-purpose) flour, plus extra for flouring

salt and ground black pepper

275g/10oz/2 cups self-raising (self-rising) flour

150g/5oz/1 cup shredded suet

finely grated rind of 1 small lemon

a little butter for greasing

about 120ml/4fl oz/½ cup beef stock or water

1 Put the stewing steak into a large mixing bowl and add the kidneys, onion and chopped herbs. Sprinkle the plain flour and seasoning over the top and mix well.

2 To make the pastry, sift the self-raising flour into another large bowl. Stir in the suet and lemon rind. Add sufficient cold water to bind the ingredients and gather into a soft dough.

3 On a lightly floured surface, knead the dough gently, and then roll out to make a circle measuring about 35cm/14in across. Cut out one quarter of the circle, roll up and put aside.

4 Lightly butter a 1.75 litre/3 pint pudding basin or heatproof bowl with a raised rim. Line the bowl with the rolled-out dough, pressing the cut edges together and allowing the pastry to overlap the top of the bowl slightly.

5 Spoon the steak mixture into the lined bowl, packing it in carefully, so as not to split the pastry.

6 Pour in sufficient stock to reach no more than three-quarters of the way up the filling. (Any stock remaining can be heated and poured into the cooked pudding to thin the gravy if desired.)

7 Roll out the reserved pastry into a circle to form a lid and lay it over the filling, pinching the edges together to seal them well.

8 Cover with greaseproof paper or baking parchment, pleated in the centre to allow the pudding to rise, and then with a large sheet of foil (again pleated at the centre). Tuck the edges under and press them tightly to the sides of the bowl until securely sealed (alternatively, tie with string). Steam for about 5 hours.

9 Carefully remove the foil and paper, slide a knife around the sides of the pudding and turn out onto a warmed serving plate.

BRAISED OXTAIL

Oxtail has been enjoyed in England for hundreds of years – oxen were sometimes listed in Anglo Saxon food rents. While oxtail requires long, slow cooking to tenderise the meat, the resulting flavour is rich and well worth the effort. Braised oxtail is traditionally served with plain boiled potatoes to soak up the rich gravy, though mashed potatoes would be good too.

SERVES 6

2 oxtails, trimmed, cut into pieces, total weight about 1.5kg/3¼lb

2 tbsp flour seasoned with salt and pepper

45ml/3 tbsp oil

2 large onions, sliced

2 celery sticks, sliced

4 medium carrots, sliced

1 litre/1¾ pints/4 cups beef stock

1 tbsp tomato purée (paste)

finely grated rind of 1 small orange

2 bay leaves

few sprigs of fresh thyme

salt and ground black pepper

chopped fresh parsley, to garnish

1 Preheat the oven to 150°C/300°F/gas 2. Coat the pieces of oxtail in the seasoned flour, shaking off and reserving any excess.

2 Heat 30ml/2 tbsp oil in a large flameproof casserole and add the oxtail in batches, cooking quickly until browned all over. Lift out and set aside. Add the remaining oil to the pan, and stir in the onions, celery and carrots.

3 Cook the vegetables quickly, stirring occasionally, until beginning to brown. Tip in any reserved flour, then add the stock, tomato purée and orange rind.

4 Heat until bubbles begin to rise to the surface, then add the bay leaves and thyme, cover and put into the hot oven. Cook for 3½–4 hours until the oxtail is very tender.

5 Remove from the oven and leave to stand, covered, for 10 minutes before skimming off the surface fat. Adjust the seasoning and garnish with parsley.

COOK'S TIP

This dish benefits from being made in advance. When cooled completely, any fat can be removed before reheating.

COLD SPICED BEEF

This is quite a traditional dish, although it is a modern version of the old recipe, as it omits the initial pickling stage and takes only three or four days to cure, in comparison with ten days for the original method. Serve on thinly sliced brown bread, with chutney (or perhaps with sour cream lightly flavoured with horseradish and black pepper).

SERVES 8

beef silverside (top rump) or tail end, weighing 1.8kg/4lb

1 tbsp coarsely ground black pepper

2 tsp ground ginger

1 tbsp juniper berries, crushed

1 tbsp coriander seeds, crushed

1 tsp ground cloves

1 tbsp ground allspice

3 tbsp soft dark brown sugar

2 bay leaves, crushed

1 small onion, finely chopped

300ml/½ pint/1¼ cups dark ale

1 First, spice the beef: blend the pepper, spices and sugar thoroughly in a pestle and mortar or small blender, then mix in the bay leaves and onion. Rub the mixture into the meat, then put it into a suitable lidded container and refrigerate for 3–4 days, turning and rubbing with the mixture daily.

2 Put the meat into a large pan and barely cover with cold water. Place a tight lid on the pan and bring to the boil. Reduce the heat and cook very gently for about 3½ hours. For the last hour, add the ale to the cooking liquid.

3 When the meat is cooked, leave it to cool in the liquid. Wrap in foil and keep in the refrigerator until required, then slice to serve. It will keep for about 1 week.

ROAST SHOULDER OF LAMB WITH MINT SAUCE

Lamb is one of the three meats (with beef and pork) that is traditionally roasted and served for Sunday lunch. It is particularly popular at Easter. Mint sauce, with its sweet and sour combination, has been lamb's customary accompaniment since at least the 17th century.

 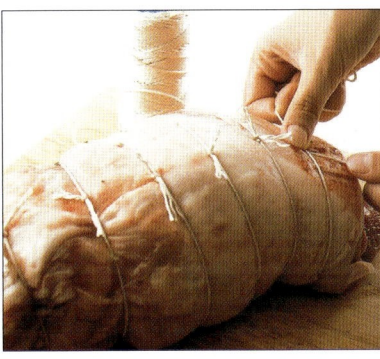 

SERVES 6–8

boned shoulder of lamb, weighing
1.5–2kg/3¼–4½lb

salt and ground black pepper

2 tbsp fresh thyme leaves

30ml/2 tbsp clear honey

150ml/¼ pint/⅔ cup dry (hard) cider
or white wine

30–45ml/2–3 tbsp double (heavy)
cream (optional)

FOR THE MINT SAUCE

large handful of fresh mint leaves

1 tbsp caster (superfine) sugar

45–60ml/3–4 tbsp cider vinegar or
wine vinegar

1 To make the mint sauce, finely chop the mint leaves with the sugar (the sugar draws the juices from the mint) and put the mixture into a bowl. Add 30ml/2 tbsp boiling water to the mint and sugar, and stir well until the sugar has dissolved. Add the vinegar to taste and leave to stand for at least 1 hour for the flavours to blend.

2 Preheat the oven to 220°C/425°F/gas 7. Open out the lamb with its skin side down. Season with salt and pepper, sprinkle with the thyme leaves and drizzle the honey over the top. Roll up and tie securely with string in several places. Place the meat in a roasting pan and put into the hot oven. Cook for 30 minutes until browned all over.

3 Pour the cider and 150ml/¼ pint/⅔ cup water into the tin. Lower the oven to 160°C/325°F/gas 3 and cook for about 45 minutes for medium (pink) or about 1 hour for well-done meat.

4 Remove the lamb from the oven, cover loosely with a sheet of foil and leave to stand for 20–30 minutes.

5 Lift the lamb onto a warmed serving plate. Skim any excess fat from the surface of the pan juices before reheating and seasoning to taste. Stir in the cream, if using, bring to the boil and remove from the heat. Carve the lamb and serve with the juices spooned over and the mint sauce.

LANCASHIRE HOTPOT

This famous hotpot was traditionally cooked in a farmhouse or communal bread oven, in time for supper at the end of the day. The ingredients would have been layered straight into the pot, but here the meat is first browned to add colour and extra flavour to the dish.

SERVES 4

8–12 lean best end of neck lamb chops

175g/6oz lamb's kidneys, skin and core removed and cut into pieces

15–30ml/1–2 tbsp oil

2 medium onions, thinly sliced

few sprigs of fresh thyme or rosemary

900g/2lb potatoes, thinly sliced

salt and ground black pepper

600ml/1 pint/2½ cups lamb or vegetable stock

25g/1oz/2 tbsp butter, cut in small pieces

1 Preheat the oven to 180°C/350°F/gas 4. Heat the oil in a large frying pan and brown the lamb chops quickly on all sides. Remove the meat from the pan and set aside.

2 Add the kidneys to the hot pan and brown lightly over a high heat. Lift out.

3 In a casserole, layer the chops and kidneys with the onions, herbs and potatoes, seasoning each layer.

4 Finish off with a layer of potatoes. Pour over the stock, sprinkle with more herbs and dot the top with butter. Cover, put into the oven and cook for 2 hours. Remove the lid, increase the oven temperature to 220°C/425°F/gas 7 and cook, uncovered, for a further 30 minutes until the potatoes are crisp.

VARIATIONS

◆ Add sliced carrots or mushrooms to the layers.

◆ Replace 150ml/¼ pint/⅔ cup of the stock with dry (hard) cider or wine.

LAMB AND PEARL BARLEY CASSEROLE

The combination of pearl barley and carrots adds texture, bulk and flavour to this comforting stew, giving a thick, tasty sauce for the meat. This is comfort food that is at its best; serve with boiled or baked potatoes or a chunk of rustic bread, and a green vegetable, such as spring cabbage.

SERVES 6

675g/1½ lb stewing lamb

15ml/1 tbsp oil

2 onions, sliced

675g/1½ lb carrots, thickly sliced

4–6 celery sticks, sliced

3 tbsp pearl barley, rinsed

about 900ml/1½ pints/3¾ cups stock or water

salt and ground black pepper

1 Trim the lamb and cut it into bite-size pieces. Heat the oil in a flameproof casserole and brown the lamb. Preheat the oven to 150°C/300°F/gas 2.

2 Add the vegetables to the casserole and fry them briefly with the meat. Add the barley and enough of the stock or water to cover, and season to taste.

3 Cover the casserole and simmer gently in the oven for 1–1½ hours until the meat is tender. You can also cook this on a very low heat on the stove top if you wish. Add extra stock during cooking if necessary. Serve.

COOK'S TIP

The best cut of lamb for stewing is neck or shoulder, with some fat on the meat to keep it moist during cooking.

BARNSLEY CHOPS WITH MUSTARD SAUCE

Named after the Yorkshire town of Barnsley, this double-sized lamb chop is cut from the saddle – the two loins with the backbone intact between them. It is served here with mustard sauce, also a Yorkshire favourite with lamb. Sprouting broccoli spears go well as a vegetable accompaniment.

SERVES 4

4 Barnsley chops or 8 lamb loin chops

1 tbsp tender rosemary leaves

60ml/4 tbsp olive oil

salt and ground black pepper

100ml/3½fl oz/scant ½ cup lamb or beef stock

2 tbsp wholegrain mustard

1 tsp Worcestershire sauce

1 Put the chops in a dish. Chop the rosemary very finely and mix with the oil. Rub the mixture over the chops and leave to stand, covered, for 30 minutes, or longer if refrigerated. Season lightly with salt and pepper.

2 Heat a large frying pan, add the chops and cook over a medium heat for 5–8 minutes on each side until cooked.

3 Lift the chops out of the pan, and keep warm. Pour the stock into the hot pan, scraping up any sediment, and add the mustard.

4 Heat until the mixture comes to the boil and leave to bubble gently until reduced by about one third. Stir in the Worcestershire sauce and adjust the seasoning.

5 Serve the chops with the mustard sauce spooned over.

VARIATION

For a richer variation of this dish, make a mustard cream sauce by stirring in 150ml/¼ pint/⅔ cup soured cream at the end of step 3 and cooking gently for 2–3 minutes.

SHEPHERD'S PIE

This dish developed during Victorian days as a thrifty way of using up leftovers. By the 1930s it had become part of a regular weekly pattern of eating, made with leftover meat from the Sunday roast and served to the family on Monday or Tuesday.

SERVES 4

450g/1lb cold cooked lamb or beef, minced (ground)

15ml/1 tbsp oil

1 large onion, finely chopped

1 medium carrot, finely chopped

150ml/¼ pint/⅔ cup lamb or beef stock

2 tbsp finely chopped fresh parsley

FOR THE MASH TOPPING

1kg/2¼lb potatoes, peeled

60ml/4 tbsp milk

about 25g/1oz/2 tbsp butter

salt and ground black pepper

1 Preheat the oven to 190°C/375°F/gas 5. Prepare the mash: boil the potatoes in salted water for about 20 minutes or until soft. Drain, and mash with the milk – you can push the potatoes through a ricer, pass them through a mouli or use a potato masher. Mix in the butter and seasoning to taste.

2 Heat the oil in a frying pan and add the onion and carrot. Cook over medium heat for 5–10 minutes, stirring occasionally, until soft. Stir in the minced meat, stock and parsley.

3 Spread the meat mixture in an ovenproof dish and spoon the mashed potato evenly over the top. Cook in the hot oven for about 30 minutes until the potato topping is crisped and browned.

VARIATIONS

◆ Add extra ingredients to the meat base, such as a clove or two of chopped garlic, a few mushrooms, a spoonful of tomato purée (paste) or ketchup, or a splash of Worcestershire sauce.

◆ You could also mix the potatoes with mashed parsnip, squash or swede (rutabaga), and add a dollop of wholegrain mustard.

LIVER AND BACON CASSEROLE

Instead of the long, slow cooking of a traditional casserole, this dish of lamb's liver and bacon is cooked in less than half an hour. You could, of course, cook calf's or pig's liver in the same way. Creamy mashed potato and cabbage make ideal accompaniments.

SERVES 4

450g/1lb lamb's liver, sliced

2 tbsp plain (all-purpose) flour, seasoned with salt and pepper

15ml/1 tbsp olive oil, plus extra if necessary

about 8 rashers of rindless streaky bacon

2 onions, thinly sliced

4 fresh sage leaves, finely chopped

150ml/¼ pint/⅔ cup chicken or vegetable stock

salt and ground black pepper

1 Pat the liver with kitchen paper, then trim it with a sharp knife, and cut on the diagonal to make thick strips. Toss the liver in the seasoned flour until it is well coated, shaking off any excess.

2 Heat the oil in a large frying pan and add the bacon. Cook over medium heat until the fat runs out of the bacon and it is browned and crisp. Lift out and keep warm.

3 Add the onions and sage to the frying pan. Cook over medium heat for about 10–15 minutes, stirring occasionally, until the onions are soft and golden brown. Lift out with a draining spoon and keep warm.

4 Increase the heat under the pan and, adding a little extra oil if necessary, add the liver in a single layer. Cook for 3–4 minutes, turning once, until browned on both sides.

5 Return the onions to the pan and pour in the stock. Bring just to the boil and bubble gently for a minute or two, seasoning to taste with salt and pepper. Serve topped with the bacon.

RISSOLES

In a 16th-century English recipe for 'rissheshewes', finely chopped cooked meat was mixed with breadcrumbs and bound into little cakes with beaten eggs and a thick gravy. These contemporary rissoles have been adapted to feature mashed potato as well as breadcrumbs, which makes the mixture easier to shape and coat with crumbs.

SERVES 4

675g/1½lb potatoes, peeled

350g/12oz cooked beef or lamb, such as the remains of a roast, trimmed of excess fat

1 small onion

1 tsp Worcestershire sauce

2 tbsp chopped fresh herbs, such as parsley, mint and chives

salt and ground black pepper

2 tbsp plain (all-purpose) flour

2 eggs, beaten

115g/4oz/2 cups fresh breadcrumbs

oil for frying

brown sauce, to serve

1 Cook the whole potatoes in boiling water for about 20 minutes or until completely soft. Meanwhile, mince (grind) or chop the meat very finely. Finely chop the onion.

2 Drain the potatoes and mash them thoroughly by pushing the potatoes through a ricer, passing them through a mouli or mashing them with a potato masher or fork.

3 In a large mixing bowl, combine the minced meat and chopped onion with the mashed potatoes, Worcestershire sauce, herbs and seasoning, beating well. Shape the mixture into eight patties or sausages.

4 Dip in the flour, then in the beaten egg and finally in the breadcrumbs, gently shaking off any excess.

5 Heat enough oil to cover the base of a large frying pan and cook the rissoles over a medium heat, turning once or twice, until crisp and golden brown. Drain and serve with brown sauce.

COOK'S TIP

Chilling the potato and meat mixture before shaping the rissoles will make it easier to handle.

ROAST PORK WITH SAGE AND ONION STUFFING

Sage and onion is such a traditional combination, and for good reason. This classic stuffing goes well with roasted duck and turkey as well as pork, with sage counteracting the fattiness of the rich meats. Serve with apple sauce, roast potatoes and vegetables.

SERVES 6–8

boneless loin of pork, weighing
1.3–1.6kg/3–3½lb
salt and ground black pepper

FOR THE STUFFING
25g/1oz/2 tbsp butter
50g/2oz bacon, finely chopped
2 large onions, finely chopped
75g/3oz/1½ cups fresh
white breadcrumbs
2 tbsp chopped fresh sage
1 tsp chopped fresh thyme
2 tsp finely grated lemon rind
1 small egg, beaten
salt and ground black pepper

FOR THE APPLE SAUCE
450g/1lb cooking apples
30ml/2 tbsp cider or water
25g/1oz/2 tbsp butter
about 25g/1oz/2 tbsp caster
(superfine) sugar

1 Preheat the oven to 220°C/425°F/gas 7.

2 Make the stuffing first. Melt the butter in a heavy-based pan and fry the bacon until it begins to brown, then add the onions and cook gently until they soften, but do not allow to brown. Mix with the breadcrumbs, sage, thyme, lemon rind and egg, then season well with salt and pepper.

3 Cut the rind off the pork in one piece and score it well. This makes crisper crackling than leaving it on the pork. Rub in 1 tsp salt.

4 Cut down the length of the meat, then open it out like a book so you can spread the stuffing over, then roll up and tie neatly. (Excess stuffing can be rolled into balls, and added to the roasting tin for the last 30 minutes of cooking.)

5 Cook the rolled pork for 25 minutes. Then, reduce the temperature to 190°C/375°F/gas 5 and cook for 20 minutes per 450g/1lb until the juices run clear and the meat is cooked through. Cover the pork with foil to rest.

6 Increase the oven temperature to 220°C/425°F/gas 7 and roast the rind on a tray for a further 20–25 minutes, until crisp. Place it back on the meat.

7 To make the apple sauce, peel, core and chop the apples, then place in a small pan with the cider or water and cook, stirring occasionally, for 5–10 minutes or until very soft. Beat well or blend in a blender or food processor until smooth, then beat in the butter and sugar to taste. Reheat the sauce just before serving, if necessary.

8 Serve the pork cut into thick slices with strips of the crisp crackling and apple sauce.

SOMERSET PORK CASSEROLE

Until the 20th century, many country folk kept and reared a pig, and not one bit of it was wasted. Apple is its perfect partner in this West Country dish. Somerset is famous for its pigs, and extensive orchards which supply the apples from which both juices and cider are made. Apple juice goes particularly well with white meats, and in this recipe imparts a delicious fruitiness to the flavour.

SERVES 4

lean belly pork, weighing 500g/1¼lb after removing rind and bones

15ml/1 tbsp oil

1 medium onion, chopped

2 celery sticks, sliced

600ml/1 pint/2½ cups chicken stock

300ml/½ pint/1¼ cups medium-dry (hard) apple juice

1 tbsp clear honey

pinch of ground cloves

1 tbsp fresh thyme leaves

4 fresh sage leaves, finely chopped

2 medium carrots, sliced

2 leeks, sliced

2 × 400g/14oz cans of haricot beans, drained

salt and ground black pepper

chopped parsley or thyme, to garnish

1 Cut the pork into 2.5cm/1in cubes. Heat the oil in a large heavy pan. Add the cubed pork to the pan and cook over a medium-high heat, turning each piece so the meat is golden brown all over.

2 Add the onion and celery and cook for about 5 minutes.

3 Add the stock, apple juice, honey, cloves, thyme and sage. Bring to the boil, cover and simmer for 1 hour, stirring occasionally. Stir in the carrots and leeks.

4 Stir in the beans and add a little seasoning. Bring just to the boil and simmer gently for a further 20–30 minutes, or until the pork is very tender.

5 Adjust the seasoning to taste and sprinkle some chopped parsley or thyme over the casserole before serving

TOAD IN THE HOLE

Early versions of toad in the hole, in the 18th century, were made with pieces of meat rather than sausages – one very grand recipe even called for fillet steak. Today the 'toads' are sausages, and the batter is the one that is used for Yorkshire pudding. There is an English pub game of the same name, where discs are thrown at a hole in the table.

SERVES 6

500g/1¼lb meaty butcher's sausages

FOR THE BATTER

175g/6oz/1½ cups plain (all-purpose) flour

½ tsp salt

2 eggs

300ml/½ pint/1¼ cups milk

300ml/½ pint/1¼ cups cold water

30ml/2 tbsp oil

1 Preheat the oven to 220°C/425°F/gas 7. To make the batter, sift the flour and salt into a bowl, make a well in the centre and break the eggs into it.

2 Mix the milk with the cold water. Using a whisk, gradually stir the milk mixture into the bowl with the eggs, incorporating the flour and beating well to make a smooth batter. Leave to stand.

3 Pour the oil into a roasting pan and add the sausages (cut in half crossways, if large). Put into the hot oven and cook for about 10 minutes until the oil is very hot and the sausages begin to brown.

4 Stir the batter and quickly pour it around the sausages and return to the oven. Cook for about 45 minutes until the batter is puffed up, set and golden brown. Serve immediately.

PORK SAUSAGES WITH MUSTARD MASH AND ONION GRAVY

Bangers and mash is a nursery favourite, but this is the grown-up version. Long, slow cooking is the trick to good onion gravy, as this reduces and caramelises the onions to create a wonderfully sweet flavour.

SERVES 4

12 pork and herb sausages

FOR THE ONION GRAVY
30ml/2 tbsp olive oil
25g/1oz/2 tbsp butter
8 onions, sliced
1 tsp caster (superfine) sugar
1 tbsp plain (all-purpose) flour
300ml/½ pint/1¼ cups beef stock
salt and ground black pepper

FOR THE MASH
1.5kg/3¼lb potatoes
50g/2oz/4 tbsp butter
150ml/¼ pint/⅔ cup double (heavy) cream
1 tbsp wholegrain mustard
salt and ground black pepper

1 First make the onion gravy. Heat the oil and butter in a large saucepan until foaming. Add the onions and mix well to coat them in the fat. Cover and cook gently for about 30 minutes, stirring frequently. Add the sugar and cook for a further 5 minutes, or until the onions are softened, reduced and caramelised.

2 Remove the pan from the heat and stir in the flour, then gradually stir in the stock. Return the pan to the heat. Bring to the boil, stirring, then simmer for 3 minutes, or until thickened. Season.

3 Meanwhile, cook the potatoes and the sausages. First, cook the potatoes in a saucepan of boiling salted water for 20 minutes, or until tender. Drain the potatoes well and mash them with the butter, cream and wholegrain mustard. Season with salt and pepper to taste.

4 While the potatoes are cooking, preheat the grill or broiler to medium. Arrange the sausages in a single layer on the grill pan and cook for 15–20 minutes, or until cooked, turning frequently so that they brown evenly.

5 Serve the sausages with the creamy mash and plenty of onion gravy.

FAGGOTS

One of the traditional, if now neglected, foods of England, this humble meatball makes use of some of the cheaper cuts but packs a rich and satisfying flavour. Faggots are believed to have originated over 100 years ago, in Birmingham and the West Midlands of England; this thrifty dish would have been a cheap and satisfying meal. Faggots are typically served with mashed potatoes and a rich gravy.

SERVES 4

400g/14oz pork liver

200ml/7fl oz/scant 1 cup milk

400g/14oz pork shoulder with a generous amount of fat (or mix of pork shoulder and belly)

2 garlic cloves, chopped

100g/3½oz/1½ cups breadcrumbs, from stale white bread

1 small onion, chopped into small pieces

¼ tsp salt

¼ tsp ground black pepper

¼ tsp dried thyme

¼ tsp ground nutmeg

¼ tsp dried sage

125g/4½oz caul fat

1 The liver can be soaked in milk ahead of making the faggots. Soak for up to 6 hours in the refrigerator, covered; discard the milk after.

2 Chop the pork shoulder and liver into rough cubes, as this will make it easier to mince in the food processor.

3 Put the shoulder into the food processor and add the garlic. Pulse the power control a few times to begin breaking the meat into smaller pieces. Add the liver and 'blitz' it for up to 1 minute on full power. It should be roughly chopped rather than a smooth paste – stop processing it once the desired texture is achieved.

4 Mix the breadcrumbs in a bowl with the chopped meat and onion. Add the salt, pepper, thyme, nutmeg and sage to the mixture, stirring them in well.

5 Unroll a length of the caul fat. Form the meat mixture into balls up to 5cm/2in in diameter. Place each ball in the centre of a piece of caul fat approximately twice as wide. Wrap up the caul to enclose each of the balls in a small parcel.

6 Preheat the oven to 180°C/350°F/gas 4. Place the faggots on a greased baking tray. Do not overcrowd the tray, but leave a small gap between them to prevent the faggots from sticking to each other. Cook for 30 minutes, turning them once or twice. Once the faggots are cooked through, they will have taken on a golden-brown colour. They do not usually shrink much during cooking. Serve at once.

COOK'S TIPS

◆ Caul fat is the thin lacy membrane surrounding an animal's internal organs, usually from a pig, used as a traditional casing or wrapping for meatballs.

◆ You can freeze the cooled baked faggots in foil freezer trays or in a container, covered with foil. Use within 3 months.

SOMERSET CIDER–GLAZED HAM

William the Conqueror is credited with bringing the art of cider-making to England from Normandy in 1066. This wonderful West Country ham glazed with cider is ideal for buffets, and for Christmas or Boxing Day, served with something fruity, perhaps peach slices or redcurrant sauce.

SERVES 8–10

middle gammon (smoked or cured ham), weighing 2kg/4½lb

2 small onions

about 30 whole cloves

3 bay leaves

10 black peppercorns

1.3 litres/2¼ pints/5⅔ cups medium-dry (hard) cider

3 tbsp soft light brown sugar

1 Weigh the ham and calculate the cooking time at 20 minutes per 450g/1lb, then place it in a large pan. Stud the onions with 5–10 cloves and add to the pan together with the bay leaves and peppercorns.

2 Add 1.2 litres/2 pints/5 cups of the cider and enough water just to cover the ham. Heat until simmering and skim off the scum that rises to the surface.

3 Start timing the cooking from the moment the stock begins to simmer. Cover with a lid or foil and simmer gently for the calculated time. Towards the end of the cooking time, preheat the oven to 220°C/425°F/gas 7.

4 Lift the ham out of the pan. Leave to stand until cool enough to handle.

5 Heat the sugar and remaining cider in a pan until the sugar dissolves. Bubble gently for about 5 minutes to make a dark glaze. Remove the pan from the heat and leave to cool for 5 minutes.

6 Carefully and evenly, cut off the rind of the ham, then score the fat to make a neat diamond pattern. Place the ham in a roasting tin. Press a clove into the centre of each diamond, then carefully spoon the glaze over. Put into the hot oven and cook for 20–25 minutes, or until brown, glistening and crisp.

7 Serve the ham sliced, hot or cold.

COOK'S TIPS

• If the ham is likely to be very salty, soak it overnight in cold water to remove excess salt before cooking.

◆ Reserve the stock used to cook the ham and use it to make a hearty split pea or lentil soup.

GRAVY

A traditional accompaniment for roast meat and poultry, gravy differs from a sauce, as it is cooked in the same tin in which meat has been cooked, using the juices from the meat. Gravy made from these roasting juices is rich in flavour and colour. Good gravy should be smooth and glossy, never heavy and floury. It's usually best to use the minimum of thickening, but this can be adjusted to taste. Providing the meat has been roasted to rich brown, the meat juices will have enough colour; if it is pale, a few drops of gravy browning could be stirred in. For a thinner sauce, an alternative method is simple deglazing, where liquid is added to skimmed pan juices and boiled to reduce.

roasting pan with juices
(for example, see page 245)

about 1 tbsp plain (all-purpose) flour

up to 600ml/1 pint/2½ cups
meat or vegetable stock

salt and black pepper

1 Spoon off most of the fat from the roasting pan. Set the pan over moderately high heat on top of the stove. When the roasting juices begin to sizzle, add the flour and stir to combine well.

2 Cook, scraping the pan well to mix in all the browned bits from the bottom, until the mixture forms a smooth brown paste, about 1–2 minutes.

3 Gradually stir in liquid (meat or vegetable stock, vegetable cooking water, or plain water), until the gravy is the desired thickness. Simmer for 2–3 minutes, stirring, until the gravy has the right consistency, then season with salt and pepper.

COOK'S TIP

Part of the beef or vegetable stock may be replaced with red wine or dark beer. You may need to add a little extra sugar to balance the acidity of the wine or beer.

POULTRY
& GAME

Most English households used to keep poultry,
if only a few hens, to provide them with eggs,
but on smallholdings and farms, ducks, turkeys
and geese would also be kept as a source of meat
for the table. Seasonal game from England's
woods and moors has always been popular,
with wild birds, venison, rabbits and hares
supplying sustenance at times when
farmed meat was expensive.

PICTURED *Deer grazing in the grounds of
a country estate, on a misty morning.*

STUFFED ROAST CHICKEN

The ancient Roman invaders of Britain enjoyed a roast stuffed chicken. Most country dwellers kept hens for their eggs, before they were eventually consigned to the cooking pot, by which time their meat would be tough and coarse; tender chicken, such as we enjoy now, was a rare treat. Add potatoes and sausages to the roasting tin if you like!

SERVES 6

1 chicken weighing about 1.8kg/4lb

15g/½oz/1½ tbsp butter

30ml/2 tbsp oil

salt and ground black pepper

6 rashers of streaky bacon

FOR THE GRAVY

1 tbsp plain (all-purpose) flour

300ml/½ pint/1¼ cups chicken stock

FOR THE STUFFING

1 onion, finely chopped

50g/2oz/4 tbsp butter

150g/5oz/2½ cups fresh white breadcrumbs

1 tbsp chopped fresh parsley

1 tbsp chopped other fresh herbs, such as thyme, marjoram and chives

grated rind and juice of ½ lemon

salt and ground black pepper

1 Preheat the oven to 200°C/400°F/gas 6. To make the stuffing, cook the onion in the butter in a large pan over low heat until soft. Remove from the heat and stir in the breadcrumbs, herbs, lemon rind and juice, salt and pepper.

2 Spoon the stuffing into the neck cavity of the chicken and secure the opening with a small skewer. Weigh the stuffed chicken and calculate the cooking time at 20 minutes per 450g/1lb, plus 20 minutes extra.

3 Spread the chicken breast with the butter, then put the oil into a roasting pan and sit the bird in it. Season and lay the bacon rashers over the breast.

4 Put the chicken into the hot oven. After 20 minutes, reduce the temperature to 180°C/350°F/gas 4 and cook for the remaining time. To check the chicken is cooked, insert a sharp knife between the body and the thigh: if the juices run clear with no hint of blood, it is done. Transfer the cooked chicken to a serving dish and allow it to rest for 10 minutes in a warm place.

5 To make the gravy, pour off the excess fat from the roasting pan, then sprinkle in the flour. Cook gently, stirring, for 1–2 minutes. Gradually add the stock, scraping the pan to lift the residue and stirring well until smooth. Bring to the boil, stirring and adding extra stock if necessary. Adjust the seasoning to taste.

6 Carve the chicken, and serve with portions of stuffing and gravy.

COOK'S TIPS

• If you prefer not to stuff the chicken, the stuffing can be formed into small balls and baked around the bird for the last 20–30 minutes of the cooking time.

• If your chicken came with neck and giblets, you could make your own chicken stock. In a pan, cover them in cold water with a sliced onion and carrot, a bunch of parsley and thyme, and seasoning. Bring to the boil and simmer for about an hour before straining.

CHICKEN WITH RED CABBAGE AND CHESTNUTS

Red cabbage is not just for pickling, though that seems to be the only way it was eaten in England until the late 20th century. Teamed with chicken and braised, it makes a delicious autumn or winter meal. Cooked chestnuts are available canned, vacuum-packed or frozen.

SERVES 4

4 chicken thighs

4 chicken drumsticks

50g/2oz/4 tbsp butter

1 onion, chopped

500g/1¼lb red cabbage, finely shredded

4 juniper berries, crushed

12 peeled, cooked chestnuts

120ml/4fl oz/½ cup red wine

salt and ground black pepper

1 Heat the butter in a heavy flameproof casserole and lightly brown the chicken pieces. Lift out.

2 Add the onion to the casserole and cook gently until soft and golden. Stir in the cabbage and juniper berries, season and cook for 6–7 minutes, stirring once or twice.

3 Add the chestnuts, then tuck the chicken under the cabbage on the bottom of the casserole. Add the wine.

4 Cover and cook gently for 40 minutes until the cabbage is very tender. Adjust the seasoning to taste. Serve up the chicken on a bed of cabbage and chestnuts.

CHICKEN WITH LEMON AND HERBS

The Crusaders encountered citrus fruits around 1191, but it was a century later when lemons and other citrus fruits arrived in England by ship in 1289 for Queen Eleanor. In the 17th century, citrus was increasingly used in meat and fish dishes, offering a refreshing zing and sharp fragrance. Tarragon, introduced into England in the 16th century, has a faint liquorice flavour that goes especially well with chicken. Vary the herbs according to what are available — try a mixture of parsley and thyme, or use fresh sage instead.

SERVES 2

4 chicken thighs

50g/2oz/4 tbsp butter

2 spring onions (scallions), white part only, finely chopped

1 tbsp chopped fresh tarragon

1 tbsp chopped fresh dill

juice of 1 lemon

salt and ground black pepper

lemon wedges and herb sprigs, to garnish

1 Preheat the grill or broiler to medium. In a small pan, heat the butter gently until melted, then remove from the heat and add the chopped spring onions, tarragon, dill and lemon juice. Season with salt and pepper.

2 Brush the chicken thighs with the herb mixture. Grill for 10–12 minutes, basting frequently. Turn over and baste again, then cook for a further 10–12 minutes or until the juices run clear.

3 Serve garnished with lemon wedges and herbs.

HINDLE WAKES

The curious name of this cold poultry dish may derive from 'Hen de la Wake' – in Lancashire dialect, a 'wake' was a fair. A medieval Lancashire recipe, it is believed to have been first brought by Flemish weavers to Bolton-le-Moor, near Wigan, in 1337. The original recipe used the blood of the fowl to bind the stuffing ingredients and an old hen would have been used instead of a chicken. The night before the dish was to be eaten, a boiling fowl was stuffed with a mixture of prunes and herbs and simmered slowly until tender. The next morning the bird was removed from the stock, coated with a lemon sauce, then decorated with prunes and slices of lemon. It was always served cold.

SERVES 4

1 chicken, weighing 2.25kg/5lb

90ml/6 tbsp white wine vinegar

4 sprigs fresh parsley

4 sprigs fresh thyme

2 bay leaves

1 tbsp light brown sugar

salt and pepper

FOR THE STUFFING

450g/1lb/2 cups ready-to-eat prunes

2 tbsp finely chopped fresh mixed herbs

2 tbsp blanched almonds, roughly chopped

salt and pepper

FOR THE SAUCE

600ml/1 pint/2¼ cups chicken stock (see method)

25g/1oz/2 tbsp butter

1½ tbsp flour

grated zest and juice of 1 lemon

150ml/¼ pint/⅔ cup double (heavy) cream

TO GARNISH

lemon slices and zest

chopped fresh parsley

1 For the stuffing, chop about half the prunes, reserving the rest for the garnish. Mix in the herbs and almonds, and season to taste. Pack into the prepared chicken (checking for and removing any giblets inside), securing the vent so that no stuffing can escape.

2 Put the chicken into a large pan with enough water to just cover the legs. Add the vinegar, herbs and sugar. Bring to the boil, cover and reduce the heat. Simmer for 1½–2 hours, until the chicken is cooked and no pink juices remain when pierced with a skewer between the breast and leg. Remove the chicken from the pan and place on a wire rack over a tray to become cold.

3 For the sauce, skim the fat from the pan and strain the chicken liquid into a measuring jug. Melt the butter in a pan and stir in the flour over a low heat until blended but still pale. Gradually whisk in 600ml/1 pint/2½ cups of the strained stock.

4 Cook gently, stirring constantly for 15–20 minutes until the sauce is very thick. Add the lemon zest and juice, and season to taste. Set aside to cool.

5 Whisk the cream until thickened, and fold into the cooled sauce.

6 Place the chicken on a serving dish. Spread the sauce over the whole chicken, using a palette knife dipped in hot water for a smooth finish.

7 Garnish the chicken dish with the remaining prunes, plus lemon slices, parsley and grated lemon zest.

CORONATION CHICKEN

Originally devised as part of the feast to celebrate the coronation of Elizabeth II in 1953, this chicken salad has been appearing on buffet tables countrywide ever since.

SERVES 8

1 chicken, weighing 2.25kg/5lb

½ lemon

1 onion, quartered

1 carrot, quartered

1 large bouquet garni

8 black peppercorns, crushed

salt

lettuce leaves and watercress sprigs, to garnish (optional)

FOR THE SAUCE

1 small onion, chopped

15g/½oz/1½ tbsp butter

1 tbsp curry paste

1 tbsp tomato purée (paste)

120ml/4fl oz/½ cup red wine

1 bay leaf

juice of ½ lemon, or to taste

2–3 tsp apricot jam

300ml/½ pint/1¼ cups mayonnaise

120ml/4fl oz/½ cup whipping cream

salt and ground black pepper

1 Put the lemon half in the chicken cavity, then place it in a close-fitting pan. Add the vegetables, bouquet garni, peppercorns and a little salt.

2 Add water to come two-thirds of the way up the chicken, bring just to the boil, cover and cook very gently for 1½ hours, until the chicken juices run clear. Leave to cool.

3 When the chicken is cold, remove all the skin and bones and chop the flesh.

4 To make the sauce, cook the onion in the butter until soft. Add the curry paste, tomato purée, wine, bay leaf and lemon juice, then cook gently for 10 minutes. Add the jam, press through a sieve and cool.

5 Beat the sauce into the mayonnaise. Whip the cream to soft peaks and fold it in; add seasoning and lemon juice, then stir in the chicken. Garnish and serve.

COOK'S TIP

A few walnut pieces or slices of celery would add some crunch and texture to the dish.

DEVILLED CHICKEN

Applying hot or spicy seasonings to food before cooking,
known as devilling, became very popular in the 1800s, and was
used to revive cold, cooked meat for serving the next day.

SERVES 4–6

6 chicken drumsticks

6 chicken thighs

15ml/1 tbsp oil

45ml/3 tbsp chutney, chopped

1 tbsp Worcestershire sauce

2 tsp English (hot) mustard

¼ tsp cayenne pepper

¼ tsp ground ginger

salt and ground black pepper

1 With a sharp knife, make several deep slashes in the chicken pieces, cutting down to the bone.

2 In a large bowl, mix the oil, chutney, Worcestershire sauce, mustard, cayenne, ginger and seasoning. Add the chicken pieces and toss them in the mixture, until well coated. Cover and leave to stand for 1 hour.

3 Preheat the oven to 200°C/400°F/gas 6. Arrange the chicken pieces in a single layer on a non-stick baking sheet, brushing them with any extra sauce.

4 Put the chicken pieces into the hot oven and cook for about 35 minutes until crisp, deep golden brown and cooked through (test by inserting a small sharp knife or skewer – the juices should run clear). Turn them over once or twice during cooking to encourage even browning. Serve.

VARIATION

Instead of chutney, try using the same quantity of tomato ketchup or mushroom ketchup.

CLASSIC ROAST TURKEY WITH COUNTRY STUFFING

The turkey was introduced to England in the early 16th century from Central America, and became a popular farmed bird. Traditionally served at Christmas, roast turkey is a splendid celebration dish. The rich herb stuffing in this recipe is made with calf's liver, but lamb's liver would be fine, too. It is usually served with a bread sauce (see page 316) and gravy, and a redcurrant jelly or cranberry sauce.

SERVES 6

1 turkey, weighing about 4.5–5.5kg/
10–12lb, washed and patted
dry with kitchen paper

salt and ground black pepper

25g/1oz/2 tbsp butter, melted

FOR THE STUFFING

200g/7oz/3½ cups fresh white
breadcrumbs

175ml/6fl oz/¾ cup milk

25g/1oz/2 tbsp butter

1 calf's liver, about 600g/
1½lb, finely chopped

2 onions, finely chopped

1 egg, separated

6 tbsp chopped fresh dill

2 tsp clear honey

salt and ground black pepper

1 To make the stuffing, put the breadcrumbs and milk in a large bowl and soak until swollen and soft.

2 Melt the butter for the stuffing in a frying pan and add the finely chopped calf's liver and onions. Fry gently for 5 minutes, until the onions are golden brown. Remove from the heat and leave to cool.

3 Preheat the oven to 180°C/350°F/gas 4. Add the cooled liver mixture to the soaked breadcrumbs and milk, then add the egg yolk, chopped dill, honey and seasoning.

4 In a clean bowl, whisk the egg white to soft peaks, then fold into the stuffing mixture, stirring gently to combine thoroughly.

5 Season the turkey inside and out with salt and pepper. Stuff the cavity with the stuffing mixture, then weigh to calculate the cooking time. Allow 20 minutes per 500g/1¼lb, plus an additional 20 minutes. Tuck the legs of the turkey inside the cavity and tie the end shut with string. Brush the outside with melted butter and transfer to a roasting pan. Place in the oven and roast for the calculated time.

6 Baste the turkey regularly during cooking, and cover with foil for the final 30 minutes if the skin becomes too brown. To test whether the turkey is cooked, pierce the thickest part of the thigh with a knife; the juices should run clear.

7 Remove the turkey from the oven, cover with foil and leave to rest for about 15 minutes. Carve into thin slices, then spoon over the juices and serve with the stuffing.

ROAST GOOSE WITH APPLES

The goose goes far back into the culinary history of England. Today, it is a seasonal treat that is popular at Christmas and New Year, but it was traditionally served on Michaelmas Day (29th September), having been fattened on barley stubble after the harvest. Apples are in season at the same time and their fresh sharp flavour offsets the richness of the goose beautifully. Serve with roast potatoes and freshly cooked seasonal vegetables.

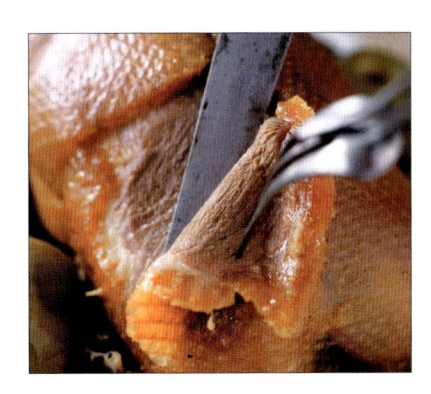

SERVES 8

1 oven-ready goose weighing about 5.5kg/12lb, with giblets

FOR THE GRAVY
1 small onion, sliced
2 small carrots, sliced
2 celery sticks, sliced
small bunch of parsley and thyme
salt and ground black pepper
about 1 tbsp flour

FOR THE APPLE STUFFING
450g/1lb black pudding (blood sausage), crumbled or chopped
1 large garlic clove, crushed
2 large cooking apples, peeled, cored and finely chopped
salt and ground black pepper
250ml/8fl oz/1 cup dry (hard) cider

1 Remove the goose liver from the giblets and put the rest of the giblets into a pan with the onion, carrots, celery and herbs. Cover with cold water, season and simmer for 30–45 minutes to make a stock for the gravy, topping up with water if necessary. Preheat the oven to 200°C/400°F/gas 6.

2 Meanwhile, for the apple stuffing, chop the goose liver finely and mix it with the black pudding, garlic and apples. Add salt and black pepper, then trickle in 75ml/5 tbsp of the cider to bind it.

3 Wipe out the goose and stuff it with this mixture. Prick the skin all over with a fork, sprinkle generously with salt and pepper and rub in well. Weigh the stuffed goose and calculate the correct cooking time at 15 minutes per 450g/1lb plus 15 minutes. Put the goose on a rack in a large roasting pan, cover with foil and put in the preheated oven.

4 After 1 hour, remove the goose from the oven and carefully pour off the hot fat that has accumulated. Pour the remaining dry cider over the goose, replace the foil and return to the oven.

5 Half an hour before the end of the estimated cooking time, remove the foil and baste the goose with the juices. Return to the oven, uncovered, and allow the skin to brown and crisp. The goose is cooked if the juices run clear when the thickest part of the thigh is pierced with a skewer. Transfer the goose to a warmed serving plate, and rest in a warm place for at least 20 minutes before carving.

6 While the goose is resting, make the gravy. Pour off any excess fat from the roasting pan, leaving about 2 tbsp, then sprinkle in enough flour to absorb it. Cook over a medium heat for 1 minute, scraping the pan to loosen the sediment. Strain the giblet stock and stir in enough to make the gravy.

7 Bring the gravy to the boil and simmer for a few minutes, stirring constantly. Add any juices that have accumulated under the cooked goose, season to taste and pour the gravy into a heated sauceboat.

8 Carve the goose into slices at the table, and serve.

DUCK WITH PLUM SAUCE

This is an updated version of an old English dish that was traditionally served in the late summer and early autumn, when Victoria plums are ripe and abundant. The sharp, fruity flavour of the plums balances the richness of the duck. Make sure the plums are very ripe; otherwise, the mixture may be too dry and the sauce too tart.

SERVES 4

4 duck quarters

1 large red onion, finely chopped

500g/1¼lb ripe plums, quartered and stoned (pitted)

2 tbsp redcurrant jelly

salt and ground black pepper

chopped thyme, to garnish

1 Prick the duck skin all over with a fork to release the fat during cooking and help give a crisp result, then place the portions in a heavy frying pan, skin side down.

2 Cook the duck pieces for 10 minutes on each side, or until golden brown and cooked right through. Remove them from the frying pan, using tongs or a draining spoon, and keep warm.

3 Pour away all but 2 tbsp of the duck fat, then stir-fry the onion for 5 minutes, or until golden. Add the plums and cook for a further 5 minutes, stirring. Add the redcurrant jelly.

4 Replace the duck portions and cook for a further 5 minutes or until thoroughly reheated. Season with salt and pepper to taste before serving, garnished with chopped thyme.

VARIATIONS

• The red onion can be replaced with a white or a brown one.

• Fine-cut orange marmalade makes a tangy alternative to the redcurrant jelly.

ROAST PHEASANT WITH GAME CHIPS

The game season begins on 1st October, when hen pheasants are in their prime. The topping of bacon helps to keep the moisture in the roasted meat. Crisp-fried thin chips (known as game chips) are the traditional, and perfect, accompaniment.

SERVES 2

1 hen pheasant
salt and ground black pepper
25g/1oz/2 tbsp butter
115g/4oz rindless
streaky bacon rashers
2 medium potatoes
oil, for deep-frying

FOR THE STUFFING

25g/1oz/2 tbsp butter
1 leek, chopped
115g/4oz peeled, cooked chestnuts,
coarsely chopped (see Cook's tip)
2 tbsp chopped fresh flat leaf parsley
salt and ground black pepper

FOR THE GRAVY

1 tbsp cornflour (cornstarch)
300ml/½ pint/1¼ cups
well-flavoured chicken stock
50ml/3 tbsp port

1 Preheat the oven to 190°C/375°F/gas 5. Pick any stray quills or stubs of feathers from the pheasant and season the bird inside and out with salt and black pepper.

2 Carefully loosen and lift the skin covering the breast and rub the butter between the skin and flesh.

3 To make the stuffing, melt the butter in a pan and cook the leek for about 5 minutes until softened but not coloured. Remove from the heat and mix in the chopped chestnuts, parsley and seasoning to taste.

4 Spoon the stuffing into the cavity of the pheasant and secure the opening with skewers. Arrange the bacon over the breast and place in a roasting pan.

5 Put into the hot oven and cook for 1–1½ hours, or until the juices run clear when the bird is pierced with a skewer in the thickest part of the leg. Lift out and cover closely with foil, then leave to stand in a warm place for 15 minutes before carving.

6 To make the gravy, heat the juices in the roasting pan on the stove and stir in the cornflour. Gradually stir in the stock and port. Bring to the boil, then reduce the heat and simmer for about 5 minutes, until the sauce is slightly thickened and glossy. Strain the sauce and keep warm.

7 Peel the potatoes and cut into matchsticks. Heat the oil in a deep-fat fryer or large pan to 190°C/375°F, or until a cube of stale bread browns in 20 seconds, and fry the chips until crisp, golden and cooked through. Drain on kitchen paper.

8 Serve the pheasant with the gravy and game chips.

COOK'S TIP

For convenience, use vacuum-packed or frozen chestnuts rather than fresh, which are fiddly to peel and cook. Simply rinse the chestnuts thoroughly with boiling water and drain before using. Whole, unsweetened canned chestnuts could be used, but they tend to be fairly dense and can be soft.

PHEASANT WITH MUSHROOMS, CHESTNUTS AND BACON

Braising is a slow, gentle cooking method, ideal for pheasants available at the end of the season, when they are no longer tender enough to roast but are full of flavour. Here they are cooked with mushrooms and chestnuts, which are in season at the same time.

SERVES 4

2 mature pheasants

salt and ground black pepper

50g/2oz/4 tbsp butter

75ml/5 tbsp brandy

50g/2oz rindless unsmoked bacon rashers

12 baby (pearl) onions, peeled

1 celery stick, chopped

3 tbsp plain (all-purpose) flour

550ml/18fl oz/2¼ cups chicken stock

175g/6oz peeled, cooked chestnuts

350g/12oz/4 cups mixed wild mushrooms, trimmed and sliced

1 tbsp lemon juice

1 Preheat the oven to 160°C/325°F/gas 3. Season the pheasants with salt and pepper. Melt half the butter in a large flameproof casserole and brown on all sides over a medium heat. Transfer them to a shallow roasting dish.

2 Pour off the excess fat from the casserole and return it to the heat. Add the brandy, stir to loosen the sediment, then pour the liquid over the pheasants.

3 Wipe out the casserole and melt the remaining butter. Cut the bacon into strips and brown in the butter with the onions and celery for 5 minutes. Sprinkle the flour into the casserole and cook, stirring, for 1 minute.

4 Gradually add the chicken stock, stirring until smooth. Add the chestnuts, mushrooms, the pheasants and their juices, and bring back to a gentle simmer. Cover the dish, put into the hot oven and cook for 1½ hours, or until the pheasants are tender.

5 Bring the sauce back to the boil, add the lemon juice and season to taste. Transfer the cooked pheasants and vegetables to a warmed serving plate. Pour over some of the sauce and serve the rest on the side.

ROAST PARTRIDGE WITH CARAMELISED PEARS AND MASH

In this recipe the partridge plays against the subtle sweetness and soft texture of pears. There are two main varieties of partridge – the English grey leg, which is slightly smaller, and the French red leg. This recipe uses the English variety, but if you have French add a couple of minutes to the cooking time. Quail, or rabbit cut into portions, would work well too. To round off the dish, it is served here with mashed swede and potatoes.

SERVES 4

4 oven-ready partridges
75g/3oz/6 tbsp butter, softened
salt and ground black pepper
30ml/2 tbsp olive oil
3 large pears, quartered and cored
8 sage leaves
1 tsp honey
150ml/¼ pint/⅔ cup perry
or dry (hard) cider

FOR THE MASH

1.2kg/2½lb floury potatoes, peeled
75g/3oz/6 tbsp butter
350g/12oz swede (rutabaga), diced
salt and ground black pepper
12–16 sage leaves, finely shredded

1 Preheat the oven to 200°C/400°F/gas 6. Put a ½ tbsp knob of the butter into the cavity of each bird. Season inside and outside with plenty of salt and pepper.

2 Heat a large ovenproof frying pan over medium heat and add the oil. Place the birds in the pan and brown evenly on all sides. Lean them against the side of the pan so they are sitting on their breastbones, and cook in the hot oven for 10 minutes.

3 Remove from the oven, roll the birds in the pan juices and remove to a warmed dish to rest and keep warm. Set aside the pan with juices.

4 Meanwhile, make the mash. Place the potatoes in a large pan of salted water, bring to the boil, reduce the heat and simmer for 12–15 minutes, until just tender but not breaking up.

5 While the potatoes are cooking, melt the butter for the mash in a frying pan, add the diced swede, season and fry gently, turning occasionally, until softened. Add the shredded sage leaves and cook for 1 minute in the butter.

6 When the potatoes are cooked, drain them in a colander, return to the pan and mash until smooth.

7 Add the mashed potato to the swede, folding the contents of the pan together. Keep warm while you cook the pears.

8 Melt the remaining butter in the pan used for the partridges, and fry the pears gently on all sides until golden, Add the sage and honey.

9 Turn the heat up, add the perry or cider, and bubble vigorously to reduce. Season, then return the birds to the pan along with any gathered juices. Serve with the mash.

VENISON STEAK PLUS TRIMMINGS

Venison is the meat of old England, whether prize of hunter or poacher. This recipe uses steaks from the rump, but loin or fillet would also be good. It is topped with an anchovy butter. Traditional accompaniments are chips, and grilled tomatoes and mushrooms.

SERVES 2

2 × 225–275g/8–10oz venison rump steaks, lightly pounded with a meat mallet or rolling pin

15ml/1 tbsp olive oil

salt and ground black pepper

FOR THE ACCOMPANIMENTS

vegetable oil, for deep-frying

675g/1½lb Maris Piper potatoes, peeled and cut lengthways into 1cm/½in wide sticks

2 large ripe tomatoes, halved

2 large field mushrooms, cleaned

salt and ground black pepper

watercress, to garnish

FOR THE ANCHOVY BUTTER

115g/4oz/½ cup butter, softened

6 anchovy fillets, chopped

grated rind and juice of ½ lemon

2 garlic cloves, crushed

1 tbsp chopped parsley

1 First make the anchovy butter. Place the softened butter, anchovy fillets, lemon rind and juice, garlic and parsley in a bowl and whisk to blend. Beating or whisking it will make the butter light and fluffy.

2 Transfer the anchovy butter to a length of cling film (plastic wrap) or baking parchment, and roll into a cylindrical shape approximately 2.5cm/1in in diameter. Secure at the ends and refrigerate. This can be done in advance and the butter chilled or frozen.

3 Half an hour before eating, start the chips. Heat a deep-fat fryer to 130°C/265°F. When the oil has reached this temperature, place the cut potatoes in the basket and blanch them for 8–10 minutes, until they are tender.

4 Remove the basket of chips from the oil and raise the heat to 180°C/350°F. Preheat the grill or broiler to medium.

5 Place the tomato halves and mushrooms on a baking sheet and lay a thin slice of the flavoured anchovy butter on each (keep some back for the steaks). Season well with salt and black pepper, then grill for 8–10 minutes, until cooked.

6 Meanwhile, heat a ridged griddle or frying pan over high heat for the venison steaks. Coat the steaks with olive oil and season well. Place the steaks on the hot griddle and cook for 2 minutes. Turn the steaks through 90 degrees and cook for 2 minutes more, turn over and repeat the process. You may want to increase the cooking time for a thick steak or if you prefer your meat well done. When the steaks are cooked to your liking, remove them from the pan and set aside to rest.

7 Refry the chips in the hot oil for 2 minutes, or until crisp on the outside and fluffy in the middle. Drain on kitchen paper and season with salt.

8 Slice the remaining anchovy butter, divide between the two steaks and place quickly under the grill, so it just starts to melt. Plate up with the chips, tomatoes and mushrooms, garnish with watercress, and serve.

VENISON STEW

Venison, both wild and (more commonly) farmed, is widely available. It is a popular meat, lean and full of flavour. This simple yet deeply flavoured stew combines the dark, rich meat of venison with red wine, sweet redcurrant jelly and bacon. Serve it with shredded greens.

SERVES 4

1.3kg/3lb stewing venison (shoulder or topside), trimmed and cut into chunks

50g/2oz/4 tbsp butter

225g/8oz streaky bacon, cut into 2cm/¾in pieces

2 large onions, chopped

1 large carrot, chopped

1 large garlic clove, crushed

1 tbsp plain (all-purpose) flour

175g/6oz/2 cups small mushrooms, trimmed

2–3 tbsp redcurrant jelly

1 bay leaf and a few sprigs of fresh parsley and thyme

150ml/¼ pint/⅔ cup red wine

about 750ml/1¼ pints/3¼ cups game or beef stock

1 Dry the venison thoroughly using kitchen paper, and set aside.

2 Melt the butter in a large, heavy pan, then cook the bacon pieces over a medium-high heat, stirring occasionally, until starting to brown. Reduce the heat to medium, add the onions and carrot and cook until the vegetables are lightly browned, stirring occasionally.

3 Add the pieces of venison to the pan together with the garlic, and stir into the mixture. Sprinkle on the flour and mix well until it has been absorbed by the fat in the pan.

4 Add the mushrooms, redcurrant jelly and herbs. Pour in the wine and sufficient dark stock to cover.

5 Cover the pan and simmer gently over a low heat for about 1½–2 hours, until the meat is cooked.

COOK'S TIPS

◆ This dish can be cooked in advance and left for a couple of days in the refrigerator, which will enhance the flavour. Simply reheat, slowly, adding a little wine if necessary, before serving.

◆ Lean beef can be used instead of venison, if preferred.

RABBIT WITH MUSTARD

For years, rabbit was a staple part of the English diet, when it made a cheap meal. Today, it is eaten less often but is lean and delicious. Wild rabbit is in season from early autumn until early spring, while farmed rabbits are available all year. Serve with cabbage wedges.

SERVES 4

4 large rabbit pieces
1 tbsp plain (all-purpose) flour
1 tbsp mustard powder
25g/1oz/2 tbsp butter
30ml/2 tbsp oil
1 onion, finely chopped
150ml/¼ pint/⅔ cup beer
300ml/½ pint/1¼ cups chicken stock
15ml/1 tbsp tarragon vinegar
25g/1oz/2 tbsp dark brown sugar
ground black pepper and salt
1 tbsp English (hot) mustard

TO FINISH

50g/2oz/4 tbsp butter
30ml/2 tbsp oil
50g/2oz/1 cup fresh breadcrumbs
1 tbsp snipped fresh chives
1 tbsp chopped fresh tarragon

1 Preheat the oven to 160°C/325°F/gas 3. Mix the flour with the mustard powder and put on a plate. Dip the rabbit pieces in the flour mixture, reserving any remaining flour.

2 Heat the butter and oil in a heavy flameproof casserole, then brown the rabbit pieces. Transfer to a plate.

3 Stir the onion into the fat remaining in the casserole and cook, stirring occasionally, until soft.

4 Stir the reserved flour mixture into the casserole, cook for 1 minute until the fat is absorbed, then gradually stir in the beer, stock and vinegar. Bring to the boil and add the sugar and some black pepper. Simmer for 2 minutes.

5 Return the rabbit pieces and their juices to the casserole. Cover the dish tightly, put into the hot oven and cook for 1 hour.

6 Stir in the prepared mustard, and salt to taste. Cover again and cook for a further 15 minutes.

7 To finish, heat the butter and oil in a frying pan and fry the breadcrumbs until crisp and golden, then stir in the chives and tarragon. Transfer the rabbit to a warmed serving dish, sprinkle over the breadcrumb mixture and serve hot.

BREAD SAUCE

The magnificent feasts of the Middle Ages were spectacular events, reflecting the wealth of the host. Each type of fish, meat and poultry was accompanied by its own particular sauce, and it was the duty of the servers to ensure that the correct sauces were provided in the small dishes placed along the length of the table. Bread was beaten with the meat juices and spices until thick and smooth. A bread sauce is still traditionally served with roast chicken or turkey, especially at Christmas.

SERVES 6–8

500ml/16fl oz/2 cups milk

1 small onion, stuck with 4 cloves

1 celery stick, chopped

1 fresh bay leaf, torn in half

6 allspice berries

1 blade of mace

85g/3½oz/1¾ cups day-old breadcrumbs, from a good-quality white loaf

salt and ground black pepper

freshly grated nutmeg

30ml/2 tbsp double (heavy) cream

15g/½oz/1½ tbsp butter

1 Place the milk, onion, celery, bay leaf, allspice and mace in a pan and bring to the boil. Take off the heat, and half cover the pan. Then set the milk aside to infuse for 30–60 minutes.

2 Strain the milk and place in a blender or food processor. Remove and discard the cloves from the onion and add it to the blender with the celery. Process until smooth, then strain the liquid back into the clean pan.

3 Bring back to the boil and stir in the breadcrumbs. Simmer gently, whisking with a small whisk, until the sauce thickens and becomes smooth. Add a little extra milk if the sauce is too thick.

4 Season to taste with salt, pepper and freshly grated nutmeg. Just before serving, whisk in the cream and butter. Serve warm rather than piping hot.

VARIATIONS

The classic bread sauce is perfect for roast poultry, just as it is. It is also good with grilled sausages or pork chops. These subtle variations make versatile use of bread-thickened sauce:

◆ Add the grated rind of 1 lemon and a good squeeze of lemon juice with the cream and butter. Serve the sauce with poached chicken. Thin it slightly with a little extra milk and serve with baked fish.

◆ Sherried bread sauce is delicious with grilled chicken, served with grilled mushrooms and bacon rolls. Add 45ml/3 tbsp dry sherry with the crumbs, simmer and finish as above.

◆ Add 1 tbsp each of finely chopped tarragon and chives, and 2 tbsp finely chopped parsley.

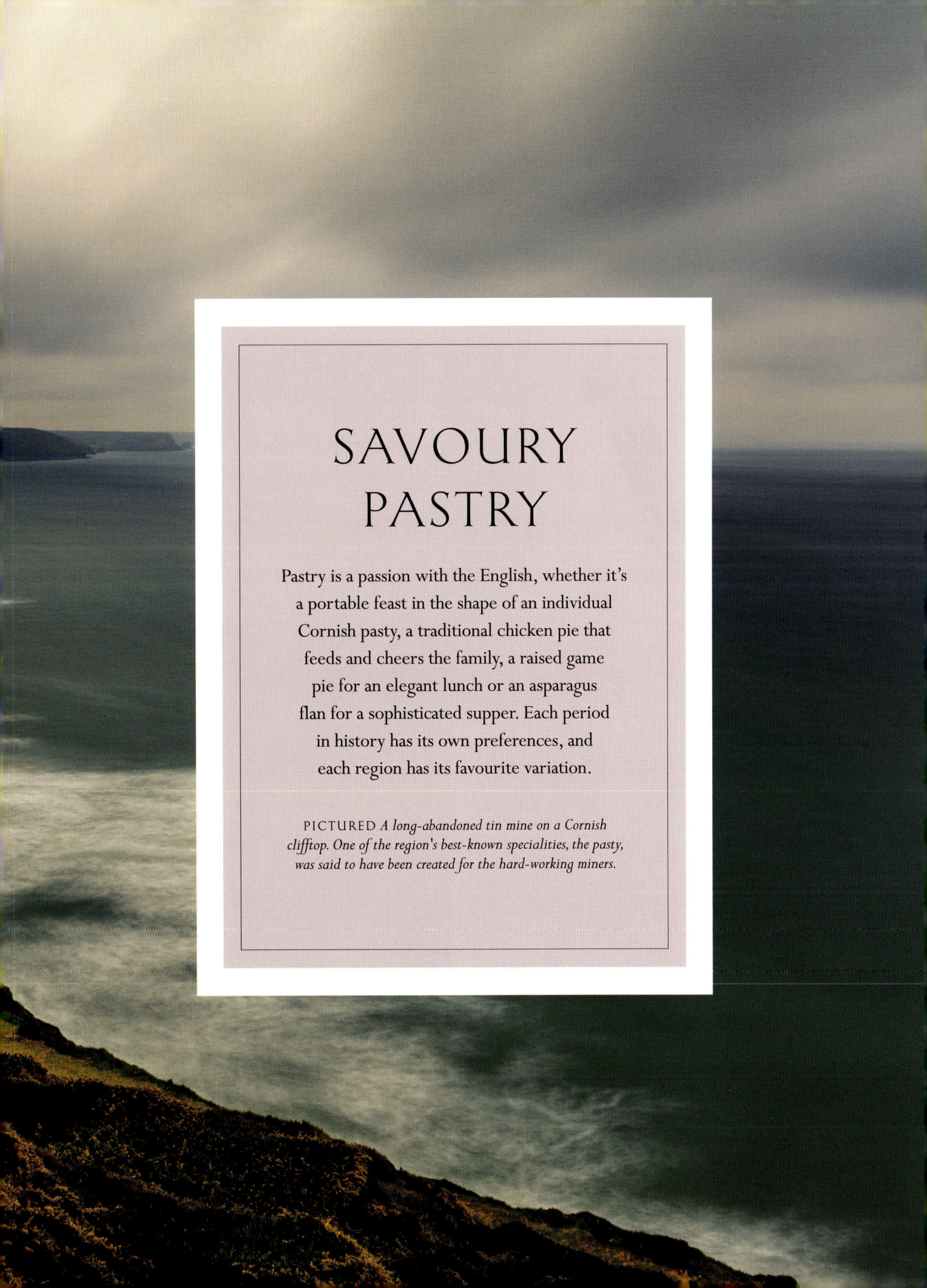

SAVOURY PASTRY

Pastry is a passion with the English, whether it's a portable feast in the shape of an individual Cornish pasty, a traditional chicken pie that feeds and cheers the family, a raised game pie for an elegant lunch or an asparagus flan for a sophisticated supper. Each period in history has its own preferences, and each region has its favourite variation.

PICTURED *A long-abandoned tin mine on a Cornish clifftop. One of the region's best-known specialities, the pasty, was said to have been created for the hard-working miners.*

STEAK AND OYSTER PIE

In the 17th century, oysters were so plentiful and cheap that, not only could the poor afford to eat them, they were even used to feed animals. When enormous beef pies were prepared for large gatherings, oysters were added to make the beef go further. Though oysters are a luxury today, they add a wonderful flavour to the filling in this pie.

SERVES 6

rump (round) steak, weighing 1kg/2¼lb, cut into 5cm/2in pieces

2 tbsp plain (all-purpose) flour, plus extra for dusting

salt and ground black pepper

45ml/3 tbsp oil

25g/1oz/2 tbsp butter

1 large onion, chopped

300ml/½ pint/1¼ cups beef stock

300ml/½ pint/1¼ cups brown ale or red wine

2 tbsp fresh thyme leaves

225g/8oz chestnut mushrooms, halved if large

12 freshly shucked oysters

375g/13oz puff pastry, thawed if frozen

beaten egg, to glaze

1 Preheat the oven if using (see step 3) to 150°C/300°F/gas 2. Season the flour with salt and pepper, and toss the steak until well coated. Heat half the oil and butter in a large pan or flameproof casserole and quickly brown the meat in batches. Set it to one side.

2 Add the remaining oil and butter to the hot pan, stir in the chopped onion and cook over a medium heat, stirring occasionally, until golden brown and beginning to soften.

3 Return the meat and any juices to the pan and stir in the stock, ale or wine, and thyme. Bring just to the boil, then cover the pan and either simmer very gently on the stove or cook in the preheated oven for about 1½ hours, until the beef is tender.

4 Using a slotted spoon, lift the meat and onion out of the liquid and put it into a 1.75 litre/3 pint pie dish. Bring the liquid in the pan to the boil and reduce to about 500ml/scant 1 pint/2 cups.

5 Season to taste and stir in the mushrooms, then pour the mixture over the meat in the dish. Leave to cool. Preheat the oven to 200°C/400°F/gas 6, if not already using.

6 Add the oysters to the cooled meat, pushing them down into the mixture. Push a pie funnel into the centre of the mixture.

7 Roll out the pastry on a lightly floured surface to a shape 2.5cm/1in larger than the dish. Trim off a 1cm/½in strip all around the edge. Brush the rim of the dish with a little beaten egg and lay the strip on it. Brush the strip with egg, lay the pastry sheet over the top, cutting a hole for the funnel, trim to fit and press the edges together well to seal them. Brush the top of the pie with beaten egg.

8 Put the pie into the hot oven and cook for about 40 minutes, until the pastry is crisp and golden brown and the filling is piping hot.

VARIATION

For a steak and kidney pie, replace the oysters with 250g/9oz lamb kidneys, diced, cooking them with the steak pieces in step 1.

BEEF WELLINGTON

This dish, a dinner party favourite, is derived from the classic French *boeuf en croûte*. The English name was applied to it in honour of the Duke of Wellington, following his victory at the Battle of Waterloo in 1815. Begin preparing the dish well in advance, to allow time for the meat to cool before it is wrapped in pastry.

SERVES 6

fillet of beef, weighing 1kg/2¼lb

45ml/3 tbsp oil

115g/4oz mushrooms, chopped

2 garlic cloves, crushed

175g/6oz smooth liver pâté

2 tbsp chopped fresh parsley

salt and ground black pepper

500g/1¼lb puff pastry, thawed if frozen

a little flour, for dusting

beaten egg, to glaze

1 Preheat the oven to 220°C/425°F/gas 7. Tie the beef fillet at intervals with string. Heat 30ml/2 tbsp of the oil in a pan, and brown the meat on all sides over a high heat. Transfer to a roasting tin and cook in the oven for 20 minutes. Leave to cool.

2 Heat the remaining oil in the pan and cook the mushrooms and garlic for 5 minutes. Beat the mushrooms into the liver pâté. Add the parsley, season and leave to cool.

3 Roll out the pastry on a lightly floured surface, reserving a small amount, into a rectangle large enough to enclose the beef. Spread the pâté mixture down the middle of the pastry, untie the beef and lay it over the pâté.

4 Brush the pastry edges with beaten egg and fold it over the meat. Place, seam side down, on a baking sheet. Cut leaves from the reserved pastry and decorate the top. Brush the parcel with beaten egg. Chill for 10 minutes. Reheat the oven to 220°C/425°F/gas 7.

5 Cook until golden and crisp – 20–25 minutes for medium-rare beef, 30 minutes for medium, 40–50 minutes for well-done, covering loosely with foil after about 30 minutes, if necessary, to prevent the pastry burning.

6 Allow to stand for 10 minutes before serving in thick slices..

MUTTON PIES

Small savoury pies were one of England's first fast foods, sold in the street during the 16th and 17th centuries on market days and holidays. Mutton pies were popular all over the country, and in Victorian times were even served as appetisers at Buckingham Palace. Using muffin tins to shape them may be unconventional, but it's very convenient.

MAKES 6

450g/1lb minced (ground) mutton or lamb, such as shoulder
3 spring onions (scallions), chopped
¼ tsp freshly grated nutmeg
salt and ground black pepper
90ml/6 tbsp meat stock

FOR THE PASTRY
275g/10oz/2 cups plain (all-purpose) flour, plus extra for dusting
generous pinch of salt
50g/2oz/4 tbsp lard
60ml/4 tbsp milk
75ml/5 tbsp water
beaten egg, to glaze

1 Preheat the oven to 190°C/375°F/gas 5. Combine the meat in a bowl with the spring onions, nutmeg and seasoning. Mix well, then stir in the stock and set aside.

2 To make the pastry, sift the flour and salt into a bowl and make a well in the centre. Heat the lard, milk and water in a small pan until just boiling. Immediately pour it into the flour and beat quickly to make a soft dough.

3 Knead the dough lightly on a floured surface until smooth, adding a little more boiling water if necessary. Working quickly, divide two-thirds of the pastry into six equal pieces. Press each into a hole in a non-stick muffin tray, with the pastry slightly above the rim.

4 Divide the meat mixture equally between the pastry cases.

5 Use the remaining pastry to make lids for the pies. Moisten the pastry edges with water and top each with a lid, pressing the edges together to seal them well. Make a small slit in the centre of each lid and brush with beaten egg.

6 Put the pies into the hot oven and cook for about 35 minutes until the pastry is crisp, golden brown and cooked through. Cool in the tin for 5 minutes, then transfer to a wire rack. Serve warm or cold.

CHICKEN, HAM AND EGG PIE

In the cold version of this pie, the filling is completely enclosed in hot water crust pastry. In this hot version, the shortcrust pastry sits on top, keeping the contents moist and the aromas sealed in until the pie is cut open.

SERVES 4

500g/1¼lb skinless boneless chicken thighs, cut into pieces

225g/8oz cooked ham, cut into cubes

1 tbsp plain (all-purpose) flour

large pinch each of dry mustard and ground black pepper

25g/1oz/2 tbsp butter

15ml/1 tbsp oil

1 onion, chopped

600ml/1 pint/2½ cups chicken or veal stock

2 eggs, hard-boiled and sliced

2 tbsp chopped fresh parsley

FOR THE PASTRY

175g/6oz/1½ cups plain (all-purpose) flour, plus extra for dusting

pinch of salt

75g/3oz/6 tbsp butter, diced

beaten egg, to glaze

1 Preheat the oven to 180°C/350°F/gas 4. Mix the chicken and ham in a bowl. Season the flour with the mustard and black pepper, then add it to the meat and toss well.

2 Heat the butter and oil in a large pan until sizzling, then cook the meat mixture in batches until golden on all sides. Use a slotted spoon to remove the meat, and set aside.

3 Cook the onion in the fat remaining in the pan until softened but not coloured. Stir in the stock and the meat. Cover and cook for about 5–6 minutes. Adjust the seasoning and leave to cool.

4 To make the pastry, sift the flour into a bowl with the salt and rub in the butter until the mixture resembles fine crumbs. Mix in just enough cold water to bind the mixture, gathering it together with your fingertips. Wrap the pastry in cling film (plastic wrap) and chill for at least 30 minutes.

5 Spoon the meat mixture into a 1.5 litre/2½ pint pie dish. Arrange the slices of hard-boiled egg on top and sprinkle with the parsley.

6 On a lightly floured surface, roll out the pastry to about 4cm/1½in larger than the top of the pie dish. Cut a strip from around the edge, dampen the rim of the dish and press the pastry strip on to it. Brush the pastry rim with beaten egg and top with the lid.

7 Trim off any excess pastry. Use the blunt edge of a knife to tap the outside edge, pressing the pastry down with your finger to seal in the filling. Pinch the pastry between your fingers to flute the edge. Roll out any trimmings and cut out shapes to decorate the pie.

8 Brush the top of the pie with beaten egg, and cut a slit in the centre to allow steam to escape. Cook for 25–35 minutes until the pastry is well risen and golden brown. Serve hot.

VARIATIONS

- Veal can be used instead of chicken if preferred.
- Puff pastry can also be used to cover the pie.

SHROPSHIRE FIDGET PIE

This classic combination of potatoes, onions, apples and bacon is packed under a pastry crust and would have been typical of the thrifty and filling food for farm workers at the end of a long, hard day in the fields. The source of the name is not known; it is also sometimes called Fitchett pie.

SERVES 4–5

225g/8oz lean bacon or gammon (smoked or cured ham)

15ml/1 tbsp oil

2 medium onions, thinly sliced

450g/1lb potatoes, thinly sliced

2 tsp sugar

2 medium cooking apples

4 fresh sage leaves, finely chopped

salt and ground black pepper

300ml/½ pint/1¼ cups vegetable stock or medium-dry (hard) cider

FOR THE PASTRY

75g/3oz/¾ cup plain (all-purpose) flour, plus extra for dusting

75g/3oz/¾ cup plain wholemeal (wholewheat) flour

pinch of salt

40g/1½oz/3 tbsp lard, diced

40g/1½oz/3 tbsp butter, diced

beaten egg or milk, to glaze

1 For the pastry, sift the two flours and salt into a bowl and rub in the fats until the mixture resembles fine crumbs. Mix in enough cold water to bind the mixture, gathering it into a ball of dough. Chill for 30 minutes.

2 Preheat the oven to 180°C/350°F/gas 4. Cut the bacon into small strips. Heat the oil in a large non-stick pan and cook the bacon until crisp. Transfer to a large mixing bowl.

3 Add the onions, potatoes and sugar to the hot pan and brown until beginning to soften. Add to the bowl.

4 Peel, core and slice the apples and add to the bowl. Stir in the sage, season with salt and pepper and mix well. Tip the mixture into a 1.5 litre/2½ pint pie dish, level the surface and pour the stock or cider over.

5 Roll out the pastry on a lightly floured surface to a shape large enough to cover the dish. Brush the edges of the dish with milk or beaten egg. Lay the pastry lid over the top, trim the edges and make a slit in the centre. Brush the lid with beaten egg or milk.

6 Put into the hot oven and cook for about 1 hour, until the crust is golden brown and the filling is cooked through.

RAISED GAME PIE

Cold game pie makes an impressive centrepiece, especially if made in a fluted raised pie mould. Not only does it look magnificent, it tastes wonderful. These pies used to be made in the country and sent to London for Christmas, so the crust had to be stoutly built.

SERVES 10

900g/2lb mixed boneless game, such as pheasant and/or pigeon breast, venison and rabbit, diced

25g/1oz/2 tbsp butter

1 onion, finely chopped

2 garlic cloves, finely chopped

2 tbsp chopped fresh herbs such as parsley, thyme and marjoram

salt and ground black pepper

FOR THE PÂTÉ

50g/2oz/4 tbsp butter

2 garlic cloves, finely chopped

450g/1lb chicken livers, rinsed, trimmed and chopped

60ml/4 tbsp brandy

1 tsp ground mace

FOR THE PASTRY

675g/1½lbs/6 cups strong plain (all-purpose) flour, plus extra for dusting

1 tsp salt

100ml/3¾fl oz/scant ½ cup milk

100ml/3¾fl oz/scant ½ cup water

115g/4oz/½ cup lard, diced

115g/4oz/½ cup butter, diced

beaten egg, to glaze

FOR THE JELLY

300ml/½ pint/1¼ cups game or beef consommé

½ tsp powdered gelatine

1 First cook the meat. Melt the butter until foaming and cook the onion and garlic until softened but not coloured. Remove from the heat and mix with the meat and herbs. Season well, cover and chill.

2 To make the pâté, melt the butter in a pan until foaming, add the garlic and chicken livers and cook until just browned. Remove from the heat and stir in the brandy and mace. Purée the mixture in a blender or food processor until smooth, then leave to cool.

3 To make the hot water crust pastry, sift the flour and salt into a bowl and make a well in the centre. Gently melt the milk, water, lard and butter together in a pan, bring to the boil, then pour into the flour and beat until smooth. Cover and leave to cool.

4 Preheat the oven to 200°C/400°F/gas 6. Roll out two-thirds of the pastry and use to line a 23cm/9in raised pie mould (or 20cm/8in springform cake pan), pressing it in with your fingers. Spoon in half the game mixture and press it down evenly. Add the pâté, then top with the remaining game.

5 Roll out the remaining pastry to form a lid. Cover the pie with the lid, using a little water to secure. Trim off excess and pinch the edges together to seal. Make two holes in the centre of the lid. Use trimmings to make leaves to garnish, and brush it all with egg.

6 Cook in the hot oven for 30 minutes, covering with foil for the last 10 minutes. Reduce the oven temperature to 150°C/300°F/gas 2. Brush the pie again with egg and cook for a further 1½ hours, keeping the top covered loosely with foil.

7 Remove from the oven and leave to stand for 15 minutes. Increase the oven temperature to 200°C/400°F/gas 6. Stand the tin on a baking sheet and remove its sides. Quickly brush the sides of the pie with beaten egg, cover the top with foil, then cook for 15 minutes to brown the sides. Leave to cool completely, then chill overnight.

8 To make the jelly, heat the consommé in a small pan until hot but not boiling, whisk in the gelatine until dissolved and leave to cool until just setting. Using a small funnel, carefully pour the jellied consommé into the holes in the pie. Chill until set.

VEAL AND EGG PIE

Pies, their crisp golden crust concealing a mouthwatering filling, are among the glories of English cuisine. Raised pies are made with a stiff hot water crust pastry, which allows it to be moulded into shape while warm. This type of pastry dates back to the Middle Ages, when a strong, pliable dough, capable of being moulded around its filling, was needed. Lard makes wonderfully crisp pastry and is essential for making the hot water pastry. This veal and egg raised pie was fashionable for picnics in the 19th century. The icing sugar in the pastry produces a crisper result.

SERVES 6–8

500g/1¼lb rose veal, minced (ground)

115g/4oz cooked ham, minced (ground)

2 tbsp chopped fresh parsley

½ tsp ground mace

finely grated zest of 1 lemon

1 onion, finely chopped

1 tsp salt

¼ tsp ground white pepper

3 eggs, hard-boiled and shelled

2 tsp aspic jelly powder

300ml/½ pint/1¼ cups water

FOR THE PASTRY

115g/4oz/½ cup lard, plus extra for greasing

200ml/7fl oz/1 scant cup water

350g/12oz/3 cups plain (all-purpose) flour, plus extra for dusting

1 tbsp icing (confectioner's) sugar

½ tsp salt

1 egg, beaten, to glaze

1 Grease a 19 x 12 x 7cm/8 x 4 x 3in loaf tin or pan, and line the base with greased greaseproof paper.

2 Put the ground meats, parsley, mace, lemon zest, onion, salt and pepper in a bowl, and mix well to combine.

3 For the hot water crust pastry, put the lard and water in a pan and heat gently until the lard has melted. Bring to the boil, remove from the heat and tip in the flour, icing sugar and salt. Beat well to form a soft dough. Put into a bowl and beat in the egg. Cover with a damp tea towel and rest in a warm place for 20 minutes, until the dough is elastic and easy to work. Do not allow the dough to cool. Preheat the oven to 180°C/350°F/gas 4.

4 Roll out two-thirds of the pastry on a lightly floured surface, to fit the base and sides of the tin. Gently press the dough into the tin, making sure it is evenly distributed.

5 Press in half of the meat mixture and place the boiled eggs down the centre. Cover with the remaining meat mixture.

6 Roll out the remaining pastry for the lid. Brush the inside of the lid with beaten egg, cover the pie with the pastry lid and seal the edges.

7 Use the pastry trimmings to decorate the top, and brush the top with more beaten egg. Make a large hole in the centre of the pie.

8 Bake for 1½ hours. If necessary, cover the pastry with foil towards the end of cooking, to prevent over-browning. Remove from the oven and leave to cool for 3–4 hours.

9 Make up the aspic jelly with the water, following the directions on the packet. Cool for about 10 minutes, then pour the liquid aspic through the hole in the top of the pie. Chill the pie for 3–4 hours until the aspic jelly has set. Leave to stand at room temperature for about 1 hour before removing from the tin.

CORNISH PASTIES

The original portable lunch, pasties made a satisfying midday meal for intrepid Cornish tin miners, who could use the crimped pastry join across the top as a handle if their hands were filthy. These contain the traditional filling of chopped steak and root vegetables.

  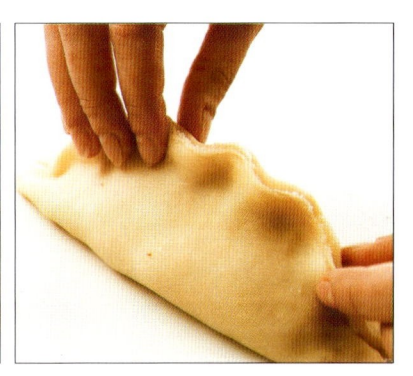

MAKES 6

450g/1lb chuck steak, cubed

about 175g/6oz potato, cubed

175g/6oz swede (rutabaga), cubed

1 onion, finely chopped

½ tsp dried mixed herbs

salt and ground black pepper

500–675g/1¼–1½lb shortcrust pastry, thawed if frozen (for home-made see recipe on page 449 and double it)

a little flour, for dusting

beaten egg, to glaze

1 Preheat the oven to 220°C/425°F/gas 7. In a bowl, mix together the steak, vegetables, herbs and seasoning,

2 On a lightly floured surface, divide the pastry into six equal pieces, then roll out each piece to form a rough circle, measuring about 20cm/8in.

3 Spoon an equal amount of meat mixture onto one half of each pastry circle.

4 Brush the edges with water, then fold the pastry over the filling. Crimp the edges firmly together.

5 Use a fish slice or spatula to transfer the pasties to a non-stick baking sheet, then brush each one with beaten egg.

6 Put into the hot oven and cook for 15 minutes, then reduce the oven temperature to 160°C/325°F/gas 3 and cook for a further 1 hour.

COOK'S TIP

Swede is the traditional vegetable in Cornish pasties, but turnip, carrot or celery could be used in its place, if you prefer.

PORK AND BACON PICNIC PIES

In the days when most country people carried their lunch with them to eat in the fields or journeying on foot along the lanes, small pies made tasty parcels that could be packed in the pocket, held in the hand and eaten anywhere.

MAKES 12

225g/8oz pork, coarsely chopped

115g/4oz cooked bacon, chopped

10ml/2 tsp oil

1 onion, finely chopped

3 tbsp chopped mixed fresh herbs, such as sage, parsley and oregano

salt and ground black pepper

6 eggs, hard-boiled and halved

20g/¾oz aspic jelly powder

300ml/½ pint/1¼ cups boiling water

FOR THE PASTRY

450g/1lb/3½ cups plain (all-purpose) flour, plus extra for dusting

115g/4oz/½ cup lard

275ml/9fl oz/generous 1 cup water

1 egg yolk, beaten, to glaze

1 Preheat the oven to 200°C/400°F/gas 6. To make the hot water crust pastry, sift the flour into a bowl and make a well in the centre. Heat the lard and water in a small pan until melted, then bring to the boil and pour into the flour, stirring. Press the mixture into a smooth ball of a dough using the back of a spoon. Cover the bowl and set it aside.

2 Now cook the meat. In a frying pan, heat the oil and cook the onion until browned. Stir in the pork and bacon, and cook until browned. Remove from the heat and add the herbs and seasoning.

3 Roll out two-thirds of the pastry on a lightly floured work surface. Using a 12cm/4½in round fluted cutter, stamp out rounds and line a 12-hole muffin tray.

4 Place a little of the meat mixture in each case, then add half an egg and top with the remaining meat.

5 Roll out the remaining pastry and use a 7.5cm/3in round cutter to stamp out lids. Dampen the rims of the bases and press the lids in place. Seal the edges, brush with egg yolk and make a hole in the top of each pie. Bake for 30–35 minutes. Cool for 15 minutes, then transfer to a rack to cool completely.

6 Meanwhile, stir the aspic powder into the boiling water until dissolved. Using a small funnel, pour a little aspic into the hole in the top of each pie. Leave the pies to cool and set, then chill for up to 24 hours before serving.

BACON AND EGG PIE

The traditional English breakfast combination encased in pastry makes an ideal lunch or supper dish. It's also excellent cold, so it can be taken on picnics (keeping it in the dish so that it travels safely) or sliced for packed lunches.

SERVES 4

4 rashers of smoked bacon, cut into 4cm/1½in pieces

30ml/2 tbsp oil

1 small onion, finely chopped

5 eggs

2 tbsp chopped fresh parsley

salt and ground black pepper

FOR THE PASTRY

275g/10oz/2 cups plain (all-purpose) flour, plus extra for dusting

pinch of salt

150g/5oz/⅔ cup butter, diced

beaten egg or milk, to glaze

1 For the pastry, sift the flour into a bowl with the salt and rub in the butter until the mixture resembles fine crumbs. Mix in just enough cold water to form a dough and chill for 30 minutes. Roll out two-thirds of the pastry on a floured surface and line a deep 20cm/8in flan tin. Preheat the oven to 200°C/400°F/gas 6.

2 Now cook the bacon. Heat the oil in a frying pan and cook the bacon until the fat runs, then add the onion and cook gently until soft. Drain on kitchen paper and leave to cool.

3 Spread the bacon mixture evenly over the pastry case, then break the eggs onto the bacon, spacing them evenly. Tilt the flan tin so the egg whites flow together. Sprinkle the eggs with the chopped fresh parsley, plenty of black pepper and just a little salt. Place a baking sheet in the oven.

4 Roll out the remaining pastry. Dampen the edges of the flan tin and top with the lid. Trim the edges and use for pastry leaves. Brush with egg or milk, and make a hole in the centre.

5 Place the pie on the hot baking sheet in the oven and cook for 10 minutes. Reduce the oven temperature to 180°C/350°F/gas 4 and cook for 20 minutes. Leave to cool before slicing and serving.

COOK'S TIP

This can also be made in a flan (pie) ring placed on a baking sheet.

CHEESE AND ASPARAGUS FLAN

The English asparagus season is short, so you need to make the most of it. The distinctive taste of fresh asparagus comes through in this flan and makes a small amount go further. It has an affinity with cheese, each ingredient enhancing the flavour of the other.

SERVES 5–6

300g/11oz small asparagus spears, weighed after trimming

75g/3oz mature (strong) Cheddar cheese, grated

3 spring onions (scallions), thinly sliced

2 eggs

300ml/½ pint/1¼ cups double (heavy) cream

freshly grated nutmeg

salt and ground black pepper

FOR THE PASTRY

175g/6oz/1½ cups plain (all-purpose) flour, plus extra for dusting

pinch of salt

40g/1½oz/3 tbsp butter, diced

40g/1½oz/3 tbsp lard (or more butter)

about 45ml/3 tbsp cold water

1 To make the pastry, sift the flour and salt into a bowl and add the butter and lard. With your fingertips, rub the fats into the flour until the mixture resembles fine breadcrumbs.

2 Stir in enough of the cold water so that the mixture can be gathered together into a ball of dough. Wrap the pastry and chill for 30 minutes.

3 Put a flat baking sheet in the oven and preheat to 200°C/400°F/gas 6. Roll out the pastry on a lightly floured work surface and use it to line a 20cm/8in flan tin.

4 Line the pastry case with baking parchment or foil and add a layer of baking beans. Put the flan tin onto the heated baking sheet in the oven and bake blind for 10–15 minutes. Carefully remove the beans and parchment or foil, return the pastry to the oven and cook for a further 5 minutes, until light golden brown on the edges. Remove the flan and reduce the temperature to 180°C/350°F/gas 4.

5 Meanwhile, cook the asparagus spears in lightly salted boiling water for 2–3 minutes or until only just tender. Drain, rinse under cold water and dry on kitchen paper. Cut the asparagus spears into 2.5cm/1in lengths, leaving the tips whole.

6 Scatter half the cheese in the base of the cooked pastry case and add the asparagus and the spring onions.

7 Beat the eggs with the cream and season with nutmeg, salt and pepper. Pour the mixture over the asparagus and top the flan with the remaining cheese.

8 Return the flan to the hot baking sheet in the oven and cook for about 30 minutes or until just set. Leave the flan to settle for 5 minutes before cutting and serving.

VEGETABLE DISHES & SALADS

Fresh vegetables, from beneath the soil
and above, are enjoyed in a myriad of dishes.
England is home to kitchen gardens with neatly
laid-out beds interspersed with herbs and
flowers, country backyards with wigwams of
runner beans and rows of potatoes, and
city allotments filled with everything
from artichokes to pumpkins.

PICTURED *Runner beans clambering up a hazel
wigwam, in a Devonshire potager garden.*

ASPARAGUS WITH HOLLANDAISE SAUCE

Since the 16th century, England has produced this 'queen of vegetables', at its finest for a short season in early summer. Serve it simply – drizzled with melted unsalted butter, with lightly boiled eggs (dip the asparagus into the egg) or with hollandaise sauce.

SERVES 4

2 bunches of asparagus

30ml/2 tbsp white wine vinegar

2 egg yolks

115g/4oz/½ cup butter, melted

juice of ½ lemon

salt and ground black pepper

1 Snap off the tough ends of the asparagus. Drop the spears into fast boiling water, cooking for 1–2 minutes until just tender. Test the thickest part of the stalk with a small sharp knife; take care not to overcook.

2 To make the hollandaise, in a pan, bring the vinegar to the boil and bubble until it has reduced to just 1 tbsp. Remove from the heat and add 1 tbsp cold water.

3 Whisk the egg yolks into the vinegar and water mixture, then put the pan over a very low heat and continue whisking until the mixture is frothy and thickened.

4 Remove from the heat again and slowly whisk in the melted butter. Add the lemon juice and seasoning, to taste. Serve the sauce immediately with the drained asparagus.

COOK'S TIPS

◆ Asparagus should be cooked and eaten as soon as possible, preferably on the day it is picked.

◆ Asparagus is also good served cold with mayonnaise.

◆ Make stock with the woody ends of the asparagus rather than throwing them away, and add it to vegetable soups or sauces.

SPRING VEGETABLES WITH TARRAGON

Boiled buttered vegetables were popular in the 17th century, a time when market gardens were becoming important, especially around London. Seasonal vegetables were sold in the capital's markets – the most famous being Covent Garden, established around 1671. Samuel Pepys mentions buying asparagus from an asparagus garden in 17th-century London. Making the most of the first fresh spring vegetables, this is almost a salad, but the vegetables are just lightly cooked, to bring out their different flavours. The tarragon adds a wonderful depth to this bright, fresh dish.

SERVES 4

5 spring onions (scallions)

50g/2oz/4 tbsp butter

1 garlic clove, crushed

115g/4oz asparagus tips

115g/4oz mangetouts (snowpeas), trimmed

115g/4oz broad (fava) beans

salt and ground black pepper

2 Little Gem (Bibb) lettuces

1 tsp finely chopped fresh tarragon

1 Cut the spring onions into quarters lengthways and fry gently over a medium-low heat in half the butter with the garlic.

2 Add the asparagus tips, mangetouts and broad beans. Mix together gently, covering all the pieces with the butter.

3 Just cover the base of the pan with water, season, and allow to simmer gently for a few minutes.

4 Cut the lettuce into quarters and add to the pan. Cook for 3 minutes then, off the heat, swirl in the remaining butter and the tarragon, and serve.

CREAMED LEEKS

Versatile leeks are a great winter vegetable, adding a subtle onion flavour to many dishes, including soups, casseroles, stews and stir-fries. Serve these creamed leeks on their own, or as a tasty accompaniment to grilled meats, such as chops, chicken or gammon.

SERVES 4–6

4 large or 6 medium leeks

300ml/½ pint/1¼ cups milk

salt and ground black pepper

a little butter, for greasing

8 streaky or fatty rashers of bacon, chopped (optional)

1 egg, lightly beaten

150ml/¼ pint/⅔ cup single (light) cream

1 tbsp wholegrain mustard

75g/3oz/¾ cup strong (mature) cheese, grated

1 Slice the leeks into fairly large chunks. Put them into a pan with the milk. Season and bring to the boil. Reduce the heat and simmer for 15–20 minutes, or until tender. Drain well and turn the leeks into a buttered shallow baking dish, reserving the cooking liquid.

2 Meanwhile, if using the bacon, put it into a frying pan and cook gently to allow the fat to run, then turn up the heat a little and cook for a few minutes until it crisps up.

3 Remove from the pan with a slotted spoon and sprinkle the bacon over the leeks. Rinse out the pan that was used for the leeks.

4 Blend the beaten egg, cream and mustard together and mix it with the reserved cooking liquid. Return to the pan and heat gently without boiling, allowing the sauce to thicken a little. Adjust the seasoning, then pour over the leeks.

5 Sprinkle the baking dish with grated cheese, and brown for a few minutes under a hot grill or broiler. Alternatively, the leeks may be served immediately without browning the top.

VARIATION

The leeks could also be spread on to toast topped with cheese, and grilled for a light lunch.

BRUSSELS SPROUTS WITH CHESTNUTS

Native to southern Europe, chestnuts arrived in England with the Romans.
The fresh nuts are available in early winter and are an indispensable
feature of Christmas dinner.

SERVES 6

350g/12oz fresh chestnuts

300ml/½ pint/1¼ cups chicken or vegetable stock or water

1 tsp sugar

675g/1½lb Brussels sprouts, trimmed

salt

50g/2oz/4 tbsp butter

115g/4oz bacon rashers, cut into strips

1 Cut a cross in the pointed end of each chestnut, then cook in boiling water for 5–10 minutes.

2 Drain the chestnuts, then peel off both the tough outer skin and the fine inner one. Return the chestnuts to the pan, add the stock or water, and add the sugar. Simmer gently for 30–35 minutes, until the chestnuts are tender, then drain thoroughly.

3 Meanwhile, cook the sprouts in lightly salted boiling water for 8–10 minutes, until tender, then drain well.

4 Melt the butter in a pan, add the bacon, cook until becoming crisp, then stir in the chestnuts for 2–3 minutes. Add the hot sprouts, toss together and serve.

BRAISED CELERY

Celery was introduced into England from Italy in the 17th century, and the leaves and stalks were included in salads. It was grown in 18th-century English kitchen gardens and was considered to be a delicacy. Use some of the celery leaves to garnish this dish.

SERVES 4

40g/1½oz/3 tbsp butter

2 rashers of bacon, chopped

1 small onion, finely chopped

1 carrot, finely chopped

1 celery head, cut into short lengths

175ml/6fl oz/¾ cup chicken or vegetable stock

1 bay leaf

1 parsley sprig

salt and ground black pepper

1 Melt the butter in a large heavy pan, then cook the bacon, onion and carrot until beginning to colour.

2 Add the celery and cook over a medium heat for 2–3 minutes. Stir in the stock, bay leaf, parsley and seasoning, and bring to the boil.

3 Cover and simmer gently for about 25 minutes, until the celery is tender and the liquid reduced to a few tablespoonfuls. Serve hot.

MUSHY PEAS

Dried marrowfat peas, cooked and served in their own juice, are
believed to have originated in the north of England. Today, they are
popular all over the country, especially with fish and chips. In the West
Riding of Yorkshire, mushy peas are served with pork pie.

SERVES 4–6

250g/9oz dried peas
1 small onion
1 small carrot
½ tsp sugar
salt and ground black pepper
25g/1oz/2 tbsp butter

1 Put the peas in a bowl and pour over boiling water to cover them
well. Soak for about 12 hours or overnight.

2 Drain and rinse the peas and put into a pan. Add the onion,
carrot, sugar and 600ml/1 pint/2½ cups cold water. Bring to the
boil and simmer gently for about 20 minutes or until the peas are
soft and the water absorbed.

3 Remove the onion and carrot from the pan. Mash the peas,
seasoning to taste with salt and black pepper, and stir in the butter.

PEASE PUDDING

'Pease pudding hot, pease pudding cold, pease pudding in the pot, nine days old…' goes
the old rhyme. This dish probably dates back to the 17th century, when puddings were
boiled, wrapped in a cloth, in a pot alongside meat (usually bacon). Once a nationwide
staple, it is still popular in the north-east. A small handful of chopped fresh mint or
a pinch of dried mint can be added to the purée in step 3, if liked.

SERVES 6

450g/1lb dried split yellow peas
40g/1½oz/3 tbsp butter,
cut into pieces
1 egg, lightly beaten
salt and ground black pepper

1 Cover the split peas with cold water and leave to soak for several
hours or overnight.

2 Drain the peas and put them into a pan. Cover with fresh cold
water, bring to the boil and simmer gently for about 45 minutes or
until very soft.

3 Preheat the oven to 180°C/350°F/gas 4. Drain and purée the
peas in a food processor or blender. Add the butter, egg and
seasoning, then mix, and spoon into a buttered ovenproof dish.

4 Bake in the hot oven for about 30 minutes until the pudding is set.
Alternatively, it can be steamed in a pudding bowl, securely covered
with baking parchment and foil, for about 45 minutes.

BROAD BEANS WITH BACON AND MINT

In early summer, tender young broad beans are a treat, and fresh mint and a smattering of crisply cooked bacon are their perfect partners. At other times of year, this recipe works well with frozen broad beans. Serve warm.

SERVES 4–6

30ml/2 tbsp oil

175g/6oz streaky bacon rashers, cut into narrow strips

1 medium onion, thinly sliced

½ tsp sugar

450g/1lb shelled broad (fava) beans

15ml/1 tbsp cider vinegar

small handful of fresh mint, finely chopped

salt and ground black pepper

1 Heat half the oil in a large pan and cook the bacon until crisp. Lift out with a slotted spoon and set aside.

2 Add the onion to the hot pan with the sugar and cook over a medium heat until soft and golden brown.

3 Meanwhile, bring a pan of water to the boil and add the beans. Cook for 5–8 minutes until tender. Drain well.

4 Add the cooked beans and bacon to the onions. Stir in the remaining oil, vinegar, mint and seasoning, transfer to a dish and serve.

BRAISED RED CABBAGE

In the English culinary tradition, red cabbage has usually been pickled. However, it is a robust winter vegetable that takes on a beautiful colour and texture when cooked slowly and gently. This spiced version goes particularly well with pork, duck or game.

SERVES 4–6

1kg/2¼lb red cabbage

2 onions, chopped

2 cooking apples, peeled, cored and coarsely grated

1 tsp freshly grated nutmeg

¼ tsp ground cloves

¼ tsp ground cinnamon

1 tbsp dark brown sugar

salt and ground black pepper

45ml/3 tbsp cider vinegar

25g/1oz/2 tbsp butter, cut into small pieces

1 Preheat the oven to 160°C/325°F/gas 3. Remove the large white ribs from the outer cabbage leaves, then shred the cabbage finely.

2 Layer the shredded cabbage in a large ovenproof dish with the onions, apples, spices, sugar and seasoning. Pour the vinegar over and dot with the butter.

3 Cover, put into the hot oven and cook for about 1½ hours, stirring a couple of times, until the cabbage is very tender. Serve hot.

COOK'S TIP

The braised cabbage can be cooked in advance and reheated in the oven for 30 minutes when needed. Leftovers can also be frozen.

ROAST BEETROOT WITH HORSERADISH CREAM

Beetroot was very popular in Elizabethan days, when its vibrant colour was added to elaborate salads. In this recipe, its sweet flavour is enhanced first by roasting and then offset by the horseradish and vinegar in the cream.

SERVES 4–6

10–12 small whole beetroot

30ml/2 tbsp oil

salt

3 tbsp grated fresh horseradish

15ml/1 tbsp white wine vinegar

2 tsp sugar

150ml/¼ pint/⅔ cup double (heavy) cream

1 Preheat the oven to 180°C/350°F/gas 4. Wash the beetroot without breaking their skins. Trim the stalks very short, but do not remove them completely.

2 Toss the beetroot in the oil and sprinkle with salt. Spread them in a roasting pan and cover with foil. Put into the hot oven and cook for about 1½ hours or until soft throughout. Leave to cool, covered, for 10 minutes.

3 Meanwhile, make the horseradish sauce. Put the grated horseradish, vinegar and sugar into a bowl and mix well. Whip the cream until thickened and fold in the horseradish mixture. Cover and chill until required.

4 When the beetroot are cool enough to handle, slip off the skins and serve with the sauce.

COOK'S TIPS

◆ If you are unable to find any fresh horseradish root, use preserved grated horseradish instead.

◆ For a lighter sauce, replace half the cream with thick plain yogurt.

ROAST PARSNIPS WITH HONEY

Parsnips were considered to be a luxury in ancient Roman times, when they were credited with a variety of medicinal and aphrodisiac qualities. Today, they are especially enjoyed when roasted around a large joint. Their sweetness mingles well with spiced honey.

SERVES 4–6

4 medium parsnips
2 tbsp plain (all-purpose) flour seasoned with salt and pepper
60ml/4 tbsp oil
1–2 tbsp clear honey
freshly grated nutmeg

1 Preheat the oven to 200°C/400°F/gas 6. Peel the parsnips and cut each one lengthways into quarters, removing any woody cores. Drop into a pan of boiling water and cook for 5 minutes until slightly softened.

2 Drain the parsnips thoroughly, then toss them in the seasoned flour, shaking off any excess.

3 Pour the oil into a roasting pan and put into the oven until hot. Add the parsnips, tossing them in the oil and arranging them in a single layer.

4 Return the pan to the oven and cook the parsnips for about 30 minutes, turning occasionally, until crisp, golden brown and cooked through.

5 Drizzle with the honey and sprinkle a little grated nutmeg. Return the parsnips to the oven for 5 minutes before serving.

PARSNIP CRISPS

Before sugar was available, parsnips were used to sweeten cakes and jams. By the 20th century, they had become an everyday item and were even dried to make 'coffee' during World War II. These crisps are particularly good served with grilled chicken or sausages.

SERVES 4

2 large parsnips
oil, for deep frying
2 tbsp plain (all-purpose) flour, seasoned with salt and a good pinch of curry powder (optional)

1 Peel the parsnips and, using a potato peeler, cut lengthways into thin strips. Put them into a pan, cover with water and bring just to the boil. Meanwhile, heat the oil in a deep, heavy pan to about 180°C/350°F.

2 Drain the parsnip strips and dry thoroughly, then toss them in the seasoned flour.

3 Fry the strips, in batches, in the hot oil until crisp and golden brown outside and soft inside. Lift out and drain on kitchen paper. Sprinkle with a little more salt and curry powder (if using) to serve.

POTATOES AND PARSNIPS WITH GARLIC AND CREAM

For the best results, cut the potatoes and parsnips very thinly — use a mandoline if you have one. This method is also ideal for cooking sweet potatoes, which Tudor cooks would have been more likely to slice and crystallise, to serve as a sweetmeat.

SERVES 4–6

3 large potatoes, total weight about 675g/1½lb

350g/12oz small to medium-sized parsnips

200ml/7fl oz/scant 1 cup single (light) cream

100ml/3½fl oz/scant ½ cup milk

2 garlic cloves, crushed

butter, for greasing

about 1 tsp freshly grated nutmeg

salt and ground black pepper

75g/3oz/¾ cup Cheddar or Red Leicester cheese, grated

1 Peel the potatoes and parsnips and cut them into thin slices. Cook in a large pan of salted boiling water for 5 minutes. Drain and cool slightly.

2 Meanwhile, pour the cream and milk into a heavy pan and add the crushed garlic. Bring to the boil over a medium heat, then remove from the heat and leave to stand for about 10 minutes.

3 Preheat the oven to 180°C/350°F/gas 4 and lightly butter the bottom and sides of a shallow ovenproof dish.

4 Arrange the potatoes and parsnips in the dish, sprinkling each layer with a little freshly grated nutmeg, salt and ground black pepper.

5 Pour the liquid into the dish and press the potatoes and parsnips down into it. Cover with lightly buttered foil and cook in the hot oven for 45 minutes.

6 Remove the foil and sprinkle the grated cheese over the vegetables in an even layer.

7 Return the dish to the oven and continue cooking, uncovered, for a further 20–30 minutes, or until the potatoes and parsnips are tender and the top is golden brown.

MASHED POTATOES

The potato arrived in England in the latter half of the 16th century and, at first,
was treated with great caution. Today, the English love them cooked in all kinds of ways.
Fluffy mashed potatoes are the traditional accompaniment to sausages – or 'bangers'.

SERVES 4

1kg/2¼lb floury potatoes,
such as Maris Piper
about 150ml/¼ pint/⅔ cup milk
115g/4oz/½ cup soft butter
salt
freshly grated nutmeg (optional)

1 Peel the potatoes and cook them whole in a large pan of boiling
water for about 20 minutes or until soft throughout. Drain. Warm
the milk and butter in a large pan.

2 Push the warm potatoes through a ricer, pass them through a
mouli or mash with a potato masher or fork.

3 Add the mashed potato to the milk and beat with a wooden spoon,
adding extra milk if necessary to achieve the desired consistency.
Season to taste with salt and a little nutmeg (if using).

VARIATIONS

◆ Cook a small onion, quartered, with the potatoes and mash it
with them.

◆ Add a spoonful of English (hot) mustard or horseradish sauce (see
page 625) to the mash.

ROAST POTATOES

Roast potatoes can be cooked in the pan with roasted meat, where they will
absorb the juices. For crisp potatoes with a soft, fluffy interior,
roast them in a separate dish in a single layer.

SERVES 4

1.3kg/3lb floury potatoes
salt
90ml/6 tbsp oil, lard or goose fat

1 Preheat the oven to 200°C/400°F/gas 6. Peel the potatoes and
cut into chunks. Boil in salted water for about 5 minutes, drain,
return to the pan, and shake them to roughen the surfaces.

2 Put the fat into a large roasting pan and put into the hot oven to
heat the fat. Add the potatoes, coating them in the fat. Return to the
oven and cook for 40–50 minutes, turning once or twice, until crisp
and cooked through.

CHIPS

In 20th-century England, serving chips with fried fish developed into a national institution, but they are eaten and enjoyed with everything. This is the secret to great chips — frying them once to cook them, and the second time to brown and crisp them.

SERVES 4

sunflower or vegetable oil, for deep frying

675g/1½lb floury potatoes, such as King Edward or Maris Piper

salt

1 Heat oil in a deep, heavy pan to 150°C/300°F. Peel the potatoes and cut them into chips about 1cm/½in thick. Rinse and dry.

2 Lower a batch of chips into the hot oil and cook for about 5 minutes or until tender but not browned. Lift out onto kitchen paper and leave to cool.

3 Just before serving, increase the temperature of the oil to 190°C/375°F. Add the par-cooked chips, in batches.

4 Cook until crisp, then lift out and drain on kitchen paper. Sprinkle with salt and serve at once.

BAKED JACKET POTATOES

When the potato, one of England's staple foods, is cooked in its skin in the oven, it can be served split and laced with butter or soured cream, or with a filling of grated cheese.

SERVES 4

4 large floury potatoes of even size, such as King Edward or Maris Piper

a little oil

salt (optional)

butter or soured cream, to serve

chopped fresh parsley or chives, to serve

1 Preheat the oven to 200°C/400°F/gas 6. Scrub and dry the potatoes, and prick the skins with a fork to prevent them bursting during cooking.

2 Rub the skins with oil and sprinkle with a little salt (if using).

3 Put the potatoes in the hot oven, either on a baking sheet or straight onto the oven shelf. Cook for about 1 hour or until soft throughout — test by inserting a sharp knife into the centre.

4 Leave the cooked potatoes to stand for 5 minutes before splitting them open. Be careful of the escaping steam.

5 Serve with a dollop of butter on top, or soured cream and a sprinkling of parsley or chives.

COOK'S TIP

If you are cooking a large number of potatoes in the oven, you will probably need to extend the cooking time by 10–15 minutes.

PAN HAGGERTY

An economical dish, the name 'haggerty' is probably derived from the French *haché*, meaning 'chopped'. This traditional Northumberland recipe works best with firm-fleshed potatoes such as Cara, Desirée or Maris Piper. Serve it cut into wedges.

SERVES 4

60ml/4 tbsp oil
450g/1lb firm potatoes, thinly sliced
1 large onion, thinly sliced
115g/4oz/1 cup mature (strong) Cheddar cheese, grated
salt and ground black pepper

1 Heat the oil in a large, heavy frying pan. Remove the pan from the heat and add alternate layers of potato, onion slices and cheese, starting and ending with potatoes, and seasoning each layer as you go. Replace the pan over a low heat.

2 Cook for 30 minutes, until the potatoes are soft and the underside has browned. Meanwhile, preheat the grill or broiler.

3 Place the pan under the grill for 5–10 minutes to brown the top. Slide the potatoes onto a warmed plate to serve.

SAVOURY POTATO CAKES

Potatoes were the main crop of Lancashire in days gone by and were included in a wide variety of savoury dishes, including these tasty fritters of grated potato, which are a favourite. Make these crisp cakes as small or as large as you like. The addition of a little bacon makes them even more appetising. Serve them just as they are, with green vegetables, salad and a spoonful of thick yogurt, or as an accompaniment.

SERVES 4

450g/1lb potatoes, grated, rinsed, drained and dried
1 small onion, grated
3 rashers of streaky bacon, finely chopped (optional)
2 tbsp self-raising (self-rising) flour
2 eggs, beaten
salt and ground black pepper
oil, for frying

1 Mix the potatoes with the onion, bacon (if using), flour, eggs and seasoning.

2 Heat 1cm/½in oil in a frying pan, then add about 1 tbsp of the potato mixture and spread it slightly with the back of the spoon.

3 Add a few more spoonfuls, leaving space between them, and cook for 4–5 minutes, until golden underneath.

4 Turn the cakes over and cook for 3–4 minutes until golden brown and cooked through. Keep warm while you cook the remaining potato mixture.

CAULIFLOWER CHEESE

The use of flour to thicken sauces began in France in the 17th century –
hence the name 'roux' for the mixture of flour and fat that forms the basis
of a white sauce. Cheese sauce as it is made here has become a staple of English cookery.
Cauliflower cheese is a traditional and comforting dish.

SERVES 4

1 medium cauliflower

25g/1oz/2 tbsp butter

25g/1oz/3 tbsp plain
(all-purpose) flour

300ml/½ pint/1¼ cups milk

115g/4oz/1 cup mature Cheddar or
Cheshire cheese, grated

salt and ground black pepper

1 Trim the cauliflower and cut it into florets. Bring a pan of lightly salted water to the boil, drop in the cauliflower and cook for 5–8 minutes or until just tender. Drain, and tip the florets into an shallow ovenproof dish.

2 To make the sauce, melt the butter in a pan, stir in the flour and cook gently, stirring constantly, for about 1 minute (do not allow it to brown). Remove from the heat and gradually stir in the milk. Return the pan to the heat and cook, stirring, until the mixture thickens and comes to the boil. Simmer gently for 1–2 minutes.

3 Stir in three-quarters of the cheese, and season to taste. Spoon the sauce over the cauliflower and scatter the remaining cheese on top. If possible, put under a hot grill or broiler to give a golden brown topping.

COOK'S TIP

Boost the cheese flavour by adding a little English (hot) mustard to the cheese sauce.

NEW POTATO AND CHIVE SALAD

The potatoes absorb the oil and vinegar dressing as they cool, and are then tossed in mayonnaise. Small, waxy potatoes, which can be kept whole, are particularly suitable for this recipe. Serve them with cold poached salmon or roast chicken.

SERVES 4–6

675g/1½lb small new potatoes, unpeeled

salt and ground black pepper

4 spring onions (scallions)

45ml/3 tbsp oil

15ml/1 tbsp cider vinegar or wine vinegar

½ tsp ready-made English (hot) mustard

175ml/6fl oz/¾ cup mayonnaise

3 tbsp chopped fresh chives

1 Cook the new potatoes in boiling salted water for about 15 minutes, or until tender.

2 Meanwhile, finely chop the white parts of the spring onions together with a little of the green part. Whisk the oil with the vinegar and mustard. Add seasoning to taste.

3 Drain the potatoes. Immediately, while the potatoes are still hot and steaming, toss them lightly with the oil mixture and the spring onions. Leave to cool.

4 Stir the mayonnaise and chives into the cooled potatoes and turn into a serving bowl. Chill the salad until you are ready to serve.

VARIATION

Instead of chives, add a handful of chopped parsley or mint to the salad with the mayonnaise.

SALMAGUNDI

Composite salads were fashionable in 16th-century England, with a range of elaborately arranged ingredients such as chopped meat, anchovies and hard-boiled eggs, dressed with lemon juice, oil and other condiments. This variation is thought to be from Northumbria.

SERVES 4–6

1 large chicken

500g/1¼lb new or baby potatoes

225g/8oz carrots, cut into small sticks

225g/8oz sugar snap peas

4 eggs

½ cucumber, cut into thin wedges

8–12 cherry tomatoes

8–12 green pitted olives

FOR THE STOCK

1 onion, 1 carrot and 1 celery stick

2 bay leaves

large sprig of thyme

10 black peppercorns

FOR THE DRESSING

75ml/5 tbsp olive oil

30ml/2 tbsp lemon juice

½ tsp sugar

¼ tsp ready-made English (hot) mustard

salt and ground black pepper

1 Put the chicken in a deep pan with the stock ingredients: the onion, carrot, celery, bay leaves, thyme and peppercorns. Add water to cover by at least 2.5cm/1in. Bring to the boil and simmer gently for 45 minutes or until the chicken is cooked, then leave to cool in the stock for several hours to keep it moist. (See Cook's Tip.)

2 Whisk together the ingredients for the dressing. Set aside.

3 Using a separate pan for each, as they will take different cooking times, cook the potatoes, carrots and peas in lightly salted boiling water until just tender. Drain and rinse under cold water. Halve the potatoes.

4 Put the eggs, in their shells, in a pan of cold water. Bring to the boil, then boil gently for 10 minutes. Cool under cold running water, then peel off the shells and cut into quarters.

5 Lift the chicken out of the stock, remove the meat and cut or tear into bite-size pieces.

6 Arrange all the vegetables, chicken and eggs on a large platter, or in a large bowl, and add the cucumber, tomatoes and olives. Just before serving, drizzle the salad dressing over the top.

COOK'S TIP

If you don't have the time to boil a chicken from scratch in a flavoured stock, you can of course use ready-cooked chicken.

COLESLAW WITH BLUE CHEESE

Lancashire, Lincolnshire and Kent, in particular, are renowned for growing cabbages. In this dish, shredded crisp white cabbage is tossed in a dressing flavoured with English blue cheese. Serve it with other salads or with hot potatoes baked in their skins.

SERVES 4–8

3 tbsp mayonnaise

3 tbsp thick natural (plain) yogurt

50g/2oz blue cheese, such as Stilton or Oxford Blue

15ml/1 tbsp lemon juice or cider vinegar

salt and ground black pepper

about 500g/1¼lb white cabbage

1 medium carrot

1 small red onion

2 small celery sticks

1 crisp eating apple

watercress sprigs, to garnish

1 Put the mayonnaise and yogurt into a large bowl and crumble in the cheese. Stir well, adding a squeeze of lemon juice and a little seasoning to taste.

2 Trim and shred the cabbage finely, grate the carrot, chop the onion finely and cut the celery into very thin slices. Core and dice the apple.

3 Add the cabbage, carrot, onion, celery and apple to the bowl and toss until all the ingredients are well mixed and coated with the dressing.

4 Cover the bowl and refrigerate for 2–3 hours, or until ready to serve. Stir before serving, garnished with watercress.

VARIATION

Try making the coleslaw with a half and half mixture of red cabbage and white cabbage.

PUDDINGS & DESSERTS

Everyone loves a pudding, and England
has many variations to enjoy. Orchard fruits
are often a main ingredient – apples, pears,
plums, apricots, cherries – stewed or baked
and made into tarts, crumbles and pies. And, of
course, the berries…There are also plenty of
nursery-style puds on the following pages,
made with sponge, suet pastry, bread, rice or
batter, as well as rich, creamy concoctions
made with products from the dairy.

PICTURED *Apple blossom in a Somerset orchard.*

APPLE AND BLACKBERRY CRUMBLE

Crumble did not appear in recipe books until the 20th century, but is a firm favourite.
Autumn heralds the harvest of apples and their perfect partners, blackberries.

SERVES 6–8

115g/4oz/½ cup butter
115g/4oz/1 cup wholemeal flour
50g/2oz/½ cup fine or
medium oatmeal
50g/2oz/4 tbsp soft light brown sugar
a little grated lemon rind (optional)
900g/2lb cooking apples
450g/1lb/4 cups blackberries
squeeze of lemon juice
175g/6oz/¾ cup caster (superfine)
sugar

1 Preheat the oven to 200°C/400°F/gas 6. To make the crumble, rub the butter into the flour, and then add the oatmeal and brown sugar and continue to rub in until the mixture begins to stick together, forming large crumbs.

2 Mix in the grated lemon rind, if using. Peel and core the cooking apples and slice into wedges.

3 Put the apples, blackberries, lemon juice, 30ml/2 tbsp water and the caster sugar in a shallow ovenproof dish, of about 2 litres/3½ pints capacity.

4 Cover the fruit with the crumble topping. Put into the hot oven and cook for 15 minutes, then reduce the heat to 190°C/375°F/gas 5 and cook for 15–20 minutes until golden brown.

WINTER FRUIT CRUMBLE

This crumble uses pears and dried fruit in its base, making it ideal for the winter months.
At other times of the year, try gooseberries or rhubarb flavoured with orange zest.

SERVES 6

175g/6oz/1½ cups plain
(all-purpose) flour
50g/2oz/½ cup ground almonds
175g/6oz/¾ cup butter, diced
115g/4oz/scant ½ cup soft light
brown sugar
40g/1½oz flaked (sliced) almonds
1 orange
about 16 ready-to-eat dried apricots
4 firm ripe pears

1 Preheat the oven to 190°C/375°F/gas 5. To make the topping, sift the flour into a bowl and stir in the ground almonds. Add the butter and rub it into the flour until the mixture resembles rough breadcrumbs. Stir in three-quarters of the sugar and the almonds.

2 Finely grate 1 tsp rind from the orange and squeeze out its juice. Halve the apricots and put them into a shallow ovenproof dish. Peel the pears, remove their cores and cut the fruit into small pieces. Scatter the pears over the apricots. Stir the orange rind into the orange juice and sprinkle over the fruit. Scatter the remaining brown sugar over the top.

3 Cover the fruit completely with the crumble mixture and smooth over. Put into the hot oven and cook for about 40 minutes until the topping is golden brown and the fruit is soft (test with the point of a sharp knife).

QUEEN OF PUDDINGS

This delicate dessert has a base made with custard and breadcrumbs flavoured with lemon. Once it is set, a layer of jam is added and covered with a light meringue topping. Mrs Beeton called this 'Queen of Bread Pudding'. It's good served as it is, or with cream.

SERVES 4

75g/3oz/1½ cups fresh breadcrumbs

50g/2oz/4 tbsp caster (superfine) sugar, plus 5ml/1 tsp

grated rind of 1 lemon

600ml/1 pint/2½ cups milk

4 eggs

3 tbsp raspberry jam, warmed

1 To make the custard pudding base, stir the breadcrumbs, 2 tbsp of the sugar and the lemon rind together in a bowl. Bring the milk to the boil in a pan, then stir it into the breadcrumb and sugar mixture.

2 Separate three of the eggs and beat the yolks with the remaining whole egg. Stir the eggs into the breadcrumb mixture, then pour into a buttered ovenproof dish and leave to stand for 30 minutes.

3 Meanwhile, preheat the oven to 160°C/325°F/gas 3. Cook the custard pudding for 50–60 minutes, until set.

4 To make the meringue topping, whisk the egg whites in a large, clean bowl until stiff but not dry, then gradually whisk in the remaining 2 tbsp caster sugar until the mixture is thick and glossy; be careful not to overwhip the mixture.

5 Spread the jam over the set custard pudding, then spoon over the meringue to cover the top. Sprinkle the remaining 1 tsp sugar over the meringue, then return to the oven for a further 15 minutes, until the meringue is light golden. Serve warm.

COOK'S TIP

The traditional recipe stipulates that raspberry jam should be used, but you could replace it with a different jam, such as strawberry or plum, or with lemon curd, marmalade or fruit purée.

JAM ROLY POLY

This warming winter pudding, with its nursery-sounding name, first appeared on English tables in the 1800s. A savoury version, known as plough pudding, had a filling of bacon, onion and sage, and was eaten by Victorian stable lads for their supper on chilly days. While boiling is the traditional cooking method for jam roly poly, baking produces a lovely crisp golden crust and a sticky jam filling. Serve it thickly sliced with custard.

SERVES 4–6

175g/6oz/1½ cups self-raising (self-rising) flour, plus extra for dusting

pinch of salt

75g/3oz/¾ cup shredded suet (or vegetarian equivalent)

finely grated rind of 1 small lemon

6 tbsp jam

1 Preheat the oven to 180°C/350°F/gas 4 and line a baking sheet with baking parchment.

2 Sift the flour and salt into a bowl and stir in the suet and lemon rind. With a round-ended knife, stir in just enough cold water to enable you to gather the mixture into a ball of soft dough, finishing off with your fingers.

3 Remove the ball of dough from the bowl and, on a lightly floured work surface or board, knead it very lightly until smooth.

4 Gently roll out the pastry into a rectangle that measures 30 x 20cm/12 x 8in.

5 Using a palette knife or metal spatula, spread the jam evenly over the pastry, leaving the side edges and ends clear.

6 Brush the edges of the pastry with a little water and, starting at one of the short ends, carefully roll up the pastry. Try to keep the roll fairly loose so that the jam is not squeezed out.

7 Place the roll, seam side down, on the prepared baking sheet. Put into the hot oven and cook for 30–40 minutes until risen, golden brown and cooked through. Leave the pudding to cool for a few minutes before cutting into thick slices to serve.

TO BOIL THE ROLY POLY

1 Shape the mixture into a roll and wrap loosely (to allow room for the pudding to rise), first in baking parchment and then in a large sheet of foil. Twist the ends of the paper and foil to seal them securely, and tie a string handle from one end to the other.

2 Lower the package into a wide pan of boiling water on the stove, cover and boil for about 1½ hours. Check the water level occasionally and top up with boiling water if necessary.

EVE'S PUDDING

The name 'Mother Eve's pudding', from the biblical Eve, was first used in
the 19th century for a boiled suet pudding filled with apples, from
which this lighter sponge version developed.

SERVES 4–6

115g/4oz/½ cup butter

115g/4oz/½ cup caster
(superfine) sugar

2 eggs, beaten

grated rind and juice of 1 lemon

90g/3¼oz/scant 1 cup self-raising
(self-rising) flour

40g/1½oz/3 tbsp ground almonds

115g/4oz/scant ½ cup brown sugar

500–675g/1¼–1½lb cooking
apples, cored and thinly sliced

25g/1oz flaked (sliced) almonds

1 Preheat the oven to 180°C/350°F/gas 4. Beat together the butter
and caster sugar in a large mixing bowl until the mixture is very
light and fluffy.

2 Gradually beat the eggs into the butter mixture, beating well after
each addition, then fold in the lemon rind, flour and ground
almonds.

3 In a separate bowl, mix the brown sugar, apples and lemon juice
together and tip then the mixture into an ovenproof dish, spreading
it out evenly.

4 Spoon the sponge mixture over the top in an even layer and right
to the edges. Sprinkle the almonds over. Put into the hot oven and
cook for 40–45 minutes until risen and golden brown.

YORKSHIRE LEMON SURPRISE

During cooking, a tangy lemon sauce collects beneath a light sponge topping. It's important
to bake this dish when it is standing in the bath of hot water, otherwise it will not work.

SERVES 4

50g/2oz/¼ cup butter,
plus extra for greasing

grated rind and juice of 2 lemons

115g/4oz/½ cup caster
(superfine) sugar

2 eggs, separated

50g/2oz/½ cup self-raising
(self-rising) flour

300ml/½ pint/1¼ cups milk

1 Preheat the oven to 190°C/375°F/gas 5. Use a little butter to
grease a 1.2 litre/2 pint ovenproof dish.

2 Beat the butter, lemon rind and caster sugar in a bowl until pale
and fluffy. Add the egg yolks and flour and beat together well.
Gradually whisk in the lemon juice and milk (the mixture may
curdle horribly, but don't be alarmed).

3 In a clean bowl, whisk the egg whites until they form stiff peaks.
Fold the egg whites lightly into the lemon mixture using a metal
spoon, then pour into the prepared dish.

4 Place the dish in a roasting pan, pour in hot water to fill halfway up the sides, put into the hot oven and cook for 45 minutes
until golden.

BREAD AND BUTTER PUDDING

Plates of white bread and butter were for many years a standard feature of an English tea or nursery supper, and frugal cooks needed to come up with ways to use up the leftovers. Bread and butter pudding is a family favourite. In the late 20th century, it was given a makeover using cream and brioche and began to appear on the menus of upmarket restaurants. This is the original version, which traditionalists prefer.

SERVES 4–6

50g/2oz/4 tbsp soft butter

about 6 large slices of day-old white bread

50g/2oz/⅓ cup dried fruit, such as raisins, sultanas (golden raisins) or chopped dried apricots

40g/1½oz/3 tbsp caster (superfine) sugar

2 large eggs

600ml/1 pint/2½ cups full fat (whole) milk

1 Preheat the oven to 160°C/325°F/gas 5. Lightly butter a 1.2-litre/2-pint ovenproof dish.

2 Butter the slices of bread and cut them into small triangles or squares.

3 Arrange half the bread pieces, buttered side up, in the prepared dish and sprinkle the dried fruit and half of the sugar over the top.

4 Lay the remaining bread slices, again buttered side up, evenly on top of the fruit. Sprinkle the remaining sugar over the top.

5 In a bowl, beat the eggs lightly together, just to break up the yolks and whites, and stir in the milk.

6 Strain the egg mixture (pushing it through a sieve) and pour it over the bread in the dish. Push the top slices down into the liquid if necessary, so that it is evenly absorbed.

7 Leave the pudding to stand for 30 minutes, to allow the bread to soak up all the liquid. This is an important step, so don't be tempted to skip it.

8 Put the dish into the hot oven and cook for about 45 minutes or until the custard is set and the top is crisp and golden brown. Serve the pudding immediately with pouring cream.

VARIATIONS

◆ To make a special-occasion chocolate bread and butter pudding, complete steps 1–4, omitting the dried fruit if you wish. Break 150g/5oz dark (bittersweet) chocolate into 525ml/17fl oz/ generous 2 cups milk and heat gently until the milk is warm and the chocolate has melted. Stir frequently during heating and do not allow the milk to boil. Stir the warm chocolate milk into the beaten eggs in step 5, and then continue with the remaining steps.

◆ You could replace the dried fruit in either version of the pudding with slices of fresh banana.

BAKED RICE PUDDING

Rice pudding can be traced back to medieval England, when rice and sugar were expensive imports. Much later, it was recommended for nursing mothers, gained a reputation as an aphrodisiac and, most enduringly, became a nursery favourite, served with a dollop of jam.

SERVES 4

50g/2oz/4 tbsp butter, diced, plus extra for greasing

50g/2oz/¼ cup pudding rice

25g/1oz/2 tbsp soft light brown sugar

900ml/1½ pints/3¾ cups milk

small strip of lemon rind

freshly grated nutmeg

1 Preheat the oven to 150°C/300°F/gas 2. Butter a 1.2 litre/2 pint shallow ovenproof dish.

2 Put the rice, sugar and butter into the dish and stir in the milk. Add the strip of lemon rind and sprinkle a little nutmeg over the surface. Put the pudding into the hot oven.

3 Cook the pudding for about 2 hours, stirring after 30 minutes and another couple of times during the next 1½ hours, until the rice is tender and the pudding is thick and creamy.

4 If you prefer skin on top, leave the pudding undisturbed for the final 30 minutes, or stir again. Serve with jam.

VARIATIONS

◆ Add some sultanas (golden raisins), raisins or ready-to-eat dried apricots and cinnamon to the pudding.

◆ Serve with fresh fruit, such as sliced peaches, raspberries or strawberries.

KENTISH CHERRY BATTER PUDDING

The south of England was already celebrated for its cherry orchards in the 16th century. Pink and white cherry blossom heralded the arrival of spring, and Kent was dubbed the 'garden of England'. They were popular fruits in London's street markets, when the fruit was brought to London on carts from Kent. Rotherhithe in London was famous for its Cherry Garden, a popular recreational area – Samuel Pepys in his diary mentions visiting here to buy cherries for his wife. The cherry season is short, and puddings like this help to make the most of it.

SERVES 4

450g/1lb cherries, pitted

45ml/3 tbsp cherry brandy or kirsch (optional)

50g/2oz/½ cup plain (all-purpose) flour

50g/2oz/4 tbsp caster (superfine) sugar, plus extra for sprinkling

2 eggs, separated

300ml/½ pint/1¼ cups milk

75g/3oz/6 tbsp butter, melted

1 Put the cherries in a bowl and sprinkle over the cherry brandy or kirsch, if using, and leave to soak for about 30 minutes.

2 Stir the flour and sugar together in a mixing bowl, then slowly stir in the egg yolks and milk to make a smooth batter. Stir half the melted butter into the mixture and leave it to rest for 30 minutes.

3 Preheat the oven to 220°C/425°F/gas 7. Pour the remaining melted butter over the bottom of a 600 ml/1 pint ovenproof dish and put it in the oven to heat up.

4 Stiffly whisk the egg whites and fold into the batter with the cherries. Pour into the dish, and bake for 15 minutes.

5 Reduce the heat to 180°C/350°F/gas 4 and cook for 20 minutes until golden and set. Serve sprinkled with sugar.

SYRUP SPONGE PUDDING

England is famous for its steamed puddings and this one is a classic. The light sponge with its golden coat of syrup brings back memories of childhood when, for many, syrup sponge pudding (probably in a more stodgy version) was one of the highlights of school dinners. Serve this one with freshly made custard or cold pouring cream.

SERVES 4–6

115g/4oz/½ cup soft butter

3 tbsp golden (light corn) syrup

115g/4oz/½ cup caster (superfine) sugar

2 eggs, beaten

1 tsp finely grated lemon rind

175g/6oz/1½ cups self-raising (self-rising) flour

30ml/2 tbsp milk

1 Butter a 1.2 litre/2 pint pudding basin (heatproof bowl with a lip) and spoon the golden syrup into the bottom of it.

2 In a large bowl, beat the butter and sugar until pale, light and fluffy.

3 Gradually beat the eggs into the butter and sugar mixture together with the lemon rind.

4 Sift the flour over the mixture and fold it in lightly using a metal spoon. Gently stir in the milk to give a soft dropping consistency.

5 Spoon the sponge mixture over the golden syrup in the basin.

6 Cover the pudding with a sheet of greaseproof (waxed) paper or baking parchment, making a pleat in the centre to give the pudding room to rise. Cover this with a large sheet of foil (again pleated in the centre).

7 Tie a length of string securely around the basin, under the lip, to hold the foil and paper in place.

8 Half-fill a large pan with water and bring it to the boil. Place an inverted saucer or trivet in the bottom and stand the basin on it. Cover the pan and steam the pudding for about 1½ hours, topping up the pan with more boiling water if necessary.

9 Remove the pudding from the steamer and leave it standing for about 5 minutes before turning out onto the warm plate to serve.

COOK'S TIPS

◆ To cook the pudding in the microwave, cover the basin with baking parchment (but do not tie it on) and cook on medium (500–600W) for 6–8 minutes until the sponge is just cooked through. Leave to stand for 5 minutes before serving.

◆ The pudding can also be baked for a drier, cakier texture. Preheat the oven to 190°C/375°F/gas 5. Cover the basin with buttered foil and cook for 35–40 minutes. Meanwhile, heat 3 tbsp golden syrup with 2 tbsp water. Pour this hot sauce into a jug and serve alongside the pudding for pouring over.

SPOTTED DICK

In the 19th century, the term 'dick' was a general term for pudding. The pudding cloth was invented in the early 17th century, when pudding mixtures were tied into the cloth and put into a pan of boiling water to cook. At the beginning of the 20th century, boiled puddings were almost always made in basins (heatproof bowls), covered with greaseproof paper or foil and partly submerged in a pan of boiling water to steam. This traditional favourite is 'spotted' with raisins or currants.

SERVES 4

225g/8oz/scant 2 cups
self-raising (self-rising) flour

pinch of salt

115g/4oz/1 scant cup shredded suet
(or vegetarian equivalent)

75g/3oz/⅓ cup caster
(superfine) sugar

225g/8oz/1 cup currants or raisins,
soaked in a little hot water

1 Sift the flour and salt into a mixing bowl. Add the shredded suet, sugar and soaked dried fruit. Add enough cold water to make a firm dough, usually about 150ml/¼ pint.

2 Put the dough into a buttered 1.2 litre/2 pint pudding basin (heatproof bowl with a lip). Cover with greaseproof (waxed) paper or baking parchment with a pleat folded in the middle, to allow the pudding to rise, and cover this with pleated foil.

3 Tie securely and put the basin into a large pan of boiling water so that the water comes halfway up the sides of the basin. Steam for 2 hours, replenishing with boiling water as needed.

4 Cool for 5–10 minutes, then turn the pudding out onto a hot dish and serve with custard.

FIGGY PUDDING

This light steamed sponge is the winter festive version of a summer pudding.
It avoids the use of suet, and the addition of fresh orange juice and rind, along
with a splash of orange liqueur, gives an intense citrus tang.

SERVES 6

grated rind and juice of 2 oranges

115g/4oz/⅔ cup ready-to-eat
dried dates, chopped

115g/4oz/⅔ cup ready-to-eat
dried figs, chopped

30ml/2 tbsp orange liqueur (optional)

175g/6oz/¾ cup unsalted butter,
plus extra for greasing

175g/6oz/scant ¾ cup
soft light brown sugar

3 eggs

75g/3oz/¾ cup self-raising wholemeal
(self-rising wholewheat) flour

115g/4oz/1 cup self-raising
(self-rising) flour

2 tbsp golden (light corn)
syrup

1 Reserve a few strips of orange rind for the decoration and put the rest in a pan with the orange juice. Add the chopped dates and figs and orange liqueur, if using. Cook, covered, over a gentle heat for 8–10 minutes, until the fruit is soft.

2 Leave the fruit mixture to cool, then transfer to a food processor or blender and process until smooth. Press through a sieve to remove the fig seeds, if you wish.

3 Cream the butter and sugar until pale and fluffy, then beat in the fig purée. Beat in the eggs, then fold in the flours and mix until combined.

4 Grease a 1.2 litre/2 pint pudding basin (heatproof bowl with a lip), and pour in the golden syrup. Tilt the basin to cover the inside with a layer of syrup. Spoon in the cake mixture.

5 Cover the top with greaseproof (waxed) paper or baking parchment, with a pleat down the centre, and then with pleated foil, and tie with string.

6 Place the basin in a large pan, and pour in enough water to come halfway up the sides of the basin. Cover with a tight-fitting lid and steam for 2 hours. Check the water occasionally and top up if necessary. Turn out and decorate with the reserved orange rind.

CHRISTMAS PUDDING

Plum pudding and figgy pudding were the forerunners of today's festive steamed concoction of mixed dried fruits. This pudding is eaten on Christmas Day, brought to the table doused in warm brandy or whisky and set alight. Christmas puddings are made at least a month in advance (traditionally on 'Stir-up Sunday' at the end of November). Serve with pouring cream and rum or brandy butter.

MAKES 2 PUDDINGS,
EACH SERVING 6–8

275g/10oz/5 cups fresh breadcrumbs

225g/8oz/1 cup soft light brown sugar

225g/8oz/1 cup currants

275g/10oz/1⅓ cups raisins

225g/8oz/1 cup sultanas
(golden raisins)

115g/4oz/½ cup glacé
(candied) cherries

50g/2oz/⅓ cup chopped
(candied) mixed peel

225g/8oz/1½ cups shredded suet
(or vegetarian equivalent)

½ tsp salt

2–4 tsp mixed (apple pie) spice

1 carrot, peeled and coarsely grated

1 apple, peeled, cored
and finely chopped

grated rind and juice of 1 orange

2 large eggs, lightly whisked

450ml/¾ pint/scant 2 cups stout
(dark ale or beer)

butter, for greasing

1 Put the breadcrumbs, sugar and dried fruits in a large mixing bowl. Add the suet, salt, mixed spice, carrot, apple and orange rind. Mix well.

2 Stir the orange juice, eggs and stout into the breadcrumb mixture. Leave overnight, stirring occasionally, if possible.

3 Butter two 1.2 litre/2 pint pudding basins (heatproof bowls with a lip) and put a circle of greaseproof (waxed) paper or baking parchment in the bottoms. Stir the mixture and turn into the basins.

4 Top with buttered circles of paper or parchment, cover tightly with more layers of paper and foil, tied securely under the rim. Steam for about 6–7 hours, top with boiling water as necessary.

5 When the puddings are cooked and cooled, re-cover them with foil and store in a cool, dry place until ready to be re-steamed and served.

CUMBERLAND RUM BUTTER

Why or when this sweet rich butter was created is unknown. Legend has it that smugglers would mix contraband spirit with butter to hide it from excise men! Another story goes that it was created when a cask of rum leaked into an old woman's stores of butter and sugar.

The recipe first appeared in print in 1887 in *Mrs A.B. Marshall's Cookery Book*. Beat 225g/8oz of unsalted butter with 225g/8oz of soft light brown sugar until soft, creamy and pale in colour. Gradually add 90ml/6 tbsp of dark rum, drop by drop (not too fast, or the mixture may curdle). When well blended, cover and chill for an hour or more. It will keep in the refrigerator for about 4 weeks.

SUSSEX POND PUDDING

The name of this traditional steamed pudding comes from the buttery lemon sauce that oozes out when the pudding is turned out onto a serving dish. The lemon becomes very soft during the cooking time and blends into the butter and sugar to produce a rich lemon-flavoured sauce when the pudding is cut open. Everyone should receive a piece of the lemon in their portion.

SERVES 4

225g/8oz/scant 2 cups self-raising (self-rising) flour, plus extra for dusting

115g/4oz/1 scant cup shredded suet (or vegetarian equivalent)

150ml/¼ pint/¾ cup milk and water, mixed

115g/4oz/½ cup butter, diced, plus extra for greasing

115g/4oz/½ cup caster (superfine) or other sugar

1 large unwaxed lemon

1 Combine the flour and suet in a mixing bowl and add the liquid. Mix to a soft dough. Generously butter a 1.5 litre/2½ pint pudding basin (or heatproof bowl with a lip).

2 Reserving a quarter of the dough for the lid, roll out the dough on a floured surface into a large circle. Line the basin completely with the pastry.

3 Put half the butter and half the sugar into the pastry-lined basin. Prick the lemon all over with a skewer and place whole on top of the butter and sugar. Cover with the rest of the butter and sugar.

4 Roll out the reserved pastry into a round to make a lid. Lay the pastry over the filling and press the edges together to seal completely.

5 Cover with greaseproof (waxed) paper or baking parchment with a pleat folded in the middle, to allow the pudding to rise, and cover this with pleated foil. Tie securely and put the basin into a large pan of boiling water so that the water comes halfway up the sides of the basin. Cover the pan and boil for 3½ hours, replenishing with boiling water as needed.

6 Take off the heat and allow to cool for a few minutes. Ease the sides of the pudding away from the basin with a palette knife. Turn out the pudding very carefully into a serving dish. Serve immediately.

STICKY TOFFEE PUDDINGS

The exact origins of this delicious pudding are disputed, but it appeared in the late 1960s–1970s and has remained popular in England ever since. This can also be made as a single large pudding, by baking in a 20 x 30cm/8 x 12in baking dish or tin, allowing an extra 10–15 minutes of baking time.

SERVES 4

175g/6oz/¾ cup pitted finely chopped Medjool dates

200ml/7fl oz/1 scant cup boiling water

½ tsp vanilla extract

1 tsp bicarbonate of (baking) soda

50g/2oz/4 tbsp butter, plus extra for greasing the moulds

175g/6oz/¾ cup soft light brown sugar

2 eggs, beaten

175g/6oz/1½ cups self-raising (self-rising) flour, plus extra for dusting

½ tsp mixed spice

FOR THE TOFFEE SAUCE

115g/4oz/½ cup unsalted butter

160g/5½oz/⅔ cup soft light brown sugar

120ml/4fl oz/½ cup double (heavy) cream

1 Preheat the oven to 180°C/350°F/gas 4.

2 Butter four small pudding basins (or dariole moulds) and dust with flour, shaking out any excess and place them on a baking tray.

3 Put the dates in a medium bowl and pour over the boiling water. Add the vanilla and bicarbonate of soda. Mix well and leave to soak.

4 Beat together the butter and sugar in a mixing bowl until light and creamy. Beat in the egg a little at a time, then gently fold in the flour and spice. Pour in the date mixture and stir well.

5 Divide the mixture equally between the prepared basins. They should be about two-thirds full.

6 Bake for 15–20 minutes, until well-risen and springy to the touch. Allow to cool for 10 minutes and then remove from the moulds.

7 Combine all the ingredients for the toffee sauce in a large pan and place over a low heat, stirring until the sugar has dissolved.

8 Place the puddings on serving dishes and pour a small amount of toffee sauce over each pudding.

POTATO HARVEST PUDDING

An early 19th-century recipe for a deliciously light pudding, similar to a soufflé.
The mild neutral taste of the potato absorbs the flavours of the other ingredients
and is unnoticeable in the cooked pudding. Potatoes were the main crop of Lancashire
and they were employed in various culinary guises in a wide variety of both savoury
and sweet dishes. A successful potato harvest was celebrated with a 'shut-in' in the
barn. Lancashire hot pot and other tasty potato dishes were enjoyed,
accompanied by the singing of traditional songs.

SERVES 4

675g/1½lb floury potatoes, peeled
and cut into chunks

115g/4oz/½ cup butter, melted

50g/2oz/4 tbsp sugar

1 tsp salt

½ tsp grated nutmeg

6 eggs, beaten

60ml/4 tbsp cider or ale

2 tbsp self-raising (self-rising) flour

75g/3oz/½ cup currants or raisins

1 Boil the potatoes for about 20 minutes until tender. Drain and mash until smooth.

2 Preheat the oven to 180°C/350°F/gas 4. Grease a 900 ml/ 1½ pint pudding basin (or heatproof bowl with a lip).

3 In a bowl, mix together the butter, sugar, salt and nutmeg with the mashed potatoes. Beat in the eggs until blended.

4 Mix together the cider and flour, and stir into the potato mixture with the currants or raisins.

5 Put the mixture into the pudding basin and bake for 40–45 minutes until risen. Serve hot.

CABINET PUDDING

A luxurious hot pudding, popular on the Victorian table.
The first recorded recipe appeared in *Cook's Oracle* in 1821. *Modern Cookery for Private Families* by Eliza Acton (1845) also included a recipe, as did *Mrs Beeton's Household Management* book, published in 1861, although she called it 'Chancellor's Pudding'. The pudding can be cooked in an ordinary baking dish if preferred, and served from the dish.

SERVES 4

25g/1oz/2½ tbsp raisins, chopped

30ml/2 tbsp brandy (optional)

25g/1oz/2½ tbsp glacé (candied) cherries, halved if large

25g/1oz/2½ tbsp candied angelica, chopped

2 trifle sponge cakes, diced

50g/2oz ratafia biscuits, crushed

2 whole eggs and 2 egg yolks

25g/1oz/2 tbsp sugar

450ml/¾ pint/scant 2 cups single (light) cream or milk

few drops of vanilla extract

1 Soak the raisins in the brandy, if using, for several hours.

2 Butter a 750 ml/1¼ pint charlotte mould and arrange some of the cherries and angelica in the base.

3 Mix the remaining cherries and angelica with the sponge cakes, ratafias and soaked raisins, and spoon into the mould.

4 Lightly whisk together the eggs, egg yolks and sugar. In a pan, bring the cream or milk just to the boil, then stir into the egg mixture with the vanilla extract.

5 Strain the egg mixture into the mould, and leave for 15–30 minutes. Preheat the oven to 160°C/325°F/gas 3.

6 Place the mould in a roasting pan, cover with baking paper and pour in boiling water around the sides, no more than halfway up the sides. Bake for 1 hour, or until set. Leave for 2–3 minutes, then turn out onto a warm plate to serve.

APPLE CHARLOTTE

This classic dessert takes its name from the straight-sided tin with heart-shaped handles in which it is baked. The buttery bread crust encases a thick and sweet yet sharp apple purée. This pudding is good served with custard.

SERVES 6

1.2kg/2½lb apples

30ml/2 tbsp water

115g/4oz/scant ½ cup soft light brown sugar

½ tsp ground cinnamon

¼ tsp freshly grated nutmeg

about 7 slices of firm-textured white bread

70g/2½oz/5 tbsp butter, melted

1 Peel, quarter and core the apples. Cut into thick slices and put in a large, heavy pan with the water. Cook, covered, over a medium-low heat for 5 minutes, and then uncover the pan and cook for 10 minutes until the apples are very soft.

2 Add the sugar, cinnamon and nutmeg and continue cooking for 5–10 minutes, stirring frequently, until the apples are soft and thick. (There should be about 750ml/1¼ pints/3 cups of apple purée.)

3 Preheat the oven to 200°C/400°F/gas 6. Trim the crusts from the bread and brush with melted butter on one side. Cut two slices into triangles and use as many as necessary to cover the base of a 1.4 litre/2¼ pint charlotte tin or soufflé dish, placing them buttered sides down and fitting them tightly. Cut wide strips of bread slices, to the same height as the tin or dish, and use them to completely line the sides, overlapping them slightly.

4 Pour in the apple purée. Cover the top with more bread slices, buttered side up, cutting them as necessary to fit.

5 Bake the charlotte for 20 minutes, then reduce the oven temperature to 180°C/350°F/gas 4 and bake for 25 minutes until well browned and firm. Leave to stand for 15 minutes. To turn out, place a serving plate over the tin or dish, hold tightly, and invert, then lift off the tin or dish.

PLUM PIE

English fruit pies are made either in a pie dish with a deep filling or on a plate with a crust both top and bottom, and even sometimes with an extra, third, pastry layer dividing the fruits inside. A range of fruits can be used, such as apples, gooseberries, blackberries, rhubarb or, as here, plums. Serve the pie with whipped cream or custard.

SERVES 6

200g/7oz/1¾ cups plain (all-purpose) flour, plus extra for dusting

25g/1oz/4 tbsp icing (confectioner's) sugar

115g/4oz/½ cup butter, diced

1 egg, lightly beaten

800g/1¾lb plums, stoned (pitted)

about 75g/3oz/⅓ cup caster (superfine) sugar, plus extra for sprinkling

beaten egg white, to frost

1 Sift the flour and icing sugar into a bowl and rub in the butter until the mixture resembles fine crumbs. Stir in the egg and gather together into a smooth dough. Chill for 30 minutes.

2 Preheat the oven to 190°C/375°F/gas 5. Place half the plums in a 1 litre/1¾ pint pie dish. Sprinkle the caster sugar over them, adjusting the amount according to the sweetness of the fruit, then add the remaining plums.

3 Roll out the pastry on a lightly floured surface to a shape slightly larger than the dish. Dampen the edges of the dish with a little egg white and cover with the pastry.

4 Trim the edges and pinch to make a decorative edging. Brush the top with egg white and sprinkle with a little caster sugar. Make a small slit in the centre to allow steam to escape.

5 Cook in the oven for 35–40 minutes until the pastry is golden brown and the plums are soft (check by inserting a knife through the slit). Serve sprinkled with extra caster sugar.

APPLE PIE

An apple pie is a taste of home across the Atlantic as well as England, of course. This traditional deep pie has melt-in-the-mouth shortcrust pastry, and the sugar, spices and flour create a deliciously thick and syrupy sauce with the apple juices. Serve with whipped cream.

SERVES 6

115g/4oz/½ cup caster (superfine) sugar

3 tbsp plain (all-purpose) flour

½ tsp ground cinnamon

finely grated rind of 1 orange

900g/2lb tart cooking apples

1 egg white, lightly beaten, to glaze

2 tbsp golden granulated sugar, for sprinkling

FOR THE PASTRY

350g/12oz/3 cups plain (all-purpose) flour, plus extra for dusting

pinch of salt

175g/6oz/¾ cup butter, diced

about 75ml/5 tbsp chilled water

1 To make the pastry, sift the flour and salt into a mixing bowl and rub or cut in the butter until the mixture resembles fine breadcrumbs. Sprinkle over the chilled water and mix to a firm, soft dough. Knead lightly for a few seconds until smooth. Wrap in cling film (plastic wrap) and chill for 30 minutes.

2 Combine the caster sugar, flour, cinnamon and orange rind in a bowl. Peel, core and thinly slice the apples. Add the apple slices to the sugar mixture in the bowl, then toss gently with your fingertips until they are all evenly coated.

3 Put a baking sheet in the oven and preheat to 200°C/400°F/gas 6. Roll out just over half the pastry on a floured surface and use to line a 23cm/9in pie dish that is 4cm/1½ in deep, allowing the pastry to overhang the edges slightly. Spoon in the filling, doming the apple slices in the centre.

4 Roll out the remaining pastry to form the lid. Lightly brush the edges of the pastry case with a little water, then place the lid over the apple filling.

5 Trim the pastry with a sharp knife. Gently press the edges together to seal, then knock up the edge. Re-roll the pastry trimmings and cut out apple and leaf shapes. Brush the top of the pie with egg white. Arrange the pastry apples and leaves on top.

6 Brush again with egg white, then sprinkle with granulated sugar. Make two small slits in the top of the pie to allow steam to escape.

7 Bake for 30 minutes, then lower the oven temperature to 180°C/350°F/gas 4 and bake for a further 15 minutes until the pastry is golden and the apples are soft – check by inserting a small sharp knife or skewer through one of the slits in the top of the pie. Serve hot or warm.

KENTISH PUDDING PIES

These unusual little pies, also known as Kent Lent pies, are light and delicate. They were made during Lent to use up spare eggs and milk before the Lenten fast and were also enjoyed at Easter. 'Going-a-pudding-pieing' was a late 19th-century Kentish custom, when groups of young people met in public houses to enjoy the pies accompanied by cherry beer. Mrs Beeton, in *The Book of Household Management* (1861), gives a similar recipe for Folkestone pudding pies.

MAKES 24

600ml/1 pint/2¼ cups milk

75g/3oz/scant ½ cup ground rice

grated zest of ½ lemon

pinch of salt

50g/2oz/4 tbsp butter

90g/3½oz/generous ⅓ cup caster (superfine) sugar

2 eggs

50g/2oz/⅓ cup raisins

grated nutmeg

FOR THE PASTRY

225g/8oz/2 cups plain (all-purpose) flour, plus extra for dusting

pinch of salt

115g/4oz/½ cup butter or lard, chilled, plus extra for greasing

45–60ml/3–4 tbsp iced water

1 For the pastry, sift the flour and salt into a mixing bowl. Rub in the butter or lard, using your fingertips until the mixture resembles coarse breadcrumbs.

2 Add iced water, a tablespoon at a time, mixing with a flat-bladed knife or your hands to form a dough. The dough should leave the bowl clean. If the mixture is too wet, add a little more flour. If it is too dry, add a little more water.

3 Gather into a ball, wrap in cling film (plastic wrap) and refrigerate for about 30 minutes. Preheat the oven to 180°C/350°F/gas 4. Grease 24 tartlet or bun tins or pans.

4 Roll out the pastry on a lightly floured surface to about 5mm/¼in thick. Cut into rounds with a 7cm/2½in cutter and line the tins with the rounds.

5 For the filling, in a bowl, mix together a quarter of the milk with the ground rice, lemon zest and salt, stirring well to ensure that no lumps form.

6 Heat the remaining milk in a pan and boil gently for 1 minute. Add the mixture in the bowl to the boiling milk and bring to the boil, stirring constantly. Simmer for about 5 minutes, still stirring. Remove from the heat.

7 Add the butter and sugar and beat well. Leave to cool slightly. Add the eggs, one at a time, beating well, then stir in the raisins.

8 Divide the mixture between the pastry cases and grate a little nutmeg over each pie. Bake for about 15 minutes until the filling is risen and firm.

9 Remove from the oven and cool in the tins for at least 15 minutes before removing. Serve warm or cold.

BAKEWELL PUDDING

Bakewell pudding has a custard-like almond filling. It is said to be the result of a 19th-century kitchen accident and is still baked in the original shop in Bakewell, Derbyshire. Made traditionally with puff pastry, this very popular, tart-like version with shortcrust pastry is simpler to make and is a favourite dessert and teatime treat all over England.

SERVES 4

2 tbsp raspberry or apricot jam
115g/4oz/½ cup butter, melted
115g/4oz/½ cup caster (superfine) sugar
2 eggs
50g/2oz/½ cup ground almonds
few drops of almond extract
icing (confectioner's) sugar, to dust

FOR THE PASTRY

175g/6oz/1½ cups plain (all-purpose) flour, plus extra for dusting
pinch of salt
75g/3oz/6 tbsp butter, diced
about 20ml/1½ tbsp iced water

1 To make the pastry, sift the flour and salt into a bowl and rub in the butter until the mixture resembles fine crumbs. Stir in a little cold water and gather into a smooth ball of dough. Wrap in cling film (plastic wrap) and chill for 30 minutes. Preheat the oven to 200°C/400°F/gas 6.

2 Roll out the pastry on a lightly floured surface and use to line a deep 20cm/8in loose-based flan tin or pan. Line the pastry case with foil and fill with baking beans. Bake blind for about 15 minutes, then remove the beans and foil and cook for a further 5 minutes to dry out the base.

3 For the filling, spread the base of the flan generously with raspberry or apricot jam.

4 Beat together the butter and sugar until light and creamy. Gradually beat in the eggs and gently stir in the ground almonds and almond extract.

5 Pour the mixture over the jam in the pastry case. Put the tart into the hot oven and cook for 25–30 minutes until golden and firm.

6 Sift a little icing sugar over the top before serving warm or at room temperature.

LEMON MERINGUE PIE

This popular dessert is a 20th-century development of older English cheesecakes – open tarts with a filling of curds. It was particularly relished in the 1950s after the years of wartime rationing, when sugar, lemons and eggs became plentiful once more. The pie is best served at room temperature, with or without cream.

SERVES 6

FOR THE PASTRY

115g/4oz/1 cup plain (all-purpose) flour, plus extra for dusting

pinch of salt

50g/2oz/4 tbsp butter, diced

about 20ml/1½ tbsp iced water

FOR THE FILLING

50g/2oz/½ cup cornflour (cornstarch)

175g/6oz/¾ cup caster (superfine) sugar

finely grated rind and juice of 2 lemons

2 egg yolks

15g/½oz/1½ tbsp butter, diced

FOR THE MERINGUE TOPPING

2 egg whites

75g/3oz/⅓ cup caster (superfine) sugar

1 To make the pastry, sift the flour and salt into a bowl and lightly rub in the butter until the mixture resembles fine crumbs. Stir in enough cold water until the mixture can be gathered together into a smooth ball of dough. (Alternatively, make the pastry using a food processor.) Wrap the pastry in cling film (plastic wrap) and chill for at least 30 minutes. Meanwhile, preheat the oven to 200°C/400°F/gas 6.

2 Roll out the pastry on a lightly floured surface and use to line a deep loose-based 20cm/8in flan tin or fluted pan. Prick the base with a fork, line with baking parchment or foil and add a layer of baking beans to prevent the pastry rising.

3 Put the pastry case into the hot oven and bake blind for 15 minutes. Remove the beans and parchment or foil, return the pastry to the oven and cook for a further 5 minutes until crisp and golden brown. Reduce the oven temperature to 150°C/300°F/gas 2.

4 To make the lemon filling, put the cornflour into a pan and add the sugar, lemon rind and 300ml/½ pint/1¼ cups water. Heat the mixture, stirring continuously, until it comes to the boil and thickens. Reduce the heat and simmer very gently for 1 minute. Remove the pan from the heat and stir in the lemon juice.

5 Add the egg yolks to the lemon mixture, one at a time and beating each addition, and then stir in the butter. Tip the mixture into the baked pastry case and level the surface.

6 To make the meringue topping, whisk the egg whites until stiff peaks form, then whisk in half the sugar. Fold in the rest of the sugar using a metal spoon.

7 Spread the meringue over the lemon filling, covering it completely. Cook for about 20 minutes until lightly browned.

TREACLE TART

The name of this tart is somewhat misleading, since golden syrup, not treacle or molasses, is used for the filling. Golden syrup became available only in the late 19th century, making this plate tart a relatively recent invention. Serve it warm or cold, with custard or cream.

SERVES 6

75g/3oz/1½ cups fresh breadcrumbs

½ tsp ground ginger (optional)

225g/8oz/1 cup golden (corn) syrup

grated rind and juice of 1 lemon

FOR THE PASTRY

175g/6oz/1½ cups plain (all-purpose) flour, plus extra for dusting

pinch of salt

40g/1½oz/3 tbsp lard, diced

40g/1½oz/3 tbsp butter, diced

45ml/3 tbsp iced water

1 For the pastry, sift the flour and salt into a bowl and add the lard and butter. With fingertips, rub the fats into the flour until the mixture resembles fine breadcrumbs. Stir in enough cold water so the mixture can be gathered together into a smooth ball of dough. Wrap the pastry in cling film (plastic wrap) and refrigerate for 30 minutes. Preheat the oven to 190°C/375°F/gas 5.

2 Roll out the pastry on a lightly floured surface and use to line a 20cm/8in flan tin or pie plate, reserving the trimmings.

3 Mix the breadcrumbs with the ginger, if using, and spread the mixture over the bottom of the pastry. Gently warm the syrup with the lemon rind and juice (on the stove or in the microwave) until quite runny, and pour evenly over the breadcrumbs.

4 Gather the reserved pastry trimmings into a ball, roll out on a lightly floured surface and cut into long, narrow strips. Twist these into spirals and arrange them in a lattice pattern on top of the tart, pressing them onto the edge to secure. Trim the ends.

5 Put into the hot oven and cook for about 25 minutes, until the pastry is golden brown and cooked through and the filling has set.

VARIATIONS

Omit the lemon rind and juice if you prefer. Sometimes finely crushed cornflakes are used in place of the breadcrumbs.

YORKSHIRE CURD TART

Also known as Yorkshire cheesecake, this tart was originally made
with curds made at home from creamy raw milk by adding buttermilk
and heating gently. The traditional flavour comes from allspice
or 'clove pepper'. Serve it plain or with cream.

SERVES 8

large pinch of ground allspice

90g/3½oz/⅓ cup soft brown sugar

3 eggs, beaten

grated rind and juice of 1 lemon

40g/1½oz/3 tbsp butter, melted

450g/1lb curd (farmer's) cheese

75g/3oz/½ cup raisins or sultanas
(golden raisins)

FOR THE PASTRY

225g/8oz/scant 2 cups plain
(all-purpose) flour,
plus extra for dusting

pinch of salt

115g/4oz/½ cup butter, diced

1 egg yolk

15–30ml/1–2 tbsp iced water

1 For the pastry, put the flour and salt in a bowl and rub in the
butter until the mixture resembles fine crumbs. Stir in the egg yolk,
with a little cold water if necessary, and gather the mixture into a
smooth ball of dough.

2 On a floured surface, roll out the pastry and use to line a
20cm/8in fluted loose-bottomed flan tin or quiche pan. Wrap in
cling film (plastic wrap) and chill for 15 minutes. Preheat the oven
to 190°C/375°F/gas 5.

3 To make the filling, mix the allspice with the sugar in a bowl, then
stir in the eggs, lemon rind and juice, butter, curd cheese and raisins
or sultanas.

4 Pour the filling into the pastry case. Bake for about 40 minutes
until the filling is lightly set and golden. Serve slightly warm, cut
into wedges.

CUMBERLAND RUM NICKY

The name of this pie comes from the traditional decoration of cuts or nicks made on top of the pastry. The rich filling ingredients – dates, spices, brown sugar and rum – were easily obtainable from the ports on the Cumbrian coast, which were a major import and trading centre for these products imported from the West Indies and the Caribbean in the 19th century.

SERVES 6

75g/3oz/6 tbsp butter

115g/4oz/⅔ cup dried dates, chopped

115g/4oz/⅔ cup currants

75g/3oz/scant ⅓ cup soft light brown sugar

25g/1oz stem ginger, finely chopped

30ml/2 tbsp dark rum

½ tsp grated nutmeg

FOR THE PASTRY

350g/12oz/3 cups plain (all-purpose) flour, plus extra for dusting

pinch salt

175g/6oz/¾ cup butter or lard, chilled

60–75ml/4–5 tbsp iced water

1 For the filling, melt the butter, then stir in the dates, currants, sugar, ginger, rum and nutmeg. Leave to stand for at least 1 hour.

2 For the pastry, sift the flour and salt into a mixing bowl. Rub in the butter or lard, using your fingertips, until the mixture resembles coarse breadcrumbs.

3 Add iced water, a tablespoon at a time, mixing with a flat-bladed knife or your hands to form a dough. The dough should leave the bowl clean. If the mixture is too wet, add a little more flour. If it is too dry, add a little more water.

4 Gather into a ball, wrap in cling film (plastic wrap) and refrigerate for about 30 minutes. Preheat the oven to 200°C/400°F/gas 6.

5 Roll out the pastry on a lightly floured surface and use half to line an 18cm/7in pie plate.

6 Stir the filling well and spread over the pastry. Cover with the remaining pastry to form a lid and press the edges together firmly to seal. Make a few small cuts across the top, or cut into a lattice pattern.

7 Bake for 30–40 minutes until the pastry is golden. Serve warm or cold.

BAKED APPLES WITH MINCEMEAT

This quintessential British fruit was once thought to have magical powers and, to this day, apples are linked with many English traditions and festivals. Here, they are baked in the oven with a filling of sweetened dried fruit. They are best served straight from the oven, while still puffed up and before they begin to crumple. Serve with custard or cream.

SERVES 4

25g/1oz/2 tbsp butter, plus extra for greasing

4 cooking apples

about 4 tbsp mincemeat (bought, or see page 617)

2 tbsp honey

1 Preheat the oven to 180°C/350°F/gas 4. Butter a shallow ovenproof dish.

2 With an apple corer or a small sharp knife, remove the cores from the apples. Run a sharp knife around the middle of each apple, cutting through the skin but not deep into the flesh. Stand the apples in the dish.

3 Fill the hollow centres of the apples with mincemeat. Drizzle the honey over the top and dot with butter. Add 60ml/4 tbsp water to the dish.

4 Bake for about 45 minutes until soft throughout, and serve at once.

VARIATION

Replace the mincemeat with chopped dried apricots or dates.

POACHED SPICED PEARS

At one time in the history of England, pears were considered by some to be poisonous. Today, the country grows several varieties, particularly in the south-east, East Anglia and the West Midlands. Serve this lightly spiced dish warm or cold, with cream and perhaps some crisp, sweet biscuits for a contrast in texture.

SERVES 4

115g/4oz/½ cup caster (superfine) sugar

grated rind and juice of 1 lemon

½ tsp ground ginger

1 small cinnamon stick

2 whole cloves

4 firm ripe pears

1 Put the sugar in a pan with 300ml/½ pint/1½ cups water, the lemon rind and juice, ginger and spices. Heat, stirring, until the sugar has dissolved.

2 Peel the pears, cut them in half lengthways and remove their cores.

3 Add the pear halves to the pan and bring just to the boil. Cover and simmer gently for about 5 minutes or until the pears are tender, turning them over in the syrup occasionally during cooking. Remove from the heat and leave to cool in the syrup before serving.

VARIATIONS

♦ Omit the spices and instead flavour the water with ginger cordial or elderflower cordial.

♦ Use white wine in place of water.

SUMMER PUDDING

This stunning dessert is an essential feature of the English summer and it is deceptively simple to make. Use a mixture of fresh seasonal soft fruits and a good-quality loaf of white bread. Serve the pudding cold with lashings of thick cream or yogurt.

SERVES 4–6

about 8 x 1cm/½in-thick slices of day-old white bread, with crusts removed

800g/1¾lb mixed berries, such as strawberries, raspberries, blackcurrants, redcurrants and blueberries

50g/2oz/4 tbsp golden caster (superfine) sugar

1 Trim a slice of bread to fit neatly in the base of a 1.2 litre/2 pint bowl, then trim another 5–6 slices to line the sides, making sure the bread stands up above the rim.

2 Place all the fruit in a pan with the sugar. Do not add any water. Cook very gently for 4–5 minutes until the juices begin to run.

3 Allow the mixture to cool, then spoon the berries, and enough of their juices to moisten the fruit, into the bread-lined bowl. Reserve any remaining juice to serve with the pudding.

4 Fold over the excess bread, then cover the fruit with the remaining slices, trimming to fit. Place a small plate or saucer that fits inside the bowl directly on top of the pudding. Weight it down with a 900g/2lb weight, if you have one, or use a couple of full food cans.

5 Chill the pudding in the refrigerator for at least 8 hours or overnight. To serve, run a knife between the pudding and the bowl and turn out onto a plate. Spoon any reserved juices over the top, and serve.

BAKED CHEESECAKE

Cheesecakes made with soft cheese were recorded in England as early as 1265, when the account books of the Countess of Leicester listed 'cheese for tarts'. Cheese tarts were great favourites at medieval summer feasts and fairs. The soft cheese was mixed with egg yolks, sugar and spices, and baked in a pastry 'coffyn'.

SERVES 8–10

675g/1½lb/3 cups low-fat soft white cheese

4 eggs, separated

150g/5oz/⅔ cup caster (superfine) sugar

3 tbsp cornflour (cornstarch)

150ml/¼ pint/⅔ cup sour cream

finely grated rind and juice of ½ lemon

1 tsp vanilla extract

FOR THE PASTRY

225g/8oz/2 cups plain (all-purpose) flour, plus extra for dusting

115g/4oz butter, diced

1 tbsp caster (superfine) sugar

finely grated rind of ½ lemon

1 egg, beaten

FOR THE FRUIT TOPPING

450g/1lb prepared red berry fruits

50g/2oz/4 tbsp caster (superfine) sugar

120ml/4fl oz/½ cup water

1 tbsp arrowroot powder

mint leaves, to decorate

1 To make the pastry, sift the flour into a large mixing bowl. Rub or cut in the butter until the mixture resembles fine breadcrumbs. Stir in the sugar and lemon rind, then add the beaten egg and mix to a dough. Wrap in cling film (plastic wrap) and chill for 30 minutes.

2 Roll out the pastry on a floured surface and use to line a 25cm/10in loose-based fluted flan or quiche tin. Chill for 1 hour. Meanwhile, place the soft white cheese in a fine sieve set over a bowl and leave to drain for 1 hour.

3 Preheat the oven to 200°C/400°F/gas 6. Prick the base of the chilled pastry case all over with a fork, fill it with crumpled foil and bake blind for about 5 minutes. Remove the foil and bake for a further 5 minutes. Remove the pastry case from the oven and lower the oven temperature to 180°C/350°F/gas 4.

4 Put the drained soft cheese in a bowl with the egg yolks and caster sugar and mix together. Blend the cornflour in a cup with a little of the sour cream, then add to the cheese mixture along with the remaining sour cream, the lemon rind and juice, and vanilla. Mix well with a wooden spoon.

5 Whisk the egg whites in a grease-free bowl until stiff, then fold into the cheese mixture, one third at a time. Pour the filling into the pastry case and bake for 1–1¼ hours, or until golden and firm. Switch off the oven and leave the door slightly ajar. Let the cheesecake cool down in the oven, then remove and chill for 2 hours.

6 To make the fruit topping, reserve a few fruits for the garnish, then put the berries, sugar and water into a pan and cook over a low heat until the sugar dissolves and the juices begin to run. Remove the fruit with a slotted spoon and put in a bowl to one side.

7 Mix the arrowroot with a little cold water in a cup. Stir the mixture into the juices in the pan and bring to the boil, stirring constantly. Return the fruit to the pan, mix, then allow to cool.

8 Serve the chilled cheesecake in slices, spooning a little of the fruit topping over each portion. Decorate with mint and fresh berries.

RASPBERRY AND HAZELNUT MERINGUE CAKE

Grace an English summer tea party with a sumptuous meringue cake, full of whipped cream and seasonal berries. Toasted and ground hazelnuts add a nutty flavour to the meringue rounds, which are sandwiched together with fresh cream and raspberries. You can store the baked meringue bases, unfilled, for one week.

SERVES 8

butter, for greasing

150g/5oz/1¼ cups hazelnuts

4 egg whites

200g/7oz/1 cup caster (superfine) sugar

½ tsp vanilla extract

FOR THE FILLING

300ml/1½ pint/1¼ cups whipping cream

700g/1lb8oz raspberries

1 Preheat the oven to 180°C/350°F/gas 4. Grease and line the bases of two 20cm/8in round cake tins or pans with baking parchment.

2 Spread the hazelnuts on a baking sheet and bake for 8 minutes, or until lightly toasted. Leave to cool slightly. Rub the hazelnuts vigorously in a clean dish towel to remove the skins. Reduce the oven temperature to 150°C/300°F/gas 2.

3 Grind the nuts in a food processor, until they are the consistency of coarse sand.

4 Put the egg whites into a clean, grease-free bowl and whisk until they form stiff peaks. Beat in 2 tbsp of the sugar, then, using a plastic spatula, fold in the remaining sugar, a few spoonfuls at a time. Fold in the vanilla and hazelnuts.

5 Divide the mixture between the cake tins and smooth the top level. Bake for 1¼ hours until firm.

6 Leave to cool in the tin for 5 minutes, then run a knife around the inside edge of the tins to loosen the meringues. Turn out to go cold on a wire rack.

7 For the filling, whip the cream. Spread half on one cake round and top with half the raspberries. Top with the other cake round. Spread the remaining cream on top and arrange the rest of the raspberries over the surface. Chill for 1 hour before serving.

FRUIT TRIFLE

Everyone's favourite, trifle is a classic English dessert. The earliest trifles were creamy confections rather like fools, but in the 18th century the dish took the form familiar today, with layers of sponge soaked in wine or sherry, topped with syllabub or whipped cream.

SERVES 6–8

15–18cm/6–7in plain sponge cake

225g/8oz/¾ cup raspberry jam

150ml/¼ pint/⅔ cup medium or sweet sherry

450g/1lb ripe fruit, such as plums, bananas and berries, prepared and sliced

300ml/½ pint/1¼ cups whipping cream

toasted flaked (sliced) almonds, or glacé (candied) cherries and angelica (optional), to decorate

FOR THE CUSTARD

450ml/¾ pint/scant 2 cups full fat (whole) milk

1 vanilla pod (bean)

3 eggs

25g/1oz/2 tbsp caster (superfine) sugar

1 To make the custard, put the milk into a pan with the vanilla pod, split along its length, and bring almost to the boil. Remove from the heat. Leave to cool a little while you whisk the eggs and sugar together lightly. Remove the vanilla pod from the milk and gradually whisk the milk into the egg mixture.

2 Rinse out the pan with cold water and return the mixture to it. (Alternatively, use a double boiler, or a bowl over a pan of boiling water.) Stir over a low heat until it thickens enough to coat the back of a wooden spoon; do not allow the custard to boil. Turn the custard into a bowl, cover and set aside while you assemble the trifle.

3 Halve the sponge cake horizontally, spread with the raspberry jam and sandwich together. Cut into slices and use to line the bottom and lower sides of a large glass serving bowl.

4 Sprinkle the sponge cake with the sherry. Spread the fruit over the sponge in an even layer. Pour the custard on top, cover with clear film (plastic wrap) to prevent a skin forming, and leave to cool and set. Chill until required.

5 To serve, whip the cream and spread it over the custard. Decorate with the almonds, cherries and angelica, if using.

FRUIT AND WINE JELLY

In 17th-century England, when making jelly was a lengthy process that involved the boiling of calf's hoof, hartshorn or isinglass, it was a centrepiece at high-class banquets. Though jelly now tends to be associated with children's parties, made from the packet, it can also be a light and elegant dessert. Allow plenty of time for sieving the fruit and cooling the jelly.

SERVES 6

600g/1½lb fresh raspberries

150g/5oz/¾ cup white sugar

100ml/3½fl oz/scant ½ cup water

5 sheets of gelatine (6 if the jelly is to be set in a mould and turned out)

300ml/½ pint/1¼ cups medium-dry white wine

mint leaf, for garnish (optional)

1 Retaining a few for garnish, put the raspberries and sugar in a pan with the water and heat gently until the fruit releases its juices and becomes very soft, and the sugar has dissolved.

2 Remove the pan from the heat, tip the mixture into a fine nylon sieve or jelly bag over a large bowl, and leave to strain – this will take some time but do not squeeze the fruit, as the resulting juice may be cloudy.

3 When the juice from the fruit has drained into the bowl, make it up to 600ml/1 pint/2½ cups with more water if necessary. Soak the gelatine in cold water for about 5 minutes to soften it.

4 Heat half the juice until very hot but not quite boiling. Remove from the heat. Squeeze the softened gelatine to remove excess water, then stir it into the hot juice until dissolved. Stir in any remaining raspberry juice, and the wine.

5 Pour into stemmed glasses and chill until set. Alternatively, set the jelly in a wetted mould and turn out onto a pretty plate for serving. Garnish with the raspberries and fresh mint if you have any.

COOK'S TIP

Instead of making your own fruit juice, use a carton of juice, such as mango, cranberry or orange, sweetened to taste.

DEVONSHIRE JUNKET

Junkets, or curds, were eaten by the medieval nobility and became universally popular in Tudor England. The name comes from a Norman word, *jonquette*, meaning 'cream cheese'. Junket featured so often at fairs held on religious holidays that the holidays themselves became known as 'junketing days'. Junket remained popular up until the 18th century, when the much easier and far less time-consuming cream-based syllabubs and fools came into vogue, although junket was still being sold in glasses or mugs from London street stalls as late as the 19th century. Junket is also known as damask cream, perhaps because of its smooth, silky consistency.

SERVES 4

600ml/1 pint/2½ cups full fat (whole) milk

40g/1½oz/3 tbsp caster (superfine) sugar

several drops of edible rosewater

2 tsp rennet

60ml/4 tbsp double (heavy) cream

sugared rose petals, to decorate (optional)

1 Gently heat the milk with 2 tbsp of the sugar, stirring, until the sugar has dissolved and the temperature reaches body heat (37°C/98.4°F).

2 Remove from the heat and stir in rosewater to taste, then the rennet.

3 Pour the junket into serving glasses and leave undisturbed at room temperature for 2–3 hours, until set. Do not move it during this time; otherwise, it will separate into curds and whey.

4 Stir the remaining sugar into the cream, then carefully spoon the mixture over the surface of the set junket. Decorate with sugared rose petals, if you wish.

COOK'S TIP

You must use fresh milk for junket; it will not set properly if homogenised or UHT milk is used. Whole milk gives a better flavour.

ALMOND AND ROSEWATER BLANCMANGE

In the Middle Ages, blancmange (literally 'white food') was a banqueting dish that contained chicken and rice as well as almonds and sugar. Later, arrowroot and cornflour were used as thickeners (and indeed are often still used). During Victoria's reign, the dessert began to be set with gelatine in fancy moulds and became very fashionable.

SERVES 6

5 sheets of gelatine

1 lemon

450ml/¾ pint/1⅔ cups milk

115g/4oz/½ cup caster (superfine) sugar

450ml/¾ pint/scant 2 cups single (light) cream

85g/3oz/¾ cup ground almonds

about 1 tsp edible rosewater

fresh or sugared rose petals, to decorate (optional)

1 Soak the gelatine leaves in cold water for about 5 minutes to soften them.

2 Thinly pare strips of rind from the lemon, taking care not to include the white pith. Heat the milk gently with the lemon rind until it just comes to the boil. Discard the rind.

3 Lift the softened sheets of gelatine out of the soaking water, squeezing out the excess. Stir the gelatine into the hot milk until dissolved. Stir in the sugar until it has dissolved. Add the cream, almonds and rosewater to taste, and mix well.

4 Pour into one large or six individual wetted moulds, put into the refrigerator and chill until completely set.

5 Turn the blancmange out of its mould(s) just before serving. Decorate with rose petals if you wish.

VARIATIONS

- Omit the lemon rind and add 1 tsp vanilla extract at step 3.
- Instead of rosewater, use your favourite liqueur.

GOOSEBERRY AND ELDERFLOWER FOOL

Little can be simpler than swirling cooked fresh fruit into whipped cream. Stewed rhubarb is another favourite seasonal flavour to use in this recipe. Be sure to serve fool in pretty glasses or dishes, accompanied by crisp biscuits to add a contrast of texture.

SERVES 4

500g/1¼lb gooseberries

300ml/½ pint/1¼ cups double (heavy) cream

about 115g/4oz/1 cup icing (confectioner's) sugar, to taste

2 tbsp elderflower cordial

mint sprigs, to decorate

crisp sweet biscuits, to serve

1 Place the gooseberries in a heavy saucepan, cover and cook over a low heat, shaking the pan occasionally, until tender. Tip the gooseberries into a bowl, crush them with a fork or potato masher, then leave to cool completely.

2 Whip the cream until soft peaks form, then fold in half the crushed fruit. Add sugar and elderflower cordial to taste. Sweeten the remaining fruit to taste.

3 Layer the cream mixture and the crushed gooseberries in dessert dishes or tall glasses, then cover and chill until ready to serve. Decorate the fool with mint sprigs and serve with crisp sweet biscuits.

VARIATIONS

• When elderflowers are in season, cook 2–3 elderflower heads with the gooseberries and omit the elderflower cordial.

• For rhubarb fool, use squeezed orange juice in place of elderflower cordial.

ETON MESS

The 'mess' consists of whipped cream, crushed meringue and sliced or mashed strawberries, all mixed together before serving. This pudding gets its name from the famous public school, Eton College, where it is served at the annual picnic on 4th June.

SERVES 4

450g/1lb ripe strawberries

45ml/3 tbsp elderflower cordial or orange liqueur

300ml/½ pint/1¼ cups double (heavy) cream

4 meringues or meringue baskets

1 Remove the green hulls from the strawberries and slice the fruit into a bowl, reserving a few for decoration.

2 Sprinkle with the elderflower cordial or fruit liqueur. Cover the bowl and chill for about 2 hours.

3 Whip the cream until soft peaks form. Crush the meringue into small pieces. Add the fruit and most of the meringue to the cream and fold in lightly.

4 Spoon into serving dishes and chill until required. Before serving, decorate with the reserved strawberries and meringue pieces.

COOK'S TIPS

◆ Serve Eton mess just as it is, or accompanied by crisp sweet biscuits.

◆ This is a useful recipe to know if you are trying to make a large meringue and it cracks, as you can just break it up completely and serve it this way. See the second Cook's Tip on page 461 for a simple meringue method.

◆ Make the dish with other soft fruit if you like, such as lightly crushed raspberries or blackcurrants.

SYLLABUB

Syllabub is a rich and creamy alcoholic concoction that dates back to Tudor times. It was reputed to have first been made by milking a cow directly into a bowl of sweetened cider, ale or wine. However, some food historians are sceptical about this; modern attempts to recreate this method resulted in a very unpleasant concoction. In the late 17th century, it was possible to purchase a special wooden 'cow', from which to squirt the milk and cream from a height into a bowl to produce a frothy top with a clear liquid underneath. As time passed cream replaced milk, and syllabub became thicker and was eaten with a spoon. Serve with sponge fingers or crisp biscuits.

SERVES 6

1 orange
65g/2½oz/5 tbsp caster (superfine) sugar
60ml/4 tbsp medium-dry sherry
300ml/½ pint/1½ cups double (heavy) cream
strips of crystallised orange, to decorate

1 Finely grate ½ tsp rind from the orange, then squeeze out all of its juice.

2 Put the orange rind and juice, sugar and sherry into a large bowl and stir until the sugar is completely dissolved.

3 Stir in the cream. Whip the mixture until it is thick and soft peaks form.

4 Spoon the syllabub into wine glasses. Chill the glasses of syllabub until ready to serve, then decorate with strips of crystallised orange.

COOK'S TIPS

◆ Syllabub is lovely spooned over a bowl of fresh soft fruit such as strawberries, apricots, raspberries or blackberries.

◆ Add a pinch of ground cinnamon to the mixture in step 2.

BURNT CREAM

Now more elegantly known as crème brûlée, this classic sweet appears on many an English restaurant menu – and the contrast between the crunchy topping and the smooth luxuriously creamy custard underneath it is irresistible.

SERVES 6

4 egg yolks

1 tbsp plus 115–150g/ 4–5oz/½–⅔ cup caster (superfine) sugar

600ml/1 pint/2½ cups double (heavy) cream

1 vanilla pod (bean), or a few drops of vanilla extract

1 In a bowl, mix the yolks well with the 1 tbsp sugar.

2 Put the cream and vanilla pod, if using, in a heavy-based pan, bring up to scalding point, remove the pod and pour the hot cream onto the yolks, blending well with a whisk. Add the vanilla extract, if using.

3 Set the bowl over a pan of hot water, or transfer to a double boiler, and cook carefully, stirring or whisking constantly, until the custard mixture thickens. Do not allow it to boil.

4 Strain the custard into a gratin dish, or divide it among six ramekins. Place the dish or ramekins in a deep roasting tin and pour in enough hot water to come halfway up the sides. Bake in the oven at 140°C/275°F/gas 1 for 25–35 minutes, until just set but still a bit wobbly in the middle.

5 Remove from the water and leave to cool, then chill in the fridge for 2–3 hours.

6 To finish, preheat the grill or broiler. Sprinkle the custard evenly with the remaining sugar so that it is completely covered, but not too thick. Grill as close as possible to the heat for 2–3 minutes, or until the sugar melts and caramelises.

7 Remove from the heat and leave in a cold place for up to 2–3 hours before serving.

CLASSIC VANILLA ICE CREAM

Nothing beats the creamy simplicity of true vanilla ice cream, the food of summertime and childhood. A dairy classic – once you've tried this luxurious home-made version, there's no going back.

SERVES 4

1 vanilla pod (bean)

300ml/½ pint/1¼ cups full fat (whole) milk

4 egg yolks

75g/3oz/⅓ cup caster (superfine) sugar

1 tsp cornflour (cornstarch)

300ml/½ pint/1¼ cups double (heavy) cream

1 Slit the vanilla pod lengthways. Pour the milk into a heavy-based pan, add the vanilla pod and bring to the boil. Remove from the heat and leave for 15 minutes.

2 Hold the pod over the pan and, with a small knife, scrape the seeds into the milk. Return the pan to the heat and bring back to the boil.

3 Whisk the egg yolks, sugar and cornflour in a bowl until thick and foamy. Gradually pour on the hot milk, whisking constantly. Return the mixture to the pan and cook over a gentle heat, stirring all the time. When the custard thickens and is smooth, pour it back into the bowl. Cover with cling film (plastic wrap) and set aside to cool.

4 Whip the cream until it has thickened but still falls from a spoon. Fold it into the custard.

5 If you are using an ice-cream maker, pour in the mixture and churn for 20–30 minutes or until it holds its shape. Transfer the ice cream to a freezerproof container and freeze until firm.

6 If you don't have an ice-cream maker, freeze the mixture in a plastic tub or similar freezerproof container for 1–2 hours until beginning to set around the edges. Tip into a bowl or food processor and beat until smooth. Return to the freezer and beat again after another 2 hours, then return to the container. Cover and freeze until firm enough to scoop.

7 To serve, scoop into dishes, bowls – or bought cones.

FRESH STRAWBERRY ICE CREAM

Aside from vanilla (chocolate was a relative latecomer), a summer ice cream doesn't get more traditional than fresh strawberry. You can make it by hand if you freeze it over a period of several hours, whisking it every hour or so, but it is easier in an ice-cream maker.

SERVES 6

300ml/½ pint/1¼ cups full fat (whole) milk

1 vanilla pod (bean)

3 large egg yolks

225g/8oz/1½–2 cups strawberries

juice of ½ lemon

75g/3oz/¾ cup icing (confectioner's) sugar

300ml/½ pint/1¼ cups double (heavy) cream

1 Pour the milk into a heavy-based pan, add the vanilla pod and bring to the boil over a low heat. Remove from the heat. Leave for 15 minutes, then remove the vanilla pod. Strain the warm milk into a bowl containing the egg yolks; whisk well.

2 Return the mixture to the clean pan and heat, stirring, until the custard just coats the back of the spoon. Pour the custard into a bowl, cover with cling film (plastic wrap) and set aside to cool.

3 Meanwhile, purée the strawberries with the lemon juice in a food processor or blender. Use a spoon to press the strawberry purée through a strainer into a bowl. Stir in the icing sugar and set aside.

4 Whip the cream to soft peaks, then gently but thoroughly fold it into the custard with the strawberry purée.

5 If you are using an ice-cream maker, pour in the mixture and churn for 20–30 minutes or until it holds its shape. Transfer the ice cream to a freezerproof container and freeze until firm.

6 If you don't have an ice-cream maker, freeze the mixture in a plastic tub or similar freezerproof container for 1–2 hours until beginning to set around the edges. Tip into a bowl or food processor and beat until smooth. Return to the freezer and beat again after another 2 hours, then return to the container. Cover and freeze until firm enough to scoop.

BROWN BREAD ICE CREAM

This was popular at the end of the 18th century and became a Victorian favourite. It was reputed to be Queen Victoria's preferred ice cream. The classic ice cream is flecked with tiny clusters of crisp, crunchy, caramelised brown breadcrumbs, which give a lovely praline flavour. It's best to use coarse-textured wholemeal (wholewheat) bread for this ice cream.

SERVES 4–6

4 egg yolks

75g/3oz/⅓ cup caster (superfine) sugar

1 tsp cornflour (cornstarch)

300ml/½ pint/1¼ cups milk

40g/1½oz/3 tbsp butter

75g/3oz/1½ cups fresh brown breadcrumbs

50g/2oz/3 tbsp soft light brown sugar

1 tsp vanilla extract

300ml/½ pint/1¼ cups double (heavy) cream

1 Whisk the egg yolks, sugar and cornflour in a bowl until thick and pale. Bring the milk to the boil in a heavy-based pan, then gradually pour it onto the egg yolk mixture, whisking constantly.

2 Return the mixture to the pan. Heat gently, stirring until thick. Pour back into the bowl, leave to cool, then chill.

3 Melt the butter in a frying pan. Add the breadcrumbs, and stir until they are evenly coated in the butter. Sprinkle the sugar over. Fry for 4–5 minutes, stirring until lightly browned. Remove from the heat and leave until cool and crisp.

4 Add the vanilla extract to the custard and mix well. Whip the cream until thick, then fold into the custard. Transfer to a freezerproof container. Freeze for 4 hours, beating once.

5 Break up the breadcrumbs with your fingers. Beat the ice cream briefly, then stir in the breadcrumbs. Return to the freezer until firm enough to scoop.

MINTED EARL GREY SORBET

Originally served in Georgian times at grand summer balls, this refreshing, slightly sharp sorbet is perfect for a lazy afternoon in the garden. It can be made as easily with tea bags as tea leaves. Only the very wealthy could afford ices and sorbets: James I had two snow pits (as they were known) built at Greenwich, and another was made at Hampton Court in 1625. Charles I had two ice houses built in St James's Park in 1660 and this was quickly copied by the nobility, who had ice houses built at their country estates – a practice which continued into the 18th and 19th centuries.

SERVES 6

200g/7oz/1 cup caster
(superfine) sugar

1 lemon, well scrubbed

3 tbsp Earl Grey tea leaves

1 egg white

2 tbsp chopped fresh mint leaves,
plus mint sprigs, to decorate

1 In a pan, bring the caster sugar and 300ml/½ pint/1¼ cups of water to the boil, stirring until the sugar has dissolved.

2 Pare the rind from the lemon directly into the pan of syrup. Simmer for 2 minutes, then pour into a bowl. Cool, then chill.

3 Put the tea into a pan and pour on 450ml/¾ pint/2 cups of boiling water. Cover and leave to stand for 5 minutes, then strain into a freezerproof container. Cool, then chill.

4 Strain in the chilled sugar syrup. Mix well. Freeze for 4 hours.

5 Lightly whisk the egg white until just frothy.

6 Transfer the ice to a bowl or food processor. Using an electric whisk or a food processor, beat the ice until smooth, then fold in the egg white and the chopped mint.

7 Spoon back into the tub and freeze for another 4 hours until firm. Serve in scoops, decorated with a few sprigs of mint.

CUSTARD

No pudding chapter in an English cookbook can overlook proper home-made custard, which is served hot or cold, with sponges, puddings, crumbles and pies. (It is also the basis for a very rich ice cream, which is essentially a frozen custard enriched with cream.) The secret for success is patience; don't try to hurry the cooking by raising the heat.

SERVES 4

450ml/¾ pint/2 cups milk

1 vanilla pod (bean), split in half

4 egg yolks

50g/2oz/4 tbsp caster (superfine) sugar, plus extra for sprinkling

1 Put the milk in a heavy-based saucepan. Hold the vanilla pod over the pan and scrape out the tiny black seeds into the milk. Add the split pod to the milk.

2 Heat the milk until bubbles appear round the edge. Remove from the heat, cover and set aside to infuse for 10 minutes. Remove the split vanilla pod.

3 In a bowl, lightly beat the egg yolks with the sugar until smoothly blended and creamy. Gradually add the hot milk to the egg yolks, stirring constantly.

4 Pour the mixture into the top of a double boiler or a bowl set over a saucepan containing hot water. Put on a moderately low heat, so the water stays below the boil.

5 Cook, stirring constantly, for 10–12 minutes or until the custard thickens to a creamy consistency that coats the spoon. Immediately remove the pan of custard from over the pan of hot water.

6 Strain the custard into a bowl. If using cold, sprinkle a little caster sugar over the surface of the custard to help prevent a skin from forming. Set the bowl in a container of iced water and leave to cool.

COOK'S TIPS

◆ If the custard gets too hot and starts to curdle, remove it from the heat immediately and pour it into a bowl. Whisk vigorously for 2–3 seconds or until smooth. Then pour it back into the pan and continue cooking.

◆ You can use the leftover egg whites to make meringues! Heat the oven to 140°C/275°F/gas 2. Whip the egg whites until they are very stiff, then fold in 200g/7oz/1 cup caster (superfine) sugar and a little vanilla extract. Pipe rosettes onto a baking tray lined with baking parchment. Bake in the oven for 1 hour, turning the heat down to 120°C/248°F/gas ½ after 30 minutes. Remove from the oven – they should peel easily away from the parchment – and cool on a wire rack.

TEATIME TREATS

Afternoon tea became an English ritual in the 19th century and is still served in many homes, hotels and teashops. It can be a simple affair or an elaborate spread with an opportunity to use the best china. A pot of tea may be accompanied by a home-made biscuit, or there may be a selection of tea infusions with a larger array of savoury and sweet goodies on offer — sandwiches, scones, buns, pastries, tarts and cakes.

PICTURED *Pretty china can be as much a feature of the traditional teatime setting as the food that is served.*

ANCHOVY TOASTS

The Victorians loved anchovies in all kinds of dishes. In the late 19th century it became fashionable to serve anchovy butter spread on fried bread and topped with Cornish clotted cream – but simple toast fingers are more suited to modern tastes.

SERVES 4–6

50g/2oz can of anchovy fillets in olive oil, well drained
75g/3oz/6 tbsp soft unsalted butter
1 tbsp finely chopped fresh parsley
generous squeeze of lemon juice
ground black pepper
4–6 slices of bread

1 Using a mortar and pestle, crush the anchovies to make a thick paste. Add the butter, parsley and lemon juice and mix well, seasoning to taste with black pepper. (Alternatively, put all the ingredients into a blender or processor and blend to a smooth paste.) Cover and chill until required.

2 Just before serving, toast the bread on both sides. Spread the anchovy butter on the hot toast, cut into fingers and serve immediately.

SAUSAGE ROLLS

Dainty sausage rolls rank high in the league of popular teatime and party foods. They are delicious when homemade, particularly if quality butcher's sausagemeat is used to fill them. Serve them hot or cold. They also make an ideal addition to a picnic or packed lunch.

MAKES ABOUT 16

175g/6oz/1½ cups plain (all-purpose) flour, plus extra for dusting
pinch of salt
40g/1½oz/3 tbsp lard, diced
40g/1½oz/3 tbsp butter, diced
250g/9oz pork sausagemeat
beaten egg, to glaze

1 To make the pastry, sift the flour and salt into a bowl and add the lard and butter. Rub the fats into the flour until the mixture resembles fine crumbs. Stir in about 45ml/3 tbsp cold water until the mixture can be gathered into a smooth ball of dough. Wrap in cling film (plastic wrap) and chill for 30 minutes.

2 Preheat the oven to 190°C/375°F/gas 5. Roll out the pastry on a lightly floured surface to make a rectangle about 30cm/12in long and 10cm/4in wide. Cut lengthways into two long strips.

3 Divide the sausagemeat into two pieces and, on a lightly floured surface, shape each into a long roll the same length as the pastry. Lay a roll on each strip of pastry. Brush the pastry edges with water and fold them over the meat, pressing together to seal them well.

4 Turn the rolls over and, with the seam side down, brush with beaten egg. Cut each roll into eight equal pieces and place on a baking sheet. Bake in the hot oven for 30 minutes until crisp and golden brown. Cool on a wire rack.

CUCUMBER SANDWICHES

Think of Edwardian England and invariably afternoon tea with dainty cucumber sandwiches comes to mind. Cucumbers were first grown in English hothouses in the 16th century, just waiting for the sandwich to be invented two hundred years later.

SERVES 4

½ cucumber
salt and ground black pepper
soft unsalted butter
8 slices of white bread

1 Peel the cucumber and cut it into thin slices. Sprinkle with salt, place in a colander and leave for about 20 minutes to drain.

2 Butter all the slices of bread on one side. Lay the cucumber over four slices of bread and sprinkle with pepper.

3 Top with the remaining bread. Press down lightly and trim off the crusts.

4 Cut the sandwiches into fingers, squares or triangles. Serve immediately.

CHEESE STRAWS

Cheese-flavoured pastries became popular when it was customary (for gentlemen, particularly) to eat a small savoury at the end of a long, sophisticated meal. Now we are more likely to eat cheese straws as an appetiser with pre-dinner drinks.

MAKES ABOUT 10

75g/3oz/¾ cup plain (all-purpose) flour, plus extra for dusting
40g/1½oz/3 tbsp butter, diced
salt and ground black pepper
40g/1½oz mature (strong) hard cheese, such as Cheddar, finely grated
1 egg
1 tsp ready-made mustard

1 Preheat the oven to 180°C/350°F/gas 4. Line a baking sheet with baking parchment.

2 Sift the flour into a bowl and rub the butter into the flour until the mixture resembles fine crumbs. Add seasoning and stir in the cheese.

3 Lightly beat the egg with the mustard. Add half the egg to the flour, stirring in well until the mixture can be gathered into a smooth ball of dough.

4 Roll the dough out on a lightly floured surface to make a square measuring about 15cm/6in. Cut into ten equal lengths. Place on the baking sheet and brush with the remaining egg.

5 Put into the hot oven and cook for about 12 minutes until golden brown. Transfer to a wire rack and serve warm.

SCONES WITH JAM AND CREAM

For many people, English afternoon tea is not the same without a plate of scones. They are perfect served with thick cream and a red jam, such as strawberry or raspberry. It's important that the scones are freshly baked, but they are quick and easy to make.

MAKES ABOUT 12

350g/12oz/3 cups self-raising (self-rising) flour, or 350g/12oz/3 cups plain (all-purpose) flour and 2 tsp baking powder, plus extra flour for dusting

¼ tsp salt

75g/3oz/⅓ cup butter, chilled and cut into small cubes

3 tbsp caster (superfine) sugar

7.5ml/½ tbsp lemon juice

about 175ml/6fl oz/¾ pint milk, plus extra to glaze

jam and whipped or clotted cream, to serve

1 Preheat the oven to 220°C/425°F/gas 7. Sift the flour, baking powder (if using) and salt into a bowl, and stir to mix. Rub the butter lightly into the flour with your fingertips until the mixture resembles fine, even-textured breadcrumbs. Stir in the sugar.

2 Whisk the lemon juice into the milk and leave for about 1 minute to thicken slightly, then pour this buttermilk into the flour mixture and mix quickly to make a soft but pliable dough. The softer it is, the lighter the resulting scones will be, but if it is too sticky they will spread during baking and lose their shape.

3 Knead the dough briefly, then roll it out on a lightly floured surface to a thickness of at least 2.5cm/1in. Using a 5cm/2in biscuit cutter, and dipping it into flour each time, stamp out 12 rounds. Place these on a floured baking sheet. Re-roll trimmings to cut more rounds.

4 Brush the tops of the scones with a little milk, then put into the hot oven and cook for about 10–15 minutes, or until risen and golden.

5 Remove from the oven and wrap the scones in a clean dish towel to keep them warm and soft until ready to eat. Eat the scones with plenty of jam and a generous dollop of cream.

VARIATION

To make savoury cheese scones, omit the sugar and add 115g/4oz/1 cup of grated Cheddar cheese to the dough.

DROP SCONES

Thin, light and spongy, drop scones are also known as girdlecakes, griddlecakes and Scotch pancakes. They can be served hot or cold with butter and honey, syrup or jam. They are good with whipped cream and fresh soft fruit too.

MAKES 8–10

115g/4oz/1 cup plain
(all-purpose) flour

1 tsp bicarbonate of soda
(baking soda)

1 tsp cream of tartar

25g/1oz/2 tbsp butter,
plus extra for greasing

1 egg, beaten

about 150ml/¼ pint/⅔ cup milk

butter and clear honey, to serve

1 Sift the flour, bicarbonate of soda and cream of tartar into a mixing bowl. Rub the butter into the flour until the mixture resembles fine breadcrumbs.

2 Make a well in the centre of the flour mixture, then stir in the egg. Stir in the milk a little at a time, adding enough to give a thick creamy consistency.

3 Lightly grease a griddle pan or heavy frying pan, and heat it.

4 Cook in batches. Drop three or four even spoonfuls of the mixture, spaced slightly apart, on the pan. Cook over a medium heat for 2–3 minutes, until bubbles rise to the surface and burst.

5 Turn the scones over and cook for a further 2–3 minutes on the other side, until golden underneath. Place the cooked scones between the folds of a clean dish towel while cooking the remaining batter. Serve warm, with butter and honey.

COOK'S TIP

Placing the freshly cooked drop scones in a clean folded dish towel keeps them soft, warm and moist. Serve them like this and invite your guests to help themselves.

SHROVE TUESDAY PANCAKES

Shrove Tuesday (the day before Ash Wednesday, the start of Lent) is the traditional day for enjoying pancakes. The custom of eating pancakes is very old – the term 'pancake' dates back to the 15th century. Along with other animal products, eggs and fat were not allowed during Lent and pancakes were a quick and tasty way to use up surplus eggs. Traditionally served spread with salty butter and sugar, and a squeeze of lemon juice, you could also top them with a few currants or other fruit.

MAKES 12–14

150ml/¼ pint/⅔ cup milk

150ml/¼ pint/⅔ cup water

225g/8oz/2 cups plain (all-purpose) flour

2 eggs

25g/1oz/2 tbsp butter, plus extra for greasing

lemon wedges, sugar, butter, and currants if liked, to serve

1 Combine the milk and water. Sift the flour into a large bowl. Make a well in the centre and break the eggs into it. With a whisk, stir in the eggs, gradually adding the milk mixture to make a smooth pouring batter.

2 Melt the butter and stir in with the whisk. Leave the batter to stand for 30 minutes and stir well before using

3 Preheat a heavy frying pan over medium heat. Lightly butter the hot surface and add a large spoonful of batter to make a pancake about 15–20cm/6–8in across. Cook for a minute or so until the underside is golden brown.

4 With a wide spatula, carefully flip the pancake over and briefly cook the second side until golden brown and set. Lift off and keep warm. Repeat with the remaining batter.

COOK'S TIP

This batter can be used to make thin, lacy pancakes by thinning it with a little extra milk, so a smaller spoonful of mixture spreads out further on the hot surface.

SUFFOLK BUNS

Caraway seeds were once a popular ingredient of breads, cakes and sweet confections, and were often chewed to sweeten the breath. Farmers traditionally gave seed cakes and buns to their labourers at the end of wheat sowing, particularly in the south-east of England.

MAKES ABOUT 12

350g/12oz/3 cups plain (all-purpose) flour, plus extra for dusting

115g/4oz/⅔ cup ground rice or semolina

2 tsp baking powder

115g/4oz/½ cup butter

75g/3oz/½ cup caster (superfine) sugar, plus extra for sprinkling

2 tbsp caraway seeds

2 eggs

about 75ml/5 tbsp milk

1 Preheat the oven to 200°C/400°F/gas 6. Line a baking sheet with baking parchment. Sift the flour, ground rice and baking powder together into a large mixing bowl.

2 Add the butter and, with your fingertips, rub it into the flour until the mixture resembles fine breadcrumbs. Stir the sugar and caraway seeds into the flour mixture.

3 Lightly beat the eggs and stir them into the flour mixture, together with sufficient milk to enable you to gather the mixture into a ball of soft dough. Transfer to a lightly floured surface.

4 Roll the dough out to about 2.5cm/1in thick. Using a 5cm/2in biscuit cutter, cut into rounds, gathering up the offcuts and re-rolling to make more until it's used up.

5 Arrange the rounds on the lined baking sheet, setting them quite close together so they support each other as they rise.

6 Put into the hot oven and cook for 15–20 minutes until risen and golden brown. Transfer to a wire rack and dust with caster sugar. Leave to cool.

COOK'S TIP

If preferred, replace the caraway seeds with 50g/2oz dried fruit, such as raisins or finely chopped apricots.

NEWCASTLE SINGIN' HINNIES

In Tyneside, 'hinny' is a term of endearment for friends or children, but these hinnies are thin, scone-like little cakes and 'singin' refers to the sound they make as they cook on the hot buttered griddle. Serve them warm, split and spread with butter.

MAKES ABOUT 20

400g/14oz/3½ cups self-raising (self-rising) flour, plus extra for dusting

1½ tsp baking powder

1 tsp salt

50g/2oz/4 tbsp butter, diced, plus extra for greasing

50g/2oz/4 tbsp lard, diced

50g/2oz/4 tbsp caster (superfine) sugar

75g/3oz/½ cup currants, raisins or sultanas (golden raisins)

about 150ml/¼ pint/⅔ cup milk

1 Sift the flour, baking powder and salt into a large bowl. Add the butter and lard and, with your fingertips, rub them into the flour until the mixture resembles fine breadcrumbs.

2 Stir in the sugar and dried fruit. Add the milk and, with a flat-bladed knife, stir the mixture until it can be gathered into a ball of soft dough.

3 Transfer to a lightly floured surface and roll out to about 5mm/¼in thick. With a 7.5cm/3in cutter, cut into rounds, gathering up the offcuts and re-rolling to make more.

4 Heat a heavy frying pan or griddle. Rub with butter and cook the scones in batches for 3–4 minutes on each side until well browned. Lift off and keep warm until all are cooked.

VARIATION

Instead of making small cakes, try cooking the dough in a large, pan-sized circle, cutting it into wedges first to facilitate easy turning.

SHROPSHIRE SOUL CAKES

These little cakes were served on All Souls' Day (2nd November), when it was customary to go 'souling' or singing prayers for the dead. In return, the singers received a soul cake. The original recipe would have included plain flour, but self-raising produces a lighter result.

MAKES ABOUT 20

450g/1lb/4 cups self-raising (self-rising) flour, plus extra for dusting

1 tsp ground mixed (apple pie) spice

½ tsp ground ginger

175g/6oz/¾ cup soft butter, plus extra for greasing

175g/6oz/¾ cup caster (superfine) sugar, plus extra for sprinkling

2 eggs, lightly beaten

50g/2oz/⅓ cup currants, raisins or sultanas (golden raisins)

about 30ml/2 tbsp milk

1 Preheat the oven to 180°C/350°F/gas 4. Lightly grease two baking sheets or line with baking parchment.

2 Sift the flour and spices into a bowl, and set aside. In another large bowl, beat the butter with the sugar until the mixture is light, pale and fluffy.

3 Gradually beat the eggs into the mixture. Fold in the flour mixture and the dried fruit, then add sufficient warm milk to bind the mixture and gather it up into a ball of soft dough.

4 Transfer to a lightly floured surface and roll out to about 5mm/¼in thick. With a floured 7.5cm/3in cutter, cut into rounds, gathering up the offcuts and re-rolling to make more.

5 Arrange the cakes on the prepared baking sheets. Prick the surface of the cakes lightly with a fork; then, with the back of a knife, mark a deep cross on top of each.

6 Put the cakes into the hot oven and cook for about 15 minutes until risen and golden brown.

7 Sprinkle the cooked cakes with a little caster sugar and then transfer to a wire rack to cool.

YORKSHIRE FAT RASCALS

These delicious teacakes from the north of England are a cross between a scone and a rock cake and are really simple to make. They would originally have been baked in a small pot oven standing over an open fire. Serve them warm or cold, just as they are or with butter.

MAKES 10

350g/12oz/3 cups self-raising (self-rising) flour

175g/6oz/¾ cup butter, diced

115g/4oz/½ cup caster (superfine) sugar

75g/3oz/½ cup mixed currants, raisins and sultanas (golden raisins)

25g/1oz/1½ tbsp chopped mixed peel

50g/2oz/⅓ cup glacé (candied) cherries

50g/2oz/⅓ cup blanched almonds, roughly chopped

1 egg

about 75ml/5 tbsp milk

1 Preheat the oven to 200°C/400°F/gas 6. Line a baking sheet with baking parchment.

2 Sift the flour into a large bowl. Add the butter and, with your fingertips, rub it into the flour until the mixture resembles fine breadcrumbs (alternatively, whizz the ingredients briefly in a food processor).

3 Stir in the sugar, dried fruit, peel, cherries and almonds.

4 Lightly beat the egg and stir into the flour mixture with sufficient milk to gather the mixture into a ball of dough.

5 With lightly floured hands, divide the dough into ten balls, press them into rough circles about 2cm/¾in thick and arrange on the prepared baking sheet.

6 Cook for 15–20 minutes until risen and golden brown. Transfer to a wire rack to cool.

MAIDS OF HONOUR

These little delicacies were allegedly being enjoyed by Anne Boleyn's maids of honour when Henry VIII first met her in Richmond Palace in Surrey, and he is said to have named them. Originally they would have been made with strained curds, made by adding rennet to milk.

MAKES 12

250g/9oz ready-made puff pastry, thawed if frozen

a little flour for dusting

250g/9oz/1¼ cups curd (farmer's) cheese

4 tbsp ground almonds

3 tbsp caster (superfine) sugar

finely grated rind of 1 small lemon

2 eggs

15g/½oz/1½ tbsp butter, melted

icing (confectioner's) sugar, to dust

1 Preheat the oven to 200°C/400°F/gas 6. Grease a 12-hole tart tin or bun tray.

2 Roll out the puff pastry very thinly on a lightly floured surface and, using a 7.5cm/3in cutter, cut out 12 circles. Press the pastry circles into the prepared tray and prick well with a fork. Chill while you make the filling.

3 Put the curd cheese into a bowl and add the almonds, sugar and lemon rind. Lightly beat the eggs with the butter and add to the cheese mixture. Mix well.

4 Spoon the mixture into the pastry cases. Bake for about 20 minutes, until the pastry is well risen and the filling is puffed up, golden brown and just firm to the touch.

5 Transfer to a wire rack (the filling will sink down as it cools). Serve warm or at room temperature, dusted with a little sifted icing sugar.

VARIATION

Sprinkle the filling with a little freshly grated nutmeg at the end of step 4.

JAM TARTS

'The Queen of Hearts, she made some tarts, all on a summer's day; the Knave of Hearts, he stole those tarts, and took them quite away!' goes the nursery rhyme. Jam tarts have long been a treat at birthday parties and are often a child's first attempt at baking.

MAKES 12

175g/6oz/1½ cups plain (all purpose) flour, plus extra for dusting

pinch of salt

2 tbsp caster (superfine) sugar

75g/3oz/6 tbsp butter, diced

1 egg, lightly beaten

about 100g/3½oz jam

1 Sift the flour and salt in a bowl and stir in the sugar. Rub in the butter until the mixture resembles fine crumbs. Stir in the egg and gather into a smooth dough ball.

2 Chill the pastry ball for 30 minutes. Meanwhile, preheat the oven to 220°C/425°F/gas 7 and lightly grease a 12-hole tart tray.

3 Roll out the pastry on a lightly floured surface to about 3mm/⅛in thick and, using a 7.5cm/3in cutter, cut out 12 circles. Press the pastry circles into the prepared tray. Put a teaspoonful of jam into each.

4 Put into the hot oven and cook for 15–20 minutes until the pastry is cooked and light golden brown. Carefully lift the tarts onto a wire rack and leave to cool before serving.

MINCE PIES

These small pies have become synonymous with Christmas. To eat one per day for the 12 days of Christmas was thought to bring happiness for the coming year.

MAKES 12

225g/8oz/2 cups plain (all-purpose) flour, plus extra for dusting

pinch of salt

3 tbsp caster (superfine) sugar, plus extra for dusting

115g/4oz/½ cup butter, diced

1 egg, lightly beaten

about 350g/12oz mincemeat (ready-made or see page 617)

icing (confectioner's) sugar, to dust

1 Sift the flour and salt in a bowl and stir in the sugar. Rub in the butter until the mixture resembles fine crumbs. Stir in the egg and gather into a smooth dough.

2 Chill the pastry for 30 minutes. Meanwhile, preheat the oven to 220°C/425°F/gas 7 and lightly grease a 12-hole tart tray.

3 Roll out the pastry on a lightly floured surface to about 3mm/⅛in thick and, using a 7.5cm/3in cutter, cut out 12 circles. Press into the prepared tray. Gather up the offcuts and roll out again, cutting slightly smaller circles to make 12 lids.

4 Spoon mincemeat into each case, dampen the edges and top with a pastry lid. Make a small slit in each pie.

5 Bake for 15–20 minutes until light golden brown. Transfer to a wire rack to cool and serve dusted with icing sugar.

ECCLES CAKES

The old meaning of the word 'eccles' was 'church', and it is likely that these fruity, buttery cakes from the Lancashire town of Eccles had a religious significance. Why the cakes are named for the town is obscure, but the cakes have a long association with the fairs or 'wakes' in the area. Strictly speaking, these traditional English bakes are a pastry rather than a cake, with warmly spiced fruit filling inside light and flaky rounds.

 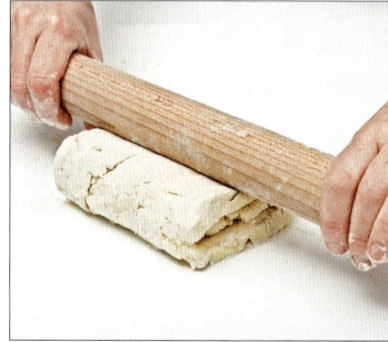 

MAKES 16

½ tsp mixed (apple pie) spice

50g/2oz/3 tbsp muscovado (molasses) sugar

175g/6oz/⅔ cup currants

50g/2oz/⅓ cup mixed chopped (candied) peel

grated rind of 1 lemon and 5ml/1 tsp lemon juice

FOR THE PASTRY

225g/8oz/2 cups plain (all-purpose) flour, plus extra for dusting

pinch of salt

200g/7oz/scant 1 cup butter, diced, plus extra for greasing

5ml/1 tsp lemon juice

100ml/3½fl oz/scant ½ cup iced water

1 egg, beaten, to glaze

caster (superfine) sugar, for dusting

1 To make the pastry, sift the flour and salt into a bowl. Add the butter, lemon juice and iced water. Mix to a soft dough using a flat-bladed knife. Add 1–2 tsp extra water if it is too dry.

2 Flour your work surface and your hands, then gently knead and shape the pastry into a rectangle 28 x 13cm/11 x 5in. (The pastry will just hold together and will still contain pieces of diced butter.)

3 Fold up the lower third of pastry and bring the top third down over it. Turn with the fold on the left, and press three times with the rolling pin to flatten. Roll out into a rectangle and fold and roll as before. Wrap in a plastic bag and chill for 20 minutes, or freeze for 5 minutes. Repeat the rolling, folding and chilling four more times.

4 Preheat the oven to 220°C/425°F/gas 7 and lightly grease two baking sheets. Mix all the filling ingredients together in a bowl.

5 Roll the pastry to 5mm/¼in thick. Using a 10cm/4in round cutter, stamp out 16 rounds and place a heaped teaspoonful of the filling in the centre of each.

6 Dampen the edges with water, gather up the pastry over the filling and press to seal. Turn the pastries so the seal is underneath, and roll each gently. Put on a baking sheet. Cut three slits across the top of each. Brush with beaten egg and sprinkle with sugar. Bake for 20 minutes, then cool on a wire rack.

CUSTARD TARTS

A vanilla custard tart has been an English favourite for hundreds of years, and was loved by Elizabeth I. Traditionally made as one big wobbly tart, little ones are easier to serve. The silky texture of the custard combined with the rich vanilla-flavoured pastry is unsurpassable. These nutmeg-dusted delights are perfect served still warm, but can be cooled and kept in the refrigerator for up to two days.

MAKES 8

600ml/1 pint/2½ cups full cream (whole) milk

6 egg yolks

75g/3oz/6 tbsp caster (superfine) sugar

freshly grated nutmeg

FOR THE PASTRY

175g/6oz/1½ cups plain (all-purpose) flour, plus extra for dusting

pinch of salt

75g/3oz/6 tbsp unsalted butter, at room temperature

75g/3oz/6 tbsp caster (superfine) sugar

3 egg yolks, at room temperature

a few drops vanilla extract

1 To make the pastry, sift the flour and salt into a bowl. In another bowl, beat together the butter, sugar, three egg yolks and vanilla extract until the mixture resembles scrambled eggs. (You can use an electric mixer or a food processor.) Add the flour and blend briefly.

2 Transfer the dough to a lightly floured surface and knead gently until smooth. Form into a ball, flatten and wrap in cling film (plastic wrap). Chill for at least 30 minutes. Bring back to room temperature before rolling out.

3 Roll out the pastry and use to line eight individual 10cm/4in loose-bottomed tartlet tins or pans. Place on a baking sheet and chill for 30 minutes.

4 Preheat the oven to 200°C/400°F/gas 6. To make the custard filling, gently heat the milk in a pan until just warmed but not yet boiling.

5 In a bowl, vigorously beat the six egg yolks and sugar together until they become pale and creamy in texture. Pour the milk onto the yolks and stir well to mix. Do not whisk, as this will produce too many bubbles.

6 Strain the milk mixture into a jug, then carefully pour the liquid into the tart cases. Liberally grate fresh nutmeg over the surface of the tartlets.

7 Bake for about 10 minutes, then lower the heat to 180°C/350°F/gas 4 and bake for another 10 minutes, or until the filling has set and is just turning golden. The tartlets should be a bit wobbly when they come out of the oven. Allow to cool a little, then remove the tarts out of the tins. Serve warm or cold.

VICTORIA SPONGE

This light cake was named in honour of Queen Victoria. Often referred to as a Victoria sandwich, it is based on equal quantities of fat, sugar, eggs and flour. It has come to be regarded as the classic English cake and remains a favourite for baking competitions.

SERVES 6–8

3 large eggs

few drops of vanilla extract

175g/6oz/¾ cup soft butter, plus extra for greasing

175g/6oz/¾ cup caster (superfine) sugar

175g/6oz/1½ cups self-raising (self-rising) flour

about 4 tbsp jam

icing (confectioner's) sugar, to dust

1 Preheat the oven to 180°C/350°F/gas 4. Butter two 20cm/8in sandwich tins or pans and line the bases with baking parchment.

2 Lightly beat the eggs with the vanilla extract. In another large mixing bowl, whisk the butter with the sugar until the mixture is pale, light and fluffy.

3 Gradually add the eggs, beating well after each addition. Sift the flour over the top and, using a metal spoon, fold in lightly until the mixture is smooth.

4 Divide the mixture between the prepared tins. Cook for 20 minutes until golden and firm to the touch.

5 Leave the cakes to cool in the tins for a few minutes, then carefully turn out onto a wire rack. Remove the paper and leave to cool completely.

6 When the cakes are cold, sandwich the two halves together with plenty of jam. Finally, sift a little icing sugar over the top.

VARIATIONS

◆ Instead of vanilla extract, beat a little finely grated lemon zest into the butter and sugar mixture in step 2. Sandwich the cake halves together with lemon curd.

◆ For a cream cake, sandwich with a thin layer of strawberry jam and a thick layer of whipped cream, topped with sliced strawberries.

CHOCOLATE CAKE

The first chocolate arrived in England in the 1500s, and the 17th century saw the opening of expensive chocolate houses, which were frequented by the rich and famous. Today, chocolate cake is a staple of every self-respecting tea table in England.

SERVES 10–12

225g/8oz/2 cups plain (all-purpose) flour

1 tsp bicarbonate of soda (baking soda)

50g/2oz/½ cup unsweetened cocoa powder

125g/4½oz/generous ½ cup soft butter, plus extra for greasing

250g/9oz/1¼ cups caster (superfine) sugar

3 eggs, beaten

250ml/8fl oz/1 cup buttermilk

FOR THE CHOCOLATE BUTTERCREAM

175g/6oz/1½ cups icing (confectioner's) sugar

115g/4oz/½ cup soft unsalted butter

few drops of vanilla extract

50g/2oz dark chocolate

1 Butter two 20cm/8in sandwich tins or pans, and line the bases with baking parchment. Preheat the oven to 180°C/350°F/gas 4.

2 Sift the flour with the bicarbonate of soda and cocoa. In another bowl, beat the butter and sugar until light and fluffy. Gradually beat in the eggs. Add the flour and buttermilk, and mix well.

3 Spoon into the prepared tins. Place into the hot oven and cook for 30–35 minutes until firm to the touch. Turn out of the tins, peel off the paper and leave on a wire rack to cool completely.

4 To make the chocolate buttercream, sift the icing sugar into a bowl. In a separate bowl, beat the butter until very soft and creamy.

5 Beat in half the sifted icing sugar until smooth and light. Gradually beat in the remaining sugar and the vanilla extract. Break the chocolate into squares. Melt in a bowl over a pan of hot water or in a microwave oven on low.

6 Mix the melted chocolate into the buttercream. Use half to sandwich the cooled cakes together, and the rest on the top.

MADEIRA CAKE

In the 19th century, this classic fine-textured cake was served with sweet wines, especially a glass of Madeira – hence the name. It is a good choice for a birthday or celebration cake as it is firm but light, which makes it the perfect base for decorating. It is ideal to serve with hot drinks, either as it is or split and sandwiched with buttercream. Store for up to one week in an airtight container.

SERVES 8–10

175g/6oz/¾ cup butter, softened, plus extra for greasing

175g/6oz/¾ cup caster (superfine) sugar

3 eggs

15ml/1 tbsp lemon juice

225g/8oz/scant 2 cups plain (all-purpose) flour

1½ tsp baking powder

1 Preheat the oven to 160°C/325°F/gas 3. Grease and line an 18cm/7in round deep cake tin or pan with baking parchment.

2 In a large bowl, beat the butter and sugar together until light and fluffy, then add the eggs one at a time, beating well after each addition. Stir in the lemon juice.

3 Sift in the flour and baking powder, and stir to combine. Spoon the mixture into the prepared tin and smooth the top level with the back of the spoon.

4 Bake in the centre of the oven for 1¼–1½ hours, until golden, or until a skewer inserted into the centre comes out clean. Leave the cake to cool in the tin for 45 minutes, then turn out onto a wire rack to go cold. Remove the lining paper.

LEMON DRIZZLE CAKE

Wonderfully moist and lemony, this classic cake is a favourite and very
easy to make. A lemon and sugar syrup is poured over the cooked cake and
allowed to soak through, so that the whole cake is sweet and tangy.
It will store in an airtight container for up to five days.

SERVES 6–8

finely grated rind of 2 lemons,
plus extra to decorate

175g/6oz/¾ cup caster
(superfine) sugar, plus
1 tsp for sprinkling

225g/8oz/1 cup unsalted butter,
softened, plus extra for greasing

4 eggs

225g/8oz/scant 2 cups self-raising
(self-rising) flour

1 tsp baking powder

FOR THE SYRUP

juice of 1 lemon

150g/5oz/⅔ cup caster
(superfine) sugar

1 Preheat the oven to 160°C/325°F/gas 3. Grease and line the base
and sides of an 18–20cm/7–8in round, deep cake tin or pan with
baking parchment.

2 Mix the lemon rind and sugar together in a bowl.

3 In a large bowl, beat the butter with the lemon and sugar mixture
until light and fluffy, then beat in the eggs one at a time.

4 Sift the flour and baking powder into the mixture in three batches
and beat well.

5 Turn the batter into the prepared tin and smooth the top level.
Bake for 1½ hours, or until golden brown and springy to the touch.

6 To make the syrup, slowly heat the juice with the sugar until
dissolved. Prick the warm cake top with a skewer and pour over
the syrup.

7 Sprinkle over the grated lemon rind and a little sugar, then leave
to cool. Remove the lining paper.

COOK'S TIP

A loaf shape is also traditional. Use a 900g/2lb loaf tin or pan, and
bake for 55–60 minutes.

WEST COUNTRY APPLE CAKE

The sweet-acid flavour of this fruity cake is refreshing,
and cooking apples produce a very moist cake, though you
can use eating apples if you prefer, for a sweeter result.

SERVES 6–8

225g/8oz cooking apples

juice of ½ lemon

225g/8oz/scant 2 cups plain
(all-purpose) flour

1½ tsp baking powder

115g/4oz/½ cup butter,
cut into small pieces,
plus extra for greasing

160g/5½oz/⅔ cup soft
light brown sugar

1 egg, beaten

about 30–45ml/2–3 tbsp milk

½ tsp ground cinnamon

1 Grease and line an 18cm/7in round cake tin or pan with baking parchment. Preheat the oven to 180°C/350°F/gas 4.

2 Peel, core and chop the apples and sprinkle them with the lemon juice to prevent browning.

3 Sift the flour and baking powder. Rub in the butter until the mixture resembles fine crumbs. Stir in 115g/4oz/½ cup of the sugar, the chopped apples and the egg. Add enough milk to give a soft dropping consistency.

4 Transfer to the prepared tin. Mix together the remaining sugar and the cinnamon and sprinkle over the cake mixture. Put into the hot oven and cook for 45–50 minutes, until firm to the touch. Leave to cool in the tin for 10 minutes, then transfer to a wire rack to cool.

YORKSHIRE PARKIN

Parkin is a dark, spicy, solid gingerbread made with oatmeal, flour, ginger and black treacle and is popular in the north of England. In Yorkshire, it's often enjoyed with a piece of cheese. It is traditionally eaten in the county on Bonfire Night, November 5th (in 19th-century Leeds, November 5th was called Parkin Day). In former days, when a quantity of parkin was being baked, one batch was sometimes eaten hot with apple sauce.

MAKES 16–20 SQUARES

300ml/½ pint/1¼ cups milk

225g/8oz/1 cup golden (light corn) syrup

225g/8oz/1 cup black treacle (molasses)

115g/4oz/½ cup butter, plus extra for greasing

50g/2oz/3 tbsp soft dark brown sugar

450g/1lb/3½ cups plain (all-purpose) flour

½ tsp bicarbonate of soda (baking soda)

1½ tsp ground ginger

350g/12oz/4 cups medium oatmeal

1 egg, beaten

icing (confectioner's) sugar, for dusting

1 Preheat the oven to 180°C/350°F/gas 4. Gently heat together the milk, syrup, treacle, butter and sugar, stirring until smooth, but do not boil.

2 Grease a 20cm/8in square cake tin or pan, and line the base and sides with baking parchment.

3 Sieve the flour into a bowl, add the bicarbonate of soda, ginger and oatmeal. Make a well in the centre and add the beaten egg, then the warmed treacle mixture, stirring to make a smooth batter.

4 Pour the batter into the tin and bake for about 45 minutes, until firm to the touch.

5 Cool slightly in the tin, then turn out onto a wire rack to cool completely. Cut into squares and dust with icing sugar.

COOK'S TIP

The flavour and texture of the cake improve if it is wrapped in foil and stored in an airtight container for several days.

HONEY CAKE

The earliest form of sweetener, honey has been an important ingredient in cooking throughout history, and there have been lots of different honey cake recipes over the centuries. Its flavour changes subtly according to the type of honey used.

MAKES 16 SQUARES

175g/6oz/¾ cup butter, plus extra for greasing

175g/6oz/¾ cup clear honey

115g/4oz/½ cup soft brown sugar

2 eggs, lightly beaten

15–30ml/1–2 tbsp milk

225g/8oz/scant 2 cups self-raising (self-rising) flour

1 Grease and line a 23cm/9in square cake tin or pan with baking parchment. Preheat the oven to 180°C/350°F/gas 4.

2 Gently heat the butter, honey and sugar, stirring frequently until well amalgamated. Set aside and leave to cool slightly.

3 Beat the eggs and milk into the cooled mixture. Sift the flour over the cake top, stir in and beat well until smooth.

4 Tip the mixture into the prepared tin, levelling the surface. Put into the hot oven and cook for about 30 minutes, until well risen, golden brown and firm to the touch.

5 Leave the cake to cool in the tin for 20 minutes then turn out, leaving the lining paper in place, onto a wire rack. Leave to cool completely.

6 Peel off the paper and cut the cake into 16 squares.

VARIATION

Add 1tsp ground cinnamon or grated nutmeg to the flour in step 3.

SEED CAKE

Caraway seeds have long been a feature of English baking, and this
old-fashioned cake, a Victorian favourite, remains popular on farmhouse
tea tables. Aromatic caraway seeds come from a herb in the
parsley family, and have a delicate aniseed flavour.

SERVES 8–10

225g/8oz/scant 2 cups plain
(all-purpose) flour

115g/4oz/½ cup butter,
at room temperature,
plus extra for greasing

115g/4oz/½ cup caster
(superfine) sugar

2 large eggs, lightly beaten

1 tsp baking powder

1 tbsp caraway seeds

30–45ml/2–3 tbsp milk, if necessary

1 Preheat the oven to 180°C/350°F/gas 4. Butter and base-line an
18cm/7in deep cake tin or pan with buttered baking parchment.

2 Sift the flour. Cream the butter and sugar together in a large bowl
until light and fluffy, then add the eggs, a little at a time, with a
spoonful of flour with each addition. Add the baking powder and
most of the caraway seeds to the remaining flour, reserving a few
seeds to sprinkle over the top of the cake.

3 Add the flour and caraway seeds mixture to the butter mixture,
and blend in lightly but thoroughly. Add a little milk to make a soft
mixture if it seems too stiff.

4 Turn the mixture into the prepared tin and sprinkle with the
reserved caraway seeds. Put the cake in the preheated oven and bake
for 15 minutes. Reduce the temperature to 160°C/325°F/gas 3
and bake for a further hour, or until the cake is well risen and
golden brown.

5 Leave the cake to cool in the tin for about 10 minutes, then
remove and finish cooling on a wire rack. When cold, remove the
baking parchment and store in an airtight tin.

BATTENBERG

Immediately identifiable, the Battenberg cake has a characteristic light sponge
that is set in a chequerboard arrangement of pink and yellow cake and encased
in a smooth cover of marzipan. It is served in dainty slices. It originates in England,
being named for Queen Victoria's granddaughter's new husband, Prince
Louis of Battenberg, on their marriage in 1884.

SERVES 14

175g/6oz/¾ cup butter, softened,
plus extra for greasing

175g/6oz/¾ cup caster
(superfine) sugar

3 large eggs, lightly beaten

175g/6oz/1½ cups self-raising
(self-rising) flour, sifted

pinch of salt

½ tsp red food colouring

½ tsp edible rosewater

½ tsp orange flower water or
almond extract

6 tbsp apricot jam

25g/1oz/2 tbsp white sugar

450g/1lb marzipan

1 Preheat the oven to 190°C/375°F/gas 5. Lightly grease a Swiss roll tin (jelly roll pan), 30 x 20 x 2.5cm (12 x 8 x 1in). Lightly grease the base and line it with baking parchment. Cut a strip of cardboard to fit the inside of the tin. Cover with foil, lightly grease and wedge in place.

2 In a large bowl, beat the butter with the caster sugar until creamy. Add the eggs and beat well. Lightly fold in the flour and salt.

3 Put half the mixture in a clean bowl and mix in the red colouring and rosewater until evenly tinted. Turn into one side of the tin.

4 Mix the orange flower water or almond extract into the remaining batter and turn into the empty side of the tin. Smooth into the corners.

5 Bake for 20 minutes until risen and firm to the touch. Leave to stand for 5 minutes. Slide the blade of a knife between cake, tin and foil strip, and turn out onto a wire rack lined with silicone paper. Remove the lining paper. Leave to go cold.

6 Trim the cake so that each half measures 28 x 9cm (11 x 3½in). Cut each slab in half lengthways so there are four equal strips.

7 In a pan, bring the jam and sugar slowly to the boil, stirring constantly. Boil for 30–60 seconds. Remove from the heat.

8 To assemble, brush the top of each plain cake strip with the cooked jam and press a pink strip on top. Brush one side of each cake stack and press them together to make a chequerboard pattern.

9 Roll out the marzipan to a 28cm/11in square. Brush the cake top with jam, and place the cake jam side down 1cm/½in from one edge of the marzipan. Brush the rest of the cake with jam. Wrap the marzipan over and around the cake, smoothing it firmly with your hand. Press firmly at the join to seal.

10 Trim away any excess marzipan and the cake is ready to serve. Cut into chequerboard slices.

BUTTERFLY CAKES

A teatime treat, these are little fairy sponge cakes with vanilla buttercream, cut to create pretty butterfly wings. In this cake-making method, the butter is beaten with the sugar until very creamy, then combined with the flour and flavourings. The resulting cake has a moist, dense crumb.

MAKES 12–15

175g/6oz/¾ cup butter, softened

175g/6oz/¾ cup caster (superfine) sugar

1 tsp vanilla extract, or 1 tsp finely grated lemon rind

4 eggs, lightly beaten

175g/6oz/1½ cups self-raising (self-rising) flour, sifted

FOR THE BUTTERCREAM

90g/3½oz/7 tbsp butter, softened

175g/6oz/1½ cups icing (confectioner's) sugar, double-sifted, plus extra for dusting

½ vanilla pod (bean), split, or a few drops of vanilla extract

a few drops of food colouring (optional)

1 Preheat the oven to 180°C/350°F/gas 4. Line cups of a bun tin or pan with paper cases.

2 Place the butter and sugar in a bowl and beat together with a spoon until very light and creamy (or use an electric mixer). Add the vanilla or lemon rind. Gradually add the eggs, beating well after each addition.

3 Add the sifted flour and fold it delicately into the mixture with a large spoon until just combined.

4 Divide the mixture among the paper cases and bake for 20 minutes, until the cakes are golden brown and the centres feel firm to the touch. Remove from the oven. Leave to cool for 5 minutes, then turn the cakes out onto a wire rack

5 When the cakes have cooled, carefully cut round the lightly domed tops with a small sharp knife and remove the top of each cake. Slice the tops in half to form two semicircles, to make the butterfly wings. Set aside.

6 To make the buttercream, beat the butter well in a bowl before beating in the sifted icing sugar. Ensure that no lumps remain. For the best vanilla flavour, split a vanilla pod in half and scrape out the seeds, then discard the pod and mix the seeds into the buttercream. Alternatively, add a few drops of vanilla extract to the mixture. Colour the icing, if you like.

7 Use a piping bag with a star nozzle to pipe a whirl of buttercream into each cake. Press the butterfly wings into the cream and dust with sifted icing sugar just before serving.

SWISS ROLL

The recipe first appeared in 1897 and became a teatime classic. Traditionally served just filled with jam, a layer of buttercream is sometimes added. Sponge cakes were latecomers to English cookery, as it was very difficult to bake such light cakes in temperamental ovens. When controllable ovens were introduced, whisked sponge cakes became favourites.

SERVES 8

oil, for greasing

115g/4oz/1 cup plain (all-purpose) flour, sifted

pinch of salt

3 eggs

115g/4oz/½ cup caster (superfine) sugar, plus extra for sprinkling

5–6 tbsp strawberry or raspberry jam

1 Preheat the oven to 200°C/400°F/gas 6. Grease and line a 33 x 23cm/13 x 9in Swiss roll tin (jelly roll pan).

2 Sift the flour and salt together three times, then set aside. Place the eggs and sugar in a mixing bowl and beat (using an electric mixer if you like) for about 10 minutes or until thick and pale. Sift the sifted flour and salt into the mixing bowl, then fold together very gently.

3 Carefully spoon the sponge mixture into the prepared tin and bake for 10–12 minutes, until well risen and springy to the touch.

4 Lay a sheet of baking parchment on a flat surface and sprinkle liberally with sugar. Turn out the cake onto the paper, and leave to cool with the tin still in place. Then lift the tin off the cooled cake and carefully peel away the lining paper from the base of the cake.

5 Spread the jam over the sponge evenly. Carefully roll up the cake from a narrow end to form a Swiss roll, using the paper to lift the sponge. Sprinkle liberally with more sugar.

COOK'S TIP

Do not leave the sponge to cool for too long, as it will be difficult to roll. If you do not want to fill it immediately, cover it with baking parchment, roll up loosely and leave until ready to fill.

YULE LOG

The ancient tradition of burning a Yule log on Christmas Eve has died out, but the custom is kept alive in the form of a chocolate log. Chocolate was first sold in London in 1657 in the form of dried cocoa nibs to make drinking chocolate. By the mid-19th century, solid chocolate was available and, together with cocoa, was sometimes used to make puddings and cakes. The sponge mixture for a Swiss roll is rolled up while it is still hot, to avoid it cracking. Eat this fresh or it could be frozen, unfilled, for two months.

SERVES 8

butter, for greasing

90g/3¼oz/scant 1 cup self-raising (self-rising) flour

2 tbsp unsweetened cocoa powder

pinch of salt

4 eggs

115g/4oz/½ cup golden caster (superfine) sugar, plus extra for dusting

FOR THE FILLING AND ICING

150ml/¼ pint/⅔ cup double (heavy) cream

50g/2oz plain (semisweet) chocolate

2 tbsp unsweetened cocoa powder

15ml/2 tbsp boiling water

115g/4oz/½ cup unsalted butter, softened

225g/8oz/2 cups icing (confectioner's) sugar, sifted, plus extra for dusting

chocolate or almond paste holly leaves, to decorate

1 Preheat the oven to 220°C/425°F/gas 7. Grease and line a 33 x 23cm/13 x 9in Swiss roll tin (jelly roll pan).

2 Sift the flour, cocoa and salt into a bowl. Put the eggs and sugar into a large heatproof bowl and place this over a pan of hot water. Whisk for 10 minutes, or until the mixture is thick. Remove the bowl from the water and whisk until the mixture is thick and pale, and leaves a trail when the beaters are lifted away

3 Using a large metal spoon, gently fold in half the flour and cocoa using a figure-of-eight movement. Fold in the remaining flour with 1 tbsp cold water. Pour the mixture into the prepared tin and smooth level.

4 Bake for 10 minutes, or until springy to the touch. Sprinkle a sheet of baking parchment with caster sugar and place this on a clean dish towel.

5 Turn the hot sponge out onto the paper. Peel away the lining paper. Trim away the crusty sponge edges. Using the dish towel, roll up the sponge loosely, with the paper inside, then leave to cool on a wire rack. Carefully unwrap the cooled cake and remove the paper.

6 For the filling, whip the cream until stiff, spread over the sponge, then roll up and chill until needed.

7 For the icing, melt the chocolate in a heatproof bowl over a pan of gently simmering water, then leave to cool. Dissolve the cocoa in the boiling water, stir until blended, then leave to cool.

8 Beat the butter until fluffy, then beat in the icing sugar and cooled cocoa along with the melted chocolate.

9 Put the cake on a long serving dish. Spread the chocolate icing over the top and sides of the cake with a metal spatula, in deep swirls and ridges. Decorate the top with edible holly leaves and dust very lightly with a sprinkle of icing sugar before serving.

CHRISTMAS CAKE

Rich cakes need at least a month to mature, so Christmas cake is best made by about Halloween. The same recipe can be used for a wedding cake. It can be finished in the traditional way, with almond paste and white royal icing, or topped as here.

SERVES 8–10

225g/8oz/scant 2 cups plain (all-purpose) flour

pinch of salt

1½ tsp mixed (apple pie) spice

900g/2lb/5 cups mixed dried fruit

50g/2oz/½ cup slivered almonds

115g/4oz/⅔ cup glacé (candied) cherries, halved

115g/4oz/⅔ cup chopped mixed (candied) peel

225g/8oz/1 cup butter, plus extra for greasing

225g/8oz/1 cup soft dark brown sugar

1 tbsp black treacle (molasses)

finely grated rind of 1 orange

1 tsp vanilla extract

4 large eggs

150ml/¼ pint/⅔ cup whisky or brandy

FOR THE TOPPING (OPTIONAL)

1 tbsp apricot jam

30ml/2 tbsp brandy

walnuts, hazelnuts and glacé cherries

1 Line a 20cm/8in round, or 18cm/7in square, loose-based cake tin or pan with three layers of greased baking parchment, extending 5cm/2in over the top of the tin. Tie a thick band of folded brown paper around the outside. Preheat the oven to 160°C/325°F/gas 3.

2 Sift the flour, salt and spice together. Put the dried fruit in a large bowl with the almonds, cherries and mixed peel and stir in 1 tbsp of the flour mixture.

3 In another bowl, beat the butter and sugar until light and fluffy, then add the treacle, orange rind and vanilla extract.

4 Add the eggs, one at a time, adding a little of the flour mixture with each egg and beating well after each addition. Fold in the fruit, remaining flour and 30ml/2 tbsp of the whisky or brandy.

5 Put the mixture into the prepared tin, levelling with the back of a spoon and making a slight hollow in the centre. Place the cake in the centre of the hot oven and cook for about 1½ hours, or until just beginning to brown.

6 Reduce the heat to 150°C/300°F/gas 2 and cook for another 3 hours until cooked. Protect the top of the cake from over-browning by covering loosely with foil or brown paper.

7 When cooked, the top of the cake will feel springy to the touch and a skewer pushed into the centre will come out clean. Leave to cool completely, then remove the lining papers and turn the cake upside down.

8 Using a skewer, make small holes all over the base of the cake and sprinkle over the remaining whisky or brandy. (Repeat this procedure after a week, if you wish.)

9 Wrap the cake in a double layer of baking parchment followed by a thick layer of foil. Store in an airtight tin in a cool place.

10 Just before Christmas, add your chosen decoration. For this glazed fruit and nut topping, heat the jam and the brandy together in a pan, whisking well until thoroughly blended. Brush the surface of the cake with some of the mixture. Arrange the nuts and cherries in rows on top and brush generously with a coating of the glaze.

SIMNEL CAKE

This cake dates back to medieval times, and was traditionally served at Easter, the balls on top representing the 11 faithful apostles. It is also made for Mothering Sunday. It is quite unlike other celebratory fruitcakes, as it has a middle and top layer of almond paste. The origins of the name are unclear, but may be derived from the Latin *simila*, which was used to describe the finest flour, or possibly from the Anglo-Saxon word for a formal feast, *symbel*.

SERVES 11

175g/6oz/¾ cup butter, plus extra for greasing

175g/6oz/scant ¾ cup soft brown sugar

3 large eggs, beaten

225g/8oz/scant 2 cups plain (all-purpose) flour

½ tsp ground cinnamon

½ tsp freshly grated nutmeg

150g/5oz/scant ¾ cup each of currants, sultanas (golden raisins) and raisins

85g/3½oz/generous ½ cup glacé (candied) cherries, quartered

85g/3½oz/generous ½ cup mixed (candied) peel, chopped

grated rind of 1 large lemon

1kg/2¼lb almond paste

icing (confectioner's) sugar, to dust

1 egg white, lightly beaten

1 Grease and line an 18cm/7in round cake tin or pan.

2 Beat the butter and sugar until pale and fluffy, then gradually beat in the eggs. Lightly fold in the flour, spices, dried fruits, cherries, mixed peel and lemon rind.

3 Preheat the oven to 160°C/325°F/gas 3. Roll out about 400g/14oz of the almond paste to a 16cm/6½in circle on a surface dusted with icing sugar.

4 Spoon half the cake mixture into the prepared tin and place the circle of almond paste on top of the mixture. Spoon the remaining cake mixture on top and level the surface.

5 Put the cake into the hot oven and cook for 1 hour. Reduce the oven temperature to 150°C/300°F/gas 2 and cook for another 2 hours. Leave to cool in the tin, then turn out on a wire rack.

6 Brush the cake with egg white. Roll out about two-thirds of the remaining almond paste to a 28cm/11in circle and use to cover the top and sides of the fruitcake. Roll the remaining paste into 11 balls and attach with egg white around the top of the cake in a circle.

7 For a dark gold topping, brush the top of the cake with more egg white and grill or broil until lightly browned.

MARMALADE TEABREAD

A cake that's perfect for serving with a cup of tea, this is especially popular in the north-west of England. The marmalade gives it a lovely flavour, at the same time as keeping it moist.

SERVES 8–10

200g/7oz/1¾ cups plain (all-purpose) flour

1 tsp baking powder

1¼ tsp ground cinnamon

90g/3½oz/7 tbsp butter, cut into small pieces, plus extra for greasing

50g/2oz/3 tbsp soft light brown sugar

1 egg

4 tbsp chunky orange marmalade

about 45ml/3 tbsp milk

4 tbsp icing (confectioner's) sugar, to decorate

shreds of orange and lemon rind, to decorate

1 Preheat the oven to 160°C/325°F/gas 3. Grease a 450g/1lb loaf tin or pan, and line with baking parchment.

2 Sift the flour, baking powder and cinnamon together, then add the butter and rub in with the fingertips until the mixture resembles fine crumbs. Stir in the sugar.

3 Beat the egg lightly in a small bowl and mix it with the marmalade and most of the milk.

4 Mix the milk mixture into the flour mixture, adding more milk if necessary to give a soft dropping consistency.

5 Transfer the mixture to the prepared tin, put into the hot oven and cook for about 1¼ hours, until the cake is firm to the touch and cooked through.

6 Leave the cake to cool for 5 minutes, then turn onto a wire rack. Carefully peel off the lining paper and leave the cake to cool completely.

7 Mix the icing sugar with just enough water to make a runny glacé icing and drizzle it over the top of the cake, then decorate with shreds of orange and lemon rind.

STICKY GINGERBREAD

Gingerbread is said to be the oldest type of cake in the world, originally dating back to ancient Greece. The English word 'gingerbread' is a corruption of Old French *gingebras*, meaning 'preserved ginger'. Early medieval gingerbread was made by simply mixing stale white breadcrumbs, honey and spices to a stiff paste; it was coloured red then pressed into moulds to dry out in a low oven. As time passed, gingerbread was made instead with flour and/or oatmeal. This dark rich and sticky gingerbread 'cake' cries out to be smothered in cool butter or swirls of cream cheese. It tastes better when kept for a few days, so prepare ahead before serving with afternoon tea on a chilly winter's day.

SERVES 8–10

225g/8oz/scant 2 cups plain (all-purpose) flour

2 tsp ground ginger

1 tsp mixed (apple pie) spice

pinch of salt

2 pieces preserved stem ginger, drained and chopped

115g/4oz/½ cup butter, softened, plus extra for greasing

115g/4oz/scant ½ cup dark muscovado (dark brown) sugar

275g/10oz/generous 1 cup black treacle (molasses)

2 eggs, beaten

½ tsp bicarbonate of soda (baking soda)

30ml/2 tbsp milk, warmed

1 Preheat the oven to 160°C/325°F/gas 3. Grease and line an 18cm/7in square cake tin or pan, about 7.5cm/3in deep.

2 Sift the flour, ground ginger, mixed spice and salt together into a bowl. Add the stem ginger and toss it in the flour to coat.

3 In a separate bowl, cream the butter and sugar together until fluffy, then gradually beat in the treacle. Add the eggs and the flour mixture.

4 Dissolve the bicarbonate of soda in the milk and gradually beat into the batter. Pour into the prepared tin, level the top and bake for about 45 minutes.

5 Reduce the oven temperature to 150°C/300°F/gas 2 and bake for a further 30 minutes. To test whether the loaf is cooked, insert a metal skewer into the middle; it should come out clean.

6 Cool for 5 minutes in the tin and then turn out onto a wire rack to cool completely. Keep for two to three days in an airtight container so that the gingerbread becomes sticky and moist.

MALT FRUIT LOAF

Dark, sticky malt loaf is a much-loved English tea bread, eaten sliced and plain or spread with butter. It was invented by a Danish man, John Sorensen, based in Manchester, who opened a bakery in Beswick in the early 1930s. In 19th-century England, malt was regarded as a healthy food for children and convalescents, as it contains some B vitamins and minerals and was added to all sorts of dishes. Malt extract, a sweet brown sticky syrup, was invented in the 19th century and gives the loaf its delectable flavour. Serve sliced, spread with butter.

SERVES 8–10

oil, for greasing

225g/8oz/scant 2 cups self-raising (self-rising) flour

pinch of salt

2 tbsp dark muscovado (dark brown) sugar

175g/6oz/¾ cup sultanas (golden raisins)

1 tbsp golden (light corn) syrup

1 tbsp black treacle (molasses)

30ml/2 tbsp malt extract

about 150ml/¼ pint/⅔ cup milk

2 eggs, beaten

1 Preheat the oven to 170°C/325°F/gas 3. Grease a 900g/2lb loaf tin or pan and line the base and sides with non-stick baking paper.

2 Put the flour, salt, sugar and sultanas in a bowl and mix together. Make a well in the centre.

3 Heat the syrup, treacle, malt extract and milk in a pan until melted. Pour into the dry ingredients and beat well, adding the beaten eggs. Add a little more milk, if necessary, to make a fairly sticky consistency.

4 Put into the tin and bake for about 1 hour 15 minutes. Cool in the tin for 10 minutes, and then place on a wire rack to cool completely.

5 Wrap the cold cake in greaseproof paper and foil, and store for a day before eating.

COOK'S TIP

Measuring syrup is easier if you dip a metal spoon in very hot water first, then quickly dry it.

OAT BISCUITS

In England, oats have been one of the principal crops since the days of the Anglo-Saxons and King Alfred the Great. By the 14th century, the grain had become a major export. These traditional country biscuits are a good store-cupboard standby – nutritious, chewy and delicious.

MAKES ABOUT 18

115g/4oz/½ cup butter, plus extra for greasing

115g/4oz/scant ½ cup soft brown sugar

115g/4oz/½ cup golden (light corn) syrup

150g/5oz/1¼ cups self-raising (self-rising) flour

150g/5oz/1 cup rolled porridge oats

1 Preheat the oven to 180°C/350°F/gas 4. Line two or three baking sheets with baking parchment, or grease them with butter.

2 Gently heat the butter, sugar and golden syrup until the butter has melted and the sugar has dissolved. Remove from the heat and leave to cool slightly.

3 Sift the flour and stir into the mixture in the pan, together with the oats, to make a soft dough.

4 Roll the dough into small balls and arrange them on the prepared baking sheets, leaving plenty of room for them to spread. Flatten each ball slightly with a palette knife or a metal spatula.

5 Put one tray into the hot oven and cook for 12–15 minutes until golden brown and cooked through.

6 Leave to cool on the baking sheet for 1–2 minutes, then carefully transfer to a wire rack to crisp up and cool completely, while you cook the remaining batches.

VARIATION

Add a handful of finely chopped toasted almonds or walnuts, or a small handful of dried fruit (such as raisins or sultanas), in step 3.

GINGER SNAPS

It was once customary to serve ginger snaps and spiced ale on Twelfth Night, the evening of 5th January and a night of parties and practical jokes. Since then, many an English tale has been written over a plate of ginger snaps and a cup of strong tea.

MAKES ABOUT 24

115g/4oz/½ cup butter, diced

115g/4oz/½ cup caster (superfine) sugar

115g/4oz/½ cup golden (light corn) syrup

225g/8oz/scant 2 cups plain (all-purpose) flour

2 tsp ground ginger

1 tsp bicarbonate of soda (baking soda)

1 Preheat the oven to 180°C/350°F/gas 4. Line two or three baking sheets with baking parchment. Gently heat the butter, sugar and syrup until the butter has melted and the sugar has dissolved. Leave to cool slightly.

2 Sift the flour, ginger and bicarbonate of soda and stir into the mixture in the pan to make a soft dough.

3 Arrange balls of the dough on the prepared baking sheets, well spaced out. Flatten each ball slightly with a palette knife or metal spatula.

4 Put one tray into the hot oven and cook for about 12 minutes until golden brown (take care not to overcook them – they burn easily). Leave to cool on the baking sheet for 1–2 minutes, then carefully transfer to a wire rack to crisp up and cool completely while you cook the remaining biscuits.

SHREWSBURY CAKES

These traditional treats are crisp, lemony shortbread biscuits with fluted edges,
which have been made and sold in the town of Shrewsbury since the 17th century.

MAKES ABOUT 20

115g/4oz/½ cup soft butter

150g/5oz/⅔ cup caster
(superfine) sugar

2 egg yolks

225g/8oz/scant 2 cups plain
(all-purpose) flour

finely grated rind of 1 lemon

1 Preheat the oven to 180°C/350°F/gas 4. Line two baking sheets
with baking parchment.

2 In a mixing bowl, beat the softened butter with the sugar until
pale, light and fluffy. Beat in each of the egg yolks one at a time,
beating thoroughly after each addition.

3 Sift the flour over the top and add the lemon rind. Stir in, and then
gather up the mixture to make a stiff dough. Knead the dough lightly
on a floured surface, then roll it out to about 5mm/¼in thick.

4 Using a 7.5cm/3in fluted biscuit cutter, cut out circles and arrange
on the baking sheets. Gather up the offcuts and roll out again to
make more biscuits.

5 Put into the hot oven and cook for about 15 minutes, until firm to
the touch and lightly browned.

6 Transfer to a wire rack and leave to crisp up and cool completely.

VARIATIONS

◆ Omit the lemon rind and sift 1 tsp ground mixed (apple pie) spice
with the flour in step 3.

◆ Add 2 tbsp of currants or raisins to the mixture in step 3.

BOSWORTH JUMBLES

Legend has it that this recipe was dropped by Richard III's cook at the
Battle of Bosworth Field in 1485, when the biscuits were called jumbals.
Originally these Leicestershire biscuits were made in interlaced ring shapes.

 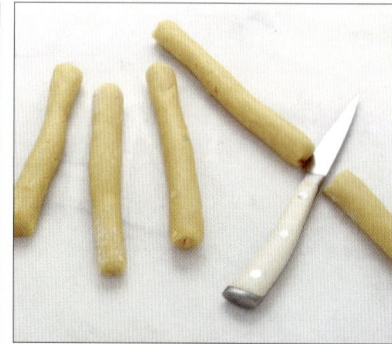 

MAKES 10–12

125g/4½oz/generous ½ cup butter

125g/4½oz/generous ½ cup sugar

1 egg, beaten

300g/11oz/2½ cups plain (all-purpose) flour, plus extra for dusting

50g/2oz/½ cup ground almonds

1 tsp finely grated lemon zest

1 Preheat the oven to 180°C/350°F/gas 4. Line two baking trays with non-stick baking paper.

2 Beat together the butter and sugar in a mixing bowl until light and fluffy.

3 Beat in the egg, followed by the flour, almonds and lemon zest, to form a soft dough.

4 With floured hands, roll pieces of the dough into sausage shapes and cut off pieces about 12cm/5in long. Put the pieces on the baking trays, curling them into S shapes.

5 Bake for 12–15 minutes. Carefully place on a wire rack to cool completely.

GOOSNARGH CAKES

These rich little biscuits come from the village of Goosnargh, near Preston in Lancashire; although their origin is unclear, they were baked specially for Easter and Whitsuntide. Caraway seeds were a common ingredient in 16th- and 17th-century recipes, as they were believed to aid digestion. Strangely, it was also believed that caraway seeds discouraged the eater from stealing.

MAKES 15

175g/6oz/¾ cup butter, plus extra for greasing

200g/7oz/1¾ cups plain (all-purpose) flour, plus extra for dusting

50g/2oz/4 tbsp caster (superfine) sugar, plus extra for sprinkling

1 tsp coriander seeds, lightly crushed

1 tsp caraway seeds

1 Grease two baking trays.

2 Rub the butter into the flour in a bowl, until well combined. Stir in the sugar and seeds and work to a fairly dry dough.

3 Roll out on a lightly floured surface, about 5mm/¼in thick, and cut into rounds using a 6cm/2½in cutter.

4 Sprinkle with sugar and place on the baking trays, leaving room for the biscuits to spread. Leave to stand for at least 2 hours. Preheat the oven to 180°C/350°F/gas 4.

5 Bake the biscuits for 10–15 minutes until pale golden. Cool on the trays for at least 15 minutes before removing carefully to a wire rack to cool completely.

DEVON FLATS

Clotted cream gives a unique texture and flavour to these delicious biscuits. Clotted or 'clouted' cream was known in the south-west from the 16th century and, as well as being considered a speciality eaten as an accompaniment, it is also used as an ingredient in many Devonshire recipes. The biscuits can be served plain, or spread with clotted cream and jam like a scone.

MAKES 15–20

a little butter for greasing

225g/8oz/scant 2 cups self-raising (self-rising) flour, plus extra for dusting

pinch of salt

125g/4½oz/generous ½ cup clotted cream

115g/4oz/½ cup caster (superfine) sugar, plus extra for sprinkling

1 egg

15–30ml/1–2 tbsp milk

1 Preheat the oven to 200°C/180°F/gas 6. Grease two baking trays.

2 Sift the flour and salt into a mixing bowl and add the clotted cream. Cut through the mixture with a knife, then rub in with your fingers. Stir in the sugar.

3 Beat together the egg and milk and gradually add to the mixture, mixing to form a soft dough – you may not need all the liquid.

4 Roll out on a lightly floured surface and cut into 15–20 rounds with a cookie cutter.

5 Place on the baking trays and sprinkle lightly with sugar.

6 Bake for 10–12 minutes until light golden. Cool on the trays for a few minutes, then place on a wire rack to cool completely.

EASTER BISCUITS

These sweet, lightly spiced cookies have fluted edges and are flecked with currants. Originally, the crisp buttery biscuits were served after church on Easter Sunday. In the West Country, they are also known as Easter cakes rather than biscuits.

MAKES 16–18

115g/4oz/½ cup soft butter, plus extra for greasing

75g/3oz/⅓ cup caster (superfine) sugar, plus extra for sprinkling

1 egg, separated

200g/7oz/1¾ cups plain (all-purpose) flour

½ tsp mixed (apple pie) spice

½ tsp ground cinnamon

50g/2oz/⅓ cup currants

1 tbsp chopped mixed (candied) peel

15–30ml/1–2 tbsp milk

1 Preheat the oven to 200°C/400°F/gas 6. Lightly grease two baking sheets or line with baking parchment.

2 Beat together the butter and sugar until light and fluffy. Beat the egg yolk into the mixture.

3 Sift the flour and spices over the mixture, then fold in the currants and peel, adding sufficient milk to make a fairly soft dough.

4 Knead the dough lightly on a floured surface, then roll out to 5mm/¼in thick. Cut out circles using a 5cm/2in fluted biscuit cutter. Arrange on the sheets and cook for 10 minutes.

5 Beat the egg white and brush gently over the biscuits. Sprinkle with sugar and return to the oven for 10 minutes until golden. Transfer to a wire rack to cool.

MACAROONS

These traditional gooey meringue-like cookies aren't to be confused with the French macaron. Finely grated creamed coconut gives the soft-centred biscuits a rich creaminess. Cooking the gooey mixture on baking parchment makes sure that they are easily removed from the baking sheet. The cooked macaroons can be stored in an airtight container for up to one week.

MAKES 16–18

50g/2oz creamed coconut, chilled

2 large egg whites

90g/3½oz/generous ⅓ cup caster (superfine) sugar

75g/3oz/1 cup desiccated (dried unsweetened shredded) coconut

1 Preheat the oven to 180°C/350°F/gas 4. Line a large baking sheet with baking parchment. Finely grate the creamed coconut.

2 Use an electric beater to whisk the egg whites in a large bowl until stiff. Whisk in the sugar, a little at a time, to make a stiff and glossy meringue. Fold in the creamed and desiccated coconut, using a large metal spoon.

3 Place dessertspoonfuls of the mixture, spaced a little apart, on the baking sheet. Bake for 15–20 minutes, until slightly risen and golden brown. Leave to cool on the parchment, then transfer to an airtight container.

VARIATION

For a tangy flavour, you could add the grated rind of one lime to the mixture in step 2.

RATAFIAS

These tiny biscuits were popular in the 18th century and would have been served with a glass of ratafia (almond liqueur), sack (sherry) or wine.

MAKES 15–20

115g/4oz/½ cup caster (superfine) sugar

50g/2oz/½ cup ground almonds

2 egg yolks

few drops edible rosewater

1 Preheat the oven to 170°C/325°F/gas 3. Line two baking trays with non-stick baking paper.

2 Mix together the sugar and almonds, then work in the egg yolks and rosewater.

3 Drop teaspoons of the mixture onto the baking trays and flatten slightly with a palette knife.

4 Bake for 15–20 minutes until golden. Place on a wire rack to cool completely.

MELTING MOMENTS

As the name suggests, these crisp biscuits really do melt in the mouth. They have a texture like shortbread, but are covered in rolled oats to give a crunchy surface and extra flavour, and traditionally topped with a nugget of glacé cherry.

MAKES 16–20

115g/4oz/½ cup soft butter

75g/3oz/⅓ cup caster (superfine) sugar

1 egg yolk, beaten

few drops of vanilla or almond extract

150g/5oz/1¼ cups self-raising (self-rising) flour

rolled oats, for coating

4–5 glacé (candied) cherries

1 Preheat the oven to 180°C/350°F/gas 4. Beat together the butter and sugar, then gradually beat in the egg yolk and the vanilla or almond extract.

2 Sift in the flour and stir to make a soft dough. Roll into 16–20 small balls.

3 Spread rolled oats on a sheet of baking parchment and toss the balls in them until evenly coated.

4 Place the balls, spaced slightly apart, on two baking sheets. Flatten each ball a little with your thumb. Cut the cherries into quarters and place a piece of cherry on top of each biscuit.

5 Put into the hot oven and cook for 15–20 minutes, until they are lightly browned. Allow the biscuits to cool for a few minutes on the baking sheets, before transferring them to a wire rack to cool completely

JAM SANDWICH BISCUITS

Inspired by a much-loved British brand, these buttery cookies are an absolute children's classic. Sandwiched with buttercream and a generous dollop of strawberry jam, they make a perfect snack served with a glass of milk at teatime.

MAKES 20

225g/8oz/scant 2 cups plain (all-purpose) flour, plus extra for flouring

175g/6oz/¾ cup unsalted butter, chilled and diced, plus extra for greasing

125g/4¼oz/generous ½ cup caster (superfine) sugar

1 egg yolk

FOR THE FILLING

90g/3½oz/scant ½ cup unsalted butter, at room temperature

1 tsp vanilla extract

150g/5oz/1½ cups icing (confectioner's) sugar

4–5 tbsp strawberry jam

1 Put the flour and butter in a bowl and rub together until the mixture resembles breadcrumbs; alternatively you can use a food processor. Mix in the sugar and egg yolk to form a dough.

2 Turn out onto a floured surface and knead until smooth. Shape into a ball, wrap in cling film (food wrap) and chill for at least 30 minutes. Preheat the oven to 180°C/350°F/gas 4.

3 Grease two baking sheets. Roll out the dough thinly on a lightly floured surface and cut out rounds using a 6cm/2½in cutter. Re-roll the trimmings and cut out more rounds until you have 40.

4 Place half the rounds on a prepared baking sheet. Using a small heart-shaped cutter, about 2cm/¾in in diameter, cut out the centres of the remaining rounds. (If you don't have a small cutter for the cookie centres, use a sharp knife to cut out triangles or squares instead.) Place on the second baking sheet.

5 Bake the biscuits for about 12 minutes until pale golden, then transfer to a wire rack and leave to cool completely.

6 To make the buttercream for the filling, beat together the butter, vanilla extract and icing sugar until smooth and creamy. Using a palette knife, spread a little buttercream on to each biscuit round.

7 Spoon a little jam onto the buttercream, then gently press the cut-out biscuits on top, so that the jam fills the heart-shaped hole.

GINGERBREAD MEN

In all its forms, gingerbread has been part of the Christmas tradition for generations. Nowhere was ginger more prized than in Germany, and it is from that country that many present-day traditions originate, but, by the 17th century, every northern European country had its regional variations of the spiced bread. In England, gingerbread was sold at country fairs, as 'fairings', and was often gilded with edible gold leaf. Cutting out gingerbread people for festive decorations and treats is ever-popular. Legend has it that the perennial children's favourites, gingerbread men, were created when Elizabeth I ordered her cooks to make caricatures of her courtiers.

MAKES ABOUT 12

350g/12oz/3 cups plain (all-purpose) flour, plus extra for flouring

1 tsp bicarbonate of soda (baking soda)

1 tsp ground ginger

115g/4oz/½ cup unsalted butter, chilled and diced

175g/6oz/scant ¾ cup light muscovado (brown) sugar

1 egg

2 tbsp black treacle (molasses) or golden (light corn) syrup

royal or thick glacé icing, to decorate

1 Preheat the oven to 180°C/350°F/gas 4. Grease two large baking sheets.

2 Put the flour, bicarbonate of soda, ginger and butter into a bowl and mix well until the mixture begins to resemble fine breadcrumbs (you can use a food processor if preferred).

3 Add the sugar, egg and black treacle or golden syrup and mix in thoroughly until it begins to form into a ball.

4 Turn the dough out on to a lightly floured surface, and knead until smooth and pliable. Roll out the dough (you might find it easier to roll half of the dough out at a time).

5 Cut out figures using people-shaped cutters, then transfer to the baking sheets. Re-roll any trimmings and cut out more figures.

6 Bake for 15 minutes until slightly risen and starting to colour around the edges. Remove the gingerbreads from the oven and, if you are planning to make a garland, immediately make two holes in the middle of each using the round end of a skewer, ensuring the holes are large enough for a ribbon to thread through. Leave for 5 minutes, then transfer the gingerbreads to a wire rack to cool.

7 To decorate, put icing into a piping bag with a small nozzle, and add little faces and clothing features of your choice. Leave to set.

COOK'S TIP

To hang a garland, use a needle to thread a long length or ribbon or strong thread through the two holds in the gingerbreads, looping from the back through the front. When they are all threaded, they are ready to hang – but don't pull the thread too tight.

BRANDY SNAPS WITH CREAM

Records show that brandy snaps were sold at fairs in the north of England in the 19th century. They were considered a special treat for high days and holidays. Every kitchen had a little pot of ground ginger ready for adding to cakes, biscuits and these lacy wafer rolls.

MAKES ABOUT 12

50g/2oz/4 tbsp butter

50g/2oz/4 tbsp caster (superfine) sugar

2 tbsp golden (light corn) syrup

50g/2oz/½ cup plain (all-purpose) flour

½ tsp ground ginger

1 tsp brandy

oil, for greasing

150ml/¼ pint/⅔ cup double (heavy) or whipping cream

1 Preheat the oven to 180°C/350°F/gas 4. Line two or three baking sheets with baking parchment.

2 Gently heat the butter, sugar and golden syrup (in a saucepan on the hob or in the microwave on low power) until the butter has melted and the sugar has dissolved.

3 Remove the pan from the heat. Sift the flour and ginger and stir into the mixture with the brandy.

4 Put small spoonfuls of the mixture on the lined baking sheets, spacing them about 10cm/4in apart to allow for spreading. Put into the hot oven and cook for 7–8 minutes or until bubbling and golden. Meanwhile, grease the handles of several wooden spoons.

5 Allow the wafers to cool on the tin for about 1 minute, then loosen with a palette knife and quickly roll around the spoon handles. Leave to set for 1 minute, before sliding them off the handles and cooling completely on a wire rack.

6 Just before serving, whip the cream until soft peaks form, spoon into a piping bag and pipe a little into both ends of each brandy snap.

COOK'S TIP

Store unfilled brandy snaps in an airtight container; they should stay crisp for up to a week. Fill with cream just before serving.

CLOTTED CREAM

Clotted cream is traditionally associated with south-west England and considered
the essential addition to a teatime scone. It is usually bought, but it is possible to make
your own. Traditionally made with raw milk by the so-called 'float-cream method',
whereby cream that rises to the surface of the milk is scalded on the stove and cooled very
slowly, this alternative method involves simply baking cream in a cool oven. The idea is not
to cook the cream, but to gently warm it so some of the liquid evaporates. For those with
an old-fashioned range, the warming oven is perfect, but a conventional or fan-assisted
oven may also be used. Clotted cream will not keep very long and is best used fresh, so it is
advisable not to make vast quantities unless you know that it will all be used up – it can be
stored in the refrigerator for up to 4 days.

MAKES ABOUT 175g/6oz

350ml/12fl oz double
(heavy) cream

1 Preheat the oven to 80°C/176°F. Pour the cream into ovenproof
ceramic dishes or ramekins and place them on a baking tray.

2 Put in a very low oven for 3 hours, or until the cream appears to
form a skin that starts to wrinkle and become more yellow.

3 Take the dish out of the oven and allow to cool at room
temperature. Don't stir or break into it. Cover with cling film
(plastic wrap) and place it in the fridge for 12 hours. There should
be a thick, slightly yellow crust.

BREADS & YEAST BAKES

Before the invention of chemical raising agents in the 19th century, yeast was the sole raising agent. Originally, wheat bread was made only for Sundays and special occasions, while sweet fruit breads were a rare treat for most people and reserved for festive celebrations. Wheat was grown in the south-east, and so wheat flour was used there for breads, while the oats grown in Staffordshire, Yorkshire and Lancashire were the staple grain in their breads and griddle cakes.

PICTURED *Wheat ready to be harvested in late summer, near Caistor, in the Lincolnshire Wolds.*

TEACAKES

These fruit-filled teatime treats, traditionally from Yorkshire, are thought to be a refinement of the original 'handbread': a shaped roll made on a flat tin. You can add a teaspoon of allspice to the flour, if you like. Serve them split and buttered, either warm from the oven or toasted.

MAKES 8–10

450g/1lb/3½ cups strong white bread flour, plus extra for dusting

1 tsp salt

1 tsp easy-blend (rapid-rise) dried yeast

40g/1½oz/3 tbsp caster (superfine) sugar

280ml/10fl oz/scant 1¼ cups lukewarm milk, plus extra for glazing

40g/1½oz/3 tbsp butter, diced

50g/2oz/⅓ cup currants

50g/2oz/⅓ cup sultanas (golden raisins)

1 Sift the flour and salt into a bowl. In a jug or pitcher, mix the yeast, 1 tsp of the sugar and the lukewarm milk, and leave to stand for 5 minutes.

2 Add the remaining sugar to the flour and make a well in the centre. Pour in the milk a little at a time and mix well, adding just enough to make a dry dough. Add the butter and knead briefly.

3 Turn the dough out onto a lightly floured surface and knead vigorously for at least 15 minutes, until the dough is no longer sticky and full of little bubbles, adding a little extra milk if necessary.

4 Shape the dough into a ball, place in a clean bowl and cover with a dampened dish towel. Leave at room temperature for 1 hour, until it has doubled in bulk. Grease two baking sheets.

5 Turn out the dough and knead in the dried fruit until it is evenly distributed.

6 Divide the dough into eight to ten portions, and shape into balls. Flatten each one into a disc about 1cm/½in thick. Place the discs on the baking sheets, 2.5cm/1in apart. Cover with oiled cling film (plastic wrap) and leave in a warm place for 30–45 minutes, or until they have almost doubled in size. Preheat the oven to 200°C/400°F/gas 6.

7 Brush the top of each teacake with milk, then bake for 15–18 minutes, or until golden. Turn out onto a wire rack to cool slightly. To serve, split open while warm and spread with butter, or let the teacakes cool, then split and toast them.

CRUMPETS

Toasting crumpets in front of an open fire became particularly popular during the reign of Queen Victoria. They are made with a yeast batter, cooked in metal rings on a griddle. Serve them freshly toasted and spread with butter and maybe a drizzle of golden syrup.

MAKES ABOUT 10

225g/8oz/scant 2 cups plain (all-purpose) flour

½ tsp salt

½ tsp bicarbonate of soda (baking soda)

1 tsp easy-blend (rapid-rise) dried yeast

150ml/¼ pint/⅔ cup milk

oil, for greasing

1 Sift the flour, salt and bicarbonate of soda into a bowl and stir in the yeast. Make a well in the centre. Heat the milk with 200ml/7fl oz/scant 1 cup water until lukewarm, and tip into the well.

2 Mix well with a whisk or wooden spoon, beating vigorously to make a thick smooth batter. Cover and leave in a warm place for about 1 hour until mixture has a spongy texture.

3 Heat a griddle or heavy frying pan. Lightly oil the hot surface and the inside of three or four metal rings, each measuring about 8cm/3½in in diameter. Place the oiled rings on the hot surface and leave for 1–2 minutes until hot.

4 Spoon the batter into the rings to a depth of about 1cm/½in. Cook over a medium-high heat for about 6 minutes until the top surface is set and bubbles have burst open to make holes.

5 When set, carefully lift off the metal rings and flip the crumpets over, cooking the second side for just 1 minute until lightly browned.

6 Lift off and leave to cool completely on a wire rack. Repeat with the remaining crumpet mixture. Just before serving, toast the crumpets on both sides, and butter generously.

ENGLISH MUFFINS

English muffins are circles of bread cooked on a griddle, and then toasted. In the past, muffins got their distinctive floury crust from being baked directly on the brick or stone oven floor. They are perfect served warm, split open and buttered for afternoon tea.

MAKES 9

450g/1lb/3½ cups strong white bread flour, plus extra for dusting

1½ tsp salt

350–375ml/12–13fl oz/1½–1⅔ cups lukewarm milk

½ tsp caster (superfine) sugar

15g/½oz fresh yeast

1 tbsp melted butter or olive oil, plus extra for greasing

rice flour or semolina, for dusting

1 Sift the flour and salt together into a large bowl and make a well in the centre.

2 Blend 150ml/¼ pint/⅔ cup of the milk, sugar and yeast together, then stir in the remaining milk and butter or oil.

3 Add the yeast mixture to the centre of the flour and beat for 4–5 minutes until smooth and elastic. The dough will be soft but just hold its shape. Cover with lightly oiled cling film (plastic wrap) and leave to rise in a warm place, for 45–60 minutes, or until doubled in bulk.

4 Turn out on a floured surface and knock back (punch down). Roll out the dough to 1cm/½in thick. Using a floured 7.5cm/3in plain cutter, cut out nine rounds.

5 Generously flour a non-stick baking sheet. Dust the muffins with rice flour or semolina and place on the prepared baking sheet. Cover and leave to rise, in a warm place, for about 20–30 minutes.

6 Warm a greased griddle pan over a medium heat. Carefully transfer the muffins in batches to the griddle. Cook slowly for about 7 minutes on each side, or until golden brown.

7 If you'd like to serve the muffins warm, transfer them to a wire rack to cool slightly before serving. Or cool, then toast like bread.

COOK'S TIPS

◆ Fresh yeast is traditional, but you can use 7g/½oz easy-blend (rapid-rise) dried yeast instead. You don't need to blend it with a little milk first; just mix it in with the flour and salt, and then add the liquid.

◆ Muffins should be cut around the outer edge only using a sharp knife and then torn apart. If toasting, toast the whole muffins first and then split them in half.

BATH BUNS

Bath buns, still made in Bath today, are made from very rich plain dough and have a sticky glaze and crushed sugar topping. They are thought to have originated in the 18th century, when they were topped with caraway seeds and sugar nibs. The first reference to Bath buns was by Jane Austen in January 1801, when she wrote of 'disordering my Stomach with Bath bunns'. Another famous bun from Bath is the Sally Lunn (see overleaf).

MAKES 10

500g/1lb2oz/4 cups
strong white bread flour

200g/7oz/scant 1 cup butter, diced

7g/¼oz easy-blend
(rapid-rise) dried yeast

2 tbsp granulated sugar

½ tsp salt

185ml/6½fl oz/generous ¾ cup
lukewarm milk

1 egg, beaten

FOR THE SUGAR SYRUP GLAZE

40g/1½oz/3 tbsp caster
(superfine) sugar

20ml/1½ tbsp water

3–4 sugar lumps, roughly crushed

1 Put the flour into a mixing bowl and rub in the butter until it resembles breadcrumbs.

2 Add the yeast, sugar, salt and the warm milk. Mix with your hands to a soft dough. Knead the dough for about 10 minutes on a lightly floured surface until smooth and elastic.

3 Place back in the bowl, cover with cling film (plastic wrap) and leave the dough to prove for about 1½ hours, until doubled in size. Line two baking trays with non-stick baking paper.

4 Knock the air out of the risen dough, then divide into ten equal pieces. Roll the pieces of dough into neat balls with your hands, then place on the baking trays, spaced apart from one another.

5 Flatten the balls slightly, cover loosely with cling film, and leave to prove for another 1½ hours. Preheat the oven to 180°C/350°F/gas 4. Brush the buns with beaten egg and bake for 25 minutes.

6 While the buns are baking, make the sugar syrup glaze. Heat the caster sugar with the water until the sugar has dissolved completely, then bring to the boil. Remove from the heat.

7 As soon as the buns come out of the oven, brush them liberally with the sugar syrup, and sprinkle with the crushed sugar lumps. Place on a wire rack to cool completely.

SALLY LUNN

The Sally Lunn is a famous yeasted enriched bun, originating from the spa town of Bath in the west of England. Sally Lunns are still made by hand in the original Bath bakery, which survives today as a popular teashop. The delicious buns are made there to a closely guarded secret recipe that came with the deeds of the house, and are served plain or with a selection of sweet and savoury fillings. It is traditionally served warm, sliced into three layers horizontally, and spread with clotted cream or butter. It looks fantastic.

SERVES 8–10

25g/1oz/2 tbsp butter, plus extra for greasing

150ml/¼ pint/⅔ cup milk or double (heavy) cream

1 tbsp caster (superfine) sugar

15g/½oz fresh yeast

275g/10oz/2 cups strong white bread flour, plus extra for dusting

½ tsp salt

finely grated rind of ½ lemon

FOR THE GLAZE AND FILLING

1 tbsp milk

1 tbsp caster (superfine) sugar

clotted cream, for filling (optional)

1 Lightly butter a 15cm/6in round cake tin or pan, 7.5cm/3in deep. Dust lightly with flour if the tin lacks a non-stick finish. Melt the butter in a small pan and then stir in the milk or cream, and sugar. The mixture should be tepid. Remove from the heat, add the yeast and blend thoroughly until the yeast has dissolved. Leave for 10 minutes, or until the yeast starts to work.

2 Sift the flour and salt together into a large bowl. Stir in the lemon rind and make a well in the centre. Add the yeast mixture to the centre of the flour and mix together to make a soft dough just stiff enough to form a shape.

3 Turn out the dough onto a lightly floured surface and knead for about 10 minutes until smooth and elastic. Shape into a ball and place in the prepared tin. Cover with lightly oiled cling film (plastic wrap) and leave in a warm place for 1¼ –1½ hours.

4 When the dough has risen almost to the top of the tin, remove the cling film. Meanwhile, preheat the oven to 220°C/425°F/gas 7.

5 Bake for 15–20 minutes or until light golden. While the loaf is baking, heat the milk and sugar for the glaze in a small pan until the sugar has dissolved, then bring to the boil. Brush the glaze over the bread.

6 Leave to cool in the tin for 10 minutes, or until the bread comes away from the side easily, then cool slightly on a wire rack before slicing and filling.

HOT CROSS BUNS

These tasty currant and sultana buns are traditionally eaten at Easter time. The cross on top probably first symbolised the four seasons; it was only later used to mark Good Friday and the Crucifixion. They became a particular Lent favourite among the Elizabethans, who enjoyed displaying their wealth and sophistication by using the expensive and sought-after spices from the Far East.

MAKES 12

450g/1lb/3½ cups strong white bread flour, plus extra for dusting

1½ tsp mixed (apple pie) spice

½ tsp ground cinnamon

½ tsp salt

50g/2oz/4 tbsp caster (superfine) sugar

7g/¼oz easy-blend (rapid-rise) dried yeast

210ml/7½fl oz/scant 1 cup milk

50g/2oz/4 tbsp butter

1 egg

75g/3oz/½ cup currants

25g/1oz/2½ tbsp sultanas (golden raisins)

25g/1oz/2½ tbsp chopped mixed (candied) peel

FOR THE PASTRY CROSSES

50g/2oz/½ cup plain (all-purpose) flour

25g/1oz/2 tbsp butter

about 1 tbsp cold water, if needed

FOR THE GLAZE

30ml/2 tbsp milk

25g/1oz/2 tbsp caster sugar

1 Put the flour, mixed spice and cinnamon in a bowl. On one side, add the salt and sugar; on the other, sprinkle over the yeast.

2 Heat the milk gently in a pan with the butter and allow to cool slightly, then mix into the flour, adding the egg to form a soft and sticky dough.

3 Add the dried fruit and peel, and knead together to form a smooth and stretchy dough. Cover with cling film (plastic wrap) and leave to rise for about 45 minutes, until doubled in size. Grease two baking sheets.

4 On a lightly floured surface, knock the dough back (punch it down) gently, then divide it into 12 pieces. Cup each piece between your hands and shape it into a ball. Place on the prepared baking sheets, cover with oiled cling film and leave to prove for another 30–45 minutes or until almost doubled in size.

5 Meanwhile, preheat the oven to 200°C/400°F/gas 6. To make the pastry for the crosses, rub the flour and butter together in a bowl until the mixture resembles fine breadcrumbs. Bind with enough cold water to make a soft pastry that can be piped (about 1 tbsp but you may need to use slightly more). Spoon the pastry into a piping bag fitted with a plain nozzle, and pipe a cross on each bun. Bake the buns for 15–18 minutes, or until golden.

6 Meanwhile, heat the milk and sugar for the glaze in a small pan. Stir thoroughly until the sugar dissolves, then brush the glaze over the top of the hot buns. Turn out onto a wire rack. Serve warm or cool.

CHELSEA BUNS

Chelsea buns are said to have been invented by the owner of the Chelsea Bun House in London at the end of the 17th century. They make the perfect accompaniment to a cup of coffee or tea.

MAKES 12

500g/1lb2oz/4 cups strong white bread flour, plus extra for dusting

½ tsp salt

7g/¼oz easy-blend (rapid-rise) dried yeast

210ml/7½fl oz/scant 1 cup milk

50g/2oz/4 tbsp butter, softened, plus extra for greasing

1 egg, beaten

FOR THE FILLING

25g/1oz/2 tbsp butter, melted

75g/3oz/⅓ cup caster (superfine) sugar

25g/1oz/2 tbsp soft light brown sugar

115g/4oz/⅔ cup sultanas (golden raisins)

25g/1oz/2½ tbsp mixed chopped (candied) peel

25g/1oz/2½ tbsp currants

1 tsp mixed (apple pie) spice

FOR THE GLAZE

50g/2oz/4 tbsp cup caster (superfine) sugar

60ml/4 tbsp water

1 tsp orange flower water

1 Mix the flour and salt in a bowl, make a well in the centre and add the yeast. Warm the milk and butter in a pan, and gradually mix into the flour mixture. Next, stir in the egg, to form a dough. Cover with a damp cloth and leave it to rise, until doubled in size (about 30–45 minutes).

2 On a lightly floured surface, knock back (punch down) the dough gently, then roll it out to form a 30cm/12in square. Grease a 23cm/9in square cake tin (pan).

3 For the filling, brush the melted butter over the dough square. Sprinkle over both the sugars, sultanas, peel, currants and mixed spice, leaving a 1cm/½in border along one long edge.

4 Starting at a covered edge, roll the dough up tightly, Swiss (jelly) roll fashion. Press the edges together to seal. Cut the roll into 12 slices and then place these cut side uppermost in the prepared tin.

5 Cover and leave for another 30 minutes to rise again. Meanwhile, preheat the oven to 200°C/400°F/Gas 6.

6 Bake the buns for 15–20 minutes, until they have risen well and are golden all over. Leave them to cool slightly in the tin before turning them out onto a wire rack to cool a little more.

7 To make the glaze, mix the caster sugar with the water in a small pan. Heat gently, stirring occasionally, until the sugar is completely dissolved. Then increase the heat and boil the mixture rapidly for 1–2 minutes without stirring, until syrupy. Stir the orange flower water into the glaze and brush the mixture over the warm buns. Serve slightly warm.

DEVONSHIRE SPLITS

A summer afternoon, another scrumptious cream tea. Devonshire splits are
less well known than the scone, the split (sometimes called a Chudleigh, after a
local market town) being a bread-type bun with a lovely soft stretchy texture,
split and filled with thick cream and jam.

MAKES 8

225g/8oz/scant 2 cups strong white
bread flour, plus extra for dusting

25g/1oz/2 tbsp caster
(superfine) sugar

½ tsp salt

7g/¼oz easy-blend
(rapid-rise) dried yeast

140ml/4½fl oz/generous ½ cup milk

a little oil, for greasing

FOR THE FILLING

clotted cream or whipped
double (heavy) cream

raspberry or strawberry jam

icing (confectioner's)
sugar, for dusting

1 Put the flour in a bowl. On one side, add the sugar and salt; on
the other, sprinkle over the yeast. Pour in the milk, mixing in
gradually to form a soft and sticky dough.

2 Knead the dough on a lightly floured surface for a few minutes
until smooth, then cover the bowl with cling film (plastic wrap) and
leave for about 45 minutes, until doubled in size. Lightly grease two
baking sheets.

3 Knock back (punch down) the dough gently, then divide into
eight equal portions. Shape each portion of dough into a ball, using
cupped hands. Place on the prepared baking sheets, and flatten the
top of each ball slightly. Cover with oiled cling film (plastic wrap)
and leave to prove again for 30–45 minutes or until the rolls have
doubled in size.

4 Meanwhile, preheat the oven to 220°C/425°F/gas 7. Bake the
buns for 15–18 minutes, or until they are light golden in colour.
Turn out onto a wire rack to cool.

5 Split the buns open and fill them with cream and jam. Dust them
with icing sugar just before serving.

LARDY CAKE

There are many different versions of this unequivocally English bread, but all go by the same name and all are very rich. A special fruit bread, it is traditional in the south of England to celebrate the harvest and other festival days. Using lard makes it authentic, but is not for vegetarians, so butter could be substituted (or non-dairy margarine for vegans).

SERVES 6–8

2 tsp sunflower oil, for greasing

450g/1lb/3½ cups white bread flour, plus extra for dusting

1 tsp salt

15g/½oz/1½ tbsp lard (shortening)

25g/1oz/2 tbsp caster (superfine) sugar, plus extra for sprinkling

20g/¾oz fresh yeast

300ml/½ pint/1¼ cups lukewarm water

FOR THE FILLING

75g/3oz/6 tbsp lard (shortening)

75g/3oz/scant ⅓ cup soft light brown sugar

115g/4oz/⅔ cup currants, slightly warmed

75g/3oz/½ cup sultanas (golden raisins), slightly warmed

25g/1oz/2½ tbsp mixed chopped (candied) peel

1 tsp mixed (apple pie) spice

1 Grease a 25 x 20cm/10 x 8in shallow roasting pan. Sift the flour and salt into a large bowl and rub in the lard. Stir in the sugar and make a well in the centre.

2 In a bowl, cream the yeast with half of the water, then blend in the remainder. Add to the centre of the flour and mix to a smooth dough.

3 Turn out onto a lightly floured surface and knead for 10 minutes until smooth and elastic. Place in a lightly oiled bowl, cover with oiled cling film (plastic wrap) and leave in a warm place, for 1 hour, or until doubled in bulk.

4 Turn the dough out on to a lightly floured surface and knock back (punch down). Knead for 2–3 minutes. Roll into a rectangle about 5mm/¼in thick.

5 Using half the lard for the filling, cover the top two-thirds of the dough with flakes of lard. Sprinkle over half the sugar, half the dried fruit and peel, and half the mixed spice. Fold the bottom third up and the top third down, sealing the edges with the rolling pin.

6 Turn the dough by 90 degrees. Repeat the rolling and cover with the remaining lard, fruit and peel, and mixed spice. Fold, seal and turn as before. Roll out the dough to fit the prepared pan. Cover with lightly oiled cling film and leave to rise, in a warm place, for 30–45 minutes, or until doubled in size.

7 Meanwhile, preheat the oven to 200°C/400°F/gas 6. Brush the top of the cake with oil and sprinkle with caster sugar, to glaze.

8 Score a criss-cross pattern on top using a sharp knife, then bake for 30–40 minutes until golden. Turn out onto a wire rack to cool slightly. Serve warm, cut into slices or squares.

COOK'S TIP

You can use dried rather than fresh yeast: use 2 x 7g/¼oz sachets or packets of easy-blend (rapid-rise) dried yeast, stirring it into the flour in step 1.

STOTTIES

This regional bread is native to the north-east of England and almost unattainable anywhere else. It's likely that they were first cooked on a griddle when most people didn't possess an oven. Later they were baked in the bottom of the oven, where the low baking temperature allowed the yeast to work longer, producing bread with a pleasant chewiness. In Yorkshire, very similar breads were known as oven-bottom cakes or scufflers – a scuffle was a tool used to clean the oven bottom.

MAKES 2 LARGE STOTTIES

675g/1½lb/6 cups strong white bread flour, plus extra for dusting

1½ tsp salt

7g/¼oz easy-blend (rapid-rise) dried yeast

1 tsp sugar

¼ tsp ground white pepper

450ml/¾ pint/scant 2 cups lukewarm water

1 Put the flour and salt into a mixing bowl and stir in the yeast with the sugar and pepper. Add the water and mix to a dough. Knead the dough for at least 10 minutes until it is smooth and elastic.

2 Cover the bowl with a clean tea towel and leave in a warm place for about 1 hour until the dough has doubled in size.

3 Preheat the oven to 200°C/400°F/gas 6. Grease two large baking trays.

4 Put the dough onto a floured surface and divide it into equal pieces. Roll out each to make two large flat discs, about 2.5cm/1in thick.

5 Make an indentation in the centre of each disc with a wooden spoon handle and prick the top of the bread with a fork.

6 Place the discs onto the baking trays and bake for 15 minutes. Turn the oven off, leaving the stotties in the oven for up to 30 minutes to continue to bake. Remove and place on a wire rack to cool completely.

STAFFORDSHIRE OATCAKES

These thick soft pancakes with a faintly sour tang are made with flour, oatmeal, yeast and salt. They were very popular in the local pottery towns in the 19th century, and the practice of making them remains widespread today. Professional bakers still guard their own unique recipes.

MAKES 12

225g/8oz/1½ cups fine oatmeal

225g/8oz/scant 2 cups plain (all-purpose) flour

1 tsp salt

15g/½oz fresh yeast

1 litre/1¾ pints/4 cups warm milk and water, mixed

1 tsp sugar

vegetable oil, for frying

1 Put the oatmeal and flour into a mixing bowl and stir to mix. Add the salt.

2 Dissolve the yeast in a little of the warm liquid and add the sugar. Set aside in a warm place until bubbles appear on the surface.

3 Stir into the flour mixture with the remaining liquid and mix to a smooth batter. Cover with a damp tea towel and leave in a warm place for 1 hour.

4 Heat a teaspoon of oil in a frying pan over a medium heat. Add a ladleful of the batter and swirl the pan to coat the bottom of it in a thin layer of the batter. Fry the oatcake for 1–2 minutes, or until golden brown on one side.

5 Turn the oatcake over and cook for a further minute, or until golden brown on both sides. Set the oatcake aside on a warm plate and cover with a sheet of greaseproof paper.

6 Repeat with the remaining batter mixture, to make about 12 oatcakes. Stack them on top of each other, separated by greaseproof paper, and keep warm.

YORKSHIRE FARLS

This is a round soda bread, cross-slashed into quarters ('farls') before being baked. Breads aerated with bicarbonate of soda instead of yeast became popular in England over a century ago, as they were quick to make. The secret of light soda bread is to work swiftly, handling the dough gently.

MAKES 4

250g/10oz/2¼ cups plain (all-purpose) flour

½ tsp salt

1 tsp sugar

1 heaped tsp bicarbonate of soda (baking soda)

250ml/8fl oz/1 cup buttermilk

1 Put the flour, salt, sugar and bicarbonate of soda into a mixing bowl and stir to combine. Make a well in the centre.

2 Pour in the buttermilk and quickly mix to a soft dough.

3 Roll out into a 20cm/8in round and cut into quarters.

4 Heat a heavy frying pan over a medium heat. Add the farls and cook for 8–10 minutes on each side until cooked through and golden brown. Leave to cool in the pan for 10 minutes.

5 Split open and eat warm with butter.

CORNISH SAFFRON BREAD

This was originally made at Easter. Its beautiful yellow colour and distinctive flavour come from saffron, used in England for this purpose for centuries. One theory is that saffron was introduced to Cornwall by Phoenicians trading in Cornish tin, but it was also cultivated, especially in the east of England. Serve sliced, spread with Cornish butter.

MAKES 1 LOAF

good pinch of saffron threads

150ml/¼ pint/⅔ cup boiling water

450g/1lb/3½ cups plain (all-purpose) flour, plus extra for dusting

½ tsp salt

50g/2oz/4 tbsp butter, diced, plus extra for greasing

50g/2oz/4 tbsp lard, diced

7g/¼oz easy-blend (rapid-rise) dried yeast

50g/2oz/4 tbsp caster (superfine) sugar

115g/4oz/⅔ cup currants, raisins or sultanas (golden raisins), or a mixture

50g/2oz/⅓ cup chopped mixed candied peel

150ml/¼ pint/⅔ cup milk

a little vegetable oil, for oiling

beaten egg, to glaze

1 Put the saffron in a bowl and add the boiling water. Cover and leave for several hours to allow the colour and flavour to develop.

2 Sift the flour and salt into a large bowl. Add the butter and lard and rub them into the flour until the mixture resembles fine breadcrumbs. Stir in the yeast, sugar, dried fruit and chopped mixed peel. Make a well in the centre.

3 Add the milk to the saffron water and warm to hand-heat. Tip the liquid into the flour and stir until it can be gathered into a ball. Cover with oiled cling film or plastic wrap and leave in a warm place for about 1 hour, until doubled in size.

4 Grease and line a 900g/2lb loaf tin with baking parchment. Turn the dough on to a lightly floured surface and knead gently and briefly.

5 Put the dough in the prepared tin, Cover and leave in a warm place for 30 minutes until nearly doubled in size. Preheat the oven to 200°C/400°F/gas 6.

6 Brush the top of the loaf with beaten egg and cook for 40 minutes or until risen and cooked through; cover with foil if it starts to brown too much. Leave in the tin for about 15 minutes before turning out onto a wire rack to cool.

LINCOLNSHIRE PLUM BREAD

This bread, always shaped into small loaves, is particularly associated with Christmas. It is sweet and rich and is eaten with cheese, sliced and buttered or toasted like rich teacake. Just as with plum pudding or plum cake, plum in this context means dried fruit, namely currants, raisins and sultanas.

MAKES 2 SMALL LOAVES

450g/1lb/3½ cups strong white bread flour

pinch of salt

1 tsp ground cinnamon

1 tsp freshly grated nutmeg

2½ tsp easy-blend (rapid-rise) dried yeast

50g/2oz/4 tbsp soft light brown sugar

115g/4oz/½ cup butter, diced, plus extra for greasing

about 100ml/3½fl oz/scant ½ cup milk

2 eggs, lightly beaten

a little vegetable oil, for oiling

225g/8oz/1 cup mixed dried fruit, such as currants, raisins, sultanas and chopped mixed (candied) peel

1 Sift together the flour, salt and spices and stir in the yeast and sugar. Gently heat the butter and milk until just melted. Add the eggs to the flour and mix well until the mixture can be gathered into a smooth ball of dough.

2 Cover with oiled cling film or plastic wrap, and leave in a warm place for about 1 hour until doubled in size. Grease and line two 450g/1lb loaf tins or pans with baking parchment and preheat the oven to 190°C/375°F/gas 5.

3 Knead the dough briefly on a lightly floured surface, working in the dried fruit evenly. Divide between the prepared tins, cover with oiled cling film and leave in a warm place for 30 minutes, or until nearly doubled in size.

4 Cook the loaves for 40 minutes, then turn them out of their tins and return to the hot oven for about 5 minutes, or until they sound hollow when tapped on the base. Cool on a wire rack.

COTTAGE LOAF

The double-ball appearance of this traditional loaf is unmistakable.
Snipping both sections of the dough at intervals looks attractive and also helps
this classic country loaf to rise and expand in the oven while it cooks.

MAKES I LARGE LOAF

a little butter or oil, for greasing

675g/1½lb/6 cups unbleached
strong white bread flour,
plus extra for dusting

2 tsp salt

20g/¾oz fresh yeast

400ml/14fl oz/1⅔ cups
lukewarm water

1 Lightly grease two baking sheets. Sift the flour and salt together into a large bowl and make a well in the centre.

2 Mix the yeast in 150ml/¼ pint/⅔ cup of the lukewarm water until dissolved. Pour into the centre of the flour with the remaining water and mix to a firm dough.

3 Knead on a lightly floured surface for 10 minutes until smooth and elastic. Place in a lightly oiled bowl, cover with lightly oiled cling film or plastic wrap and leave to rise, in a warm place, for about 1 hour, or until doubled in bulk.

4 Turn out onto a lightly floured surface and knock back (punch down). Knead for 2–3 minutes, then divide into two-thirds and one third and shape into balls.

5 Place the balls of dough on the baking sheets. Cover with inverted bowls and leave to rise, in a warm place, for about 30 minutes. Gently flatten the top of the larger round of dough and, with a sharp knife, cut a cross in the centre, about 4cm/1½in across. Brush with a little water and place the smaller round on top.

6 Press a hole through the middle of the top ball with your thumb and first two fingers. Snip both balls round the sides at 5cm/2in intervals. Cover with lightly oiled cling film and rest for about 10 minutes.

7 Set the oven to 220°C/425°F/gas 7 and place the bread on the lower shelf. It will finish expanding as the oven heats up. Bake for 35–40 minutes, or until golden brown. Cool on a wire rack.

COOK'S TIPS

♦ To ensure a well-shaped cottage loaf, the dough needs to be dry and firm enough to support the weight of the top ball. Alternatively, make smaller, individual rolls – bake them for 25 minutes.

♦ You can use dried rather than fresh yeast: use a 7g/¼oz sachet or packet of easy-blend (rapid-rise) dried yeast, stirring it into the flour in step 1.

GRANARY COB

The word 'cob' is an old English word for a head, and plain round loaves made with coarse, brown meal would have been the basic loaf for many families for generations. Cobs today can be white, but are usually brown, wholemeal (wholewheat) or granary.

MAKES 1 LOAF

450g/1lb/3½ cups granary (wholewheat) or malthouse flour, plus extra for dusting

2½ tsp salt

15g/½oz fresh yeast

300ml/½ pint/1¼ cups lukewarm water

a little oil, for greasing

wheat flakes, cracked wheat or rolled oats for sprinkling

1 Lightly flour a baking sheet. Mix the flour and 2 tsp of the salt together in a large bowl and make a well in the centre. Place in a very low oven for 5 minutes to warm.

2 In a bowl, mix the yeast with a little of the lukewarm water, then blend in the rest. Pour the yeast mixture into the centre of the flour and mix to a dough.

3 Turn out onto a lightly floured surface and knead for about 10 minutes, until smooth and elastic. Place in a lightly oiled bowl, cover with lightly oiled cling film (plastic wrap) and leave to rise in a warm place for 1¼ hours, or until doubled in bulk.

4 Turn the dough out onto a floured surface. Knead for 2–3 minutes, then roll into a ball. Place on the baking sheet. Cover with a bowl and leave to rise in a warm place for 30–45 minutes.

5 Preheat the oven to 230°C/450°F/gas 8 towards the end of the rising time. Mix 30ml/2 tbsp water with the remaining ½ tsp salt and brush evenly over the bread. Sprinkle the loaf with wheat flakes, cracked wheat or a handful of rolled oats.

6 Bake the bread for 15 minutes, then reduce the oven temperature to 200°C/400°F/gas 6 and bake for a further 20 minutes, or until the loaf is firm to the touch and sounds hollow when tapped on the bottom.

SPLIT TIN WHITE LOAF

The deep centre split down this loaf gives it its name and characteristic appearance. The split tin loaf slices well for making thick-cut sandwiches, or for serving hearty chunks of bread to accompany robust cheese and relish.

  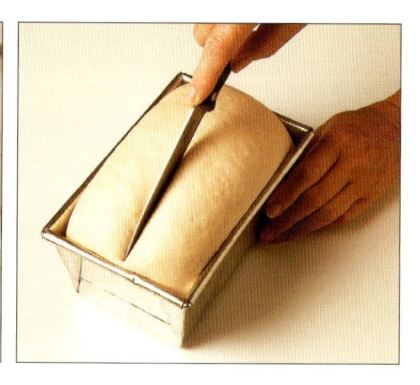

MAKES 1 LOAF

a little oil, for greasing

500g/1lb 2oz/4 cups unbleached strong white bread flour, plus extra for dusting

2 tsp salt

15g/½oz fresh yeast

300ml/½ pint/1¼ cups lukewarm water

60ml/4 tbsp lukewarm milk

1 Grease a 900g/2lb loaf tin (pan). Sift the flour and salt into a bowl and make a well in the centre. Mix the yeast with half the lukewarm water in a bowl, then stir in the remaining water.

2 Pour the yeast mixture into the flour and, using your fingers, mix in a little flour to form a smooth batter. Sprinkle a little more flour from around the edge over the batter and leave in a warm place for about 20 minutes to 'sponge'. Add the milk and remaining flour, and mix to a firm dough.

3 Lay the dough on a lightly floured surface and knead for about 10 minutes, until smooth and elastic. Place it in a lightly oiled bowl, cover with lightly oiled cling film (plastic food wrap) and leave to rise in a warm place for 1–1¼ hours, until nearly doubled in bulk.

4 Knock back (punch down) the dough and turn out onto a lightly floured surface. Shape into a rectangle, the length of the tin. Roll the dough up lengthways, tuck the ends under and place, seam side down, in the tin. Cover and leave to rise for about 20–30 minutes.

5 Using a sharp knife, make one deep, central slash. Dust the top of the loaf with a little sifted flour. Leave for 10–15 minutes. Meanwhile, preheat the oven to 230°C/450°F/gas 8.

6 Bake for 15 minutes, then reduce the oven temperature to 200°C/400°F/gas 6. Bake for 20–25 minutes, until golden and it sounds hollow when tapped on the base. Cool on a wire rack.

BLOOMER

This loaf is baked without a tin, either on a tray or on the bottom of the oven. It has a plump, oval shape and is distinguished by five or six diagonal slashes across the upper crust. A good bloomer has a soft crumb and a fragile and sharp crust. It can be made using brown wheat flour, rye or multigrain. However, the most popular type is white. Poppy seeds weren't originally added, but are often sprinkled over nowadays for flavour and crunch.

MAKES 1 LOAF

675g/1½lb/6 cups unbleached strong white bread flour, plus extra for dusting

2 tsp salt

15g/½oz fresh yeast

450ml/¾ pint/scant 2 cups lukewarm water

a little oil, for greasing

FOR THE GLAZE

½ tsp salt

30ml/2 tbsp water

1 tbsp poppy seeds (optional)

1 Sift the flour and salt together into a large bowl and make a well in the centre. Mix the yeast and a third of the water, then mix in the remaining water. Add to the centre of the flour. Mix, gradually incorporating the surrounding flour, until it forms a firm dough.

2 Turn out onto a lightly floured surface and knead very well, for at least 10 minutes, until smooth and elastic. Place in a lightly oiled bowl, cover with lightly oiled cling film (plastic wrap) and leave at cool room temperature for 5–6 hours or until doubled in bulk.

3 Knock back (punch down) the dough, turn out onto a lightly floured surface and knead it thoroughly and quite hard for about 5 minutes. Return the dough to the bowl, and re-cover. Leave to rise, at cool room temperature, for a further 2 hours or slightly longer.

4 Knock back again and repeat the thorough kneading. Leave the dough to rest for 5 minutes, then roll out into a rectangle 2.5cm/1in thick. Roll the dough up from one long side and shape it into a square-ended thick baton shape about 33 x 13cm/13 x 5in.

5 Place it seam side up on a lightly floured baking sheet, cover and leave to rest for 15 minutes. Turn the loaf over and place on a greased baking sheet. Plump up by tucking the dough under the sides and ends. Using a sharp knife, cut six diagonal slashes on the top. Leave to rest, covered, in a warm place, for 10 minutes. Meanwhile, preheat the oven to 230°C/450°F/gas 8.

6 For the glaze, mix the salt and water together and brush over the bread. Sprinkle with poppy seeds, if using. Spray the oven with water, bake the bread immediately for 20 minutes, then reduce the oven temperature to 200°C/400°F/gas 6 and bake for 25 minutes more, or until golden. Transfer to a wire rack to cool.

7 The traditional cracked appearance of this loaf is difficult to achieve in a domestic oven. However, if the underneath of the loaf is not crusty at the end of baking, turn it over on the sheet, switch off the heat and leave in the oven for a further 5–10 minutes.

OATMEAL BREAD

Oats have always been an important crop in England, although mainly for animal feed. Oatmeal contains no gluten, so breads made entirely using oats were inevitably flat, baked on stones or on a griddle. Many regions have their own traditional oatmeal cakes, but the oats can be used for baking loaves if mixed with wheat flour.

MAKES 2 LOAVES

500ml/16fl oz/2 cups milk

25g/1oz/2 tbsp butter

50g/2oz/3 tbsp soft dark brown sugar

2 tsp salt

1 tbsp easy-blend (rapid-rise) dried yeast

45ml/3 tbsp lukewarm water

300g/11oz/3 cups rolled oats

500g/1lb 2oz/4 cups strong white bread flour, plus extra for dusting

a little oil, for greasing

1 Put the milk in a small pan and bring to boiling point. Quickly remove from the heat and stir in the butter, brown sugar and salt. Leave the mixture to cool until lukewarm.

2 Combine the yeast and warm water in a large bowl and leave for about 15 minutes until frothy.

3 Stir the milk mixture into the bowl with the yeast. Keeping back a handful to sprinkle over later, add the rolled oats, and add enough flour to obtain a soft dough.

4 Transfer the dough to a floured surface and knead until smooth and elastic. Place in a greased bowl, cover with cling film (plastic wrap), and leave until doubled in volume (about 2–3 hours).

5 Grease a large baking sheet. Transfer the dough to a lightly floured surface and divide in half, then shape into rounds. Place the rounds on the baking sheet, cover with a clean dish towel or oiled cling film and leave to rise until doubled in volume, which will take about an hour.

6 Preheat the oven to 200°C/400°F/gas 6. Score the tops of the loaves and sprinkle with the remaining oats.

7 Bake the loaves in the oven for about 45–50 minutes, until the base of each one sounds hollow when tapped. Turn out onto wire racks to cool.

WHOLEMEAL BREAD

A simple wholesome bread to be enjoyed at any time. Wholemeal (wholewheat) bread has a denser texture than white bread. Wholemeal flour dates back to the early 17th century and contains all the bran and wheatgerm (which are removed from white flour), and is more nutritious than white flour. At the end of the 19th century, a growing interest in 'natural' foods increased its popularity.

MAKES 1 LOAF

525g/1lb 5oz/4¼ cups strong wholemeal (wholewheat) bread flour

2 tsp salt

4 tsp easy-blend (rapid-rise) dried yeast

450ml/¾ pint/scant 2 cups lukewarm water

2 tbsp honey

30ml/2 tbsp oil, plus extra for greasing

40g/1½oz/3 tbsp wheatgerm

milk, to glaze

1 Warm the flour and salt in a bowl in the oven at its lowest setting for 10 minutes.

2 Meanwhile, combine the yeast with half of the water in a bowl. Leave to dissolve and for the yeast to become frothy.

3 Make a central well in the flour. Pour in the yeast mixture, the remaining water, honey, oil and wheatgerm. Stir in the flour from the centre, incorporating it as you go, until smooth.

4 Grease a 23 x13cm/9 x 5in loaf tin (pan). Knead the dough just enough to shape into a loaf. Put it in the tin and cover with cling film (plastic wrap). Leave in a warm place to rise, until the dough is about 2.5cm/1in higher than the tin rim (about 1 hour).

5 Preheat the oven to 200°C/400°F/gas 6. Brush the loaf with milk, and bake until the base sounds hollow when tapped (about 35–40 minutes). Cool on a wire rack.

COOK'S TIP

Strong bread flours have a high gluten content, which allows yeast to rise well, and breads made with strong flours are light and have an airy crumb. Most yeast recipes use strong bread flour rather than plain (all-purpose) or self-raising (self-rising) flours.

HARVEST FESTIVAL SHEAF

Celebratory loaves, such as this centrepiece, often signal the start of harvest time. Harvest loaves are not really intended for eating, but are made by bakers in the autumn to coincide with harvest festivals in churches and schools. It is a tradition that has happily endured in many of the smaller villages of England, and bakers clearly enjoy the opportunity to demonstrate their skill and expertise.

MAKES 1 LOAF

900g/2lb/7 cups unbleached strong white bread flour, plus extra for dusting

1 tbsp salt

15g/½oz fresh yeast

75ml/5 tbsp lukewarm milk

400ml/14fl oz/1⅔ cups cold water

a little oil, for greasing

FOR THE GLAZE

1 egg

15ml/1 tbsp milk

1 Sift the flour and salt together into a bowl. Cream the yeast with the milk in a bowl. Add to the centre of the flour with the cold water and mix to a stiff dough. Knead on a floured surface for 10–15 minutes until smooth. Place in an oiled bowl, cover and leave for about 2 hours, or until doubled in size.

2 Turn the dough out onto a floured surface, knock back (punch down) and knead for 1 minute. Cover and leave for 10 minutes.

3 Divide the dough in two. Roll out one piece to a large oblong. Fold loosely in half lengthways. Cut out a half-mushroom shape, reserving the dough trimmings for the plaited tie. Place the half-mushroom shape on a greased baking sheet and open it out. Prick with a fork and brush with water. Cover and set aside.

4 Divide the remaining dough into two. Shape one piece on a floured surface into a rectangle, and cut into 30 thin strips and place on the base.

5 Preheat the oven to 220°C/425°F/gas 7. Take the last piece of dough and divide into four, then divide each into 25 to make 100 wheat ears. Make each roll pointed at one end. Arrange the ears around the outer edge of the top of the mushroom shape. Repeat until they are all used.

6 Beat the egg and milk for the glaze, and brush most of it all over the sheaf.

7 Braid the trimmings for the tie. Place across the wheat stalks and brush with glaze. Prick the tie using a sharp knife and bake for 15 minutes.

8 Reduce the oven to 180°C/350°F/gas 4. Brush the bread with the remaining glaze and bake for a further 30–35 minutes, or until golden. Leave to cool on the baking sheet.

CONDIMENTS, DRINKS & SWEETS

In olden times, foods in season were pickled, potted and dried to preserve them for the winter, when food was scarce. A wide variety of vegetables and fruits were cultivated, and any surplus was thriftily used to make a tempting variety of jams, jellies, condiments, chutneys, pickles and drinks. Some old-fashioned sweets and candies are included here as well, a delicious trip down memory lane for many.

PICTURED *Winter was the time to reap the benefits of the hard work preserving foods during the summer.*

MARMALADE

An English breakfast wouldn't be the same without marmalade on your toast. This is a classic recipe. To save time, you could shred the citrus peel in a food processor rather than by hand.

MAKES ABOUT 2.5kg/5½lb

900g/2lb Seville oranges

1 large lemon

2.4 litres/4 pints/10 cups water

1.8kg/4lb/9 cups granulated white sugar, warmed

1 Wash and dry the fruits. If you are using waxed fruit, scrub the skins. Halve the fruits and squeeze out the juice and pips (seeds), then pour into a muslin- or cheesecloth-lined sieve set over a bowl. Remove some of the pith from the citrus peels and reserve, then cut the peel into narrow strips.

2 Add the reserved pith to the pips in the muslin and tie together to make a loose bag. Allow plenty of room so that the water can bubble through the bag and extract the pectin from the pith and pips.

3 Place the shredded peel, juices and the muslin bag in a large preserving pan and pour in the water. Using a clean ruler, measure the depth of the contents in the pan and make a note of it.

4 Slowly bring the mixture to the boil and simmer gently for 1½–2 hours, or until the peel is soft and the contents have reduced by about one third of their depth. To check that the peel is cooked, remove a piece from the pan and, allowing it to cool, press between finger and thumb; it should feel very soft.

5 Using a slotted spoon, remove the muslin bag from the pan and set it aside until cool enough to handle. Then, squeeze as much liquid as possible back into the pan in order to extract all the pectin.

6 Add the warmed sugar to the pan and stir constantly over a low heat until the sugar has completely dissolved. It is important to keep stirring, to prevent the sugar burning on the bottom of the pan and your marmalade becoming caramelised.

7 Bring the marmalade to the boil, then boil rapidly for about 5–10 minutes until setting point is reached (105°C/220°F). You can use the wrinkle test to check the set, by pouring a tablespoon into a saucer and leaving to cool slightly. If a wrinkle forms on the surface when pushed with a fingertip, the marmalade will set.

8 Using a slotted spoon, remove any scum from the surface of the marmalade, then leave to cool until a thick skin starts to form on the surface of the preserve. Meanwhile, warm the sterilised jars and lids by leaving in a low oven at 140°C/275°F/gas 1 for 10–15 minutes.

9 Stir the marmalade gently to distribute the peel evenly. Ladle into the warmed sterilised jars, then cover and seal.

STRAWBERRY JAM

In England, wild strawberries were eagerly sought out in woods and undergrowth, and gradually the wild plants were transplanted into cottage gardens and smallholdings. London's street sellers were selling the luscious fruits as early as 1430. This classic soft fruit jam is always popular, and a great way to use surplus or over-ripe strawberries. Make sure the jam is allowed to cool before pouring into jars; otherwise, the fruit will float to the top.

MAKES ABOUT 2.25kg/5lb

1kg/2¼lb/8½ cups strawberries
juice of 2 lemons
900g/2lb/4½ cups granulated white sugar

1 Hull the strawberries by squeezing slightly and pulling out the stalk. Put the strawberries in a pan with the lemon juice. Mash a few of the strawberries. Let the fruit simmer for 20 minutes or until softened.

2 Add the sugar and let it dissolve slowly over a gentle heat. Then let the jam boil rapidly until a setting point is reached. To test for setting, pour about 1 tbsp into a saucer and leave to cool slightly. If a wrinkle forms on the surface when pushed with a fingertip, a set is reached. Leave to stand until the strawberries are well distributed through the jam.

3 Pour into warmed, sterilised jars, cover and seal. Store in a cool dark place; the jam may be kept unopened for up to a year. Once opened, keep in the refrigerator and consume within 2 weeks.

BRAMBLE JAM

Blackberrying is a traditional autumn activity and leads to a range
of culinary delights – including this jam, perfect on hot buttered toast.
Blackberries are Britain's most common wild fruit and one of the
oldest; references to them date back at least a thousand years. Cultivated
blackberries don't have the same depth of flavour as wild berries, but are
still very good to eat and also have the advantage of having fewer pips
than the wild variety. The name of the bush is derived from
brambel, or *brymbyl*, signifying 'prickly'.

MAKES ABOUT 3.6kg/8lb

2.75kg/6lb/13½ cups granulated
white sugar, warmed

2.75kg/6lb blackberries

juice of 2 lemons

150ml/¼ pint/⅔ cup water

1 Put the sugar to warm either in a low oven or in a pan over a low heat. The heating of the sugar in advance helps speed up the jam-making process and gives a brighter, more intense flavour.

2 Rinse the blackberries and place in a large pan with the lemon juice and water. Bring to the boil and simmer for about 5 minutes.

3 Stir in the sugar, bring to the boil and boil rapidly. Check for the setting point by placing a spoonful of jam on a plate, and allow to cool. If it wrinkles when pressed, it's ready. Ladle into warmed, sterilised jam jars and seal. Store in a dark place.

REDCURRANT JELLY

This is one of the best fruit jellies you can make. It is traditionally served
with meats such as lamb or venison, or try it with goat's cheese.

MAKES ABOUT 1.3kg/3lb

1.3kg/3lb just-ripe redcurrants

600ml/1 pint/2½ cups water

about 900g/2lb/4½ cups preserving
or granulated sugar

1 Check the fruit is clean. If necessary, rinse in cold water and use a little less water in the recipe. Remove the currants from the stalks.

2 Place the redcurrants in a large heavy pan with the water and simmer gently for about 30 minutes, or until the fruit is very soft and pulpy. Stir occasionally during cooking, to prevent the fruit from catching and burning.

3 Pour the cooked fruit and juices into a sterilised jelly bag suspended over a large bowl. Leave to drain for about 4 hours, or until the juice stops dripping. (Do not press or squeeze the fruit in the bag, because this will result in a cloudy jelly.)

4 Discard the pulp remaining in the bag. Pour the juice into the cleaned pan and add 450g/1lb/2¼ cups warmed sugar for each 600ml/1 pint/2½ cups of juice.

5 Heat the mixture gently, stirring frequently, until the sugar has completely dissolved, then increase the heat and bring to the boil.

6 Boil the jelly rapidly for about 10 minutes, or until setting point is reached. You can check this using the flake test or wrinkle test, or you can use a jam thermometer. The jelly should be heated to 105°C/220°F.

7 Remove the pan from the heat, then skim any froth from the surface of the jelly using a slotted spoon. Carefully remove the last traces of froth using a piece of kitchen paper.

8 Pot the jelly into sterilised jars immediately, because it will start to set fairly quickly. Seal and cover the jelly while it is hot, then leave to cool completely. (Do not move or tilt the jars until the jelly is completely cold and set.) Label the jars and store in a cool, dark place.

COOK'S TIP

When making jellies with low-pectin fruit or vegetables, stir in a little lemon juice or vinegar to improve the set. This will also help to offset the sweetness of the jelly.

RHUBARB AND MINT JELLY

Rhubarb began to be cultivated as an ornamental plant in English gardens in the early 17th century, but it wasn't until the late 18th century that someone discovered that the thick fleshy stems were edible. This recipe is a good way to use up older dark red or green-stemmed rhubarb, which is usually too tough to use for desserts.

MAKES ABOUT 2kg/4½lb

1kg/2¼lb rhubarb

about 1.3kg/3lb/6½ cups preserving or granulated white sugar, warmed

large bunch fresh mint and 2 tbsp finely chopped fresh mint

1 Using a sharp knife, cut the rhubarb into chunks and place in a large, heavy pan. Pour in just enough water to cover, cover the pan with a lid, and cook until the rhubarb is soft.

2 Remove the pan from the heat and leave to cool slightly. Pour the stewed fruit and juices into a sterilised jelly bag suspended over a non-metallic bowl and leave to drain overnight.

3 Measure the strained juice into a preserving pan and add 450g/1lb/2¼ cups warmed sugar for each 600ml/1 pint/2½ cups strained juice.

4 Add the bunch of mint to the pan. Bring to the boil, stirring until the sugar has dissolved. Boil to setting point (105°C/220°F).

5 Remove the bunched mint. Leave to stand for 10 minutes, stir in the chopped mint, then pot into sterilised jars and seal.

RED GOOSEBERRY JELLY

Perfect for spreading on toast at any time of the day. Choose small dark red gooseberries to produce a jelly with the best colour and flavour. The amount of pectin in gooseberries diminishes as the fruit ripens, so select firm, just-ripe fruit to achieve a really good set.

MAKES ABOUT 2kg/4½lb

1.3kg/3lb red gooseberries

2 red skinned eating apples, washed and chopped with skins and cores intact

2.5cm/1in piece fresh root ginger, sliced

about 1.3kg/3lb/6½ cups preserving or granulated white sugar, warmed

1 Put the fruit and ginger in a pan and pour over just enough water to cover the fruit. Cover and simmer for 45 minutes.

2 Remove from the heat, cool slightly, then pour the fruit and juices into a sterilised jelly bag suspended over a non-metallic bowl and leave to drain overnight.

3 Measure the strained juice into a pan and add 450g/1lb/2¼ cups warmed sugar for every 600ml/1 pint/2½ cups juice.

4 Stir over a low heat until the sugar has dissolved. Boil for about 10 minutes, or to setting point (105°C/220°F). Skim off any scum, then pot into sterilised jars, seal and label.

LEMON AND LIME CURD

Home-made classic English lemon curd is irresistible. Serve this intense creamy citrus spread with toast or muffins, as an alternative to jam. It can also be used to make tarts or as a tangy filling for a sponge cake.

MAKES ABOUT 1.3kg/3lb

3 eggs

115g/4oz/½ cup unsalted butter

grated rind and juice of 2 lemons

grated rind and juice of 2 limes (or more lemons, if you prefer)

225g/8oz/generous 1 cup caster (superfine) sugar

1 Set a large heatproof mixing bowl over a pan of simmering water. Lightly beat the eggs in another bowl.

2 Add the butter to the bowl above the pan, and then pour in the beaten eggs.

3 Add the lemon and lime rinds and juices to the beaten egg and butter, then add the sugar.

4 Stir the mixture with a wooden spoon constantly until it thickens, then pour into sterilised jars. Seal and store in a cool, dark place. The curd will keep unopened for up to a month. Once opened, keep in the refrigerator and consume within a week.

COOK'S TIP

Buy unwaxed lemons and limes, if possible. If not, before grating the zest, wash the fruit in warm water to remove the wax.

APPLE BUTTER

Fruit butters are old country recipes for potted thick fruit pastes. Despite the name, they don't contain butter – the fruit is simmered with sugar until thick and concentrated. Spices were often added, too. Spread onto bread, toast and teacakes.

MAKES ABOUT 1.8kg/4lb

500ml/16fl oz/2 cups dry (hard) cider

450g/1lb tart cooking apples, peeled, cored and sliced

450g/1lb eating apples, peeled, cored and sliced

grated rind and juice of 1 lemon

675g/1½lb/scant 3½ cups granulated white sugar, warmed

1 tsp ground cinnamon

1 Pour the cider into a large pan and bring to the boil. Boil hard until the volume is reduced by half, then add the apples and lemon rind and juice.

2 Cover the pan and cook for 10 minutes. Uncover and continue cooking for 20–30 minutes, or until the apples are very soft.

3 Leave the mixture to cool slightly, then pour into a blender or food processor and blend to a purée. Press through a fine sieve into a bowl.

4 Measure the purée into a large heavy pan, adding 275g/10oz/ 1⅓ cups warmed sugar for every 600ml/1 pint/2½ cups of purée. Add the ground cinnamon and stir well to combine.

5 Gently heat the mixture, stirring continuously, until the sugar has completely dissolved. Increase the heat and boil steadily for about 20 minutes, stirring frequently, until the mixture forms a thick purée that hold its shape when spooned onto a cold plate.

6 Spoon the apple and cinnamon butter into warmed, sterilised jars. Seal and label, then store in a cool, dark place for 2 days to allow the flavours to develop before serving.

PLUM CHEESE

Sweet fruit jellies became known as cheeses because they are firm enough to be cut into slices and wedges, and can be set in shaped moulds and turned out. You can use hard cooking plums for this cheese, or damsons for the most intense flavour. This wonderfully fragrant fruit cheese is good with cheeses, roast lamb, duck and game.

MAKES ABOUT 1kg/2¼lb

1.5kg/3¼lb hard plums or damsons, washed, destoned and halved

800g/1¾lb/4 cups granulated or preserving sugar, warmed

a little vegetable oil, for greasing

1 Put the plums or damsons in a large, heavy pan, and pour in enough water to come halfway up the fruit. Bring to a boil, cover and simmer for 30 minutes.

2 Press the fruit and juices through a sieve into a bowl. Measure the purée into the cleaned large pan, adding 400g/14oz/2 cups sugar for every 600ml/1 pint/2½ cups of purée.

3 Gently heat the purée, stirring, until the sugar has dissolved. Increase the heat slightly and cook for about 45 minutes, stirring frequently with a wooden spoon, until very thick. When the cheese is ready, you should be able to see the base of the pan when a wooden spoon is drawn through the mixture. To test the set, spoon a small amount onto a chilled plate – it should be very stiff.

4 Spoon the mixture into greased moulds or ramekins, and leave to set before turning out and serving. Keep refrigerated and use within 2 weeks.

VARIATIONS

Try the cheese set in squares, dusted with sugar and served as a sweetmeat. It is also good bottled in jars and spooned out as required; it will keep for up to 6 months in sealed, sterilised jars.

GREEN TOMATO CHUTNEY

This is a classic chutney for using the last tomatoes of summer that just never seem to ripen. Autumn apples and onions contribute essential flavour, which is enhanced by the addition of sultanas and ginger.

MAKES ABOUT 1.5kg/3½lb

900g/2lb green tomatoes, chopped

450g/1lb cooking apples, peeled, cored and chopped

450g/1lb onions, chopped

2 large garlic cloves, chopped

1 tsp salt

300ml/½ pint/1¼ cups cider vinegar or pickling vinegar

150g/5oz/scant ¾ cup sultanas (golden raisins)

2.5cm/1in piece fresh root ginger, grated

350g/12oz/1½ cups light muscovado (brown) sugar

1 Place the tomatoes, apples, onions and garlic in a heavy pan and add the salt.

2 Add about a third of the vinegar to the pan and bring to the boil. Reduce the heat, then simmer for 1 hour, or until the chutney is reduced and thick, stirring frequently.

3 Remove from the heat. Add the sultanas, ginger, sugar and remaining vinegar to the chutney. When the sugar has dissolved completely, return to the heat and bring to the boil.

4 Reduce the heat and simmer gently for 1½ hours until thick, stirring the mixture occasionally.

5 Spoon the hot chutney into warmed, sterilised jars with non-metal lids. Cover and seal immediately. Allow the chutney to mature for at least 1 month before using.

SWEET PICCALILLI

Undoubtedly one of the most popular English relishes, piccalilli can be eaten with grilled sausages, ham, chops or cold meats, or a strong, well-flavoured cheese such as Cheddar. It should contain a good selection of fresh, crunchy vegetables in a smooth mustard sauce.

MAKES ABOUT 1.8kg/4lb

1 large cauliflower

450g/1lb pickling (pearl) onions

900g/2lb mixed vegetables, such as marrow (large zucchini), cucumber, green beans

225g/8oz/scant 1 cup salt

2.4 litres/4 pints/10 cups cold water

200g/7oz/1 cup granulated white sugar

2 garlic cloves, peeled and crushed

2 tsp mustard powder

1 tsp ground ginger

1 litre/1¾ pints/4 cups distilled (white) vinegar

25g/1oz/3 tbsp plain (all-purpose) flour

1 tbsp ground turmeric

1 Prepare the vegetables. Divide the cauliflower into small florets; peel and quarter the pickling onions; seed and finely dice the marrow and cucumber; trim the green beans, then cut them into 2.5cm/1in lengths.

2 Layer the vegetables in a large glass or stainless-steel bowl, generously sprinkling each layer with salt. Pour over the water, cover the bowl with cling film (plastic wrap) and leave to soak for about 24 hours.

3 Drain the soaked vegetables and discard the brine. Rinse well in several changes of cold water to remove as much salt as possible, then drain them thoroughly.

4 Put the sugar, garlic, mustard, ginger and 900ml/1½ pints/ 3¾ cups of the vinegar in a preserving pan. Heat gently, stirring occasionally, until the sugar has dissolved.

5 Add the vegetables to the pan, bring to the boil, reduce the heat and simmer for 10–15 minutes, or until they are almost tender.

6 Mix the flour and turmeric with the remaining vinegar and stir into the vegetables. Bring to the boil, stirring, and simmer for 5 minutes, until the piccalilli is thick.

7 Spoon the piccalilli into warmed, sterilised jars with non-metal lids, cover and seal. Store in a cool, dark place for at least 2 weeks. Use within 1 year. Once opened, store in the refrigerator for up to 2 weeks.

COOK'S TIP

Traditional preserving pans are copper, but if you don't have a preserving pan, any stainless-steel, shallow and wide-topped pan will be suitable – the large surface area will help evaporation during cooking, which gives a good result.

MINCEMEAT

Originally mincemeat was, as its name implies, made from minced meat, as a way of preserving the last scraps of meat; the mixture, which also included fresh and dried fruits, spices and sugar, was simmered for several days and then stored in sealed jars in the cellar or in an outhouse. A 17th-century writer described the contemporary mince pie, a huge dish called 'Christmas pie', as 'a most learned mixture of Neats-tongues [ox tongues], chicken, eggs, sugar, raisins, lemon and orange peel, various kinds of Spicery, etc'. Today's mincemeat no longer contains meat or poultry, and the suet is usually substituted with vegetable fat. The mixture may be used to fill open lattice tarts and small mince pies. Mincemeat should be made at least four weeks before Christmas and left in a cool, dry, dark place to mature.

MAKES ABOUT 1.75kg/4lb

225g/8oz/1⅓ cups currants

225g/8oz/1 cup
sultanas (golden raisins)

450g/1lb/2 cups seedless raisins

450g/1lb cooking apples,
peeled, cored and chopped

225g/8oz/1 cup candied
citrus peel, chopped

100g/4oz/⅔ cup blanched
almonds, chopped

225g/8oz/1½ cups vegetarian suet

225g/8oz/1 cup soft dark brown sugar

1 tsp ground cinnamon

1 tsp ground allspice

1 tsp ground ginger

½ tsp grated nutmeg

grated rind and juice of 2 oranges

grated rind and juice of 2 lemons

about 150ml/¼ pint/⅔ cup
brandy or port (optional)

1 Place all the ingredients except the brandy or port in a large mixing bowl. Stir well, cover the bowl with a cloth and set aside in a cool place overnight.

2 The following day, stir in enough brandy or port (if using) to make a mixture moist enough to drop from a spoon. Spoon the mixture into sterilised jars and cover and store in a cool, dry place.

VARIATION

Other fruits can be used in the mincemeat mixture if you like – dessert apples to replace some of the cooking apples; dried apricots, figs and prunes instead of some of the currants, sultanas and raisins; fresh green grapes.

WINDFALL PEAR CHUTNEY

The bullet-hard pears that litter the ground underneath old pear trees after high winds are ideal for this tasty chutney. Serve with cold meats or bread and cheese.

MAKES ABOUT 2kg/4½lb

675g/1½lb pears, peeled and cored

3 onions, chopped

175g/6oz/¾ cup raisins

1 cooking apple, peeled, cored and chopped

50g/2oz/⅓ cup preserved stem ginger

115g/4oz/1 cup walnuts, chopped

1 garlic clove, chopped

grated rind and juice of 1 lemon

600ml/1 pint/2½ cups cider vinegar

175g/6oz/¾ cup soft brown sugar

2 cloves

1 tsp salt

1 Peel the pears, then chop roughly and put them in a bowl. Add the onions, raisins, apple, ginger, walnuts and garlic, as well as the lemon rind and juice.

2 Put the vinegar, sugar, cloves and salt into a pan. Gently heat, stirring until the sugar has dissolved, then bring to the boil briefly and pour over the fruit. Cover and leave overnight. The following day, transfer the mixture to a preserving pan and boil gently for 1½ hours until soft.

3 Spoon into warm, sterilised jars with non-metallic lids. Seal and store in a dark, cool place for up to a year. Once opened, store in the refrigerator.

CUCUMBER DILL PICKLES

Pickling in vinegar was very popular in 16th-century England. Cucumbers were grown on a grand scale, eaten fresh in summer and pickled for winter, flavoured with fennel or dill.

MAKES ABOUT 1kg/2¼lb

1kg/2¼lb small cucumbers

100g/3½oz/⅓ cup coarse sea salt

750ml/¾ pint/generous 3 cups white wine vinegar

100g/3½oz/scant ½ cup white sugar

3 bay leaves

2 tbsp dill seeds

1 tbsp coriander seeds

2 cloves garlic, slivered

dill flowerheads

1 Slice the cucumbers into medium to thick slices. Layer with the salt in a large bowl, cover and leave overnight. Drain off the brine, then rinse and dry with kitchen paper.

2 Put the vinegar, sugar, bay leaves, dill seeds and coriander seeds into a pan and heat gently until the sugar has dissolved. Bring to the boil, then remove immediately from the heat.

3 Layer the garlic and dill flowerheads between slices of cucumber in sterilised preserving jars, until the jars are full, then cover with the warm vinegar mixture.

4 Seal with vinegar-proof (non-metallic) lids. If using metal lids, line them with a disc of waxed paper first. Leave for a week before using.

TRADITIONAL PICKLED ONIONS

Once, pickling was an important way of storing vegetables through the winter months, but nowadays onions are pickled because people like the taste. Although onions (and shallots and garlic) keep well in their natural state, pickling has always been popular because their naturally strong flavour survives the pickling process so well. Crunchy and pungent, pickled onions are essential for a ploughman's lunch.

MAKES ABOUT 1kg/2¼lb

1kg/2¼lb pickling (pearl) onions

about 750ml/1¼ pints/3 cups water

115g/4oz/½ cup salt

750ml/1¼ pints/3 cups malt vinegar

1 tbsp sugar

2–3 dried red chillies

1 tsp brown mustard seeds

1 tbsp coriander seeds

1 tsp allspice berries

1 tsp black peppercorns

a piece of cinnamon stick

5cm/2in piece fresh root ginger, sliced

2–3 blades of mace

2–3 fresh bay leaves

1–2 star anise (optional)

1 To peel the onions, trim off the root ends, but leave the onion layers attached. Cut a thin slice off the top (neck) end of the onion. Place the onions in a non-metallic bowl, then cover with boiling water. Leave to stand for about 4 minutes, then drain. The skins should then be easy to peel using a small, sharp knife.

2 Pour the water into a large pan. Add the salt and heat to dissolve, then cool before pouring the brine over the onions.

3 Place a plate inside the top of the bowl and weigh it down slightly so that it keeps all the onions submerged in the brine. Leave to stand for 24 hours.

4 Meanwhile, pour the vinegar into a large pan. Add the sugar. Wrap all the spices and herbs in a piece of muslin (cheesecloth), and add to the pan.

5 Bring to the boil, simmer for about 5 minutes, then remove the pan from the heat. Set aside, cover and leave in a cool place overnight to infuse.

6 The next day, drain the onions from their brine, rinse and pat dry. Pack them into sterilised jars. Pour the infused vinegar over to cover. (You can store leftover vinegar in a bottle for another batch of pickles.)

7 Seal the jars with non-metallic lids and store in a cool, dark place for at least 6 weeks before eating so the flavours develop.

COOK'S TIP

The longer you heat the flavourings with the vinegar, the stronger the taste will become. For a sweeter vinegar, dissolve an additional 30ml/2 tbsp of muscovado (molasses) sugar in the vinegar.

POACHED SPICED PLUMS IN BRANDY

Bottling spiced fruit is a traditional way to preserve summer flavours for eating in winter. Serve these with whipped cream as a dessert, or on top of muesli and yogurt for breakfast.

MAKES 1kg/2¼lb

600ml/1 pint/2½ cups brandy
rind of 1 lemon, peeled in a long strip
350g/12oz/1½ cups caster (superfine) sugar
1 cinnamon stick
1kg/2¼lb plums

1 Put the brandy, lemon rind, sugar and cinnamon in a pan and heat gently to dissolve the sugar. Add the plums and poach for 15 minutes, or until soft.

2 Remove the plums with a slotted spoon and set aside. Reduce the syrup by a third by rapid boiling. Strain it over the plums, then bottle them in sterilised jars. Seal tightly. Store for up to 6 months.

SPICED PICKLED PEARS

These delicious pears not only make a delicious dessert, but are also the perfect accompaniment for cooked ham. They will keep for up to a year unopened.

MAKES 1kg/2¼lb

1kg/2¼lb pears
600ml/1 pint/2½ cups white wine vinegar
225g/8oz/generous 1 cup sugar
1 cinnamon stick
5 star anise
10 whole cloves

1 Peel the pears, keeping them whole and leaving on the stalks. Heat the vinegar and sugar together in a large pan until the sugar has dissolved. Add the pears and poach for 15 minutes, covered, turning occasionally.

2 Add the cinnamon, star anise and cloves, and simmer for 10 minutes. Remove the pears and pack tightly into sterilised jars. Simmer the syrup for 15 minutes more and pour over the pears.

3 Seal the jars tightly with non-metallic lids and store in a cool, dark place. Once opened, store in the refrigerator for up to a week.

MINT SAUCE

In England, mint sauce is the traditional and inseparable accompaniment to roast lamb. Its fresh, tart and astringent flavour is the perfect foil to the rich, strongly flavoured meat. Extremely simple to make, this mint sauce keeps for up to six months when stored in the refrigerator, but is best when used within three weeks.

MAKES ABOUT 250ml/8fl oz

1 large bunch mint
105ml/7 tbsp boiling water
150ml/¼ pint/⅔ cup wine vinegar
25g/1oz/2 tbsp granulated white sugar

1 Using a sharp knife, chop the mint very finely and place it in a large heatproof jug or pitcher. Pour the boiling water over the mint and leave to infuse for about 10 minutes.

2 When the mint infusion has cooled and is lukewarm, stir in the wine vinegar and sugar. Continue stirring (but do not mash up the mint leaves) until the sugar has dissolved completely.

3 Pour the mint sauce into a warmed, sterilised bottle or jar. Seal the jar, label it with the date and store in the refrigerator or a cool, dark place.

REAL HORSERADISH SAUCE

Fiery, peppery horseradish sauce is the essential accompaniment to English roast beef, and is also delicious with smoked salmon. Take care when handling it, and wash your hands afterwards. To counteract the potent fumes of the horseradish, keep the root submerged in water while you chop and peel it. Use a food processor to do the fine chopping or grating, and avert your head when removing the lid.

MAKES ABOUT 200ml/7fl oz

3 tbsp freshly grated horseradish root
15ml/1 tbsp white wine vinegar
1 tsp granulated white sugar
pinch of salt
150ml/¼ pint/⅔ cup thick double (heavy) cream

1 Place the grated horseradish in a bowl, then add the white wine vinegar, sugar and just a pinch of salt.

2 Stir the ingredients together, mixing them well until they are thoroughly combined and smooth.

3 Pour the mixture into a sterilised jar. (It will keep in the refrigerator in this form for up to 6 months.)

4 A few hours before you intend to serve the sauce, stir the cream into the horseradish and leave to infuse. Stir once again before serving.

CUMBERLAND SAUCE

This citrus-based savoury sauce is considered to be quintessentially English, and it features in Mrs Beeton's famous cookbook. However, it originated in Hanover, Germany; the Duke of Cumberland became ruler of Hanover at a time when fruit sauces were served with meat and game in Germany. Spicy fruit sauces served with meat have been popular since medieval times, of course. This one goes well with cold cuts, pâtés and terrines, and Christmas turkey.

MAKES ABOUT
750ml/1¼ PINTS

4 oranges

2 lemons

450g/1lb redcurrant or rowan jelly

150ml/¼ pint/⅔ cup port

4 tsp cornflour (cornstarch)

pinch of ground ginger

1 Scrub the oranges and lemons, then remove the rind thinly, paring away any white pith.

2 Cut the orange and lemon rind into very thin matchstick strips. Put the strips in a heavy pan, cover them with cold water and bring the water to the boil.

3 Simmer the rind for 2 minutes, then drain, cover with cold water, bring to the boil and simmer for about 3 minutes. Drain well and return the rind to the pan.

4 Squeeze the juice from the fruits, then add it to the pan with the redcurrant or rowan jelly. Reserve 30ml/2 tbsp of the port and add the rest to the pan.

5 Slowly bring the mixture to the boil, stirring until the jelly has melted. Simmer for 10 minutes until slightly thickened.

6 Blend the cornflour and ginger with the reserved port and stir into the sauce. Cook over a low heat, stirring until the sauce thickens and boils. Simmer for 2 minutes. Leave the sauce to cool for about 5 minutes, then stir again briefly.

7 Pour into warmed, sterilised bottles or jars, cover and seal. The sauce will keep for several weeks in the refrigerator, but use within 3 weeks once opened.

HERB MUSTARD

Introduced into England by the ancient Romans, mustard was originally made by mixing the hot seeds of plants of the cabbage family with unfermented grape juice, or 'must'. It was very popular in the Middle Ages and became even more so in the 19th century, with the manufacture of yellow mustard powder, a blend of mustard seeds, turmeric and flour.

MAKES ABOUT 200g/7oz

75g/3oz/scant ½ cup white mustard seeds

50g/2oz/3 tbsp soft light brown sugar

1 tsp salt

1 tsp whole peppercorns

½ tsp ground turmeric

200ml/7fl oz/scant 1 cup distilled malt vinegar

4 tbsp chopped fresh mixed herbs, such as parsley, sage, thyme and rosemary

1 Put the mustard seeds, sugar, salt, whole peppercorns and ground turmeric into a food processor or blender and process for about 1 minute, or until the peppercorns are coarsely chopped.

2 Gradually add the vinegar to the mustard mixture, 1 tbsp at a time, processing well between each addition, then continue processing until a coarse paste forms.

3 Add the chopped fresh herbs to the mustard and mix well, then leave to stand for 10–15 minutes until the mustard thickens slightly.

4 Spoon the mustard into a sterilised jar. Cover the surface of the mustard with a baking parchment disc, then seal with a screw-top lid or a cork, and label. Store unopened in a cool, dark place for up to 3 months.

HONEY MUSTARD

Delicious home-made mustards mature to make the most aromatic of condiments. This honey mustard is richly flavoured and is wonderful served with meats and cheeses, or stirred into sauces and salad dressings to give an extra-peppery bite.

MAKES ABOUT 250g/9oz

225g/8oz/1 cup mustard seeds

1 tbsp ground cinnamon

½ tsp ground ginger

300ml/½ pint/1¼ cups white wine vinegar

90ml/6 tbsp dark clear honey

1 Put the mustard seeds in a bowl with the cinnamon and ginger, and pour over the white wine vinegar. Stir well to mix, then cover and leave to soak overnight in a cool place.

2 The next day, put the mustard mixture in a mortar and pound with a pestle, adding the honey very gradually.

3 Continue pounding and mixing until the mustard resembles a stiff paste. If the mixture becomes too stiff, add a little extra vinegar to achieve the desired consistency.

4 Spoon the mustard into four warmed, sterilised jars. Seal and label the jars, then store in a cool, dark place or in the refrigerator.

LEMON BARLEY WATER

Like lemonade, barley water has long been widely enjoyed as a refreshing summer drink and, until a generation ago, it would have been home-made. Lemon barley water is the traditional drink at the Wimbledon tennis tournament. Usually served cold, it is also good warmed, and served as a cold remedy.

MAKES ABOUT 10 GLASSES

50g/2oz/⅓ cup pearl barley

1 lemon

sugar, to taste

ice cubes and mint sprigs, to serve

1 Wash the pearl barley, then put it into a large stainless-steel pan and cover with cold water. Bring to the boil and simmer gently for 2 minutes, then strain the liquid. Return the barley to the rinsed pan.

2 Wash the lemon and pare the rind from it with a vegetable peeler. Squeeze the juice.

3 Add the lemon rind and 600ml/1 pint/2½ cups cold water to the pan containing the barley. Bring to the boil over a medium heat, then simmer the mixture very gently for 1½–2 hours, stirring occasionally.

4 Strain the liquid into a jug or pitcher, add the lemon juice, and sweeten to taste with sugar. Leave to cool. Pour the liquid into a bottle and keep in the refrigerator to use as required.

5 To serve, dilute to taste with cold water, and add ice cubes or crushed ice and a sprig of mint, if you like.

SUMMER PUNCH

Summertime means a long, cool drink in the garden. Quintessentially English, Pimm's is a gin-based spirit with a fruity flavour, a delicate combination of herbal botanicals, caramelised orange and spices. James Pimm created No. 1 Cup around 1840 and it was so popular that it had to be bottled to satisfy demand. The secret recipe has remained unchanged to this day. The beautiful borage flowers add the final flourish.

SERVES 4–6

1 small orange

¼ cucumber, thinly sliced

¼ bottle Pimm's ('No. 1 Cup' is traditional), chilled

several sprigs of mint and/ or lemon balm

several sprigs of borage

ice cubes

1 large bottle lemonade or ginger beer

1 Chop the orange into small chunks, leaving the skin on. Put in a large jug or pitcher with the sliced cucumber.

2 Pour the Pimm's into the jug, and add the mint and/or lemon balm, followed by the borage and ice cubes. (To prepare the flowers, remove each flowerhead from the green calyx by gently teasing it out. It should come away easily.)

3 Slowly pour in the lemonade or ginger beer, making sure it doesn't fizz up too much. Stir to mix through, check if it is cold enough, and add more ice if needed.

4 Serve the Pimm's in tall glasses, with flowers on top of each glass.

SLOE GIN

The small, purple fruit of the blackthorn shrub grow widely in
English country hedgerows. The tart, astringent berries are not much
used, except for infusing in alcohol to make sloe gin, as here.

MAKES 2–3 BOTTLES

450g/1lb ripe sloes (black plums)

225g/8oz/generous 1 cup
caster (superfine) sugar

1 litre/1¾ pints/4 cups gin

1 Check through the sloes and discard any damaged or unsound
fruit. Rinse the sloes and remove the stalks. Prick each sloe at least
once with a silver or stainless-steel fork, or use a wooden cocktail
stick or toothpick.

2 Select several wide-necked screw-top or easy-to-seal sterilised
jars and arrange alternate layers of fruit and sugar in them. Top up
the jars with gin, and close them tightly. Store for at least 3 months
in a cool, dark place.

3 Shake the jars gently every now and then to help extract and
distribute the flavour evenly. When ready, strain into a jug or
pitcher, and then pour into sterilised bottles and store for another 3
months if possible.

MULLED CIDER

This hot cider cup is easy to make and traditional at Halloween. However, it makes a
good, inexpensive warming brew for winter gatherings and celebrations, and
for 'wassail', drunk during the Yuletide tradition of door-to-door visiting.

MAKES ABOUT 20 GLASSES

2 lemons

1 litre/1¾ pints/4 cups apple juice

2 litres/3½ pints/9 cups
medium-sweet cider

3 small cinnamon sticks

4–6 whole cloves

slices of lemon, to serve (optional)

1 Wash the lemons and pare the rinds with a vegetable peeler. Mix
all the ingredients together in a large stainless-steel pan.

2 Set over a low heat and heat through to infuse (steep) the mixture
for 15 minutes. Do not allow it to boil.

3 Strain the liquid and serve, with extra slices of lemon, if you like.

ELDERFLOWER CORDIAL

The rank scent of the elderflower bush gives no clue to the delicate flavour of this cordial made from its flowers. It makes a wonderfully refreshing summer drink and a delicious sorbet. A spoonful of the cordial added to cooked gooseberries gives them a subtle muscatel flavour. To serve, dilute to taste with still or sparkling mineral water. Will keep indefinitely in a cool place.

MAKES 2.5 LITRES/
4¼ PINTS

1.5kg/3½lb/7½ cups granulated
white sugar
1.5 litres/2½ pints/6¼ cups hot water
50g/2oz citric acid
25 elderflower heads,
washed and gently shaken dry
2 lemons, unwaxed, sliced

1 Dissolve the sugar in the hot water and leave to cool. When cool, stir in the citric acid, and add the elderflower heads and lemons.

2 Cover and leave to infuse for 2 days, stirring occasionally.

3 Strain and pour into clean, dry, sterilised bottles and seal. Store in a cool place, and open the lid every now and then to release any build-up of pressure in the bottles.

ROSEHIP SYRUP

Rosehips are a rich source of vitamin C, so this is an ideal winter drink to ward off coughs and colds. Dilute before drinking!

MAKES ABOUT
400ml/14fl oz

400g/14oz ripe but firm rosehips
about 750ml/1¼ pints/3¼ cups water
200g/7oz/1 cup sugar

1 Wash the rosehips thoroughly, then top and tail them. Place them in a food processor and chop coarsely. Tip them into a pan, barely cover with water and bring to the boil. Turn down the heat and leave to simmer gently for about 10–20 minutes, until tender.

2 Remove from the heat and then allow to stand for a further 10 minutes. Leave to strain overnight through a sterilised thick jelly bag. The juice should be clear. However, if it is not, strain it through several thicknesses of muslin (cheesecloth) to remove any particles.

3 Pour back into the pan and add the sugar. Bring to the boil, and boil until the syrup thickens, then pour into warm, dry, sterilised bottles and seal securely with a cork.

4 To drink, dilute the syrup with water, to taste.

QUINCE PASTE

Quince must be cooked in order to bring out its delicious flavour and deep jewel colouring. The fruit was once very popular and was usually added to apple pies and puddings to give them a nice pink colour. Quinces were also cored and stuffed with sugar and baked like apples, but were most often served in the form of a paste, as here. For some reason they lost popularity in the late 18th century, but are delectable.

MAKES ABOUT 1kg/2¼lb

butter, for greasing

4 or 5 large quinces (about 1kg/2¼lb in weight)

100ml/3¾fl oz/scant ½ cup water

about 1.2kg/2½lb/6 cups granulated white or preserving sugar

45ml/3 tbsp fresh lemon juice, strained

caster (superfine) sugar, for coating

1 Grease a Swiss roll tin (jelly roll pan) and line with baking parchment.

2 Wash the quinces well to remove any fuzz. Quarter and core the fruit, but leave the peel on. Cut into smaller chunks and place the fruit in a large, heavy pan.

3 Add the water, cover and simmer over a low heat for about 1 hour, or until the fruit is soft and tender. Stir occasionally. Add more water, if necessary.

4 Remove the pan from the heat and pass the fruit through a food mill or sieve. Weigh the fruit pulp and place it back into the pan. Measure an equal weight of sugar and stir it into the puréed quince.

5 Place the pan over a very low heat and, stirring occasionally, cook for 1½–2 hours until the paste is a dark garnet colour.

6 To test the mixture, put a spoonful on a plate. It should firm up and, when it cools, it should be matte and not sticky. Stir in the lemon juice.

7 Spread the paste out in the tin. Leave to cool. Once cooled, cut into squares using a knife (or into shapes using a cutter) and coat in caster sugar. Store in an airtight container in the refrigerator for 3 weeks.

RASPBERRY JELLIES

Jellies of fresh fruit purées have been made in England since the Middle Ages and were a real luxury. Dense little fruit sweets such as these are different from the wobbly jellies that are served as dessert. These have just a slight bite and, because of the additional gelatine, they maintain their shape. They dissolve in your mouth, releasing their fresh fruit flavour.

MAKES ABOUT 1kg/2¼lb

500g/1¼lb/4½ cups raspberries

25g/1oz powdered gelatine

200g/7oz/1 cup preserving or granulated white sugar

20ml/4 tsp fresh lemon juice, strained

caster (superfine) sugar, for rolling (optional)

1 Put the raspberries in a heavy pan and heat gently until the fruits soften and the juices run. Do not stir. Strain through a sieve placed over a large bowl to catch the juices, pushing the pulp through with the back of a spoon. You should have about 300ml/½ pint/1¼ cups raspberry purée.

2 Put the gelatine in a small bowl with 60ml/4 tbsp cold water.

3 Put the sugar and 150ml/¼ pint/⅔ cup water in a pan. Cook over a low heat, stirring, until the sugar has dissolved. Then bring to the boil and cook until it reaches the soft-ball stage (114°C/238°F).

4 Add the softened gelatine, the raspberry purée and the lemon juice to the reduced sugar syrup.

5 Sprinkle a 20cm/8in square cake tin or pan with a little water. Pour the purée into the tin through a sieve. Leave to set for 5 hours.

6 Once set, run a small knife around the edge of the tin and turn the jelly out onto a marble slab or a cool solid surface, dusted with caster sugar. If the jelly sticks in the tin, run a warm, damp cloth over the bottom of the tin.

7 Cut into shapes with an oiled cookie cutter or a knife. Serve immediately, rolled in caster sugar, if you like. If you are not serving them on the day, dust with caster sugar and store in a cool place in an airtight container for 1–2 days. Roll in sugar again before serving.

VANILLA FUDGE

This classic sweetshop favourite has many variants, from the firmer Scottish tablet to the softer fudge found in America, but traditional English fudge has a firmer, grainy texture, which comes from the beating of the mixture.

MAKES ABOUT 1kg/2¼lb

300ml/½ pint/1¼ cups
full-fat (whole) milk

½ vanilla pod (bean), seeds scraped

900g/2lb/4½ cups caster
(superfine) sugar

125g/4½oz/generous ½ cup unsalted
butter, diced, plus extra for greasing

2 tsp vanilla extract

tiny pinch of salt

1 Grease a 20cm/8in square baking tin or pan and line with baking parchment. Prepare an ice bath: fill a large pan or a sink with crushed ice or ice cubes and cold water. Ensure that there's enough space for the pan, so that the iced water won't flow over the sides.

2 Put the milk, scraped vanilla seeds and pod, sugar and butter in a large, heavy saucepan and cook over a moderate heat, stirring constantly, until the sugar has completely dissolved and the butter has melted.

3 Increase the heat and bring the mixture to the boil. Cover with a tight-fitting lid and cook for 2 minutes, then remove the lid.

4 Without stirring, let the mixture cook at a slow-rolling boil for about 10 minutes, or until it reaches the soft-ball stage (114°C/238°F).

5 Immediately place the pan over the ice-water bath for a few seconds. Remove the vanilla pod with a fork or slotted spoon and discard. Stir in the vanilla extract and salt.

6 Place the pan in a cool part of the kitchen until it is lukewarm or about 43°C/110°F. Do not stir. Once it reaches this temperature, beat with a wooden spoon until it is thick, smooth and creamy.

7 Pour into the prepared tin and leave it to cool completely. Cut it into squares in the tin, then lift it out by the sides of the parchment and serve. Store in an airtight container.

DONCASTER BUTTERSCOTCH

There are many opinions as to which is the most traditional of the English sweets, but butterscotch will certainly be a popular choice. This hard buttery toffee was famous in Doncaster in Yorkshire in the 19th century and was sold to the racegoers who attended the horse racing there. The name comes from the English word 'scotch', to cut or notch.

MAKES ABOUT 450g/1lb

450g/1lb/2 cups demerara (raw) sugar

75g/3oz/6 tbsp butter, plus extra for greasing

45ml/3 tbsp water

150ml/¼ pint/⅔ cup milk

pinch of cream of tartar

1 Grease a 23cm/9in square cake tin or pan, and line it with baking parchment so that the paper comes all the way up the sides.

2 Place the sugar, butter, water and milk in a heavy-based pan and heat gently, stirring until the sugar has dissolved completely. Add the cream of tartar, stirring.

3 Bring to the boil and boil steadily, stirring occasionally until a little of the mixture dropped into a cup of cold water forms a hard crack and will break easily between your fingers (140°C/280°F on a sugar thermometer).

4 Remove from the heat and pour into the prepared tin or pan. When almost set, mark into squares. Leave in the tin until cold, then break and wrap the pieces in squares of cellophane or waxed paper.

BONFIRE TOFFEE

Dark, intensely flavoured and satisfyingly hard and brittle to crunch
on, this traditional English hard toffee is the perfect accompaniment to fireworks
and fun on Guy Fawkes Night, or Bonfire Night. In 1605, Guy Fawkes was arrested
for trying to blow up Parliament on that night, 5th November.

MAKES ABOUT 600g/1½lb

125g/4½oz/generous ½ cup unsalted
butter, plus extra for greasing

225g/8oz/1 cup black treacle
(molasses)

200g/7oz/scant 1 cup
demerara (raw) sugar

tiny pinch of salt

1 Grease a shallow baking tray. Melt the butter in a large, heavy pan over a low heat. Add the black treacle, the demerara sugar and salt to the pan, and let them gently dissolve into the butter.

2 Once they have completely dissolved, turn the heat up to medium and bring to the boil. Boil until the mixture is just below the hard-crack stage (154°C/310°F on a sugar thermometer). Carefully pour the syrup into the baking sheet.

3 Leave the toffee to cool – this should only take about 20 minutes. When it is cold, break into shards. As this is very sticky toffee, wrap the shards individually in pieces of baking parchment, if you wish, before storing in an airtight container.

TOFFEE CARAMEL APPLES

These delicious treats are a favourite with children at country fairs and village fêtes, especially around harvest time, as well as for Bonfire Night. The sweet caramel shell contrasts wonderfully with the crisp apple inside.

MAKES 8

8 small or medium eating apples

115g/4oz/½ cup unsalted butter

200g/7oz/1 cup granulated white sugar

150ml/¼ pint/⅔ cup double (heavy) cream

1 tbsp soft light brown sugar

125g/4¼oz/scant ½ cup golden (light corn) syrup

½ tsp vanilla extract

¼ tsp salt

1 Wash and dry the apples. Push lollipop (or ice lolly/popsicle) sticks or wooden dowels into the stem end of the apples.

2 Prepare an ice-water bath (see page 642) and line a shallow baking tray with baking parchment.

3 Place all of the remaining ingredients in a large, heavy pan and heat gently over a medium heat. Stir, until everything is dissolved together into an emulsified mass. Once the sugar has completely dissolved, increase the heat and bring the mixture to the boil. Cook until it reaches the soft-ball stage (114°C/238°F).

4 Remove the toffee from the heat and halt the cooking by placing the pan over the ice-water bath. Leave the mixture to cool to 82°C/180°F before dipping the apples into the toffee, holding them by their sticks and rolling them to coat in toffee all the way round.

5 Place the apples on the prepared baking sheet, stick end up, until the toffee hardens. If it slips off, leave it to cool slightly and dip again into the pan. Eat the toffee apples immediately or store in an airtight container at room temperature for up to 3 days.

BARLEY SUGAR TWISTS

Barley sugar was originally made with the water left over from cooking pearl barley, but it is essentially a hard-boiled sweet flavoured with lemon. You could try making them using the strained cooking water from boiled pearl barley, if you like (see page 630). The flavour will be rich and earthy, and will also make the sweets more nutritious.

 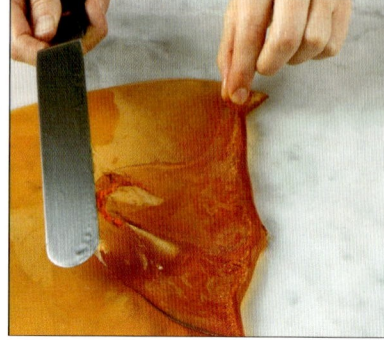 

MAKES ABOUT 600g/1½lb

oil, for greasing

450g/1lb/2¼ cups granulated white sugar

150ml/¼ pint/⅔ cup water

thinly peeled rind of 1 lemon

¼ tsp cream of tartar

juice of ½ lemon

1 Grease a marble slab, a palette knife or metal spatula, and a pair of kitchen scissors. Prepare an ice-water bath (see page 642).

2 Place the sugar and water in a heavy pan and bring to the boil. Add the lemon rind and cream of tartar.

3 Boil the syrup until it reaches the soft-ball stage (114°C/238°F). Add the lemon juice, then continue to boil until it reaches the hard-crack stage (154°C/310°F).

4 Remove the pan from the heat. Arrest the cooking by placing it momentarily over the ice-water bath. Remove the lemon rind with a fork, and discard.

5 Pour the syrup onto the marble and allow it to cool for 1 minute. Using the oiled palette knife or metal spatula, fold each side into the centre of the pool.

6 Gently pull the two ends to make a longer, thinner, flat piece of syrup. Using oiled scissors, cut 1cm/½in strips.

7 Working quickly, twist the strips into corkscrew shapes. Serve immediately, or wrap the sweets in baking parchment or waxed paper and store in an airtight container.

PEPPERMINT HUMBUGS

'Humbug', meaning 'a hoax'. or 'hypocrite' was a term first used in the 18th and 19th centuries, most famously by Dickens in *A Christmas Carol*. Developed in England around the same time, the sweet is a hard brown- or black-and-white confection with a chewy centre.

MAKES ABOUT 600g/1½lb

oil, for greasing

450g/1lb/2¼ cups granulated white sugar

150ml/¼ pint/⅔ cup water

¼ tsp cream of tartar

1 tbsp golden (light corn) syrup

2 tsp peppermint extract

2–3 drops black food colouring

1 Grease a marble slab, a metal scraper and a pair of kitchen scissors. Prepare an ice-water bath. Preheat the oven to 150°C/300°F/gas 2.

2 Combine the sugar, water, cream of tartar and syrup in a heavy pan. Heat gently until the sugar dissolves, then bring to the boil. Reduce the heat to medium and cook, without stirring, until it reaches the soft-crack stage (143°C/290°F). Add the peppermint.

3 Remove from the heat and arrest the cooking by momentarily placing the base of the pan in the ice-water bath. Pour the syrup onto the oiled marble slab and leave it to cool until a skin forms.

4 Using the oiled scraper, cut off one third of the syrup and place it back in the pan. Put in the warm oven to prevent it hardening.

5 Using the scraper, begin to fold the edges of the larger portion of syrup into its centre until cool enough to handle. Oil your hands and, with the aid of the scraper, lift the syrup up off the marble and work it into a cylinder. Pull from both ends to form a long strand.

6 Take hold of the ends of the syrup strand and pull them up toward you to form a 'U' shape. Twist the two sides together into a rope, then pull again from both ends to make the shape. Repeat these steps for 15–20 minutes, until the rope becomes opaque and lighter in colour. You need to work it constantly so that it remains supple. If it becomes too hard, put it in the oven for a few minutes to soften.

7 Divide the pulled syrup into four sections and pull these out to form strands of equal length and thickness.

8 Remove the un-pulled piece of syrup from the pan. Working quickly, add the black colouring to it with the scraper, and shape it into a log the same length as the white pieces but quite a lot thicker.

9 Press the four white ropes alongside and around the black log, spacing them evenly around the central black piece. Pull the whole thing gently at both ends until the combined piece is the required thickness of the sweets. Twist it once or twice so that the white strands spiral around the black. If the humbug taffy is still too soft, let it cool slightly and firm up a bit more, then cut it into small, even pieces. Wrap in waxed paper and store in an airtight container.

SOUR DROPS

Sour drops were originally called acidulated drops in 19th-century Britain. They are also known as acid drops and sourballs. The sour taste comes from the addition of tartaric acid. Although it sounds like a chemical, tartaric acid is actually an organic by-product of wine-making. If you cannot find it, you can use citric acid; the two are interchangeable.

MAKES ABOUT 600g/1½lb

oil, for greasing

450g/1lb/2¼ cups caster (superfine) sugar

150ml/¼ pint/⅔ cup water

½ tsp cream of tartar

½ tsp lemon juice

1 tsp tartaric acid

icing (confectioner's) sugar, for dusting

1 Grease a marble slab. Prepare an ice-water bath (see page 642) or fill the sink with a little cold water.

2 Put the sugar, water and cream of tartar in a heavy pan over a moderate heat, and leave for about 5 minutes until the sugar has dissolved.

3 Once the sugar has dissolved completely, turn the heat up to high and boil the mixture until it begins to turn yellow in colour and reaches the soft-ball stage (116°C/240°F).

4 Add the lemon juice to the syrup, but resist the temptation to stir it, as this could cause the syrup to crystallize. Continue boiling until it reaches the hard-crack stage (154°C/310°F), then remove from the heat. Place the pan briefly over the ice-water bath or cold water, to arrest the cooking.

5 Sprinkle over the tartaric acid and quickly stir it into the syrup.

6 Holding the pan of syrup low over the marble, carefully pour it out to form small drops, about the size of a large coin, or spoon it onto the marble with a spoon.

7 Allow the discs to harden and cool. Using an offset spatula, loosen the discs from the marble. Dust with icing sugar, then shake off any excess. Serve immediately, or wrap in baking parchment or waxed paper and store in an airtight container.

PONTEFRACT-STYLE CAKES

The original soft and intense liquorice cakes are from Pontefract, in the north of England, and date back to the 17th century. Pontefract was at the heart of the English liquorice industry, with manufacture soaring in the 19th century. Originally, a seal with a depiction of Pontefract Castle was applied to the top of each cake. If you have some little madeleine, tartlet or jelly moulds, try using the bottom of those. Or, if you have a wax seal stamp, that would look appealing.

MAKES ABOUT 550g/1¼lb

100g/3¾oz/8 tbsp butter, plus extra for greasing

200g/7oz/1 cup caster (superfine) sugar

75ml/5 tbsp golden (light corn) syrup

45ml/3 tbsp black treacle (molasses)

120ml/4fl oz/7 tbsp sweetened condensed milk

½ tsp salt

1½ tsp anise extract

a few drops of black food colouring

1 tsp bicarbonate of soda (baking soda)

1 Grease a 23 x 33cm/9 x 13in baking tray and line with baking parchment.

2 Place all of the ingredients in a heavy pan. Heat gently, stirring, until dissolved.

3 Turn up the heat and bring the syrup up to 112°C/233°F, stirring constantly, without scraping down the sides of the pan.

4 Pour the mixture into the prepared tray. Leave to cool, then chill for 10 minutes.

5 Remove from the refrigerator and stamp out small rounds with a small plain cutter. Transfer the rounds to a sheet of baking parchment.

6 Press the tops of the cakes with a stamp or mould. Serve immediately, or wrap in waxed paper and store in an airtight container for 1 month.

NUTRITIONAL NOTES

The nutritional analysis given for each recipe is calculated per portion (i.e. serving or item), unless otherwise stated. If the recipe gives a range, such as Serves 4–6, then the nutritional analysis will be for the smaller portion, i.e. 6 servings. The analysis does not include optional ingredients, such as salt added to taste.

p121 Full English Breakfast Energy 731kcal/3046kJ; Protein 32.7g; Carbohydrate 35.3g, of which sugars 7.6g; Fat 52.2g, of which saturates 16.5g; Cholesterol 288mg; Calcium 185mg; Fibre 3.1g; Sodium 2049mg

p122 Scrambled Eggs Energy 240kcal/995kJ; Protein 12.6g; Carbohydrate 0.1g, of which sugars 0.1g; Fat 21.4g, of which saturates 9.6g; Cholesterol 407mg; Calcium 60mg; Fibre 0g; Sodium 216mg

p122 Poached Eggs Energy 74kcal/306kJ; Protein 6.3g; Carbohydrate 0g, of which sugars 0g; Fat 5.6g, of which saturates 1.6g; Cholesterol 190mg; Calcium 29mg; Fibre 0g; Sodium 70mg

p125 Boiled Eggs Energy 74kcal/306kJ; Protein 6.3g; Carbohydrate 0g, of which sugars 0g; Fat 5.6g, of which saturates 1.6g; Cholesterol 190mg; Calcium 29mg; Fibre 0g; Sodium 70mg

p125 Coddled Eggs Energy 92kcal/383kJ; Protein 6.3g; Carbohydrate 0g, of which sugars 0g; Fat 7.6g, of which saturates 2.9g; Cholesterol 196mg; Calcium 29mg; Fibre 0g; Sodium 85mg

p126 Omelette Arnold Bennett Energy821kcal/ 3396kj; Protein 36.1g; Carbohydrate 2.6g, of which sugars 2.6g; Fat 74g, of which saturates 42.6g; Cholesterol 577mg; Calcium 280mg; Fibre 0g; Sodium 1123mg

p129 Bubble and Squeak Energy 219kcal/908kJ; Protein 2.5g; Carbohydrate 17.2g, of which sugars 2.5g; Fat 15.9g, of which saturates 1.9g; Cholesterol 0mg; Calcium 33mg; Fibre 2.6g; Sodium 14mg

p130 Gateshead Bacon Floddies Energy 214kcal/891kJ; Protein 8.8g; Carbohydrate 17.1g, of which sugars 3.5g; Fat 12.7g, of which saturates 3.4g; Cholesterol 82mg; Calcium 38mg; Fibre 1.4g; Sodium 397mg

p133 Mushrooms on Toast Energy 350kcal/1460kJ; Protein 6.8g; Carbohydrate 25.7g, of which sugars 2.1g; Fat 25.3g, of which saturates 14.2g; Cholesterol 57mg; Calcium 78mg; Fibre 2g; Sodium 318mg

p134 Poor Knights of Windsor Energy 250kcal/1043kJ; Protein 7.9g; Carbohydrate 22.2g, of which sugars 7.2g; Fat 14.2g, of which saturates 7.4g; Cholesterol 146mg; Calcium 75mg; Fibre 1g; Sodium 290mg

p137 Grilled Kippers with Marmalade Toast Energy 518kcal/2155kJ; Protein 33.9g; Carbohydrate 17.6g, of which sugars 5.9g; Fat 35.1g, of which saturates 7.6g; Cholesterol 121mg; Calcium 126mg; Fibre 0.4g; Sodium 1640mg

p138 Kedgeree Energy 320kcal/1337kJ; Protein 15.6g; Carbohydrate 46.6g, of which sugars 0g; Fat 7.6g, of which saturates 3.2g; Cholesterol 149mg; Calcium 39mg; Fibre 0g; Sodium 357mg

p141 Devilled Kidneys Energy 520kcal/2174kJ; Protein 29.9g; Carbohydrate 35.1g, of which sugars 3.8g; Fat 27.9g, of which saturates 15.9g; Cholesterol 449mg; Calcium 203mg; Fibre 4.3g; Sodium 604mg

p145 London Particular Energy 378kcal/1584kJ; Protein 20.2g; Carbohydrate 34.9g, of which sugars 3.1g; Fat 18.5g, of which saturates 8.7g; Cholesterol 47mg; Calcium 45mg; Fibre 3.4g; Sodium 527mg

p146 Cream of Tomato Soup Energy 107kcal/447kJ; Protein 2.3g; Carbohydrate 11.4g, of which sugars 10.9g; Fat 6.1g, of which saturates 3.5g; Cholesterol 13mg; Calcium 50mg; Fibre 3.9g; Sodium 71mg

p149 Jerusalem Artichoke Soup Energy 310kcal/1277kJ; Protein 2.7g; Carbohydrate 4.7g, of which sugars 4.3g; Fat 31.3g, of which saturates 19.4g; Cholesterol 80mg; Calcium 116mg; Fibre 1.5g; Sodium 168mg

p150 Watercress Soup Energy 68kcal/280kJ; Protein 1.5g; Carbohydrate 1.4g, of which sugars 1g; Fat 6.3g, of which saturates 2.4g; Cholesterol 8mg; Calcium 79mg; Fibre 0.9g; Sodium 45mg

p153 Country Vegetable Soup Energy 160kcal/665kJ; Protein 3.6g; Carbohydrate 11.5g, of which sugars 10g; Fat 11.4g, of which saturates 6.8g; Cholesterol 27mg; Calcium 72mg; Fibre 5.4g; Sodium 106mg

p154 Celery Soup with Stilton Energy 199kcal/826kJ; Protein 5.9g; Carbohydrate 7.5g, of which sugars 2.4g; Fat 16.2g, of which saturates 10.4g; Cholesterol 44mg; Calcium 117mg; Fibre 1.4g; Sodium 233mg

p157 Parsnip and Apple Soup Energy 130kcal/548kJ; Protein 3.4g; Carbohydrate 18.5g, of which sugars 12.6g; Fat 5.3g, of which saturates 2.9g; Cholesterol 12mg; Calcium 101mg; Fibre 4g; Sodium 56mg

p158 Shropshire Pea and Mint Soup Energy 376kcal/ 1560kJ; Protein 9.3g; Carbohydrate 15.3g, of which sugars 5.2g; Fat 29.4g, of which saturates 17.7g; Cholesterol 85mg; Calcium 64mg; Fibre 6.7g; Sodium 549mg

p161 Celeriac Soup with Cabbage, Bacon and Herbs Energy 462Kcal/1919kJ; Protein 12.3g; Carbohydrate 24.3g, of which sugars 7.3g; Fat 35.7g, of which saturates 20.4g; Cholesterol 97mg; Calcium 144mg; Fibre 4.3g; Sodium 954mg

p162 Mushroom Soup Energy 155Kcal/648kJ; Protein 3.2g; Carbohydrate 13.6g, of which sugars 3.4g; Fat 7.6g, of which saturates 3.2g; Cholesterol 11mg; Calcium 23mg; Fibre 2.1g; Sodium 44mg

p165 Oxtail Soup Energy 459kcal/1914kJ; Protein 45.4g; Carbohydrate 6.5g, of which sugars 2.6g; Fat 26.8g, of which saturates 11.8g; Cholesterol 176mg; Calcium 36mg; Fibre 0.7g; Sodium 403mg

p166 Brown Windsor Soup Energy 182kcal/757kJ; Protein 13.8g; Carbohydrate 8g, of which sugars 3.4g; Fat 10.7g, of which saturates 5.5g; Cholesterol 46mg; Calcium 25mg; Fibre 1.7g; Sodium 81mg

p169 Bacon and Barley Broth Energy 276Kcal/1166kJ; Protein 26.6g; Carbohydrate 33.6g, of which sugars 8.4g; Fat 4.8g, of which saturates 1.6g; Cholesterol 13mg; Calcium 87mg; Fibre 4.8g; Sodium 765mg

p170 Split Pea and Gammon Soup Energy 244kcal/ 1033kJ; Protein 17.2g; Carbohydrate 35.2g, of which sugars 3.4g; Fat 4.8g, with saturates 2.5g; Cholesterol 19mg; Calcium 40mg; Fibre 3.5g; Sodium 254mg

p173 Devon Crab Soup Energy 209kcal/867kJ; Protein 7.8g; Carbohydrate 4.6g, of which sugars 1.2g; Fat 17.3g, of which saturates 10.6g; Cholesterol 70mg; Calcium 69mg; Fibre 0.3g; Sodium 241mg

p177 Smoked Mackerel Pâté Energy 344kcal/1421kJ; Protein 10.7g; Carbohydrate 0.5g, of which sugars 0.4g; Fat 33.3g, of which saturates 14.3g; Cholesterol 88mg; Calcium 57mg; Fibre 0.1g; Sodium 518mg

p178 Salmon Mousse Energy 285kcal/1183kJ; Protein 12.6g; Carbohydrate 5.8g, of which sugars 3.2g; Fat 22.7g, of which saturates 8.7g; Cholesterol 57mg; Calcium 73mg; Fibre 0.2g; Sodium 103mg

p180 Potted Shrimps Energy 460kcal/1895kJ; Protein 9.6g; Carbohydrate 0.4g, of which sugars 0.4g; Fat 46.7g, of which saturates 29.4g; Cholesterol 193mg; Calcium 83mg; Fibre 0g; Sodium 555mg

p180 Prawn Cocktail Energy 193kcal/802kJ; Protein 13.9g; Carbohydrate 4g, of which sugars 3.9g; Fat 13.6g, of which saturates 4.6g; Cholesterol 167mg; Calcium 79mg; Fibre 0.4g; Sodium 374mg

p183 Devilled Whitebait Energy 696kcal/2881kJ; Protein 25.8g; Carbohydrate 7g, of which sugars 0.1g; Fat 63g, of which saturates 5.8g; Cholesterol 0mg; Calcium 1140mg; Fibre 0.3g; Sodium 305mg

p184 Sussex Smokies Energy 363kcal/1525kJ; Protein 30.1g; Carbohydrate 21.8g, of which sugars 5.8g; Fat 17.4g, of which saturates 10.8g; Cholesterol 79mg; Calcium 396mg; Fibre 0.5g; Sodium 1073mg

p187 Angels on Horseback Energy 326kcal/1365kJ; Protein 20.3g; Carbohydrate 26.4g, of which sugars 1.4g; Fat 16.2g, of which saturates 6.9g; Cholesterol 79mg; Calcium 147mg; Fibre 0.8g; Sodium 1483mg

p187 Devils on Horseback Energy 309kcal/1303kJ; Protein 14.7g; Carbohydrate 41.7g, of which sugars 18.3g; Fat 10.4g, of which saturates 3.5g; Cholesterol 30mg; Calcium 75mg; Fibre 3.6g; Sodium 1132mg

p188 Salad with Warm Black Pudding Energy 683kcal/2858kJ; Protein 16.4g; Carbohydrate 66.5g, of which sugars 9.5g; Fat 41g, of which saturates 9g; Cholesterol 43mg; Calcium 234mg; Fibre 3.5g; Sodium 1156mg

p191 Pears with Stilton, Cream and Walnuts Energy 527kcal/2175kJ; Protein 12.4g; Carbohydrate 2.8 g, of which sugars 2.7g; Fat 51g, of which saturates 15.3g; Cholesterol 50mg; Calcium 156mg; Fibre 3.4g; Sodium 249mg

p192 Potted Cheese Energy 262kcal/1082kJ; Protein 10.7g; Carbohydrate 0.2g, of which sugars 0.2g; Fat 23.6g, of which saturates 15.2g; Cholesterol 70mg; Calcium 290mg; Fibre 0g; Sodium 363mg

p195 Chicken Liver Pâté Energy 614kcal/2532kJ; Protein 11.9g; Carbohydrate 2.6g, of which sugars 2.4g; Fat 60.7g, of which saturates 37.6g; Cholesterol 390mg; Calcium 61mg; Fibre 0.1g; Sodium 276mg

p196 Game Pâté with Red Onion Marmalade Energy 324kcal/1350kJ; Protein 25g; Carbohydrate 10.6g, of which sugars 8.6g; Fat 18g, of which saturates 4.2g; Cholesterol 28mg; Calcium 38mg; Fibre 1.2g; Sodium 197mg

p199 Devilled Eggs Energy 149kcal/620kJ; Protein 12.8g; Carbohydrate 0.5g, of which sugars 0.4g; Fat 10.5g, of which saturates 2.5g; Cholesterol 311mg; Calcium 44mg; Fibre 0.2g; Sodium 278mg

p200 Scotch Eggs Energy 514kcal/2141kJ; Protein20.8 g; Carbohydrate 30.7g, of which sugars 2.5g; Fat 33.5g, of which saturates 8.9g; Cholesterol 294mg; Calcium 143mg; Fibre 3.2g; Sodium 515mg

p203 Cheese Pudding Energy 534kcal/2232kJ; Protein 27.5g; Carbohydrate 29.5g, of which sugars 7.9g; Fat 33.9g, of which saturates 20.2g; Cholesterol 227mg; Calcium 656mg; Fibre 0.6g; Sodium 803mg

p204 Baked Macaroni Cheese Energy 798kcal/3348kJ; Protein 31g; Carbohydrate 93.6g, of which sugars 8.7g; Fat 32.5g, of which saturates 19.3g; Cholesterol 85mg; Calcium 535mg; Fibre 3.5g; Sodium 505mg

p209 Fresh Mackerel with Gooseberry Relish Energy 576kcal/2390kJ; Protein 38.1g; Carbohydrate 8.4g, of which sugars 8.4g; Fat 43.5g, of which saturates 8.2g; Cholesterol 108mg; Calcium 43mg; Fibre 1.5g; Sodium 128mg

p210 Halibut Fillets with Parsley Sauce Energy 594kcal/2493kJ; Protein 58.2g; Carbohydrate 30.4g, of which sugars 5g; Fat 27.6g, of which saturates 14.1g; Cholesterol 227mg; Calcium 234mg; Fibre 0.9g; Sodium 487mg

p213 Pan-Cooked Salmon with Sorrel Sauce Energy 549kcal/2274kJ; Protein 36.7g; Carbohydrate 1.1g, of which sugars 1g; Fat 44.2g, of which saturates 18.1g; Cholesterol 147mg; Calcium 98mg; Fibre 0.5g; Sodium 145mg

p214 Poached Salmon with Hollandaise Sauce Energy 450kcal/1868kJ; Protein 34.6g; Carbohydrate 0.5g, of which sugars 0.5g; Fat 34.4g, of which saturates 12.8g; Cholesterol 182mg; Calcium 44mg; Fibre 0g; Sodium 183mg

p217 Soused Herrings Energy 332kcal/1384kJ; Protein 30.5g; Carbohydrate 2.2g, of which sugars 1.9g; Fat 22.5g, of which saturates 5.6g; Cholesterol 85mg; Calcium 106mg; Fibre 0.2g; Sodium 205mg

p219 Trout with Almonds Energy 475kcal/1978kJ; Protein 39.2g; Carbohydrate 7.6g, of which sugars 0.8g; Fat 32.2g, of which saturates 12.4g; Cholesterol 187mg; Calcium 101mg; Fibre 1.2g; Sodium 249mg

p220 Pan-Fried Dover Sole Energy 177kcal/739kJ; Protein 18.6g; Carbohydrate 3g, of which sugars 0.2g; Fat 10.2g, of which saturates 1.2g; Cholesterol 50mg; Calcium 42mg; Fibre 0.3g; Sodium 101mg

p223 Skate with Black Butter Energy 246kcal/1029kJ; Protein 35.5g; Carbohydrate 0.5g, of which sugars 0.4g; Fat 11.2g, of which saturates 6.5g; Cholesterol 27mg; Calcium 125mg; Fibre 0.8g; Sodium 356mg

p224 Fish and Chips Energy 803kcal/3352kJ; Protein 35.5g; Carbohydrate 51g, of which sugars 1.7g; Fat 49.9g, of which saturates 3.6g; Cholesterol 88mg; Calcium 113mg; Fibre 4.5g; Sodium 257mg

p227 Haddock in Cheese Sauce Energy 430kcal/1809kJ; Protein 58.2g; Carbohydrate 9.6g, of which sugars 4.5g; Fat 17.4g, of which saturates 10.6g; Cholesterol 136mg; Calcium 351mg; Fibre 0.4g; Sodium 446mg

p228 Salmon Fishcakes Energy 586kcal/2453kJ; Protein 29.8g; Carbohydrate 49.9g, of which sugars 3.2g; Fat 31g, of which saturates 7.2g; Cholesterol 117mg; Calcium 79mg; Fibre 1.3g; Sodium 266mg

p231 Fish Pie Energy 458kcal/1921kJ; Protein 29.4g; Carbohydrate 32.8g, of which sugars 5.8g; Fat 25g, of which saturates 3.7g; Cholesterol 74mg; Calcium 216mg; Fibre 1g; Sodium 867mg

p232 Smoked Fish Soufflé Energy 325kcal/1356kJ; Protein 24.4g; Carbohydrate 11.4g, of which sugars 3.8g; Fat 20.3g, of which saturates 10.7g; Cholesterol 272mg; Calcium 247mg; Fibre 0.3g; Sodium 706mg

p235 Fisherman's Casserole Energy 583kcal/2439kJ; Protein 49.3g; Carbohydrate 25.3g, of which sugars 6.1g; Fat 30.2g, of which saturates 16.5g; Cholesterol 354mg; Calcium 199mg; Fibre 2.5g; Sodium 404mg

p236 Dressed Crab with Asparagus Energy 207kcal/859kJ; Protein 19.5g; Carbohydrate 3g, of which sugars 2.8g; Fat 13g, of which saturates 1.9g; Cholesterol 72mg; Calcium 157mg; Fibre 2.6g; Sodium 540mg

p239 Scallops with Bacon Energy 208kcal/867kJ; Protein 15.6g; Carbohydrate 2.4g, of which sugars 0.7g; Fat 14.5g, of which saturates 5.9g; Cholesterol 53mg; Calcium 19mg; Fibre 0g; Sodium 445mg

p240 Mussels in Tomato Broth Energy 211kcal/891kJ; Protein 21.1g; Carbohydrate 9.3g, of which sugars 4.9g; Fat 9g, of which saturates 1.2g; Cholesterol 72mg; Calcium 77mg; Fibre 1.2g; Sodium 444mg

p245 Rib of Beef with Yorkshire Puddings Energy 1037kcal/4338kJ; Protein 129g; Carbohydrate 15.1g, of which sugars 4.1g; Fat 51.5g, of which saturates 24.3g; Cholesterol 352mg; Calcium 123mg; Fibre 0.5g; Sodium 249mg

p246 Pot-Roasted Beef with Stout Energy 415kcal/1743kJ; Protein 36g; Carbohydrate 35.6g, of which sugars 13.1g; Fat 14g, of which saturates 4.4g; Cholesterol 81mg; Calcium 66mg; Fibre 4.2g; Sodium 284mg

p249 Braised Beef Stew with Herb Dumplings Energy 754kcal/3148kJ; Protein 60.8g; Carbohydrate 36.6g, of which sugars 3.8g; Fat 41.4g, of which saturates 14.9g; Cholesterol 163mg; Calcium 147mg; Fibre 2.1g; Sodium 700mg

p250 Steak and Kidney Pudding Energy 436kcal/1835kJ; Protein 31.1g; Carbohydrate 49.5g, of which sugars 4.8g; Fat 13.9g, of which saturates 3.6g; Cholesterol 166mg; Calcium 201mg; Fibre 1.9g; Sodium 380mg

p253 Braised Oxtail Energy 341kcal/1426kJ; Protein 30.9g; Carbohydrate 13.6g, of which sugars 7.7g; Fat 18.6g, of which saturates 0.7g; Cholesterol 0mg; Calcium 54mg; Fibre 2.3g; Sodium 203mg

p254 Cold Spiced Beef Energy 309Kcal/1301kJ; Protein 53.6g; Carbohydrate 2g, of which sugars 2g; Fat 9.7g, of which saturates 3.6g; Cholesterol 137mg; Calcium 15mg; Fibre 0g; Sodium 140mg

p257 Roast Shoulder of Lamb with Mint Sauce Energy 351kcal/1468kJ; Protein 36.9g; Carbohydrate 2.5g, of which sugars 2.5g; Fat 21g, of which saturates 9.8g; Cholesterol 143mg; Calcium 23mg; Fibre 0g; Sodium 202mg

p258 Lancashire Hotpot Energy 810kcal/3400kJ; Protein 76.7g; Carbohydrate 43.7g, of which sugars 9.3g; Fat 37.8g, of which saturates 13.2g; Cholesterol 363mg; Calcium 140mg; Fibre 6.2g; Sodium 285mg

p261 Lamb and Pearl Barley Casserole Energy 304Kcal/1263kJ; Protein 23.2g; Carbohydrate 13g, of which sugars 11.3g; Fat 18g, of which saturates 7.5g; Cholesterol 84mg; Calcium 53mg; Fibre 3.6g; Sodium 110mg

p262 Barnsley Chops with Mustard Sauce Energy 582kcal/2401kJ; Protein 18.8g; Carbohydrate 0.9g, of which sugars 0.9g; Fat 55.9g, of which saturates 23.6g; Cholesterol 96mg; Calcium 17mg; Fibre 0g; Sodium 313mg

p265 Shepherd's Pie Energy 487kcal/2045kJ; Protein 29.4g; Carbohydrate 50.1g, of which sugars 15.2g; Fat 20.2g, of which saturates 8.4g; Cholesterol 69mg; Calcium 54mg; Fibre 5.3g; Sodium 379mg

p266 Liver and Bacon Casserole Energy 310kcal/1293kJ; Protein 28.7g; Carbohydrate 13.7g, of which sugars 5.7g; Fat 15.9g, of which saturates 4.4g; Cholesterol 500mg; Calcium 44mg; Fibre 1.6g; Sodium 400mg

p269 Rissoles Energy 519kcal/2184kJ; Protein 27.4g; Carbohydrate 56.7g, of which sugars 4.1g; Fat 22g, of which saturates 6.5g; Cholesterol 162mg; Calcium 86mg; Fibre 2.8g; Sodium 363mg

p270 Roast Pork with Sage and Onion Stuffing Energy 599kcal/2497kJ; Protein 38.5g; Carbohydrate 16.1g, of which sugars 10.9g; Fat 41.7g, of which saturates 16.5g; Cholesterol 147mg; Calcium 70mg; Fibre 2.6g; Sodium 274mg

p273 Somerset Pork Casserole Energy 619kcal/2594kJ; Protein 39g; Carbohydrate 52g, of which sugars 22.8g; Fat 29.7g, of which saturates 9.8g; Cholesterol 89mg; Calcium 189mg; Fibre 15g; Sodium 891mg

p274 Toad in the Hole Energy 497kcal/2070kJ; Protein 14.5g; Carbohydrate 32.1g, of which sugars 3.8g; Fat 35.4g, of which saturates 13.6g; Cholesterol 109mg; Calcium 141mg; Fibre 1.3g; Sodium 616mg

p277 Pork Sausages with Mustard Mash and Onion Gravy Energy 888kcal/3694kJ; Protein 21.5g; Carbohydrate 68g, of which sugars 18g; Fat 56.2g, of which saturates 25g; Cholesterol 133mg; Calcium 209mg; Fibre 11.6g; Sodium 886mg

p278 Faggots Energy 569kcal/2372kJ; Protein 46.2g; Carbohydrate 14.6g, of which sugars 4g; Fat 35.9g, of which saturates 12.6g; Cholesterol 352mg; Calcium 122mg; Fibre 1.1g; Sodium 283mg

p281 Somerset Cider-Glazed Ham Energy 368kcal/1541kJ; Protein 39.6g; Carbohydrate 15.2g, of which sugars 15.2g; Fat 16.9g, of which saturates 5.6g; Cholesterol 52mg; Calcium 25mg; Fibre 0.6g; Sodium 1982mg

p282 Gravy Energy 164kcal/682kJ; Protein 5.6g; Carbohydrate 9.6g, of which sugars 0.2g; Fat 11.4g, of which saturates 5.2g; Cholesterol 19mg; Calcium 13mg; Fibre 0.3g; Sodium 1348mg

p287 Stuffed Roast Chicken Energy 823kcal/3420kJ; Protein 55.7g; Carbohydrate 21.1g, of which sugars 19.1g; Fat 57.8g, of which saturates 19.7g; Cholesterol 383mg; Calcium 113mg; Fibre 4.9g; Sodium 252mg

p288 Chicken with Red Cabbage and Chestnuts Energy 405kcal/1697kJ; Protein 44.9g; Carbohydrate 18.6g, of which sugars 9.2g; Fat 14.9g, of which saturates 7.7g; Cholesterol 189mg; Calcium 94mg; Fibre 4.1g; Sodium 229mg

p291 Chicken with Lemon and Herbs Energy 406kcal/1692kJ; Protein 42.1g; Carbohydrate 0.5g, of which sugars 0.4g; Fat 26.2g, of which saturates 14.7g; Cholesterol 263mg; Calcium 22mg; Fibre 0.3g; Sodium 333mg

p292 Hindle Wakes Energy 811kcal/3376kJ; Protein 50.3g; Carbohydrate 32.1g, of which sugars 30.1g; Fat 51.9g, of which saturates 19.2g; Cholesterol 294mg; Calcium 117mg; Fibre 5.2g; Sodium 250mg

p295 Coronation Chicken Energy 587kcal/2429kJ; Protein 10.1g; Carbohydrate 17.1g, of which sugars 4.7g; Fat 51.6g, of which saturates 8.8g; Cholesterol 228mg; Calcium 97mg; Fibre 1.1g; Sodium 401mg

p296 Devilled Chicken Energy 299kcal/1254kJ; Protein 47.4g; Carbohydrate 0.3g, of which sugars 0.3g; Fat 12g, of which saturates 2.6g; Cholesterol 236mg; Calcium 41mg; Fibre 0.6g; Sodium 207mg

p298 Classic Roast Turkey with Country Stuffing Energy 740kcal/3126kJ; Protein 112.3g; Carbohydrate 35.9g, of which sugars 7.3g; Fat 13.5g, of which saturates 6.6g; Cholesterol 507mg; Calcium 122mg; Fibre 1.7g; Sodium 517mg

p301 Roast Goose with Apples Energy 822kcal/3437kJ; Protein 54.8g; Carbohydrate 44.1g, of which sugars 21.8g; Fat 48.7g, of which saturates 0.9g; Cholesterol 0mg; Calcium 87mg; Fibre 3.1g; Sodium 486mg

p302 Duck with Plum Sauce Energy 608kcal/2515kJ; Protein 15.1g; Carbohydrate 17.4g, of which sugars 17g; Fat 53.5g, of which saturates 14.5g; Cholesterol 0mg; Calcium 35mg; Fibre 2.2g; Sodium 102mg

p305 Roast Pheasant with Game Chips Energy 897kcal/3742kJ; Protein 70.6g; Carbohydrate 34.3g, of which sugars 9.1g; Fat 50.8g, of which saturates 20g; Cholesterol 524mg; Calcium 127mg; Fibre 4.5g; Sodium 946mg

p306 Pheasant with Mushrooms, Chestnuts and Bacon Energy 883kcal/3699kJ; Protein 86.8g; Carbohydrate 32.3g, of which sugars 6.9g; Fat 41.6g, of which saturates 15.8g; Cholesterol 35mg; Calcium 205mg; Fibre 2.9g; Sodium 920mg

p309 Roast Partridge with Caramelised Pears and Mash Energy 1126kcal/4730kJ; Protein 127.2g; Carbohydrate 64.9g, of which sugars 20.4g; Fat 40.3g, of which saturates 16.5g; Cholesterol 43mg; Calcium 237mg; Fibre 7.1g; Sodium 523mg

p310 Venison Steak Energy 1995kcal/8331kJ; Protein 70.4g; Carbohydrate 143.1g, of which sugars 5.8g; Fat 132.3g, of which saturates 47.3g; Cholesterol 245mg; Calcium 176mg; Fibre 11.9g; Sodium 1315mg

p313 Venison Stew Energy 727kcal/3045kJ; Protein 83.8g; Carbohydrate 17.5g, of which sugars 14.4g; Fat 31.3g, of which saturates 13.8g; Cholesterol 226mg; Calcium 70mg; Fibre 2.9g; Sodium 985mg

p314 Rabbit with Mustard Energy 531kcal/2209kJ; Protein 31.8g; Carbohydrate 21.3g, of which sugars 8.7g; Fat 35g, of which saturates 14.6g; Cholesterol 187mg; Calcium 48mg; Fibre 0.6g; Sodium 247mg

p317 Bread Sauce Energy 99kcal/415kJ; Protein 3.3g; Carbohydrate 8.4g, of which sugars 3.6g; Fat 5.7g, of which saturates 3.5g; Cholesterol 17mg; Calcium 97mg; Fibre 0.6g; Sodium 89mg

p320 Steak and Oyster Pie Energy 689kcal/2874kJ; Protein 49.4g; Carbohydrate 29.8g, of which sugars 1g; Fat 39g, of which saturates 9.1g; Cholesterol 144mg; Calcium 145mg; Fibre 0.4g; Sodium 674mg

p323 Beef Wellington Energy 511kcal/2131kJ; Protein 41.7g; Carbohydrate 19.3g, of which sugars 1.2g; Fat 30.6g, of which saturates 7.2g; Cholesterol 128mg; Calcium 41mg; Fibre 0.4g; Sodium 320mg

p324 Mutton Pies Energy 369kcal/1547kJ; Protein 18.7g; Carbohydrate 33g, of which sugars 1.2g; Fat 19g, of which saturates 8.2g; Cholesterol 66mg; Calcium 85mg; Fibre 1.4g; Sodium 58mg

p327 Chicken, Ham and Egg Pie Energy 646kcal/2696kJ; Protein 43.1g; Carbohydrate 37.9g, of which sugars 3.3g; Fat 35g, of which saturates 17.2g; Cholesterol 330mg; Calcium 93mg; Fibre 2.7g; Sodium 1092mg

p328 Shropshire Fidget Pie Energy 436kcal/1824kJ; Protein 12.7g; Carbohydrate 42.7g, of which sugars 8.2g; Fat 25g, of which saturates 10.7g; Cholesterol 48mg; Calcium 43mg; Fibre 4g; Sodium 754mg

p331 Raised Game Pie Energy 448kcal/1871kJ; Protein 28.3g; Carbohydrate 29.5g, of which sugars 5.3g; Fat 24.9g, of which saturates 9.5g; Cholesterol 55mg; Calcium 67mg; Fibre 1.5g; Sodium 393mg

p332 Veal and Egg Pie Energy 446kcal/1864kJ; Protein 24g; Carbohydrate 34.9g, of which sugars 2.6g; Fat 22.9g, of which saturates 8.9g; Cholesterol 161mg; Calcium 71mg; Fibre 2.2g; Sodium 201mg

p335 Cornish Pasties Energy 414kcal/1731kJ; Protein 10.4g; Carbohydrate 38.8g, of which sugars 1.4g; Fat

25.3g, of which saturates 9.2g; Cholesterol 51mg; Calcium 93mg; Fibre 1.4g; Sodium 620mg

p336 Pork and Bacon Picnic Pies Energy 311kcal/1302kJ; Protein 12.1g; Carbohydrate 30.4g, of which sugars 1.6g; Fat 16.4g, of which saturates 5.5g; Cholesterol 135mg; Calcium 77mg; Fibre 1.5g; Sodium 74mg

p339 Bacon and Egg Pie Energy 756kcal/3149kJ; Protein 20.5g; Carbohydrate 51.9g, of which sugars 1.6g; Fat 51.2g, of which saturates 24.2g; Cholesterol 354mg; Calcium 113mg; Fibre 3.1g; Sodium 762mg

p340 Cheese and Asparagus Flan Energy 547kcal/2266kJ; Protein 10.4g; Carbohydrate 24.7g, of which sugars 2.4g; Fat 45.6g, of which saturates 26.2g; Cholesterol 165mg; Calcium 184mg; Fibre 1.8g; Sodium 167mg

p344 Asparagus with Hollandaise Sauce Energy 276kcal/1135kJ; Protein 5.3g; Carbohydrate 2.7g, of which sugars 2.6g; Fat 27.1g, of which saturates 15.9g; Cholesterol 162mg; Calcium 51mg; Fibre 2.1g; Sodium 180mg

p347 Spring Vegetables with Tarragon Energy 149kcal/619kJ; Protein 4.7g; Carbohydrate 6.1g, of which sugars 3g; Fat 12g, of which saturates 7.3g; Cholesterol 29mg; Calcium 55mg; Fibre 3.5g; Sodium 89mg

p348 Creamed Leeks Energy 238Kcal/993kJ; Protein 18.6g; Carbohydrate 9g, of which sugars 7.9g; Fat 14.4g, of which saturates 7.3g; Cholesterol 90mg; Calcium 172mg; Fibre 3.5g; Sodium 830mg

p351 Brussels Sprouts with Chestnuts Energy 256kcal/1070kJ; Protein 8.3g; Carbohydrate 26g, of which sugars 7.6g; Fat 13.9g, of which saturates 6.6g; Cholesterol 30mg; Calcium 59mg; Fibre 7g; Sodium 364mg

p351 Braised Celery Energy 120kcal/496kJ; Protein 3g; Carbohydrate 3.4g, of which sugars 3g; Fat 10.6g, of which saturates 6g; Cholesterol 28mg; Calcium 61mg; Fibre 1.9g; Sodium 332mg

p352 Mushy Peas Energy 68kcal/288kJ; Protein 4.8g; Carbohydrate 11.5g, of which sugars 1.4g; Fat 0.6g, of which saturates 0.1g; Cholesterol 0mg; Calcium 12mg; Fibre 1.5g; Sodium 283mg

p352 Pease Pudding Energy 300kcal/1270kJ; Protein 18.9g; Carbohydrate 42.3g, of which sugars 1.8g; Fat 7.4g, of which saturates 3.9g; Cholesterol 46mg; Calcium 44mg; Fibre 3.7g; Sodium 79mg

p355 Broad Beans with Bacon and Mint Energy 162kcal/674kJ; Protein 7.9g; Carbohydrate 9.6g, of which sugars 1.8g; Fat 10.5g, of which saturates 2.2g; Cholesterol 9mg; Calcium 45mg; Fibre 4.5g; Sodium 190mg

p355 Braised Red Cabbage Energy 74kcal/309kJ; Protein 2.1g; Carbohydrate 10.1g, of which sugars 9.5g; Fat 3g, of which saturates 0.4g; Cholesterol 0mg; Calcium 53mg; Fibre 3.1g; Sodium 38mg

p356 Roast Beetroot with Horseradish Cream Energy 254kcal/1052kJ; Protein 2.1g; Carbohydrate 10g, of which sugars 9.1g; Fat 22.2g, of which saturates 3.2g; Cholesterol 1mg; Calcium 26mg; Fibre 2.3g; Sodium 143mg

p359 Roast Parsnips with Honey Energy 144kcal/600kJ; Protein 2g; Carbohydrate 16.2g, of which sugars 6.7g; Fat 8.3g, with saturates 1g; Cholesterol 0mg; Calcium 41mg; Fibre 4g; Sodium 9mg

p359 Parsnip Crisps Energy 230kcal/956kJ; Protein 2.3g; Carbohydrate 16.8g, of which sugars 5.1g; Fat 17.6g, of which saturates 2.1g; Cholesterol 0mg; Calcium 47mg; Fibre 4.3g; Sodium 9mg

p360 Potatoes and Parsnips with Garlic and Cream Energy 241kcal/1012kJ; Protein 7.8g; Carbohydrate 27.2g, of which sugars 6.4g; Fat 11.7g, of which saturates 7.2g; Cholesterol 31mg; Calcium 173mg; Fibre 3.9g; Sodium 126mg

p363 Mashed Potatoes Energy 338kcal/1424kJ; Protein 5.9g; Carbohydrate 50.4g, of which sugars 3.3g; Fat 14g, of which saturates 9.1g; Cholesterol 39mg; Calcium 42mg; Fibre 3.6g; Sodium 140mg

p363 Roast Potatoes Energy 484kcal/2048kJ; Protein 9.4g; Carbohydrate 84.2g, of which sugars 2g; Fat 14.6g, of which saturates 5.9g; Cholesterol 13mg; Calcium 26mg; Fibre 5.9g; Sodium 29mg

p364 Chips Energy 403kcal/1689kJ; Protein 5.4g; Carbohydrate 51.5g, of which sugars 2.9g; Fat 14.5g, of which saturates 6.1g; Cholesterol 0mg; Calcium 19mg; Fibre 3.7g; Sodium 59mg

p364 Baked Jacket Potatoes Energy 182kcal/772kJ; Protein 3.8g; Carbohydrate 36.2g, of which sugars 2.9g; Fat 3.4g, of which saturates 0.6g; Cholesterol 0mg; Calcium 14mg; Fibre 2.3g; Sodium 25mg

p367 Pan Haggerty Energy 271kcal/1128kJ; Protein 9.8g; Carbohydrate 21.1g, of which sugars 3.6g; Fat 16.9g, of which saturates 7.5g; Cholesterol 30mg; Calcium 215mg; Fibre 1.7g; Sodium 206mg

p367 Savoury Potato Cakes Energy 186kcal/776kJ; Protein 6g; Carbohydrate 12.3g, of which sugars 1.2g; Fat 12.6g, of which saturates 4.2g; Cholesterol 38mg; Calcium 126mg; Fibre 1g; Sodium 246mg

p368 Cauliflower Cheese Energy 318kcal/1318kJ; Protein 17.4g; Carbohydrate 4.4g, of which sugars 3.9g; Fat 25.8g, of which saturates 16.3g; Cholesterol 71mg; Calcium 371mg; Fibre 1.8g; Sodium 453mg

p371 New Potato and Chive Salad Energy 182kcal/761kJ; Protein 2.5g; Carbohydrate 22.5g, of which sugars 1.9g; Fat 9.7g, of which saturates 1.5g; Cholesterol 0mg; Calcium 20mg; Fibre 1.7g; Sodium 17mg

p372 Salmagundi Energy 397kcal/1664kJ; Protein 41.2g; Carbohydrate 24.9g, of which sugars 8.7g; Fat 15.5g, of which saturates 3g; Cholesterol 220mg; Calcium 63mg; Fibre 4.6g; Sodium 155mg

p375 Coleslaw with Blue Cheese Energy 86kcal/359kJ; Protein 2.7g; Carbohydrate 5.1g, of which sugars 4.8g; Fat 6.3g, of which saturates 1.9g; Cholesterol 9mg; Calcium 78mg; Fibre 1.6g; Sodium 116mg

p378 Apple and Blackberry Crumble Energy 336kcal/1413kJ; Protein 4g; Carbohydrate 53.1g, of which sugars 30.8g; Fat 13.4g, of which saturates 6.8g; Cholesterol 27mg; Calcium 72mg; Fibre 3g; Sodium 81mg

p378 Winter Fruit Crumble Energy 615kcal/2569kJ; Protein 9.4g; Carbohydrate 65.7g, of which sugars 42.9g; Fat 36.7g, of which saturates 16.2g; Cholesterol 62mg; Calcium 150mg; Fibre 6.6g; Sodium 190mg

p381 Queen of Puddings Energy 297kcal/1259kJ; Protein 13.7g; Carbohydrate 45g, of which sugars 31g; Fat 8.5g, of which saturates 3.2g; Cholesterol 199mg; Calcium 242mg; Fibre 0.4g; Sodium 281mg

p382 Jam Roly Poly Energy 240kcal/1008kJ; Protein 2.8g; Carbohydrate 33.7g, of which sugars 10.7g; Fat 11.3g, of which saturates 5.7g; Cholesterol 0mg; Calcium 104mg; Fibre 0.9g; Sodium 111mg

p385 Eve's Pudding Energy 507kcal/2128kJ; Protein 6.9g; Carbohydrate 65.5g, of which sugars 52.7g; Fat 26.1g, of which saturates 12g; Cholesterol 114mg; Calcium 91mg; Fibre 2.8g; Sodium 159mg

p385 Yorkshire Lemon Surprise Energy 319kcal/1341kJ; Protein 7g; Carbohydrate 43.1g, of which sugars 33.8g; Fat 14.5g, of which saturates 8.1g; Cholesterol 126mg; Calcium 166mg; Fibre 0.4g; Sodium 190mg

p386 Bread and Butter Pudding Energy 622kcal/2597kJ; Protein 10.5g; Carbohydrate 55.6g, of which sugars 37.8g; Fat 39g, of which saturates 23g; Cholesterol 186mg; Calcium 203mg; Fibre 1.6g; Sodium 350mg

p389 Baked Rice Pudding Energy 298kcal/1252kJ; Protein 8.8g; Carbohydrate 54.3g, of which sugars 21.5g; Fat 5.2g, of which saturates 1.4g; Cholesterol 143mg; Calcium 71mg; Fibre 0g; Sodium 185mg

p390 Kentish Cherry Batter Pudding Energy 357kcal/1493kJ; Protein 8.1g; Carbohydrate 39.4g, of which sugars 29.8g; Fat 19.7g, of which saturates 11.4g; Cholesterol 140mg; Calcium 147mg; Fibre 1.4g; Sodium 183mg

p393 Syrup Sponge Pudding Energy 480kcal/2005kJ; Protein 16.2g; Carbohydrate 48.2g, of which sugars 23.7g; Fat 27g, of which saturates 15.8g; Cholesterol 173mg; Calcium 153mg; Fibre 1.2g; Sodium 451mg

p394 Spotted Dick Energy 667kcal/2801kJ; Protein 6.8g; Carbohydrate 100.8g, of which sugars 57.4g; Fat 25g, of which saturates 14.9g; Cholesterol 23mg; Calcium 212mg; Fibre 6.1g; Sodium 202mg

p397 Figgy Pudding Energy 556kcal/2351kJ; Protein 9g; Carbohydrate 73g, of which sugars 51g; Fat 28g, of which saturates 17g; Cholesterol 183mg; Calcium 145mg; Fibre 4g; Sodium 142mg

p398 Christmas Pudding Energy 448kcal/1902kJ; Protein 2.4g; Carbohydrate 99.8g, of which sugars 92.5g; Fat 7.1g, of which saturates 3.6g; Cholesterol 20mg; Calcium 67mg; Fibre 0.9g; Sodium 123mg

p401 Sussex Pond Pudding Energy 759kcal/3165kJ; Protein 6.6g; Carbohydrate 73.2g, of which sugars 29.9g; Fat 48.1g, of which saturates 28.7g; Cholesterol 83mg; Calcium 214mg; Fibre 3.7g; Sodium 404mg

p402 Sticky Toffee Puddings Energy 1013kcal/4240kJ; Protein 9.4g; Carbohydrate 126.6g, of which sugars 95.2g; Fat 51.4g, of which saturates 31.2g; Cholesterol 235mg; Calcium 218mg; Fibre 3.2g; Sodium 607mg

p405 Potato Harvest Pudding Energy 575kcal/2405kJ; Protein 15.4g; Carbohydrate 56g, of which sugars 27g; Fat 30.9g, of which saturates 16.5g; Cholesterol 363mg; Calcium 85mg; Fibre 4.2g; Sodium 364mg

p406 Cabinet Pudding Energy 466kcal/1944kJ; Protein 10.9g; Carbohydrate 37.4g, of which sugars 29.9g; Fat 28.9g, of which saturates 15.9g; Cholesterol 299mg; Calcium 157mg; Fibre 0.9g; Sodium 146mg

p409 Apple Charlotte Energy 369kcal/1551kJ; Protein 4.7g; Carbohydrate 60.1g, of which sugars 42.6g; Fat 10.7g, of which saturates 6.1g; Cholesterol 25mg; Calcium 89mg; Fibre 6.4g; Sodium 363mg

p410 Plum Pie Energy 360kcal/1516kJ; Protein 4.1g; Carbohydrate 57g, of which sugars 25.5g; Fat 14.5g, of which saturates 7.5g; Cholesterol 26mg; Calcium 73mg; Fibre 2.9g; Sodium 61mg

p413 Apple Pie Check Energy 591Kcal/2488kJ; Protein 7.4g; Carbohydrate 89.9g, of which sugars 39.8g; Fat 25g, of which saturates 15.3g; Cholesterol 62mg; Calcium 117mg; Fibre 4.4g; Sodium 193mg

p414 Kentish Pudding Pies Energy 138kcal/577kJ; Protein 2.7g; Carbohydrate 15.6g, of which sugars 6.3g; Fat 7.1g, of which saturates 4.3g; Cholesterol 34mg; Calcium 46mg; Fibre 0.5g; Sodium 68mg

p417 Bakewell Pudding Energy 700kcal/2919kJ; Protein 10.8g; Carbohydrate 57.1g, of which sugars 36.7g; Fat 49.9g, of which saturates 17.1g; Cholesterol 257mg; Calcium 110mg; Fibre 0.9g; Sodium 394mg

p418 Lemon Meringue Pie Energy 357kcal/1497kJ; Protein 6.8g; Carbohydrate 42.8g, of which sugars 25.1g; Fat 18.9g, of which saturates 9g; Cholesterol 129mg; Calcium 108mg; Fibre 0.7g; Sodium 137mg

p421 Treacle Tart Energy 420kcal/1764kJ; Protein 4.1g; Carbohydrate 63.5g, of which sugars 35.1g; Fat 18.4g, of which saturates 11.3g; Cholesterol 46mg; Calcium 62mg; Fibre 1.1g; Sodium 344mg

p422 Yorkshire Curd Tart Energy 480kcal/2005kJ; Protein 16.2g; Carbohydrate 48.2g, of which sugars 23.7g; Fat 27g, of which saturates 15.8g; Cholesterol 173mg; Calcium 153mg; Fibre 1.2g; Sodium 451mg

p425 Cumberland Rum Nicky Energy 690kcal/2886kJ; Protein 7g; Carbohydrate 81.4g, of which sugars 38.6g; Fat 35.2g, of which saturates 22g; Cholesterol 89mg; Calcium 100mg; Fibre 5g; Sodium 314mg

p426 Baked Apples with Mincemeat Energy 70kcal/301kJ; Protein 0.7g; Carbohydrate 17.4g, of which sugars 17.4g; Fat 0.3g, with saturates 0g; Cholesterol 0mg; Calcium 30mg; Fibre 2.4g; Sodium 9mg

p429 Poached Spiced Pears Energy 93kcal/392kJ; Protein 0.5g; Carbohydrate 23.6g, of which sugars 23.6g; Fat 0.2g, of which saturates 0g; Cholesterol 0mg; Calcium 17mg; Fibre 3.3g; Sodium 6mg

p430 Summer Pudding Energy 192kcal/815kJ; Protein 5.2g; Carbohydrate 43.1g, of which sugars 22.1g; Fat 1g, of which saturates 0g; Cholesterol 0mg; Calcium 82mg; Fibre 2.5g; Sodium 245mg

p433 Baked Cheesecake Energy 296kcal/1238kJ; Protein 7.6g; Carbohydrate 27.1g, of which sugars 19g; Fat 18g, of which saturates 9g; Cholesterol 83mg; Calcium 56mg; Fibre 1.1g; Sodium 139mg

p434 Raspberry and Hazelnut Meringue Cake Energy 298kcal/1252kJ; Protein 3.2g; Carbohydrate 39.5g, of which sugars 39.5g; Fat 15.3g, of which saturates 9.5g; Cholesterol 39mg; Calcium 55mg; Fibre 1.4g; Sodium 44mg

p437 Fruit Trifle Energy 631kcal/2615kJ; Protein 8.4g; Carbohydrate 24.9g, of which sugars 18.4g; Fat 53.1g, of which saturates 28.4g; Cholesterol 258mg; Calcium 155mg; Fibre 1.4g; Sodium 116mg

p438 Fruit and Wine Jelly Energy 178kcal/758kJ; Protein 8.6g; Carbohydrate 29.3g, of which sugars 29.3g; Fat 0.3g, of which saturates 0.1g; Cholesterol 0mg; Calcium 42mg; Fibre 2.5g; Sodium 6mg

p441 Devonshire Junket Energy 196kcal/824kJ; Protein 7.5g; Carbohydrate 19.1g, of which sugars 19.1g; Fat 10.6g, of which saturates 6.6g; Cholesterol 29mg; Calcium 193mg; Fibre 0g; Sodium 69mg

p442 Almond and Rosewater Blancmange Energy 350kcal/1462kJ; Protein 10.2g; Carbohydrate 26.2g, of which sugars 25.0g; Fat 23.5g, of which saturates 10.6g; Cholesterol 46mg; Calcium 201mg; Fibre 1.1g; Sodium 57mg

p445 Gooseberry and Elderflower Fool Energy 366kcal/1521kJ; Protein 3.5g; Carbohydrate 24.2g, of which sugars 21.8g; Fat 28.4g, of which saturates 16.7g; Cholesterol 70mg; Calcium 111mg; Fibre 1.9g; Sodium 41mg

p446 Eton Mess Energy 526kcal/2182kJ; Protein 3.5g; Carbohydrate 32.8g, of which sugars 32.8g; Fat 40.4g, of which saturates 25.1g; Cholesterol 103mg; Calcium 60mg; Fibre 1.4g; Sodium 53mg

p449 Syllabub Energy 310kcal/1282kJ; Protein 1.1g; Carbohydrate 14.5g, of which sugars 14.5g; Fat 26.9g, of which saturates 16.7g; Cholesterol 69mg; Calcium 41mg; Fibre 0.3g; Sodium 15mg

p450 Burnt Cream Energy 547Kcal/2251kJ; Protein 3.6g; Carbohydrate 4.3g, of which sugars 4.3g; Fat 57.4g, of which saturates 34.4g; Cholesterol 272mg; Calcium 66mg; Fibre 0g; Sodium 28mg

p453 Classic Vanilla Ice Cream Energy 546kcal/2264kJ; Protein 6.8g; Carbohydrate 25.6g, of which sugars 24.4g; Fat 47.1g, of which saturates 27.4g; Cholesterol 309mg; Calcium 160mg; Fibre 0g; Sodium 60mg

p454 Fresh Strawberry Ice Cream Energy 244kcal/1012kJ; Protein 2.4g; Carbohydrate 12.2g, of which sugars 10.4g; Fat 20.4g, of which saturates 12.1g; Cholesterol 51mg; Calcium 73mg; Fibre 0.7g; Sodium 32mg

p457 Brown Bread Ice Cream Energy 418kcal/1735kJ; Protein 4.2g; Carbohydrate 28g, of which sugars 17.2g; Fat 32.5g, of which saturates 19.2g; Cholesterol 125mg; Calcium 62mg; Fibre 0.3g; Sodium 144mg

p458 Minted Earl Grey Sorbet Energy 135kcal/578kJ; Protein 0.8g; Carbohydrate 35.1g, of which sugars 34.8g; Fat 0g, of which saturates 0g; Cholesterol 0mg; Calcium 29mg; Fibre 0g; Sodium 13mg

p461 Custard Energy 163kcal/689kJ; Protein 5.8g; Carbohydrate 25.5g, of which sugars 16.3g; Fat 5g, of which saturates 2.1g; Cholesterol 108mg; Calcium 169mg; Fibre 0g; Sodium 64mg

p464 Anchovy Toasts Energy 159kcal/661kJ; Protein 4g; Carbohydrate 10.4g, of which sugars 0.7g; Fat 11.5g, of which saturates 6.7g; Cholesterol 32mg; Calcium 55mg; Fibre 0.4g; Sodium 512mg

p464 Sausage Rolls Energy 125kcal/521kJ; Protein 2.5g; Carbohydrate 10.3g, of which sugars 0.5g; Fat 8.4g, of which saturates 3.9g; Cholesterol 14mg; Calcium 23mg; Fibre 0.4g; Sodium 142mg

p467 Cucumber Sandwiches Energy 174kcal/735kJ; Protein 6.8g; Carbohydrate 29.2g, of which sugars 3.3g; Fat 4.2g, of which saturates 1.1g; Cholesterol 5mg; Calcium 92mg; Fibre 1g; Sodium 307mg

p467 Cheese Straws Energy 49kcal/206kJ; Protein 1.5g; Carbohydrate 3.9g, of which sugars 0.1g; Fat 3.1g, of which saturates 1.9g; Cholesterol 13mg; Calcium 32mg; Fibre 0.2g; Sodium 39mg

p468 Scones with Jam and Cream Check Energy 177kcal/746kJ; Protein 3.4g; Carbohydrate 25.1g, of which sugars 3.9g; Fat 6.8g, of which saturates 4.2g; Cholesterol 17mg; Calcium 109mg; Fibre 1.2g; Sodium 237mg

p471 Drop Scones Energy 60kcal/252kJ; Protein 2g; Carbohydrate 11.1g, of which sugars 1.8g; Fat 1.1g, of which saturates 0.2g; Cholesterol 11mg; Calcium 66mg; Fibre 0.4g; Sodium 56mg

p472 Shrove Tuesday Pancakes Energy 84kcal/352kJ; Protein 2.8g; Carbohydrate 13g, of which sugars 0.8g; Fat 2.7g, of which saturates 1.3g; Cholesterol 32mg; Calcium 40mg; Fibre 0.5g; Sodium 26mg

p475 Suffolk Buns Energy 244kcal/1026kJ; Protein 5.1g; Carbohydrate 36.9g, of which sugars 7.3g; Fat 9.5g, of which saturates 5.4g; Cholesterol 53mg; Calcium 60mg; Fibre 1.1g; Sodium 75mg

p476 Newcastle Singin' Hinnies Energy 132kcal/557kJ; Protein 2.3g; Carbohydrate 21.1g, of which sugars 5.8g; Fat 4.9g, of which saturates 2.4g; Cholesterol 8mg; Calcium 42mg; Fibre 0.7g; Sodium 118mg

p479 Shropshire Soul Cakes Energy 191kcal/803kJ; Protein 2.9g; Carbohydrate 28.4g, of which sugars 11.3g; Fat 8.1g, of which saturates 4.8g; Cholesterol 38mg; Calcium 45mg; Fibre 0.7g; Sodium 62mg

p481 Yorkshire Fat Rascals Energy 375kcal/1574kJ; Protein 5.6g; Carbohydrate 50g, of which sugars 23.2g; Fat 18.4g, of which saturates 9.6g; Cholesterol 57mg; Calcium 93mg; Fibre 1.8g; Sodium 129mg

p482 Maids of Honour Energy 182kcal/758kJ; Protein 5.2g; Carbohydrate 12.6g, of which sugars 5.1g; Fat 12.9g, of which saturates 3g; Cholesterol 43mg; Calcium 31mg; Fibre 0.4g; Sodium 85mg

p485 Jam Tarts Energy 114kcal/479kJ; Protein 1.1g; Carbohydrate 18.8g, of which sugars 12.5g; Fat 4.3g, of which saturates 2.6g; Cholesterol 18mg; Calcium 16mg; Fibre 0.3g; Sodium 39mg

p485 Mince Pies Energy 236kcal/993kJ; Protein 2.5g; Carbohydrate 36.7g, of which sugars 22.4g; Fat 9.8g, of which saturates 5.2g; Cholesterol 37mg; Calcium 43mg; Fibre 1g; Sodium 70mg

p486 Eccles Cakes Energy 201kcal/842kJ; Protein 1.7g; Carbohydrate 23.5g, of which sugars 12.8g; Fat 11.8g, of which saturates 7.4g; Cholesterol 30mg; Calcium 38mg; Fibre 0.8g; Sodium 96mg

p489 Custard Tarts Energy 336kcal/1409kJ; Protein 7.9g; Carbohydrate 40g, of which sugars 23.4g; Fat 17.1g, of which saturates 8.6g; Cholesterol 257mg; Calcium 157mg; Fibre 0.7g; Sodium 101mg

p490 Victoria Sponge Energy 368kcal/1543kJ; Protein 4.6g; Carbohydrate 44.7g, of which sugars 28.5g; Fat 20.3g, of which saturates 12g; Cholesterol 118mg; Calcium 104mg; Fibre 0.7g; Sodium 241mg

p493 Chocolate Cake Energy 430kcal/1790kJ; Protein 7.8g; Carbohydrate 29.5g, of which sugars 28.8g; Fat 32.1g, of which saturates 13.6g; Cholesterol 96mg; Calcium 92mg; Fibre 1.9g; Sodium 125mg

p494 Madeira Cake Energy 453kcal/1894kJ; Protein 6.1g; Carbohydrate 51.4g, of which sugars 30g; Fat 26.3g, of which saturates 15.5g; Cholesterol 155mg; Calcium 74mg; Fibre 0.9g; Sodium 208mg

p497 Lemon Drizzle Cake Energy 659kcal/2765kJ; Protein 8g; Carbohydrate 84.1g, of which sugars 56.2g; Fat 34.8g, of which saturates 21.4g; Cholesterol 213mg; Calcium 184mg; Fibre 1.2g; Sodium 466mg

p498 West Country Apple Cake Energy 3810kcal/16031kJ; Protein 35.7g; Carbohydrate 596.6g, of which sugars 451.9g; Fat 159g, of which saturates 68.4g; Cholesterol 260mg; Calcium 617mg; Fibre 16.4g; Sodium 839mg

p501 Yorkshire Parkin Energy 273kcal/1152kJ; Protein 5.3g; Carbohydrate 50g, of which sugars 20.1g; Fat 7.1g, of which saturates 3.3g; Cholesterol 23mg; Calcium 127mg; Fibre 1.9g; Sodium 102mg

p502 Honey Cake Energy 152kcal/639kJ; Protein 1.9g; Carbohydrate 23.5g, of which sugars 13g; Fat 6.3g, of which saturates 3.8g; Cholesterol 26mg; Calcium 30mg; Fibre 0.4g; Sodium 49mg

p505 Seed Cake Energy 281kcal/1181kJ; Protein 4.6g; Carbohydrate 36.9g, of which sugars 15.5g; Fat 13.8g, of which saturates 8g; Cholesterol 87mg; Calcium 58mg; Fibre 0.8g; Sodium 109mg

p506 Battenberg Energy 355kcal/1492kJ; Protein 4.4g; Carbohydrate 51.2g, of which sugars 41.7g; Fat 15.7g, of which saturates 7.5g; Cholesterol 70mg; Calcium 55mg; Fibre 1g; Sodium 117mg

p509 Butterfly Cakes Energy 455kcal/1905kJ; Protein 4.8g; Carbohydrate 55.3g, of which sugars 40.9g; Fat 25.4g, of which saturates 15.7g; Cholesterol 148mg; Calcium 106mg; Fibre 0.6g; Sodium 312mg

p510 Swiss Roll Energy 183kcal/772kJ; Protein 4.3g; Carbohydrate 33.6g, of which sugars 23.1g; Fat 3.3g, of which saturates 0.8g; Cholesterol 76mg; Calcium 27mg; Fibre 0.7g; Sodium 38mg

p513 Yule Log Energy 478kcal/2003kJ; Protein 7.1g; Carbohydrate 55.4g, of which sugars 44.1g; Fat 26.1g, of which saturates 15g; Cholesterol 130mg; Calcium 75mg; Fibre 1.4g; Sodium 47mg

p514 Christmas Cake with Topping Energy 8751kcal/36742kJ; Protein 107.1g; Carbohydrate 1267.0g, of which sugars 1076.8g; Fat 298.6g, of which saturates 132.6g; Cholesterol 1432mg; Calcium 1787mg; Fibre 102.6g; Sodium 3004mg

p514 Christmas Cake without Topping Energy 7784 kcal/32714kJ; Protein 93g; Carbohydrate 1180.2g, of which sugars 989.9g; Fat 245.2g, of which saturates 127.4g; Cholesterol 1432mg; Calcium 1641mg; Fibre 94.8g; Sodium 2964mg

p517 Simnel Cake Energy 8108kcal/34162kJ; Protein 104g; Carbohydrate 1323.3g, of which sugars 1113.8g; Fat 303.9g, of which saturates 132.5g; Cholesterol 1442mg; Calcium 1557mg; Fibre 33.4g; Sodium 2080mg

p518 Marmalade Teabread Energy 250kcal/1049kJ; Protein 3.5g; Carbohydrate 38g, of which sugars 19g; Fat 10.4g, of which saturates 6.2g; Cholesterol 48mg; Calcium 56mg; Fibre 0.8g; Sodium 86mg

p521 Sticky Gingerbread Energy 373kcal/1572kJ; Protein 5.2g; Carbohydrate 60.9g, of which sugars 38.7g; Fat 13.9g, of which saturates 8.1g; Cholesterol 78.5mg; Calcium 253.6mg; Fibre 0.9g; Sodium 170.5mg

p522 Malt Fruit Loaf Energy 188kcal/796kJ; Protein 4.8g; Carbohydrate 37g, of which sugars 20.9g; Fat 2g, of which saturates 0.8g; Cholesterol 42mg; Calcium 110mg; Fibre 1.4g; Sodium 114mg

p525 Oat Biscuits Energy 151kcal/637kJ; Protein 1.8g; Carbohydrate 23.9g, of which sugars 11.9g; Fat 6g, of which saturates 3.3g; Cholesterol 14mg; Calcium 22mg; Fibre 0.8g; Sodium 59mg

p526 Ginger Snaps Energy 101kcal/424kJ; Protein 1g; Carbohydrate 16.1g, of which sugars 9g; Fat 4.1g, of which saturates 2.5g; Cholesterol 10mg; Calcium 17mg; Fibre 0.3g; Sodium 43mg

p529 Shrewsbury Cakes Energy 115kcal/482kJ; Protein 1.4g; Carbohydrate 16.1g, of which sugars 7.5g; Fat 5.4g, of which saturates 3.2g; Cholesterol 32mg; Calcium 23mg; Fibre 0.4g; Sodium 37mg

p530 Bosworth Jumbles Energy 242kcal/1012kJ; Protein 4.2g; Carbohydrate 29.2g, of which sugars 10.8g; Fat 11.7g, of which saturates 5.8g; Cholesterol 39mg; Calcium 39mg; Fibre 1.5g; Sodium 85mg

p533 Goosnargh Cakes Energy 150kcal/626kJ; Protein 1.5g; Carbohydrate 13.4g, of which sugars 3.5g; Fat 9.9g, of which saturates 6.2g; Cholesterol 25mg; Calcium 19mg; Fibre 0.7g; Sodium 86mg

p534 Devon Flats Energy 100kcal/418kJ; Protein 1.6g; Carbohydrate 13.3g, of which sugars 5.4g; Fat 4.4g, of which saturates 2.6g; Cholesterol 21mg; Calcium 36mg; Fibre 0.4g; Sodium 56mg

p537 Easter Biscuits Energy 116kcal/485kJ; Protein 1.5g; Carbohydrate 15.4g, of which sugars 7g; Fat 5.7g, of which saturates 3.4g; Cholesterol 24mg; Calcium 25mg; Fibre 0.4g; Sodium 46mg

p538 Ratafias Energy 41kcal/173kJ; Protein 0.9g; Carbohydrate 5g, of which sugars 4.9g; Fat 1.9g, of which saturates 0.3g; Cholesterol 22mg; Calcium 9mg; Fibre0.3 g; Sodium 1mg

p538 Macaroons Energy 83Kcal/344kJ; Protein 1g; Carbohydrate 6g, of which sugars 6g; Fat 10g, of which saturates 5g; Cholesterol 29mg; Calcium 7mg; Fibre 0.6g; Sodium 100mg

p541 Melting Moments Energy 88kcal/370kJ; Protein 0.7g; Carbohydrate 10.9g, of which sugars 5.4g; Fat 5g, of which saturates 2.4g; Cholesterol 7mg; Calcium 30mg; Fibre 0.3g; Sodium 40mg

p542 Jam Sandwich Biscuits Energy 207kcal/864kJ; Protein 1.4g; Carbohydrate 23.8g, of which sugars 15.5g; Fat 11.7g, of which saturates 7.3g; Cholesterol 40mg; Calcium 16mg; Fibre 0.5g; Sodium 4mg

p545 Gingerbread Men Energy 261kcal/1100kJ; Protein 3.6g; Carbohydrate 41.5g, of which sugars 19.9g; Fat 8.7g, of which saturates 5.2g; Cholesterol 37mg; Calcium 47mg; Fibre 1.2g; Sodium 107mg

p546 Brandy Snaps with Cream Energy 121kcal/505kJ; Protein 0.6g; Carbohydrate 11.7g, of which sugars 10g; Fat 7.9g, with saturates 5g; Cholesterol 21mg; Calcium 16mg; Fibre 0.1g; Sodium 24mg

p549 Clotted Cream Energy 1540kcal/6332kJ; Protein 5.5g; Carbohydrate 5.5g, of which sugars 5.5g; Fat 166.1g, of which saturates 103.1g; Cholesterol 533mg; Calcium 190mg; Fibre 0g; Sodium 86mg

p552 Teacakes Energy 285kcal/1183kJ; Protein 12.6g; Carbohydrate 5.8g, of which sugars 3.2g; Fat 22.7g, of which saturates 8.7g; Cholesterol 57mg; Calcium 73mg; Fibre 0.2g; Sodium 103mg

p555 Crumpets Energy 93kcal/393kJ; Protein 3g; Carbohydrate 16.5g, of which sugars 1g; Fat 2.1g, of which saturates 1g; Cholesterol 21mg; Calcium 48mg; Fibre 0.6g; Sodium 21mg

p556 English Muffins Energy 201kcal/852kJ; Protein 6g; Carbohydrate 40.7g, of which sugars 2.6g; Fat 2.7g, of which saturates 1.4g; Cholesterol 6mg; Calcium 117mg; Fibre 1.6g; Sodium 356mg

p559 Bath Buns Energy 376kcal/1576kJ; Protein 8g; Carbohydrate 44g, of which sugars 8.1g; Fat 18.3g, of which saturates 11.2g; Cholesterol 65mg; Calcium 98mg; Fibre 1.8g; Sodium 280mg

p560 Sally Lunn Per loaf: Energy 1250kcal/5290kJ; Protein 31g; Carbohydrate 236.9g, of which sugars 27.3g; Fat 26.6g, of which saturates 15.6g; Cholesterol 66mg; Calcium 577mg; Fibre 8.5g; Sodium 1262mg

p563 Hot Cross Buns Energy 155kcal/657kJ; Protein 3.7g; Carbohydrate 29.3g, of which sugars 11.7g; Fat 3.4g, of which saturates 1.1g; Cholesterol 16mg; Calcium 55mg; Fibre 0.9g; Sodium 60mg

p564 Chelsea Buns Energy 287kcal/1208kJ; Protein 6.1g; Carbohydrate 43.5g, of which sugars 16.6g; Fat 11.1g, of which saturates 2.3g; Cholesterol 26mg; Calcium 85mg; Fibre 1.3g; Sodium 243mg

p567 Devonshire Splits Energy 116kcal/495kJ; Protein 3.2g; Carbohydrate 26g, of which sugars 4.6g; Fat 0.7g, of which saturates 0.2g; Cholesterol 1mg; Calcium 62mg; Fibre 0.9g; Sodium 134mg

p568 Lardy Cake Per loaf: Energy 3499kcal/14750kJ; Protein 47.5g; Carbohydrate 598.9g, of which sugars 256g; Fat 117.9g, of which saturates 40.7g; Cholesterol 84mg; Calcium 872mg; Fibre 18.8g; Sodium 2087mg

p571 Stotties Energy 1216kcal/5156kJ; Protein 43.3g; Carbohydrate 245.4g, of which sugars 3.7g; Fat 4.1g, of which saturates 1.1g; Cholesterol 0mg; Calcium 457mg; Fibre 11.9g; Sodium 1742mg

p572 Staffordshire Oatcakes Energy 210kcal/881kJ; Protein 5.7g; Carbohydrate 27.4g, of which sugars 2.5g; Fat 8.2g, of which saturates 1.7g; Cholesterol 5mg; Calcium 80mg; Fibre 0.9g; Sodium 214mg

p575 Yorkshire Farls Energy 247kcal/1047kJ; Protein 8.1g; Carbohydrate 49.8g, of which sugars 4g; Fat 1.2g, of which saturates 0.4g; Cholesterol 1mg; Calcium 127mg; Fibre 2.5g; Sodium 650mg

p576 Cornish Saffron Bread Energy 3041kcal/12821kJ; Protein 50.7g; Carbohydrate 516.8g, of which sugars 173.9g; Fat 99.9g, of which saturates 48.7g; Cholesterol 162mg; Calcium 1018mg; Fibre 18.5g; Sodium 541mg

p579 Lincolnshire Plum Bread Energy 1710kcal/7211kJ; Protein 32.2g; Carbohydrate 285.2g, of which sugars 113.7g, of which saturates 32.5g; Cholesterol 316mg; Calcium 535mg; Fibre 9.1g; Sodium 465mg

p580 Cottage Loaf Per loaf: Energy 2302kcal/9794kJ; Protein 77.6g; Carbohydrate 508.3g, of which sugars 9.4g; Fat 9.4g, of which saturates 1.4g; Cholesterol 0mg; Calcium 946mg; Fibre 20.9g; Sodium 3950mg

p583 Granary Cob Per loaf: Energy 1395kcal/5931kJ; Protein 57.1g; Carbohydrate 287.6g, of which sugars 9.4g; Fat 9.9g, of which saturates 1.4g; Cholesterol 0mg; Calcium 172mg; Fibre 40.5g; Sodium 4926mg

p584 Split Tin White Loaf Energy 1223kcal/5185kJ; Protein 30.7g; Carbohydrate 256.4g, of which sugars 7.5g; Fat 15.2g, of which saturates 6.3g; Cholesterol 0mg; Calcium 457mg; Fibre 10.1g; Sodium 1.48g

p587 Bloomer Per loaf: Energy 2272kcal/9638kJ; Protein 91.2g; Carbohydrate 431.6g, of which sugars 14.3g; Fat 32.3g, of which saturates 4.5g; Cholesterol 0mg; Calcium 459mg; Fibre 63.1g; Sodium 4939mg

p588 Oatmeal Bread Per loaf: Energy 2254kcal/9556kJ; Protein 64.8g; Carbohydrate 445.2g, of which sugars 42.4g; Fat 36.1g, of which saturates 9.8g; Cholesterol 41mg; Calcium 883mg; Fibre 24.1g; Sodium 256mg

p591 Wholemeal Bread Per loaf: Energy 1933kcal/8198kJ; Protein 47.2g; Carbohydrate 409.5g, of which sugars 28.5g; Fat 23g, of which saturates 11.4g; Cholesterol 43mg; Calcium 715mg; Fibre 15.5g; Sodium 1120mg

p592 Harvest Festival Sheaf Per loaf: Energy 3104kcal/13196kJ; Protein 87.1g; Carbohydrate 703g, of which sugars 17.3g; Fat 13g, of which saturates 2.5g; Cholesterol 4mg; Calcium 1352mg; Fibre 27.9g; Sodium 5963mg

p597 Marmalade Energy 7520kcal/31958kJ; Protein 8.7g; Carbohydrate 1856.3g, of which sugars 1856.3g; Fat 2.1g, of which saturates 0.5g; Cholesterol 0mg; Calcium 463mg; Fibre 21.4g; Sodium 216mg

p598 Strawberry Jam Energy 3816kcal/16,259kJ; Protein 12.5g; Carbohydrate 1000.5g, of which sugars 1000.5g; Fat 1g, of which saturates 0g; Cholesterol 0mg; Calcium 637mg; Fibre 11g; Sodium 114mg

p601 Bramble Jam Energy 12570kcal/53550kJ; Protein 42g; Carbohydrate 3288g, of which sugars 3288g; Fat 6g, of which saturates 0g; Cholesterol 0mg; Calcium 2820mg; Fibre 93g; Sodium 240mg

p602 Redcurrant Jelly Energy 561kcal/2391kJ; Protein 4.2g; Carbohydrate 144.9g, of which sugars 144.9g; Fat 0g, of which saturates 0g; Cholesterol 0mg; Calcium 153mg; Fibre 14.7g; Sodium 13mg

p605 Rhubarb and Mint Jelly Energy 5366kcal/22805kJ; Protein 12.8g; Carbohydrate 1313.3g, of which sugars 1313.3g; Fat 1.7g, of which saturates 0.2g; Cholesterol 0mg; Calcium 1270mg; Fibre 24.8g; Sodium 185mg

p605 Red Gooseberry Jelly Energy 5717kcal/24238kJ; Protein 14.4g; Carbohydrate 1368.7g, of which sugars 1367.2g; Fat 5.6g, of which saturates 1.4g; Cholesterol 0mg; Calcium 507mg; Fibre 62.4g; Sodium 171mg

p606 Lemon and Lime Curd Energy 1927kcal/8056kJ; Protein 20.7g; Carbohydrate 212.1g, of which sugars 212.1g; Fat 116.8g, of which saturates 66.2g;

Cholesterol 1029mg; Calcium 294mg; Fibre 0g; Sodium 871mg

p609 Apple Butter Energy 3057kcal/12972kJ; Protein 2.7g; Carbohydrate 720g, of which sugars 719.5g; Fat 1.3g, of which saturates 0.3g; Cholesterol 0mg; Calcium 247mg; Fibre 12.4g; Sodium 78mg

p610 Plum Cheese Energy 483kcal/2063kJ; Protein 1.6g; Carbohydrate 126.8g, of which sugars 126.8g; Fat 0.2g, of which saturates 0g; Cholesterol 0mg; Calcium 46mg; Fibre 2.7g; Sodium 8mg

p613 Green Tomato Chutney Energy 1436kcal/6100kJ; Protein 17.4g; Carbohydrate 353.1g, of which sugars 342.8g; Fat 4.7g, of which saturates 0.9g; Cholesterol 0mg; Calcium 329mg; Fibre 31g; Sodium 2100mg

p614 Sweet Piccalilli Energy 1358kcal/5757kJ; Protein 34.1g; Carbohydrate 300.8g, of which sugars 266g; Fat 12g, of which saturates 1.2g; Cholesterol 0mg; Calcium 555mg; Fibre 20.6g; Sodium 4011mg

p617 Mincemeat Energy 7149Kcal/30087kJ; Protein 55.6g; Carbohydrate 1114g, of which sugars 1088.3g; Fat 267.7g, of which saturates 106.3g; Cholesterol 0mg; Calcium 1228mg; Fibre 47.3g; Sodium 774mg

p618 Windfall Pear Chutney Energy 2496kcal/10480kJ; Protein 32g; Carbohydrate 415g, of which sugars 400g; Fat 82g, of which saturates 7g; Cholesterol 0mg; Calcium 512mg; Fibre 24.3g; Sodium 2205mg

p618 Cucumber Dill Pickles Energy 823kcal/3484kJ; Protein 13.8g; Carbohydrate 123.3g, of which sugars 117g; Fat 9.7g, of which saturates 2.2g; Cholesterol 0mg; Calcium 494mg; Fibre 13.9g; Sodium 4733mg

p621 Traditional Pickled Onions Energy 109kcal/454kJ; Protein 3.1g; Carbohydrate 24.5g, of which sugars 18.6g; Fat 0.5g, of which saturates 0g; Cholesterol 0mg; Calcium 67mg; Fibre 3.6g; Sodium 8mg

p622 Poached Spiced Plums in Brandy Energy 3035kcal/12,792kJ; Protein 7.1g; Carbohydrate 444.9g, of which sugars 444.9g; Fat 0.9g, of which saturates 0g; Cholesterol 0mg; Calcium 302mg; Fibre 14.4g; Sodium 39mg

p622 Spiced Pickled Pears Energy 1379kcal/5835kJ; Protein 6g; Carbohydrate 330g, of which sugars 330g; Fat 2g, of which saturates 0g; Cholesterol 0mg; Calcium 187mg; Fibre 0.0 g; Sodium 76mg

p625 Mint Sauce Energy 161kcal/685kJ; Protein 3.9g; Carbohydrate 36.6g, of which sugars 31.3g; Fat 0.7g, of which saturates 0g; Cholesterol 0mg; Calcium 226mg; Fibre 0g; Sodium 17mg

p625 Real Horseradish Sauce Energy 774kcal/3190kJ; Protein 2.8g; Carbohydrate 9.9g, of which sugars 9.8g; Fat 80.7g, of which saturates 50.1g; Cholesterol 206mg; Calcium 98mg; Fibre 1.1g; Sodium 40mg

p626 Cumberland Sauce Energy 1697kcal/7205kJ; Protein 9.1g; Carbohydrate 359.4g, of which sugars 350.8 g; Fat 2.1g, of which saturates 0.6g; Cholesterol 0mg; Calcium 387mg; Fibre 19g; Sodium 71mg

p629 Herb Mustard Energy 553kcal/2324kJ; Protein 23.4g; Carbohydrate 69.1g, of which sugars 53.4g; Fat 34.5g, of which saturates 1.1g; Cholesterol 3mg; Calcium 374mg; Fibre 2.5g; Sodium 23mg

p629 Honey Mustard Energy 1276kcal/5345kJ; Protein 65.4g; Carbohydrate 115.3g, of which sugars 68.8g; Fat 101.5g, of which saturates 3.4g; Cholesterol 9mg; Calcium 747mg; Fibre 0g; Sodium 21mg

p630 Lemon Barley Water Per glass: Energy 37.9Kcal/161.6kJ; Protein 0.43g; Carbohydrate 9.44g, of which sugars 5.26g; Fat 0.08g, of which saturates 0g; Cholesterol 0mg; Calcium 3.8mg; Fibre 0g; Sodium 0.5mg

p633 Summer Punch Per glass: Energy 90kcal/380kJ; Protein 0g; Carbohydrate 17g, of which sugars 17g; Fat 0g, of which saturates 0g; Cholesterol 0mg; Calcium 26mg; Fibre 0.6g; Sodium 21mg

p634 Sloe Gin Per bottle: Energy 1554Kcal/6486kJ; Protein 0.6g; Carbohydrate 117.6g, of which sugars 117.6g; Fat 0g, of which saturates 0g; Cholesterol 0mg; Calcium 60mg; Fibre 0g; Sodium 7mg

p634 Mulled Cider Per glass: Energy 61Kcal/258kJ; Protein 0.1g; Carbohydrate 9.3g, of which sugars 9.3g; Fat 0.1g, of which saturates 0g; Cholesterol 0mg; Calcium 12mg; Fibre 0g; Sodium 8mg

p637 Rosehip Syrup Energy 810kcal/3442kJ; Protein 0.1g; Carbohydrate 201.5g, of which sugars 201.5g; Fat 0.1g, of which saturates 0g; Cholesterol 0mg; Calcium 27mg; Fibre 1.4g; Sodium 765mg

p637 Elderflower Cordial Energy 6145kcal/26129kJ; Protein 0.3g; Carbohydrate 1501.5g, of which sugars 1501g; Fat 0g, of which saturates 0g; Cholesterol 0mg; Calcium 157mg; Fibre 0.4g; Sodium 76mg

p638 Quince Paste Energy 86kcal/369kJ; Protein 0.2g; Carbohydrate 22.8g, of which sugars 22.8g; Fat 0g, of which saturates 0g; Cholesterol 0mg; Calcium 11mg; Fibre 0.3g; Sodium 2mg

p641 Raspberry Jellies Energy 999kcal/4270kJ; Protein 28g; Carbohydrate 233g, of which sugars 233g; Fat 2g, of which saturates 1g; Cholesterol 0mg; Calcium 209mg; Fibre 34g; Sodium 108mg

p642 Vanilla Fudge 4665kcal/19743kJ; Protein 15g; Carbohydrate 955g, of which sugars 955g; Fat 114g, of which saturates 75g; Cholesterol 330mg; Calcium 841mg; Fibre 0g; Sodium 1157mg

p645 Doncaster Butterscotch Energy 2454kcal/10347kJ; Protein 7.8g; Carbohydrate 454g, of which sugars 454.7g; Fat 67.2g, of which saturates 42.6g; Cholesterol 178mg; Calcium 329mg; Fibre 0g; Sodium 637mg

p646 Bonfire Toffee Energy 2386kcal/10037kJ; Protein 4.5g; Carbohydrate 386g, of which sugars 386g; Fat 102g, of which saturates 68g; Cholesterol 288mg; Calcium 1263mg; Fibre 0g; Sodium 1167mg

p649 Toffee Caramel Apples Energy 366kcal/1534kJ; Protein 0.8g; Carbohydrate 47g, of which sugars 47g; Fat 22g, of which saturates 13.4g; Cholesterol 57mg; Calcium 33mg; Fibre 1.1g; Sodium 160mg

p650 Barley Sugar Twists Energy 1777kcal/7579kJ; Protein 0g; Carbohydrate 473g, of which sugars 473g; Fat 0g, of which saturates 0g; Cholesterol 0mg; Calcium 47mg; Fibre 0g; Sodium 23mg

p653 Peppermint Humbugs Energy 1621kcal/6914kJ; Protein 2g; Carbohydrate 429.9g, of which sugars 429.9g; Fat 0g, of which saturates 0g; Cholesterol 0mg; Calcium 216mg; Fibre 0g; Sodium 65mg

p654 Sour Drops Energy 1862kcal/7984kJ; Protein 1g; Carbohydrate 476g, of which sugars 475g; Fat 0g, of which saturates 0g; Cholesterol 0mg; Calcium 59mg; Fibre 0g; Sodium 25mg

p657 Pontefract-Style Cakes Energy 1668kcal/7114kJ; Protein 3.1g; Carbohydrate 441.2g, of which sugars 441.2g; Fat 0g, of which saturates 0g; Cholesterol 0mg; Calcium 785mg; Fibre 0g; Sodium 1690mg

INDEX

COOK'S NOTES

- Terms in parentheses are intended for American readers.
- For all recipes, quantities are given in both metric and imperial measures and, where appropriate, in standard cups and spoons. Follow one set of measures, but not a mixture, because they are not interchangeable.
- Standard spoon and cup measures are level.
- 1 tsp = 5ml, 1 tbsp = 15ml, 1 cup = 250ml/8fl oz.
- Australian standard tablespoons are 20ml. Australian readers should use 3 tsp in place of 1 tbsp for measuring small quantities.
- American pints are 16fl oz/2 cups. The pint measures for the recipes in this book are given in imperial measures, so American readers should use 20fl oz/2½ cups in place of 1 pint when measuring liquids.
- Medium (US large) eggs are used unless otherwise stated.
- Since ovens vary, you should check with your manufacturer's book for guidance.

ABOUT THE EDITOR

Editor Carol Wilson is a food writer and historian who has contributed to many publications, including *The Times*, *Illustrated London News*, *Heritage*, *Food and Wine* and *Gastronomica*. She has appeared on television promoting British food and discussing the history and usage of traditional ingredients. Other books include *Scottish Heritage Food and Cooking*, *The Liquorice Cookbook* and *The Bacon Cookbook*. She is a member of the Guild of Food Writers.

LEFT Oak tree with view of hills, in Herefordshire.

PAGE 4 Village with church in the Cotswolds.

ENDPAPERS Castle Combe in the Cotswolds, Wiltshire; the Seven Sisters (white cliffs) in the South Downs, East Sussex.

This edition is published by Lorenz Books
an imprint of Anness Publishing Ltd
www.annesspublishing.com
info@anness.com

© Anness Publishing Ltd 2023

A CIP catalogue record for this book is available from the British Library.

Publisher: Joanna Lorenz
Design and art direction: Simon Daley
Photography: Ian Garlick and Craig Robertson
Food styling: Felicity Barnum-Bobb and Fergal Connelly
Map artwork: Simon Daley
Readers: Susan Low, Nicola Twyman
Nutritional consultants: Clare Emery and Catherine Atkinson
Index: Marie Lorimer

With thanks to the additional research and recipe contributors (Annette Yates, Carol Pastor, Jennie Shapter, Maggie Mayhew, Ann Nicol, Claire Ptak, Biddy White Lennon and Antony Wild), photographers (Nicky Dowey and Willliam Lingwood) and the team of stylists.

A substantial part of this book was previously published as *English Heritage Food & Cooking*, by Annette Yates.

With thanks to picture agencies Alamy (7, 12, 13, 14, 19.1, 19.2, 21, 23, 25, 28, 29, 30, 31, 32t, 32b, 33, 35, 36, 37t, 40, 42, 43, 47, 49, 51, 52, 53, 54, 55t, 55b, 56, 57, 58, 59, 61, 62.2, 64, 66, 68, 70, 71t, 71b, 72, 74, 75, 76t, 76b, 79, 80, 81, 82, 83, 84, 85, 86, 87, 88, 89, 91, 93t, 93b, 94, 95, 96, 98, 103, 104, 105, 106, 107, 109, 112, 113, 114, 115, 116, 142, 594), Bridgeman (20, 24, 26, 27, 34) and Shutterstock (4, 8, 10, 11, 16, 17, 18, 22, 37b, 39, 44, 48, 50, 60, 62.1, 63, 65, 67, 69, 77, 78, 90, 92, 99, 100, 101, 110, 117, 118, 174, 206, 242, 284, 318, 342, 376, 462, 554, 664, 672, endpapers).

All other images © Anness Publishing Ltd